System Design Interview

An Insider's Guide
Volume 2

Alex Xu | Sahn Lam

ByteByteGo

SYSTEM DESIGN INTERVIEW - AN INSIDER'S GUIDE (VOLUME 2)

System Design Newsletter

Subscribe to the ByteByteGo weekly newsletter to get a Free System Design PDF (158 pages): blog.bytebytego.com

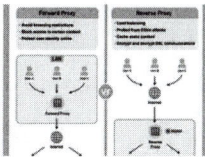

EP26: Proxy vs reverse proxy

In this issue, we will cover: Why is Nginx called a "reverse" proxy? CAP theorem How Does Live Streaming Platform Work? CDN Postman the API platform for...

ALEX XU   OCT 1   ♡ 225   ⬭ 6   ⤳

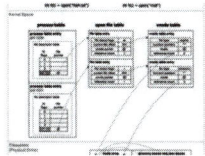

EP17: Design patterns cheat sheet. Also...

For this week's newsletter, we will cover: Design patterns cheat sheet 6 ways to turn code into beautiful architecture diagrams What is a File...

ALEX XU   JUL 30   ♡ 166   ⬭ 7   ⤳

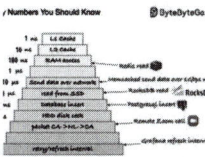

EP22: Latency numbers you should know. Also...

In this newsletter, we'll cover the following topics: Latency numbers you should know Microservice architecture Handling hotspot accounts E-commerce...

ALEX XU   SEP 3   ♡ 153   ⬭ 9   ⤳

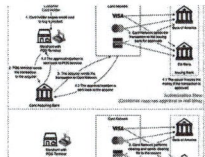

EP15: What happens when you swipe a credit card? Also...

For this week's newsletter, we will cover: How does VISA work when we swipe a credit card at a merchant's shop? What are the differences between bare...

ALEX XU   JUL 16   ♡ 141   ⬭ 8   ⤳

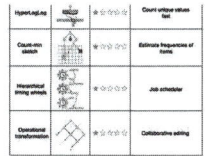

EP14: Algorithms you should know for System Design. Also...

In this newsletter, we'll cover the following topics: Algorithms you should know before taking System Design Interviews How to store passwords safely in...

ALEX XU   JUL 9   ♡ 185   ⬭ 2   ⤳

YouTube Channel

Check us out on YouTube: https://www.youtube.com/@ByteByteGo

ByteByteGo ✓
@ByteByteGo
251K subscribers

HOME   VIDEOS   PLAYLISTS   COMMUNITY   CHANNELS   ABOUT   🔍

Recently uploaded   Popular

| Why is Kafka fast?
5:02

SYSTEM DESIGN FUNDAMENTALS
System Design: Why is Kafka fast?
504K views · 5 months ago

| HTTP/1 -> HTTP/2 -> HTTP/3
HTTP/1 HTTP/1.1 HTTP/2 HTTP/3
4:07

SYSTEM DESIGN FUNDAMENTALS
HTTP/1 to HTTP/2 to HTTP/3
285K views · 3 months ago

| Microservice Architecture
4:45

SYSTEM DESIGN FUNDAMENTALS
**What Are Microservices Really All About?
(And When Not To Use It)**
227K views · 2 months ago

| Why is RESTful API so popular
Client   REST API   Server
5:21

SYSTEM DESIGN INTERVIEW
**What Is REST API? Examples And How To
Use It**
184K views · 3 months ago

| Why is Redis so fast
redis
3:39

SYSTEM DESIGN FUNDAMENTALS
**System Design: Why is single-threaded
Redis so fast?**
171K views · 4 months ago

| Design a proximity service
24:41

SYSTEM DESIGN INTERVIEW
**FAANG System Design Interview: Design A
Location Based Service (Yelp, Google...**
168K views · 4 months ago

To Julia.
ALEX XU

To Esther, who loves to read my code out LOUD.
And to the Lam Fam Jam Band.
SAHN LAM

Contents

Foreword

We are delighted you are joining us to become better equipped for system design interviews. System design interviews are the most difficult to tackle of all technical interview questions. The questions test the interviewees' ability to design a scalable software system. This could be a news feed, Google search, chat application, or any other system. These questions are intimidating and there is no fixed pattern to follow when tackling them. The questions are usually very broad and vague. They are open-ended, with several plausible angles of attack, and often no perfect answer.

Many companies ask system design interview questions because the communication and problem-solving skills they test for are similar to the skills that software engineers use in their daily work. A candidate is evaluated on how they analyze a vague problem and how they solve it, step by step.

System design questions are open-ended. As in the real world, a design can have numerous variations. The desired outcome is an architecture that satisfies the agreed design goals. The discussions may go in different directions. Some interviewers may choose high-level architecture to cover all aspects of the challenge, whereas others might focus on one or more specific areas. Typically, system requirements, constraints, and bottlenecks should be well understood by the candidate, to shape the direction of the interview.

The objective of this book is to provide a reliable strategy and knowledge base for approaching a broad range of system design questions. The right strategy and knowledge are vital for the success of an interview.

This book also provides a step-by-step framework for how to tackle a system design question. It provides many examples to illustrate the systematic approach, with detailed steps that you can follow. With regular practice, you will be well-equipped to tackle system design interview questions.

This book can be seen as a sequel to the book: System Design Interview - An Insider's Guide (Volume 1: https://bit.ly/systemdesigning). Although reading Volume 1 is helpful, it is not a necessity to do so before you read this. This book should be accessible to readers who have a basic understanding of distributed systems. Let's get started!

Additional Resources

This book contains references at the end of each chapter. The following Github repository contains all the clickable links.

https://bit.ly/systemDesignLinks

You can connect with Alex on social media, where he shares system design interview tips every week.

twitter.com/alexxubyte

bit.ly/linkedinaxu

Acknowledgements

We wish we could say all the designs in this book are original. The truth is that most of the ideas discussed here can also be found elsewhere; in engineering blogs, research papers, code, tech talks, and other places. We have collected these elegant ideas and considered them, then added our personal experiences, to present them here in an easy-to-understand way. Additionally, this book has been written with the significant input and reviews of more than a dozen engineers and managers, some of whom made large writing contributions to the chapters. Thank you so much!

- Proximity Service, Meng Duan (Tencent)
- Nearby Friends, Yan Guo (Amazon)
- Google Maps, Ali Aminian (Adobe, Google)
- Distributed Message Queue, Lionel Liu (eBay)
- Distributed Message Queue, Tanmay Deshpande (Schlumberger)
- Metrics Monitoring and Alerting System, Neeraj Gupta
- Ad Click Event Aggregation, Xinda Bian (Ant Group)
- Real-time Gaming Leaderboard, Jossie Haines (Tile)
- Distributed Email Servers, Kevin Henrikson (Instacart)
- Distributed Email Servers, JJ Zhuang (Instacart)
- S3-like Object Store, Zhiteng Huang (eBay)

We are particularly grateful to those who provided detailed feedback on an earlier draft of this book:

- Darshit Dave (Bloomberg)
- Dwaraknath Bakshi (Twitter)
- Fei Nan (Gusto, Airbnb)
- Richard Hsu (Amazon)

- Simon Gao (Google)

- Stanly Mathew Thomas (Microsoft)

- Tian Qin (NYU)

- Wenhan Wang (Tiktok)

- Shiwakant Bharti (Amazon)

A huge thanks to our editors, Dominic Gover and Doug Warren. Your feedback was invaluable.

Last but not least, very special thanks to Elvis Ren and Hua Li for their invaluable contributions. This book wouldn't be what it is without them.

1   Proximity Service

In this chapter, we design a proximity service. A proximity service is used to discover nearby places such as restaurants, hotels, theaters, museums, etc., and is a core component that powers features like finding the best restaurants nearby on Yelp or finding k-nearest gas stations on Google Maps. Figure 1.1 shows the user interface via which you can search for nearby restaurants on Yelp [1]. Note the map tiles used in this book are from Stamen Design [2] and data are from OpenStreetMap [3].

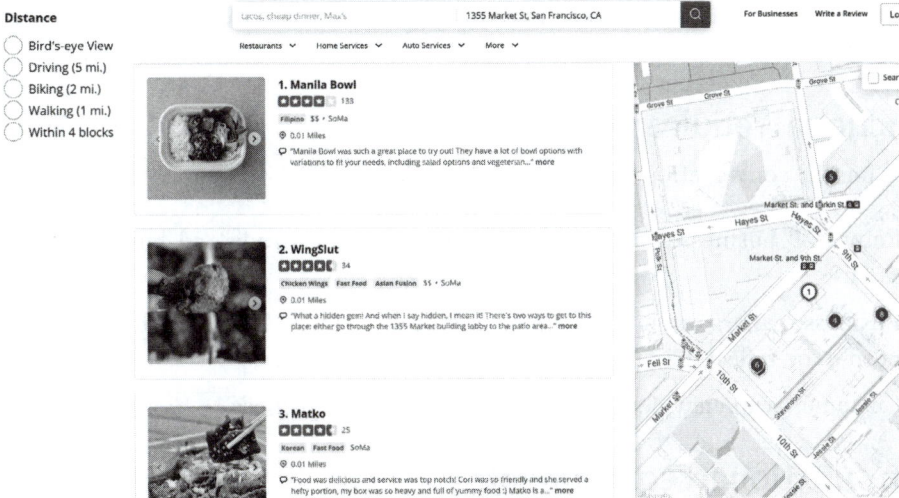

Figure 1.1: Nearby search on Yelp

Step 1 - Understand the Problem and Establish Design Scope

Yelp supports many features and it is not feasible to design all of them in an interview session, so it's important to narrow down the scope by asking questions. The interactions between the interviewer and the candidate could look like this:

Candidate: Can a user specify the search radius? If there are not enough businesses within the search radius, does the system expand the search?
Interviewer: That's a great question. Let's assume we only care about businesses within a specified radius. If time allows, we can then discuss how to expand the search if there are not enough businesses within the radius.

Candidate: What's the maximal radius allowed? Can I assume it's 20km (12.5 miles)?
Interviewer: That's a reasonable assumption.

Candidate: Can a user change the search radius on the UI?
Interviewer: Yes, we have the following options: 0.5km (0.31 mile), 1km (0.62 mile), 2km (1.24 mile), 5km (3.1 mile), and 20km (12.42 mile).

Candidate: How does business information get added, deleted, or updated? Do we need to reflect these operations in real-time?
Interviewer: Business owners can add, delete or update a business. Assume we have a business agreement upfront that newly added/updated businesses will be effective the next day.

Candidate: A user might be moving while using the app/website, so the search results could be slightly different after a while. Do we need to refresh the page to keep the results up to date?
Interviewer: Let's assume a user's moving speed is slow and we don't need to constantly refresh the page.

Functional requirements

Based on this conversation, we focus on 3 key features:

- Return all businesses based on a user's location (latitude and longitude pair) and radius.

- Business owners can add, delete or update a business, but this information doesn't need to be reflected in real-time.

- Customers can view detailed information about a business.

Non-functional requirements

From the business requirements, we can infer a list of non-functional requirements. You should also check these with the interviewer.

- Low latency. Users should be able to see nearby businesses quickly.

- Data privacy. Location info is sensitive data. When we design a location-based service (LBS), we should always take user privacy into consideration. We need to comply with data privacy laws like General Data Protection Regulation (GDPR) [4] and California Consumer Privacy Act (CCPA) [5], etc.

- High availability and scalability requirements. We should ensure our system can handle the spike in traffic during peak hours in densely populated areas.

Back-of-the-envelope estimation

Let's take a look at some back-of-the-envelope calculations to determine the potential scale and challenges our solution will need to address. Assume we have 100 million daily active users and 200 million businesses.

Calculate QPS
• Seconds in a day $= 24 \times 60 \times 60 = 86{,}400$. We can round it up to 10^5 for easier calculation. $\mathbf{10^5}$ **is used throughout this book** to represent seconds in a day.
• Assume a user makes 5 search queries per day.
• Search QPS $= \dfrac{100 \text{ million} \times 5}{10^5} = 5{,}000$

Step 2 - Propose High-level Design and Get Buy-in

In this section, we discuss the following:

- API design
- High-level design
- Algorithms to find nearby businesses
- Data model

API design

We use the RESTful API convention to design a simplified version of the APIs.

GET /v1/search/nearby

This endpoint returns businesses based on certain search criteria. In real-life applications, search results are usually paginated. Pagination [6] is not the focus of this chapter, but is worth mentioning during an interview.

Request Parameters:

Field	Description	Type
latitude	Latitude of a given location	decimal
longitude	Longitude of a given location	decimal
radius	Optional. Default is 5000 meters (about 3 miles)	int

Table 1.1: Request parameters

```
{
  "total": 10,
  "businesses":[{business object}]
}
```

The business object contains everything needed to render the search result page, but we may still need additional attributes such as pictures, reviews, star rating, etc., to render the business detail page. Therefore, when a user clicks on the business detail page, a new endpoint call to fetch the detailed information of a business is usually required.

APIs for a business

The APIs related to a business object are shown in the table below.

API	Detail
GET /v1/businesses/:id	Return detailed information about a business
POST /v1/businesses	Add a business
PUT /v1/businesses/:id	Update details of a business
DELETE /v1/businesses/:id	Delete a business

Table 1.2: APIs for a business

If you are interested in real-world APIs for place/business search, two examples are Google Places API [7] and Yelp business endpoints [8].

Data model

In this section, we discuss the read/write ratio and the schema design. The scalability of the database is covered in deep dive.

Read/write ratio

Read volume is high because the following two features are very commonly used:

- Search for nearby businesses.
- View the detailed information of a business.

On the other hand, the write volume is low because adding, removing, and editing business info are infrequent operations.

For a read-heavy system, a relational database such as MySQL can be a good fit. Let's take a closer look at the schema design.

Data schema

The key database tables are the business table and the geospatial (geo) index table.

Business table

The business table contains detailed information about a business. It is shown in Table 1.3 and the primary key is business_id.

business	
business_id	PK
address	
city	
state	
country	
latitude	
longtitude	

Table 1.3: Business table

Geo index table

A geo index table is used for the efficient processing of spatial operations. Since this table requires some knowledge about geohash, we will discuss it in the "Scale the database" section on page 23.

High-level design

The high-level design diagram is shown in Figure 1.2. The system comprises two parts: location-based service (LBS) and business-related service. Let's take a look at each component of the system.

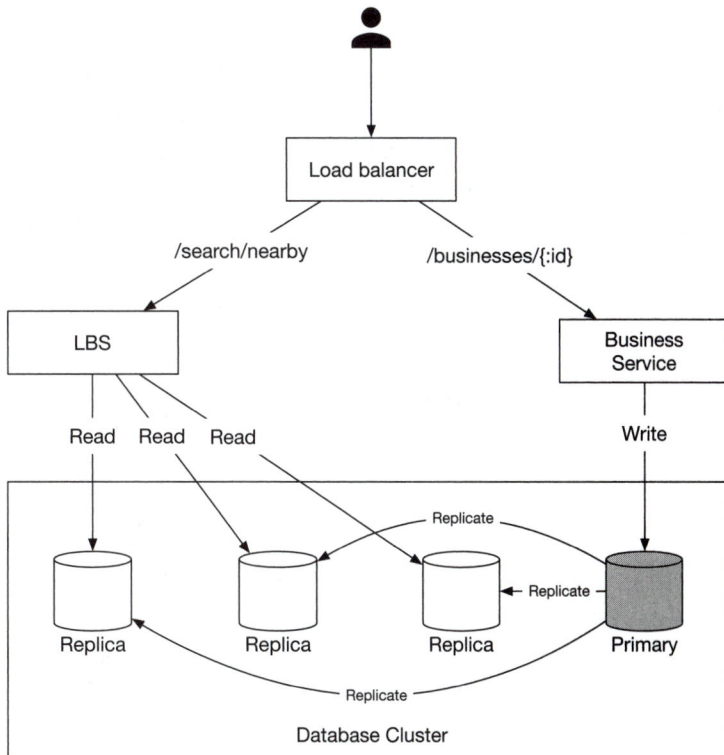

Figure 1.2: High-level design

Load balancer

The load balancer automatically distributes incoming traffic across multiple services. Normally, a company provides a single DNS entry point and internally routes the API calls to the appropriate services based on the URL paths.

Location-based service (LBS)

The LBS service is the core part of the system which finds nearby businesses for a given radius and location. The LBS has the following characteristics:

- It is a read-heavy service with no write requests.
- QPS is high, especially during peak hours in dense areas.
- This service is stateless so it's easy to scale horizontally.

Business service

Business service mainly deals with two types of requests:

- Business owners create, update, or delete businesses. Those requests are mainly write operations, and the QPS is not high.
- Customers view detailed information about a business. QPS is high during peak hours.

Database cluster

The database cluster can use the primary-secondary setup. In this setup, the primary database handles all the write operations, and multiple replicas are used for read operations. Data is saved to the primary database first and then replicated to replicas. Due to the replication delay, there might be some discrepancy between data read by the LBS and the data written to the primary database. This inconsistency is usually not an issue because business information doesn't need to be updated in real-time.

Scalability of business service and LBS

Both the business service and LBS are stateless services, so it's easy to automatically add more servers to accommodate peak traffic (e.g. mealtime) and remove servers during off-peak hours (e.g. sleep time). If the system operates on the cloud, we can set up different regions and availability zones to further improve availability [9]. We discuss this more in the deep dive.

Algorithms to fetch nearby businesses

In real life, companies might use existing geospatial databases such as Geohash in Redis [10] or Postgres with PostGIS extension [11]. You are not expected to know the internals of those geospatial databases during an interview. It's better to demonstrate your problem-solving skills and technical knowledge by explaining how the geospatial index works, rather than to simply throw out database names.

The next step is to explore different options for fetching nearby businesses. We will list a few options, go over the thought process, and discuss trade-offs.

Option 1: Two-dimensional search

The most intuitive but naive way to get nearby businesses is to draw a circle with the pre-defined radius and find all the businesses within the circle as shown in Figure 1.3.

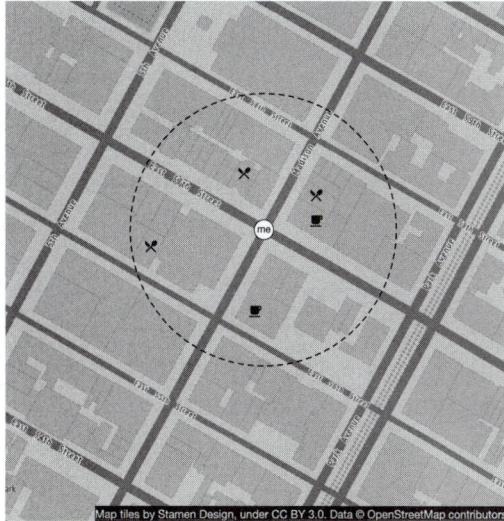

Figure 1.3: Two dimensional search

This process can be translated into the following pseudo SQL query:

```
SELECT business_id, latitude, longitude,
FROM business
WHERE (latitude BETWEEN {:my_lat} - radius AND {:my_lat} + radius)
AND
   (longitude BETWEEN {:my_long} - radius AND {:my_long} + radius)
```

This query is not efficient because we need to scan the whole table. What if we build indexes on longitude and latitude columns? Would this improve the efficiency? The answer is not by much. The problem is that we have two-dimensional data and the dataset returned from each dimension could still be huge. For example, as shown in Figure 1.4, we can quickly retrieve dataset 1 and dataset 2, thanks to indexes on longitude and latitude columns. But to fetch businesses within the radius, we need to perform an intersect operation on those two datasets. This is not efficient because each dataset contains lots of data.

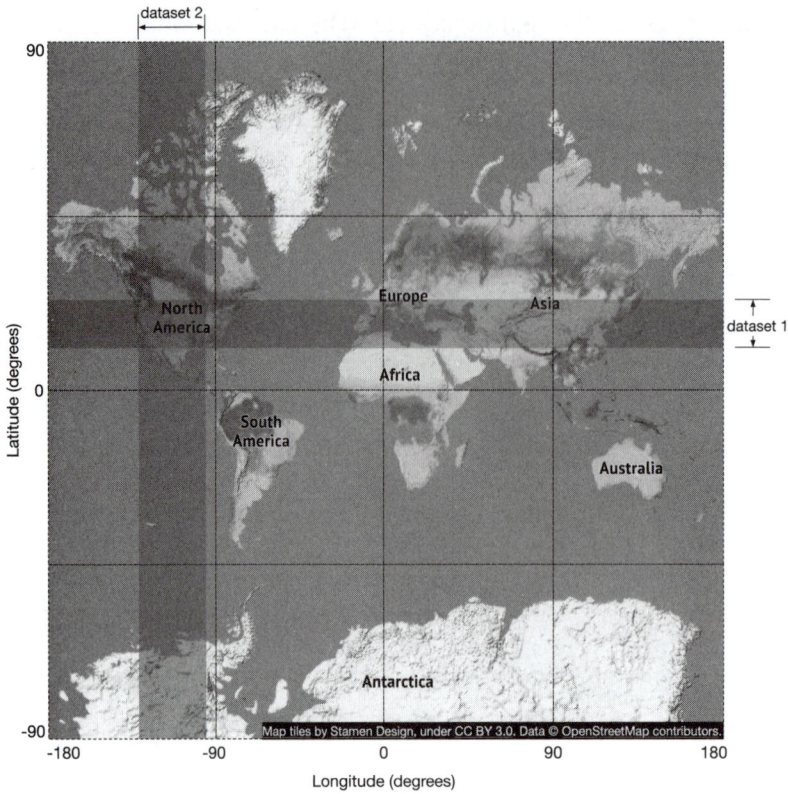

Figure 1.4: Intersect two datasets

The problem with the previous approach is that the database index can only improve search speed in one dimension. So naturally, the follow-up question is, can we map two-dimensional data to one dimension? The answer is yes.

Before we dive into the answers, let's take a look at different types of indexing methods. In a broad sense, there are two types of geospatial indexing approaches, as shown in Figure 1.5. The highlighted ones are the algorithms we discuss in detail because they are commonly used in the industry.

- Hash: even grid, geohash, cartesian tiers [12], etc.
- Tree: quadtree, Google S2, RTree [13], etc.

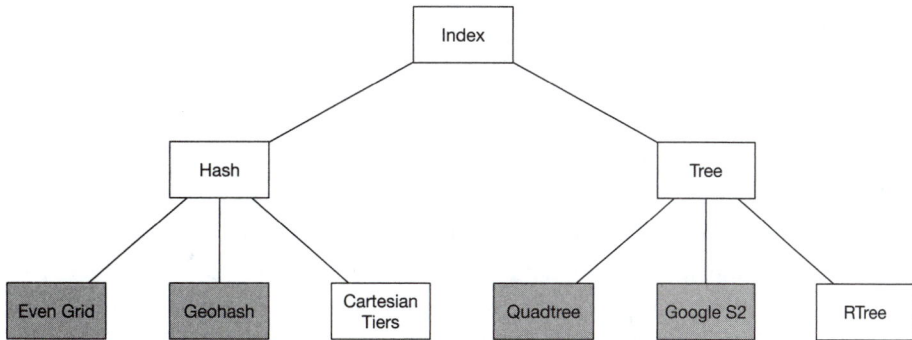

Figure 1.5: Different types of geospatial indexes

Even though the underlying implementations of those approaches are different, the high-level idea is the same, that is, **to divide the map into smaller areas and build indexes for fast search**. Among those, geohash, quadtree, and Google S2 are most widely used in real-world applications. Let's take a look at them one by one.

Reminder
In a real interview, you usually don't need to explain the implementation details of indexing options. However, it is important to have some basic understanding of the need for geospatial indexing, how it works at a high level, and also its limitations.

Option 2: Evenly divided grid

One simple approach is to evenly divide the world into small grids (Figure 1.6). This way, one grid could have multiple businesses, and each business on the map belongs to one grid.

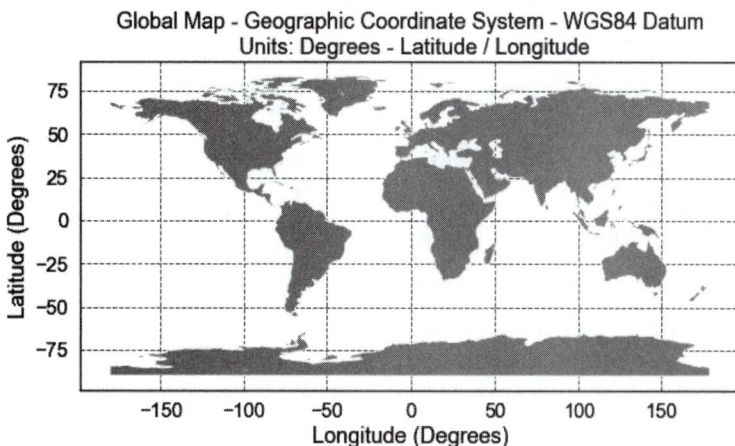

Figure 1.6: Global map (source: [14])

This approach works to some extent, but it has one major issue: the distribution of businesses is not even. There could be lots of businesses in downtown New York, while other grids in deserts or oceans have no business at all. By dividing the world into even grids, we produce a very uneven data distribution. Ideally, we want to use more granular grids for dense areas and large grids in sparse areas. Another potential challenge is to find neighboring grids of a fixed grid.

Option 3: Geohash

Geohash is better than the evenly divided grid option. It works by reducing the two-dimensional longitude and latitude data into a one-dimensional string of letters and digits. Geohash algorithms work by recursively dividing the world into smaller and smaller grids with each additional bit. Let's go over how geohash works at a high level.

First, divide the planet into four quadrants along with the prime meridian and equator.

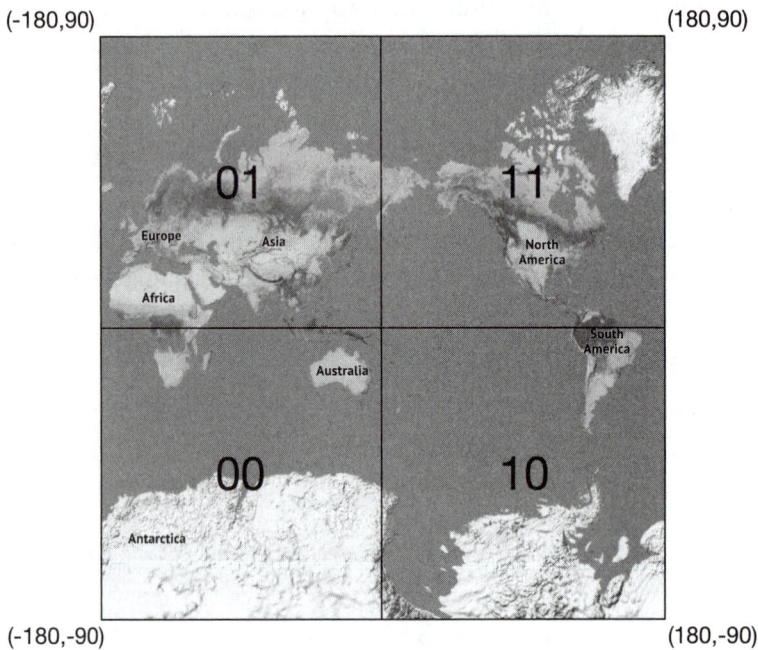

Figure 1.7: Geohash

- Latitude range $[-90, 0]$ is represented by 0
- Latitude range $[0, 90]$ is represented by 1
- Longitude range $[-180, 0]$ is represented by 0
- Longitude range $[0, 180]$ is represented by 1

Second, divide each grid into four smaller grids. Each grid can be represented by alternating between longitude bit and latitude bit.

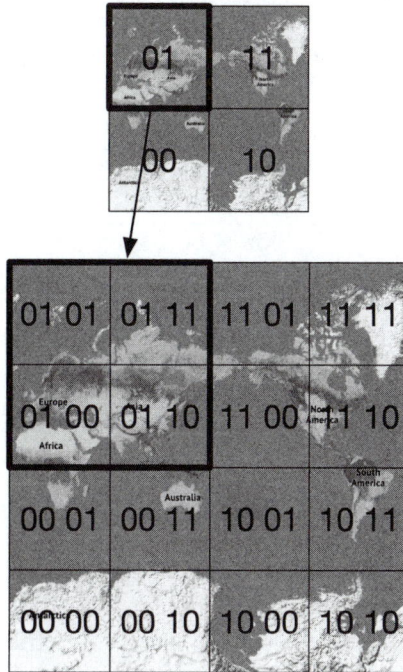

Figure 1.8: Divide grid

Repeat this subdivision until the grid size is within the precision desired. Geohash usually uses base32 representation [15]. Let's take a look at two examples.

- geohash of the Google headquarter (length = 6):
  `1001 10110 01001 10000 11011 11010` (base32 in binary) →
  9q9hvu **(base32)**
- geohash of the Facebook headquarter (length = 6):
  `1001 10110 01001 10001 10000 10111` (base32 in binary) →
  9q9jhr **(base32)**

Geohash has 12 precisions (also called levels) as shown in Table 1.4. The precision factor determines the size of the grid. We are only interested in geohashes with lengths between 4 and 6. This is because when it's longer than 6, the grid size is too small, while if it is smaller than 4, the grid size is too large (see Table 1.4).

geohash length	Grid width × height
1	5,009.4km × 4,992.6km (the size of the planet)
2	1,252.3km × 624.1km
3	156.5km × 156km
4	39.1km × 19.5km
5	4.9km × 4.9km
6	1.2km × 609.4m
7	152.9m × 152.4m
8	38.2m × 19m
9	4.8m × 4.8m
10	1.2m × 59.5cm
11	14.9cm × 14.9cm
12	3.7cm × 1.9cm

Table 1.4: Geohash length to grid size mapping (source: [16])

How do we choose the right precision? We want to find the minimal geohash length that covers the whole circle drawn by the user-defined radius. The corresponding relationship between the radius and the length of geohash is shown in the table below.

Radius (Kilometers)	Geohash length
0.5km (0.31 mile)	6
1km (0.62 mile)	5
2km (1.24 mile)	5
5km (3.1 mile)	4
20km (12.42 mile)	4

Table 1.5: Radius to geohash mapping

This approach works great most of the time, but there are some edge cases with how the geohash boundary is handled that we should discuss with the interviewer.

Boundary issues

Geohashing guarantees that the longer a shared prefix is between two geohashes, the closer they are. As shown in Figure 1.9, all the grids have a shared prefix: 9q8zn.

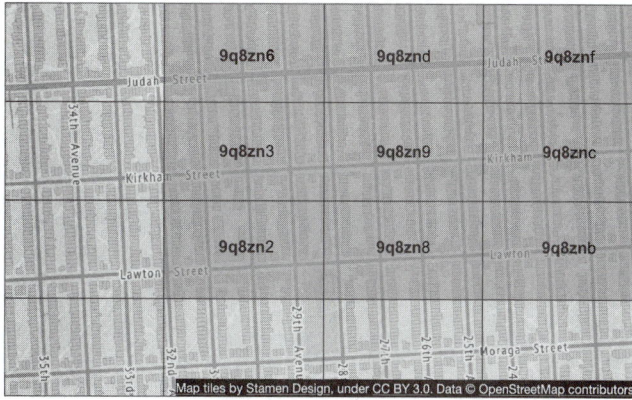

Figure 1.9: Shared prefix

Boundary issue 1

However, the reverse is not true: two locations can be very close but have no shared prefix at all. This is because two close locations on either side of the equator or prime meridian belong to different "halves" of the world. For example, in France, La Roche-Chalais (geohash: u000) is just 30km from Pomerol (geohash: ezzz) but their geohashes have no shared prefix at all [17].

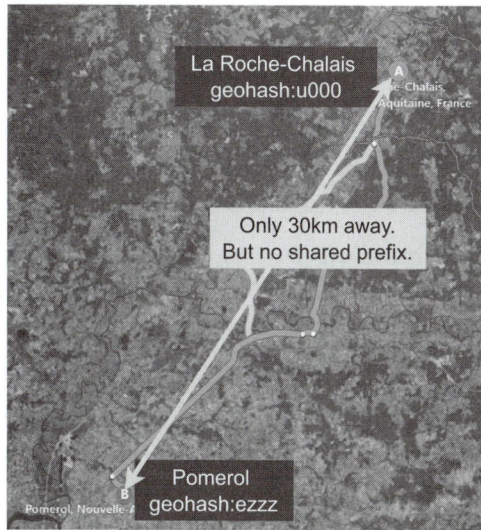

Figure 1.10: No shared prefix

Because of this boundary issue, a simple prefix SQL query below would fail to fetch all nearby businesses.

```
SELECT * FROM geohash_index WHERE geohash LIKE '9q8zn%'
```

Boundary issue 2

Another boundary issue is that two positions can have a long shared prefix, but they belong to different geohashes as shown in Figure 1.11.

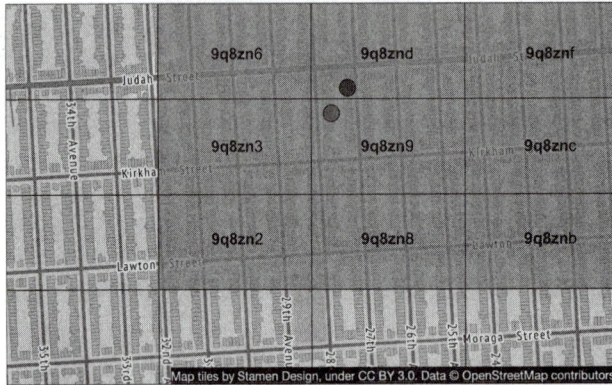

Figure 1.11: Boundary issue

A common solution is to fetch all businesses not only within the current grid but also from its neighbors. The geohashes of neighbors can be calculated in constant time and more details about this can be found here [17].

Not enough businesses

Now let's tackle the bonus question. What should we do if there are not enough businesses returned from the current grid and all the neighbors combined?

Option 1: only return businesses within the radius. This option is easy to implement, but the drawback is obvious. It doesn't return enough results to satisfy a user's needs.

Option 2: increase the search radius. We can remove the last digit of the geohash and use the new geohash to fetch nearby businesses. If there are not enough businesses, we continue to expand the scope by removing another digit. This way, the grid size is gradually expanded until the result is greater than the desired number of results. Figure 1.12 shows the conceptual diagram of the expanding search process.

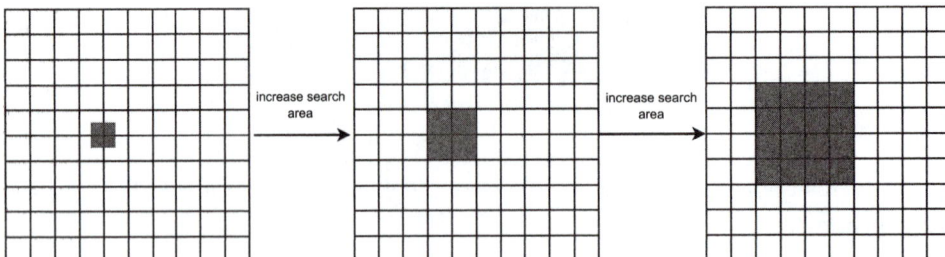

Figure 1.12: Expand the search process

Option 4: Quadtree

Another popular solution is quadtree. A quadtree [18] is a data structure that is commonly used to partition a two-dimensional space by recursively subdividing it into four quadrants (grids) until the contents of the grids meet certain criteria. For example, the criterion can be to keep subdividing until the number of businesses in the grid is not more than 100. This number is arbitrary as the actual number can be determined by business needs. With a quadtree, we build an in-memory tree structure to answer queries. Note that quadtree is an in-memory data structure and it is not a database solution. It runs on each LBS server, and the data structure is built at server start-up time.

The following figure visualizes the conceptual process of subdividing the world into a quadtree. Let's assume the world contains 200m (million) businesses.

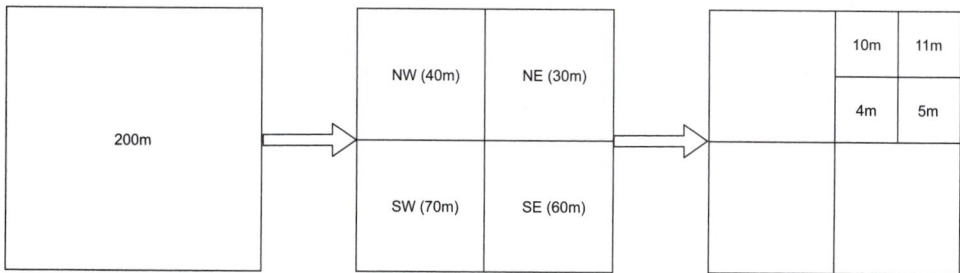

Figure 1.13: Quadtree

Figure 1.14 explains the quadtree building process in more detail. The root node represents the whole world map. The root node is recursively broken down into 4 quadrants until no nodes are left with more than 100 businesses.

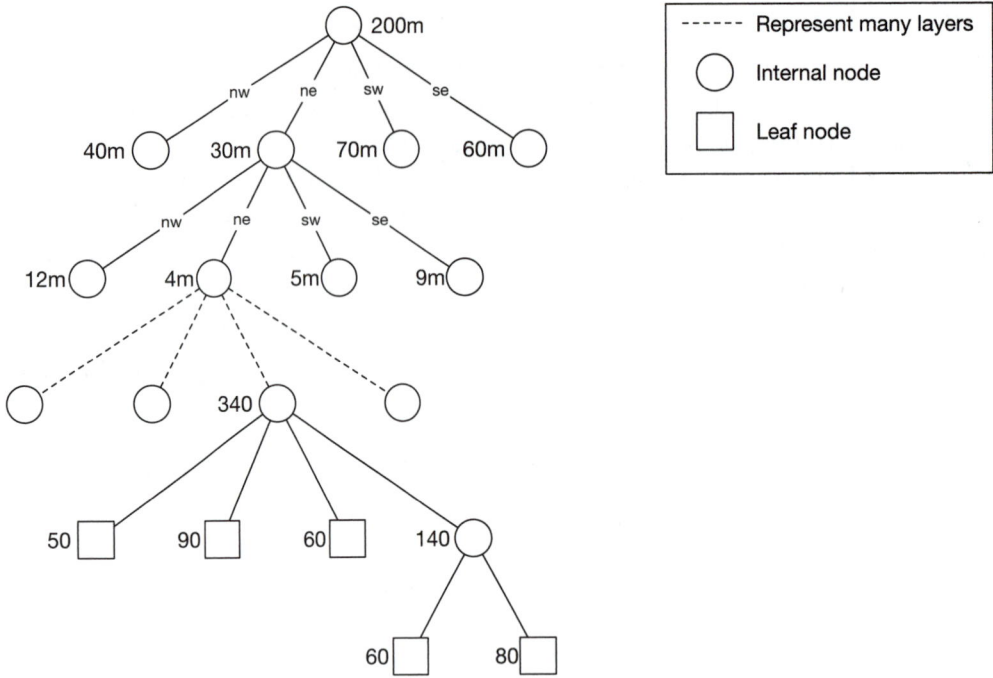

Figure 1.14: Build quadtree

The pseudocode for building quadtree is shown below:

```
public void buildQuadtree(TreeNode node) {
  if (countNumberOfBusinessesInCurrentGrid(node) > 100) {
    node.subdivide();
    for (TreeNode child : node.getChildren()) {
      buildQuadtree(child);
    }
  }
}
```

How much memory does it need to store the whole quadtree?

To answer this question, we need to know what kind of data is stored.

Data on a leaf node

Name	Size
Top left coordinates and bottom-right coordinates to identify the grid	32 bytes (8 bytes ×4)
List of business IDs in the grid	8 bytes per ID × 100 (maximal number of businesses allowed in one grid)
Total	832 bytes

Table 1.6: Leaf node

Data on internal node

Name	Size
Top left coordinates and bottom-right coordinates to identify the grid	32 bytes (8 bytes ×4)
Pointers to 4 children	32 bytes (8 bytes ×4)
Total	64 bytes

Table 1.7: Internal node

Even though the tree-building process depends on the number of businesses within a grid, this number does not need to be stored in the quadtree node because it can be inferred from records in the database.

Now that we know the data structure for each node, let's take a look at the memory usage.

- Each grid can store a maximal of 100 businesses
- Number of leaf nodes $=\sim \dfrac{200 \text{ million}}{100} =\sim 2$ million
- Number of internal nodes $= 2$ million $\times \dfrac{1}{3} =\sim 0.67$ million. If you do not know why the number of internal nodes is one-third of the leaf nodes, please read the reference material [19].
- Total memory requirement $= 2$ million $\times$ 832 bytes $+ 0.67$ million $\times$ 64 bytes $= \sim$ 1.71GB. Even if we add some overhead to build the tree, the memory requirement to build the tree is quite small.

In a real interview, we shouldn't need such detailed calculations. The key takeaway here is that the quadtree index doesn't take too much memory and can easily fit in one server. Does it mean we should use only one server to store the quadtree index? The answer is no. Depending on the read volume, a single quadtree server might not have enough CPU or network bandwidth to serve all read requests. If that is the case, it will be necessary to spread the read load among multiple quadtree servers.

How long does it take to build the whole quadtree?

Each leaf node contains approximately 100 business IDs. The time complexity to build the tree is $\frac{n}{100} \log \frac{n}{100}$, where n is the total number of businesses. It might take a few minutes to build the whole quadtree with 200 million businesses.

How to get nearby businesses with quadtree?

1. Build the quadtree in memory.
2. After the quadtree is built, start searching from the root and traverse the tree, until we find the leaf node where the search origin is. If that leaf node has 100 businesses, return the node. Otherwise, add businesses from its neighbors until enough businesses are returned.

Operational considerations for quadtree

As mentioned above, it may take a few minutes to build a quadtree with 200 million businesses at the server start-up time. It is important to consider the operational implications of such a long server start-up time. While the quadtree is being built, the server cannot serve traffic. Therefore, we should roll out a new release of the server incrementally to a small subset of servers at a time. This avoids taking a large swath of the server cluster offline and causes service brownout. Blue/green deployment [20] can also be used, but an entire cluster of new servers fetching 200 million businesses at the same time from the database service can put a lot of strain on the system. This can be done, but it may complicate the design and you should mention that in the interview.

Another operational consideration is how to update the quadtree as businesses are added and removed over time. The easiest approach would be to incrementally rebuild the quadtree, a small subset of servers at a time, across the entire cluster. But this would mean some servers would return stale data for a short period of time. However, this is generally an acceptable compromise based on the requirements. This can be further mitigated by setting up a business agreement that newly added/updated businesses will only be effective the next day. This means we can update the cache using a nightly job. One potential problem with this approach is that tons of keys will be invalidated at the same time, causing heavy load on cache servers.

It's also possible to update the quadtree on the fly as businesses are added and removed. This certainly complicates the design, especially if the quadtree data structure could be accessed by multiple threads. This will require some locking mechanism which could dramatically complicate the quadtree implementation.

Real-world quadtree example

Yext [21] provided an image (Figure 1.15) that shows a constructed quadtree near Denver [21]. We want smaller, more granular grids for dense areas and larger grids for sparse areas.

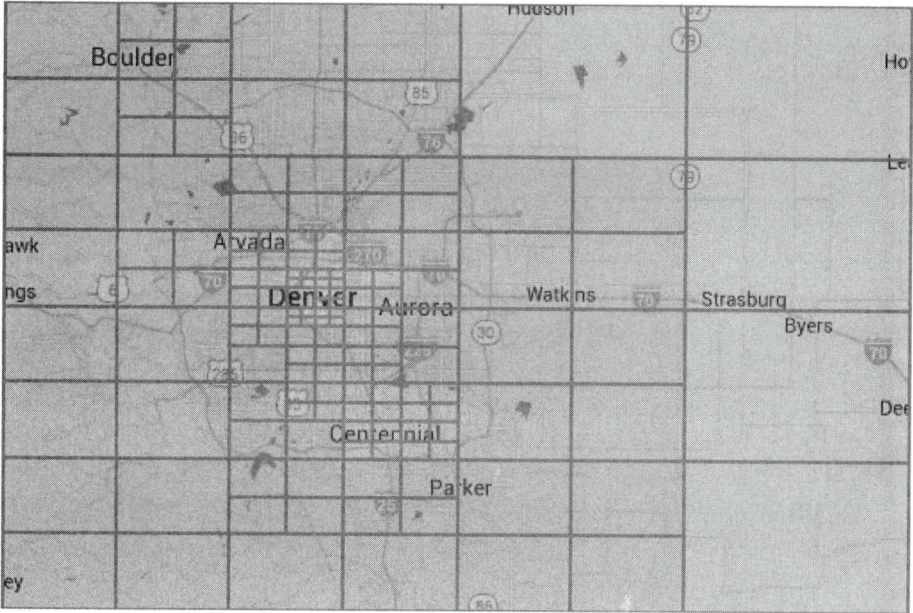

Figure 1.15: Real-world example of a quadtree

Option 5: Google S2

Google S2 geometry library [22] is another big player in this field. Similar to Quadtree, it is an in-memory solution. It maps a sphere to a 1D index based on the Hilbert curve (a space-filling curve) [23]. The Hilbert curve has a very important property: two points that are close to each other on the Hilbert curve are close in 1D space (Figure 1.16). Search on 1D space is much more efficient than on 2D. Interested readers can play with an online tool [24] for the Hilbert curve.

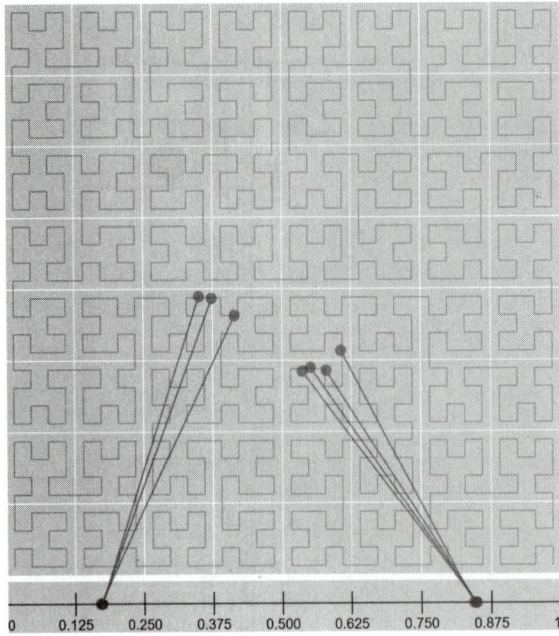

Figure 1.16: Hilbert curve (source: [24])

S2 is a complicated library and you are not expected to explain its internals during an interview. But because it's widely used in companies such as Google, Tinder, etc., we will briefly cover its advantages.

- S2 is great for geofencing because it can cover arbitrary areas with varying levels (Figure 1.17). According to Wikipedia, "A geofence is a virtual perimeter for a real-world geographic area. A geo-fence could be dynamically generated—as in a radius around a point location, or a geo-fence can be a predefined set of boundaries (such as school zones or neighborhood boundaries)" [25].

  Geofencing allows us to define perimeters that surround the areas of interest and to send notifications to users who are out of the areas. This can provide richer functionalities than just returning nearby businesses.

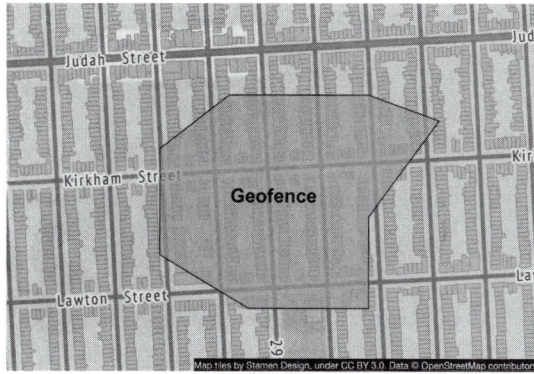

Figure 1.17: Geofence

- Another advantage of S2 is its Region Cover algorithm [26]. Instead of having a fixed level (precision) as in geohash, we can specify min level, max level, and max cells in S2. The result returned by S2 is more granular because the cell sizes are flexible. If you want to learn more, take a look at the S2 tool [26].

Recommendation

To find nearby businesses efficiently, we have discussed a few options: geohash, quadtree and S2. As you can see from Table 1.8, different companies or technologies adopt different options.

Geo Index	Companies
geohash	Bing map [27], Redis [10], MongoDB [28], Lyft [29]
quadtree	Yext [21]
Both geohash and quadtree	Elasticsearch [30]
S2	Google Maps, Tinder [31]

Table 1.8: Different types of geo indexes

During an interview, we suggest choosing **geohash or quadtree** because S2 is more complicated to explain clearly in an interview.

Geohash vs quadtree

Before we conclude this section, let's do a quick comparison between geohash and quadtree.

Geohash

- Easy to use and implement. No need to build a tree.

- Supports returning businesses within a specified radius.

- When the precision (level) of geohash is fixed, the size of the grid is fixed as well. It cannot dynamically adjust the grid size, based on population density. More complex logic is needed to support this.

- Updating the index is easy. For example, to remove a business from the index, we just need to remove it from the corresponding row with the same geohash and `business_id`. See Figure 1.18 for a concrete example.

geohash	business_id
9q8zn	3
~~9q8zn~~	~~8~~
9q8zn	4

Figure 1.18: Remove a business

Quadtree

- Slightly harder to implement because it needs to build the tree.
- Supports fetching k-nearest businesses. Sometimes we just want to return k-nearest businesses and don't care if businesses are within a specified radius. For example, when you are traveling and your car is low on gas, you just want to find the nearest k gas stations. These gas stations may not be near you, but the app needs to return the nearest k results. For this type of query, a quadtree is a good fit because its subdividing process is based on the number k and it can automatically adjust the query range until it returns k results.
- It can dynamically adjust the grid size based on population density (see the Denver example in Figure 1.15).
- Updating the index is more complicated than geohash. A quadtree is a tree structure. If a business is removed, we need to traverse from the root to the leaf node, to remove the business. For example, if we want to remove the business with ID = 2, we have to travel from the root all the way down to the leaf node, as shown in Figure 1.19. Updating the index takes $O(\log n)$, but the implementation is complicated if the data structure is accessed by a multi-threaded program, as locking is required. Also, rebalancing the tree can be complicated. Rebalancing is necessary if, for example, a leaf node has no room for a new addition. A possible fix is to over-allocate the ranges.

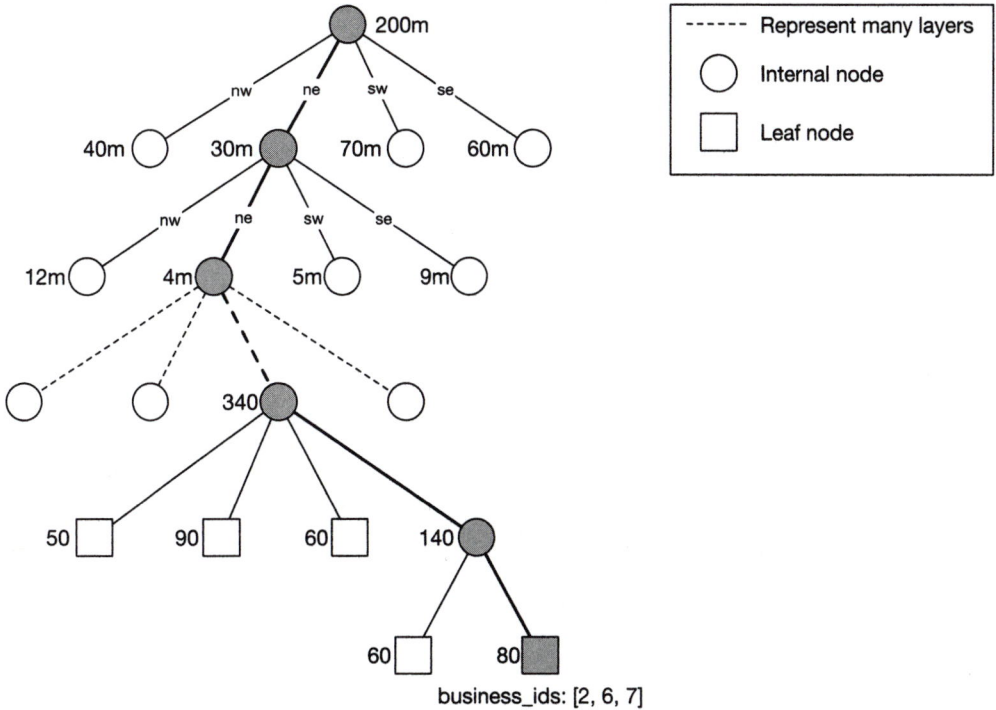

Figure 1.19: Update quadtree

Step 3 - Design Deep Dive

By now you should have a good picture of what the overall system looks like. Now let's dive deeper into a few areas.

- Scale the database
- Caching
- Region and availability zones
- Filter results by time or business type
- Final architecture diagram

Scale the database

We will discuss how to scale two of the most important tables: the business table and the geospatial index table.

Business table

The data for the business table may not all fit in one server, so it is a good candidate for sharding. The easiest approach is to shard everything by business ID. This sharding scheme ensures that load is evenly distributed among all the shards, and operationally it is easy to maintain.

Geospatial index table

Both geohash and quadtree are widely used. Due to geohash's simplicity, we use it as an example. There are two ways to structure the table.

Option 1: For each geohash key, there is a JSON array of business IDs in a single row. This means all business IDs within a geohash are stored in one row.

geospatial_index
geohash
list_of_business_ids

Table 1.9: `list_of_business_ids` is a JSON array

Option 2: If there are multiple businesses in the same geohash, there will be multiple rows, one for each business. This means different business IDs within a geohash are stored in different rows.

geospatial_index
geohash
business_id

Table 1.10: `business_id` is a single ID

Here are some sample rows for option 2.

geohash	business_id
32feac	343
32feac	347
f3lcad	112
f3lcad	113

Table 1.11: Sample rows of the geospatial index table

Recommendation: we recommend option 2 because of the following reasons:

For option 1, to update a business, we need to fetch the array of `business_ids` and scan the whole array to find the business to update. When inserting a new business, we have to scan the entire array to make sure there is no duplicate. We also need to lock the row to prevent concurrent updates. There are a lot of edge cases to handle.

For option 2, if we have two columns with a compound key of (`geohash`, `business_id`), the addition and removal of a business are very simple. There would be no need to lock anything.

Scale the geospatial index

One common mistake about scaling the geospatial index is to quickly jump to a sharding scheme without considering the actual data size of the table. In our case, the full dataset for the geospatial index table is not large (quadtree index only takes 1.71G memory and storage requirement for geohash index is similar). The whole geospatial index can easily fit in the working set of a modern database server. However, depending on the read volume, a single database server might not have enough CPU or network bandwidth to handle all read requests. If that is the case, it is necessary to spread the read load among multiple database servers.

There are two general approaches for spreading the load of a relational database server. We can add read replicas, or shard the database.

Many engineers like to talk about sharding during interviews. However, it might not be a good fit for the geohash table as sharding is complicated. For instance, the sharding logic has to be added to the application layer. Sometimes, sharding is the only option. In this case, though, everything can fit in the working set of a database server, so there is no strong technical reason to shard the data among multiple servers.

A better approach, in this case, is to have a series of read replicas to help with the read load. This method is much simpler to develop and maintain. For this reason, scaling the geospatial index table through replicas is recommended.

Caching

Before introducing a cache layer we have to ask ourselves, do we really need a cache layer?

It is not immediately obvious that caching is a solid win:

- The workload is read-heavy, and the dataset is relatively small. The data could fit in the working set of any modern database server. Therefore, the queries are not I/O bound and they should run almost as fast as an in-memory cache.
- If read performance is a bottleneck, we can add database read replicas to improve the read throughput.

Be mindful when discussing caching with the interviewer, as it will require careful benchmarking and cost analysis. If you find out that caching does fit the business requirements, then you can proceed with discussions about caching strategy.

Cache key

The most straightforward cache key choice is the location coordinates (latitude and longitude) of the user. However, this choice has a few issues:

- Location coordinates returned from mobile phones are not accurate as they are just the best estimation [32]. Even if you don't move, the results might be slightly different each time you fetch coordinates on your phone.
- A user can move from one location to another, causing location coordinates to change slightly. For most applications, this change is not meaningful.

Therefore, location coordinates are not a good cache key. Ideally, small changes in location should still map to the same cache key. The geohash/quadtree solution mentioned earlier handles this problem well because all businesses within a grid map to the same geohash.

Types of data to cache

As shown in Table 1.12, there are two types of data that can be cached to improve the overall performance of the system:

Key	Value
geohash	List of business IDs in the grid
business_id	Business object

Table 1.12: Key-value pairs in cache

List of business IDs in a grid

Since business data is relatively stable, we precompute the list of business IDs for a given geohash and store it in a key-value store such as Redis. Let's take a look at a concrete example of getting nearby businesses with caching enabled.

1. Get the list of business IDs for a given geohash.

```
SELECT business_id FROM geohash_index WHERE geohash LIKE `{:
geohash}%`
```

2. Store the result in the Redis cache if cache misses.

```
public List<String> getNearbyBusinessIds(String geohash) {
  String cacheKey = hash(geohash);
  List<string> listOfBusinessIds = Redis.get(cacheKey);
  if (listOfBusinessIDs == null) {
    listOfBusinessIds = Run the select SQL query above;
    Cache.set(cacheKey, listOfBusinessIds, "1d");
  }
  return listOfBusinessIds;
}
```

When a new business is added, edited, or deleted, the database is updated and the cache invalidated. Since the volume of those operations is relatively small and no locking mechanism is needed for the geohash approach, update operations are easy to deal with.

According to the requirements, a user can choose the following 4 radii on the client: 500m, 1km, 2km, and 5km. Those radii are mapped to geohash lengths of 4, 5, 5, and 6, respectively. To quickly fetch nearby businesses for different radii, we cache data in Redis on all three precisions (geohash_4, geohash_5, and geohash_6).

As mentioned earlier, we have 200 million businesses and each business belongs to 1 grid in a given precision. Therefore the total memory required is:

- Storage for Redis values: 8 bytes × 200 million × 3 precisions = ~ 5GB
- Storage for Redis keys: negligible
- Total memory required: ~ 5GB

We can get away with one modern Redis server from the memory usage perspective, but to ensure high availability and reduce cross continent latency, we deploy the Redis cluster across the globe. Given the estimated data size, we can have the same copy of cache data deployed globally. We call this Redis cache "Geohash" in our final architecture diagram (Figure 1.21).

Business data needed to render pages on the client

This type of data is quite straightforward to cache. The key is the business_id and the value is the business object which contains the business name, address, image URLs, etc. We call this Redis cache "Business info" in our final architecture diagram (Figure 1.21).

Region and availability zones

We deploy a location-based service to multiple regions and availability zones as shown in Figure 1.20. This has a few advantages:

- Makes users physically "closer" to the system. Users from the US West are connected to the data centers in that region, and users from Europe are connected with data centers in Europe.

- Gives us the flexibility to spread the traffic evenly across the population. Some regions such as Japan and Korea have high population densities. It might be wise to put them in separate regions, or even deploy location-based services in multiple availability zones to spread the load.

- Privacy laws. Some countries may require user data to be used and stored locally. In this case, we could set up a region in that country and employ DNS routing to restrict all requests from the country to only that region.

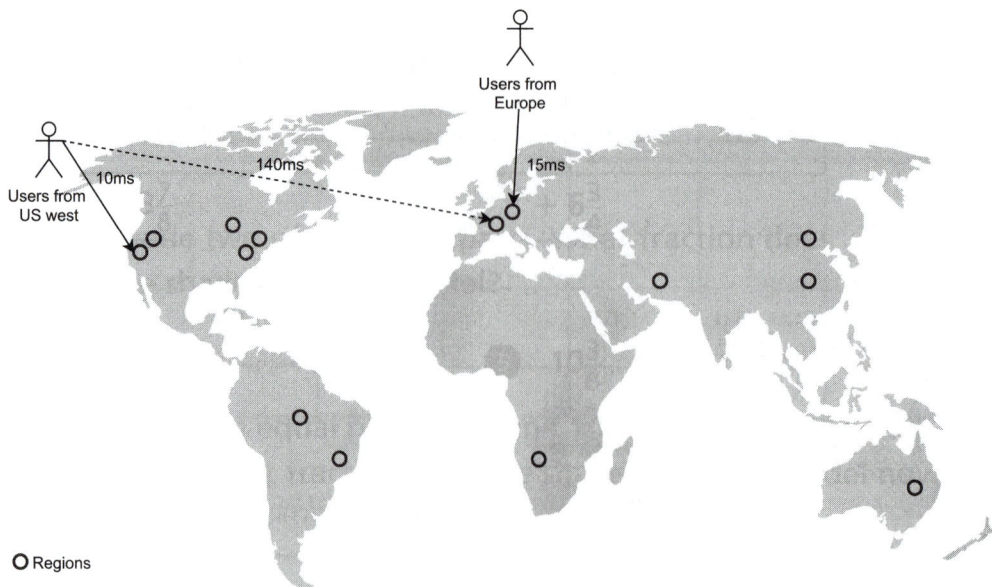

Figure 1.20: Deploy LBS "closer" to the user

Follow-up question: filter results by time or business type

The interviewer might ask a follow-up question: how to return businesses that are open now, or only return businesses that are restaurants?

Candidate: When the world is divided into small grids with geohash or quadtree, the number of businesses returned from the search result is relatively small. Therefore, it is acceptable to return business IDs first, hydrate business objects, and filter them based on opening time or business type. This solution assumes opening time and business type are stored in the business table.

Final design diagram

Putting everything together, we come up with the following design diagram.

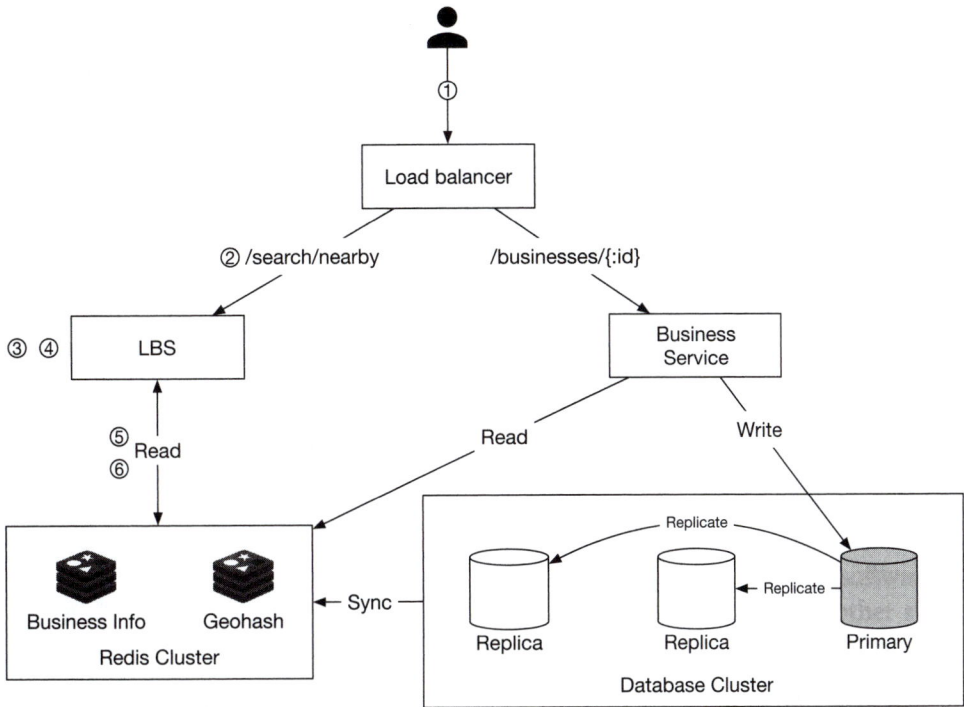

Figure 1.21: Design diagram

Get nearby businesses

1. You try to find restaurants within 500 meters on Yelp. The client sends the user location (latitude $= 37.776720$, longitude $= -122.416730$) and radius (500m) to the load balancer.

2. The load balancer forwards the request to the LBS.

3. Based on the user location and radius info, the LBS finds the geohash length that matches the search. By checking Table 1.5, 500m map to geohash length $= 6$.

4. LBS calculates neighboring geohashes and adds them to the list. The result looks like this:
   list_of_geohashes = [my_geohash, neighbor1_geohash, neighbor2_geohash, ..., neighbor8_geohash].

5. For each geohash in list_of_geohashes, LBS calls the "Geohash" Redis server to fetch corresponding business IDs. Calls to fetch business IDs for each geohash can be made in parallel to reduce latency.

6. Based on the list of business IDs returned, LBS fetches fully hydrated business information from the "Business info" Redis server, then calculates distances between a user and businesses, ranks them, and returns the result to the client.

View, update, add or delete a business

All business-related APIs are separated from the LBS. To view the detailed information about a business, the business service first checks if the data is stored in the "Business info" Redis cache. If it is, cached data will be returned to the client. If not, data is fetched from the database cluster and then stored in the Redis cache, allowing subsequent requests to get results from the cache directly.

Since we have an upfront business agreement that newly added/updated businesses will be effective the next day, cached business data is updated by a nightly job.

Step 4 - Wrap Up

In this chapter, we have presented the design for proximity service. The system is a typical LBS that leverages geospatial indexing. We discussed several indexing options:

- Two-dimensional search
- Evenly divided grid
- Geohash
- Quadtree
- Google S2

Geohash, quadtree, and S2 are widely used by different tech companies. We choose geohash as an example to show how a geospatial index works.

In the deep dive, we discussed why caching is effective in reducing the latency, what should be cached and how to use cache to retrieve nearby businesses fast. We also discussed how to scale the database with replication and sharding.

We then looked at deploying LBS in different regions and availability zones to improve availability, to make users physically closer to the servers, and to comply better with local privacy laws.

Congratulations on getting this far! Now give yourself a pat on the back. Good job!

Chapter Summary

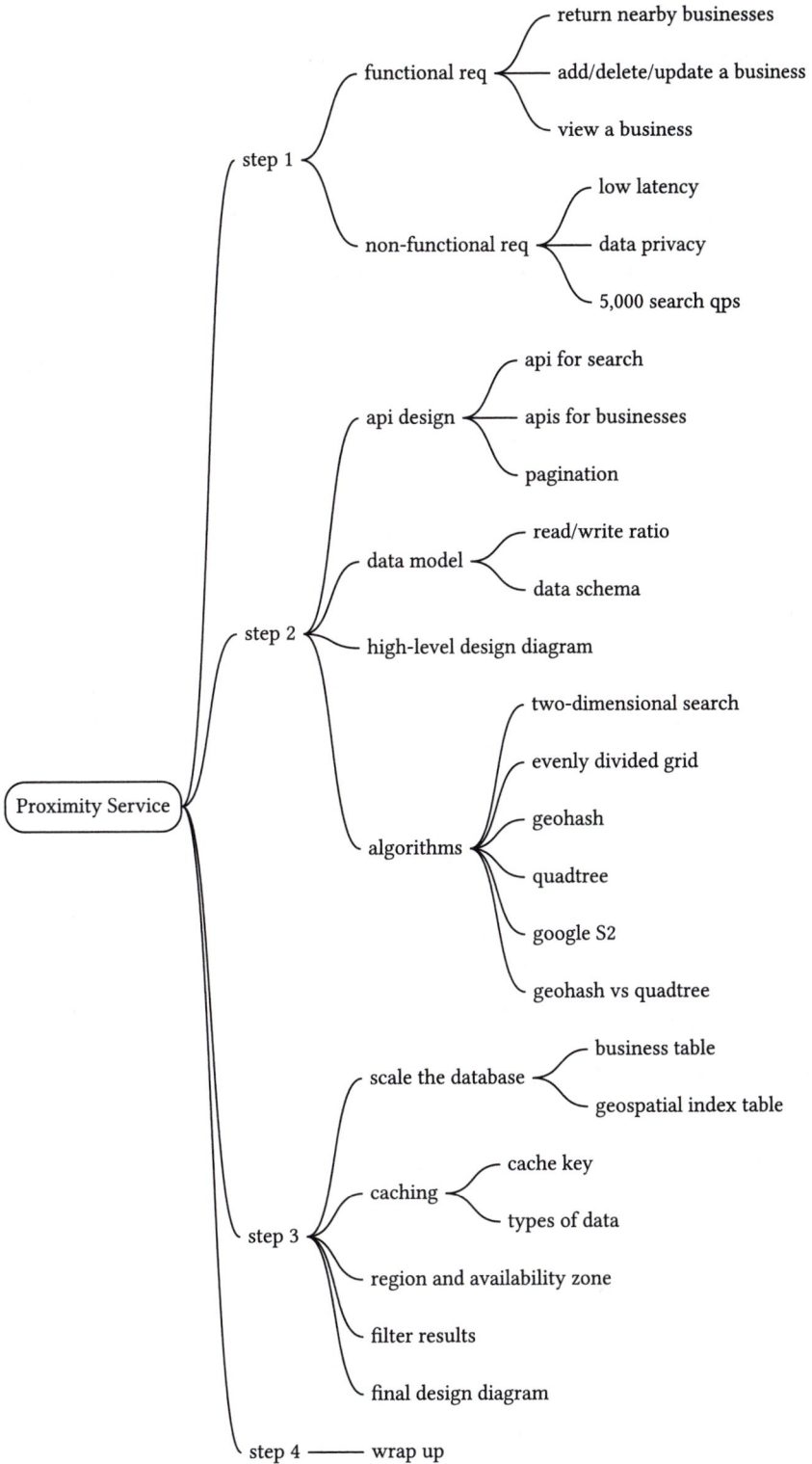

Proximity Service

- step 1
  - functional req
    - return nearby businesses
    - add/delete/update a business
    - view a business
  - non-functional req
    - low latency
    - data privacy
    - 5,000 search qps
- step 2
  - api design
    - api for search
    - apis for businesses
    - pagination
  - data model
    - read/write ratio
    - data schema
  - high-level design diagram
  - algorithms
    - two-dimensional search
    - evenly divided grid
    - geohash
    - quadtree
    - google S2
    - geohash vs quadtree
- step 3
  - scale the database
    - business table
    - geospatial index table
  - caching
    - cache key
    - types of data
  - region and availability zone
  - filter results
  - final design diagram
- step 4 — wrap up

Reference Material

[1] Yelp. https://www.yelp.com/.

[2] Map tiles by Stamen Design. http://maps.stamen.com/.

[3] OpenStreetMap. https://www.openstreetmap.org.

[4] GDPR. https://en.wikipedia.org/wiki/General_Data_Protection_Regulation.

[5] CCPA. https://en.wikipedia.org/wiki/California_Consumer_Privacy_Act.

[6] Pagination in the REST API. https://developer.atlassian.com/server/confluence/pagination-in-the-rest-api/.

[7] Google places API. https://developers.google.com/maps/documentation/places/web-service/search.

[8] Yelp business endpoints. https://www.yelp.com/developers/documentation/v3/business_search.

[9] Regions and Zones. https://docs.aws.amazon.com/AWSEC2/latest/UserGuide/using-regions-availability-zones.html.

[10] Redis GEOHASH. https://redis.io/commands/GEOHASH.

[11] POSTGIS. https://postgis.net/.

[12] Cartesian tiers. http://www.nsshutdown.com/projects/lucene/whitepaper/localluc ene_v2.html.

[13] R-tree. https://en.wikipedia.org/wiki/R-tree.

[14] Global map in a Geographic Coordinate Reference System. https://bit.ly/3DsjAwg.

[15] Base32. https://en.wikipedia.org/wiki/Base32.

[16] Geohash grid aggregation. https://bit.ly/3kKl4e6.

[17] Geohash. https://www.movable-type.co.uk/scripts/geohash.html.

[18] Quadtree. https://en.wikipedia.org/wiki/Quadtree.

[19] How many leaves has a quadtree. https://stackoverflow.com/questions/35976444/how-many-leaves-has-a-quadtree.

[20] Blue green deployment. https://martinfowler.com/bliki/BlueGreenDeployment.html.

[21] Improved Location Caching with Quadtrees. https://engblog.yext.com/post/geolocation-caching.

[22] S2. https://s2geometry.io/.

[23] Hilbert curve. https://en.wikipedia.org/wiki/Hilbert_curve.

[24] Hilbert mapping. http://bit-player.org/extras/hilbert/hilbert-mapping.html.

[25] Geo-fence. https://en.wikipedia.org/wiki/Geo-fence.

[26] Region cover. https://s2.sidewalklabs.com/regioncoverer/.

[27] Bing map. https://bit.ly/30ytSfG.

[28] MongoDB. https://docs.mongodb.com/manual/tutorial/build-a-2d-index/.

[29] Geospatial Indexing: The 10 Million QPS Redis Architecture Powering Lyft. https://www.youtube.com/watch?v=cSFWlF96Sds&t=2155s.

[30] Geo Shape Type. https://www.elastic.co/guide/en/elasticsearch/reference/1.6/mapping-geo-shape-type.html.

[31] Geosharded Recommendations Part 1: Sharding Approach. https://medium.com/tinder-engineering/geosharded-recommendations-part-1-sharding-approach-d5d54e0ec77a.

[32] Get the last known location. https://developer.android.com/training/location/retrieve-current#Challenges.

2   Nearby Friends

In this chapter, we design a scalable backend system for a new mobile app feature called "Nearby Friends". For an opt-in user who grants permission to access their location, the mobile client presents a list of friends who are geographically nearby. If you are looking for a real-world example, please refer to this article [1] about a similar feature in the Facebook app.

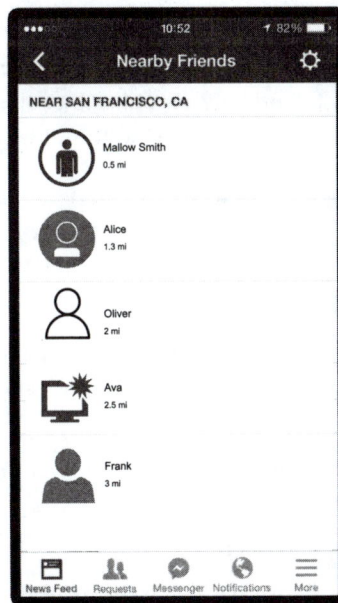

Figure 2.1: Facebook's nearby friends

If you read Chapter 1 Proximity Service, you may wonder why we need a separate chapter for designing "nearby friends" since it looks similar to proximity services. If you think carefully though, you will find major differences. In proximity services, the addresses for businesses are static as their locations do not change, while in "nearby friends", data is more dynamic because user locations change frequently.

Step 1 - Understand the Problem and Establish Design Scope

Any backend system at the Facebook scale is complicated. Before starting with the design, we need to ask clarification questions to narrow down the scope.

Candidate: How geographically close is considered to be "nearby"?
Interviewer: 5 miles. This number should be configurable.

Candidate: Can I assume the distance is calculated as the straight-line distance between two users? In real life, there could be, for example, a river in between the users, resulting in a longer travel distance.
Interviewer: Yes, that's a reasonable assumption.

Candidate: How many users does the app have? Can I assume 1 billion users and 10% of them use the nearby friends feature?
Interviewer: Yes, that's a reasonable assumption.

Candidate: Do we need to store location history?
Interviewer: Yes, location history can be valuable for different purposes such as machine learning.

Candidate: Could we assume if a friend is inactive for more than 10 minutes, that friend will disappear from the nearby friend list? Or should we display the last known location?
Interviewer: We can assume inactive friends will no longer be shown.

Candidate: Do we need to worry about privacy and data laws such as GDPR or CCPA?
Interviewer: Good question. For simplicity, don't worry about it for now.

Functional requirements

- Users should be able to see nearby friends on their mobile apps. Each entry in the nearby friend list has a distance and a timestamp indicating when the distance was last updated.
- Nearby friend lists should be updated every few seconds.

Non-functional requirements

- Low latency. It's important to receive location updates from friends without too much delay.
- Reliability. The system needs to be reliable overall, but occasional data point loss is acceptable.
- Eventual consistency. The location data store doesn't need strong consistency. A few seconds delay in receiving location data in different replicas is acceptable.

Back-of-the-envelope estimation

Let's do a back-of-the-envelope estimation to determine the potential scale and challenges our solution will need to address. Some constraints and assumptions are listed below:

- Nearby friends are defined as friends whose locations are within a 5-mile radius.
- The location refresh interval is 30 seconds. The reason for this is that human walking speed is slow (average $3 \sim 4$ miles per hour). The distance traveled in 30 seconds does not make a significant difference on the "nearby friends" feature.
- On average, 100 million users use the "nearby friends" feature every day.
- Assume the number of concurrent users is 10% of DAU (Daily Active Users), so the number of concurrent users is 10 million.
- On average, a user has 400 friends. Assume all of them use the "nearby friends" feature.
- The app displays 20 nearby friends per page and may load more nearby friends upon request.

Calculate QPS
• 100 million DAU
• Concurrent users: $10\% \times 100$ million $= 10$ million
• Users report their locations every 30 seconds.
• Location update QPS $= \dfrac{10 \text{ million}}{30} = \sim 334{,}000$

Step 2 - Propose High-level Design and Get Buy-in

In this section, we will discuss the following:

- High-level design
- API design
- Data model

In other chapters, we usually discuss API design and data model before the high-level design. However, for this problem, the communication protocol between client and server might not be a straightforward HTTP protocol, as we need to push location data to all friends. Without understanding the high-level design, it's difficult to know what the APIs look like. Therefore, we discuss the high-level design first.

High-level design

At a high level, this problem calls for a design with efficient message passing. Conceptually, a user would like to receive location updates from every active friend nearby. It could in theory be done purely peer-to-peer, that is, a user could maintain a persistent connection to every other active friend in the vicinity (Figure 2.2).

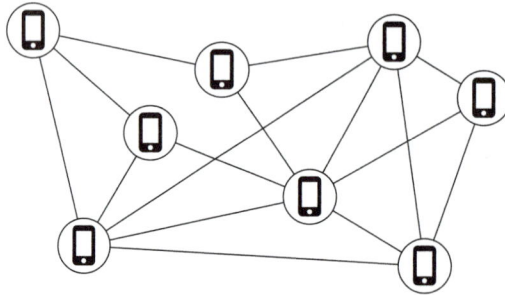

Figure 2.2: Peer-to-peer

This solution is not practical for a mobile device with sometimes flaky connections and a tight power consumption budget, but the idea sheds some light on the general design direction.

A more practical design would have a shared backend and look like this:

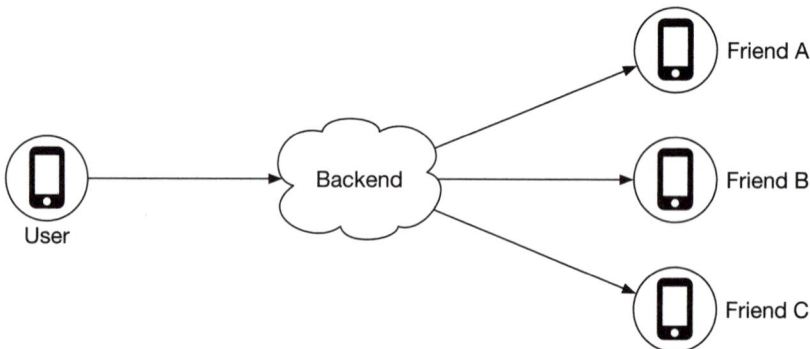

Figure 2.3: Shared backend

What are the responsibilities of the backend in Figure 2.3?

- Receive location updates from all active users.
- For each location update, find all the active friends who should receive it and forward it to those users' devices.
- If the distance between two users is over a certain threshold, do not forward it to the recipient's device.

This sounds pretty simple. What is the issue? Well, to do this at scale is not easy. We have 10 million active users. With each user updating the location information every 30 seconds, there are 334K updates per second. If on average each user has 400 friends, and we further assume that roughly 10% of those friends are online and nearby, every second the backend forwards $334K \times 400 \times 10\% = 14$ million location updates per second. That is a lot of updates to forward.

Proposed design

We will first come up with a high-level design for the backend at a lower scale. Later in the deep dive section, we will optimize the design for scale.

Figure 2.4 shows the basic design that should satisfy the functional requirements. Let's go over each component in the design.

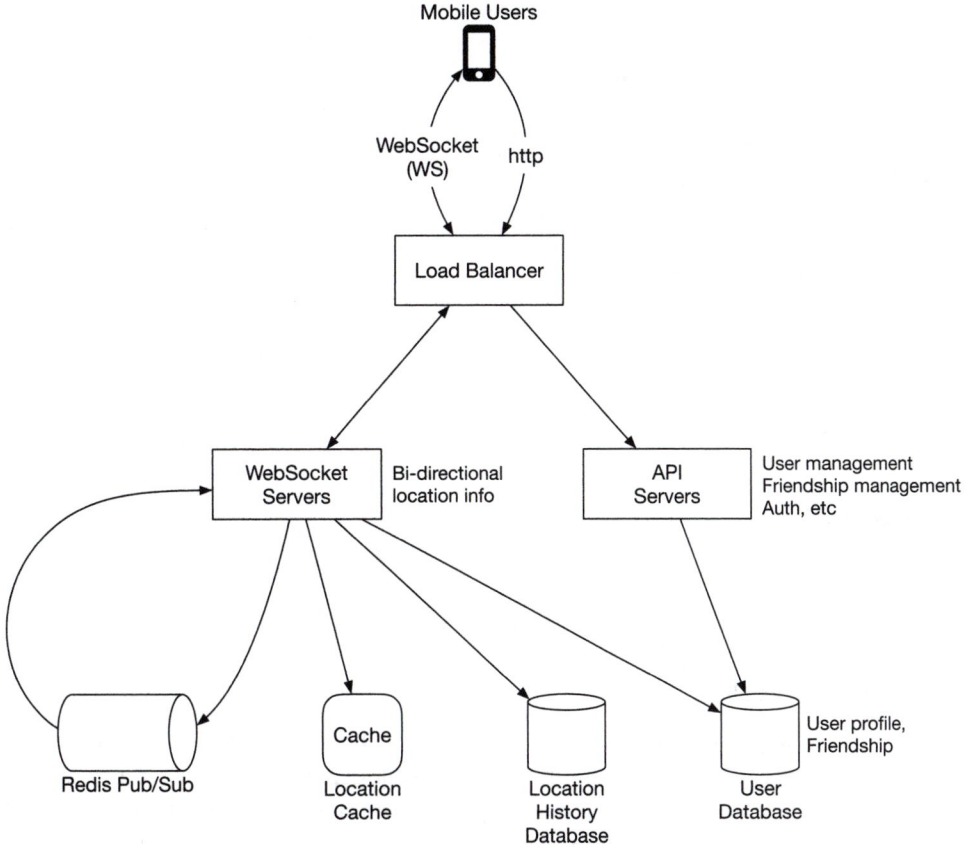

Figure 2.4: High-level design

Load balancer

The load balancer sits in front of the RESTful API servers and the stateful, bi-directional WebSocket servers. It distributes traffic across those servers to spread out load evenly.

RESTful API servers

This is a cluster of stateless HTTP servers that handles the typical request/response traffic. The API request flow is highlighted in Figure 2.5. This API layer handles auxiliary tasks like adding/removing friends, updating user profiles, etc. These are very common and we will not go into more detail.

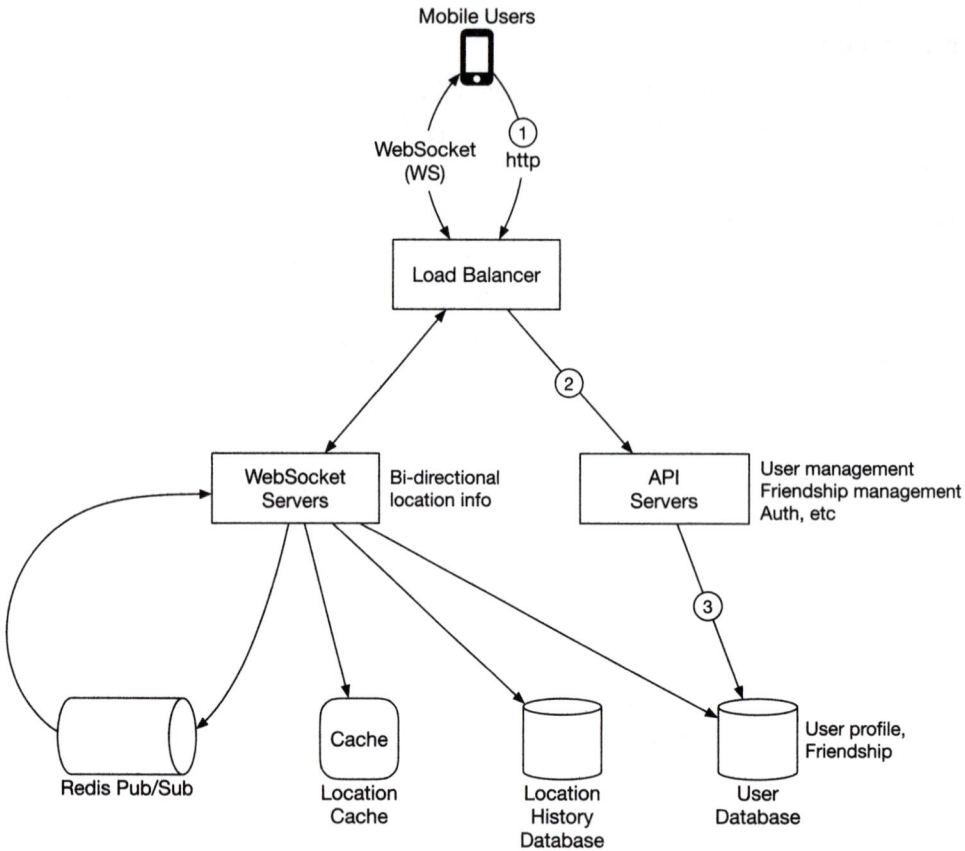

Figure 2.5: RESTful API request flow

WebSocket servers

This is a cluster of stateful servers that handles the near real-time update of friends' locations. Each client maintains one persistent WebSocket connection to one of these servers. When there is a location update from a friend who is within the search radius, the update is sent on this connection to the client.

Another major responsibility of the WebSocket servers is to handle client initialization for the "nearby friends" feature. It seeds the mobile client with the locations of all nearby online friends. We will discuss how this is done in more detail later.

Note "WebSocket connection" and "WebSocket connection handler" are interchangeable in this chapter.

Redis location cache

Redis is used to store the most recent location data for each active user. There is a Time to Live (TTL) set on each entry in the cache. When the TTL expires, the user is no longer active and the location data is expunged from the cache. Every update refreshes the TTL.

Other KV stores that support TTL could also be used.

User database

The user database stores user data and user friendship data. Either a relational database or a NoSQL database can be used for this.

Location history database

This database stores users' historical location data. It is not directly related to the "nearby friends" feature.

Redis Pub/Sub server

Redis Pub/Sub [2] is a very lightweight message bus. Channels in Redis Pub/Sub are very cheap to create. A modern Redis server with GBs of memory could hold millions of channels (also called topics). Figure 2.6 shows how Redis Pub/Sub works.

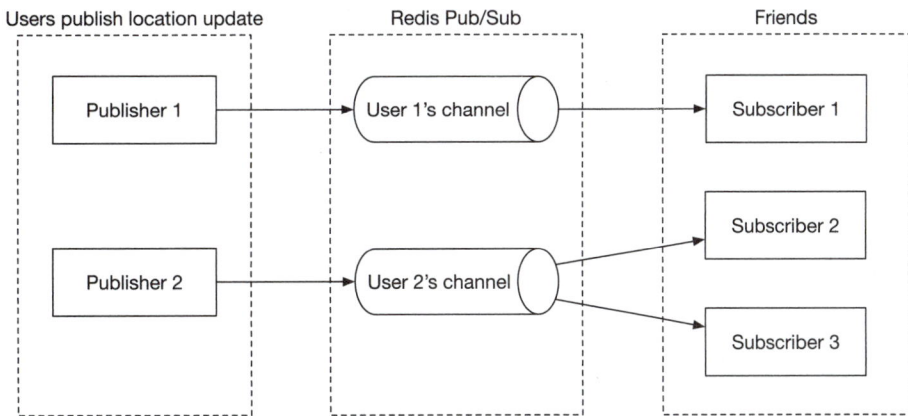

Figure 2.6: Redis Pub/Sub

In this design, location updates received via the WebSocket server are published to the user's own channel in the Redis Pub/Sub server. A dedicated WebSocket connection handler for each active friend subscribes to the channel. When there is a location update, the WebSocket handler function gets invoked, and for each active friend, the function recomputes the distance. If the new distance is within the search radius, the new location and timestamp are sent via the WebSocket connection to the friend's client. Other message buses with lightweight channels could also be used.

Now that we understand what each component does, let's examine what happens when a user's location changes from the system's perspective.

Periodic location update

The mobile client sends periodic location updates over the persistent WebSocket connection. The flow is shown in Figure 2.7.

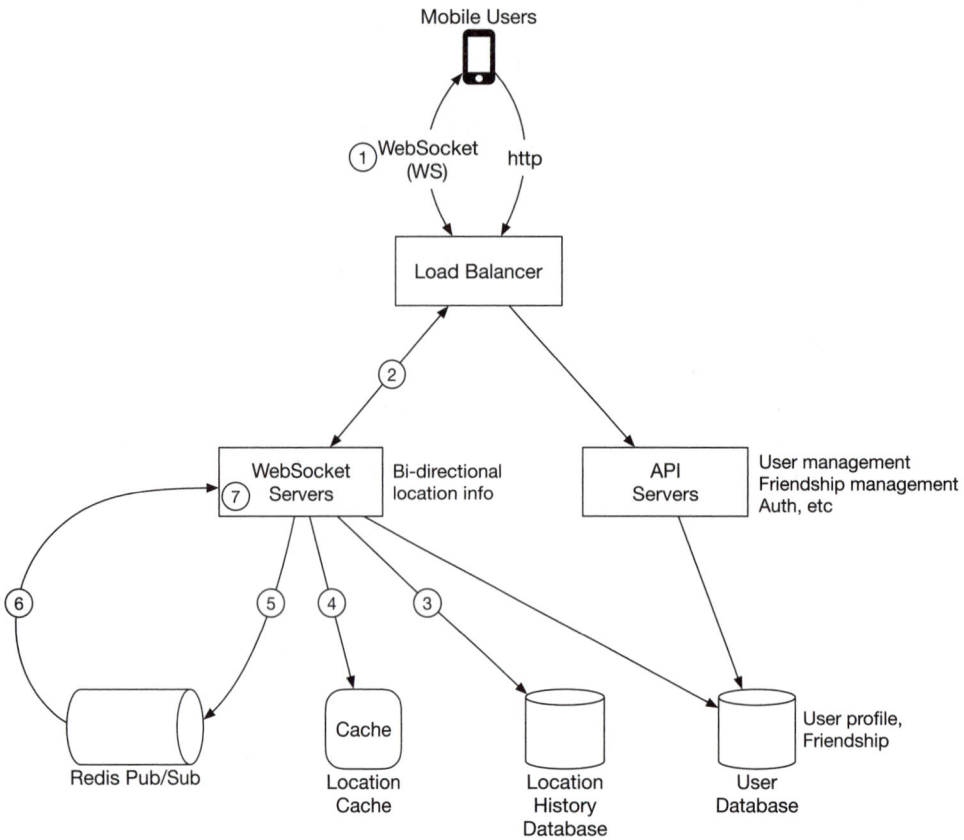

Figure 2.7: Periodic location update

1. The mobile client sends a location update to the load balancer.

2. The load balancer forwards the location update to the persistent connection on the WebSocket server for that client.

3. The WebSocket server saves the location data to the location history database.

4. The WebSocket server updates the new location in the location cache. The update refreshes the TTL. The WebSocket server also saves the new location in a variable in the user's WebSocket connection handler for subsequent distance calculations.

5. The WebSocket server publishes the new location to the user's channel in the Redis Pub/Sub server. Steps 3 to 5 can be executed in parallel.

6. When Redis Pub/Sub receives a location update on a channel, it broadcasts the update to all the subscribers (WebSocket connection handlers). In this case, the subscribers are all the online friends of the user sending the update. For each subscriber (i.e., for each of the user's friends), its WebSocket connection handler would receive the user location update.

7. On receiving the message, the WebSocket server, on which the connection handler lives, computes the distance between the user sending the new location (the location data is in the message) and the subscriber (the location data is stored in a variable

with the WebSocket connection handler for the subscriber).

8. This step is not drawn on the diagram. If the distance does not exceed the search radius, the new location and the last updated timestamp are sent to the subscriber's client. Otherwise, the update is dropped.

Since understanding this flow is extremely important, let's examine it again with a concrete example, as shown in Figure 2.8. Before we start, let's make a few assumptions.

- User 1's friends: User 2, User 3, and User 4.
- User 5's friends: User 4 and User 6.

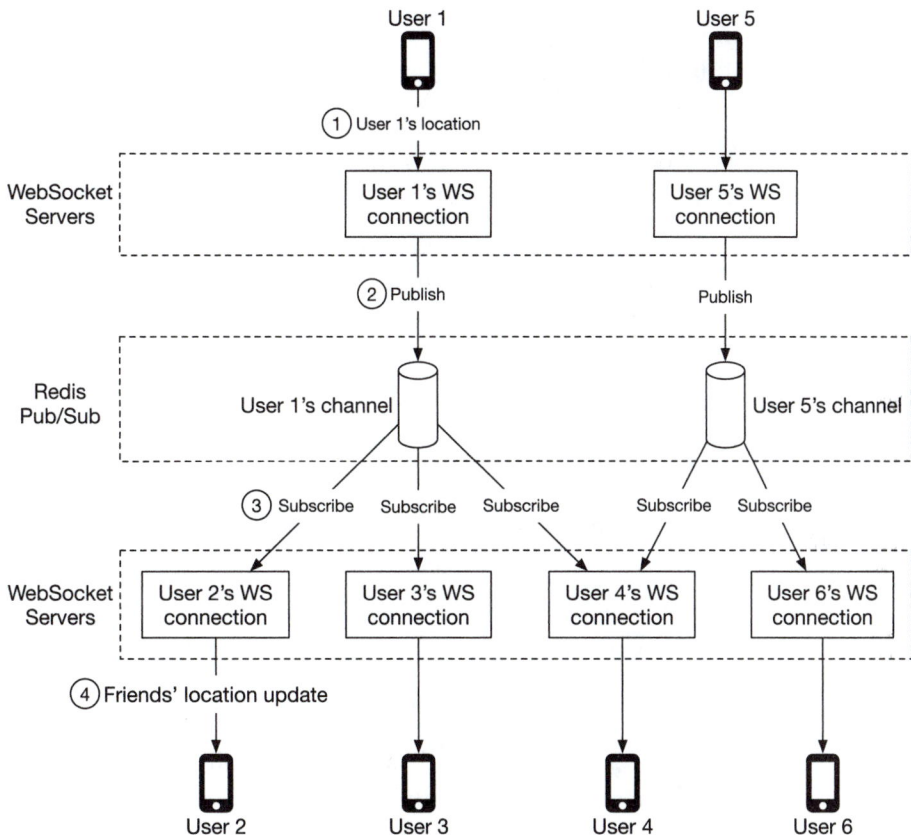

Figure 2.8: Send location update to friends

1. When User 1's location changes, their location update is sent to the WebSocket server which holds User 1's connection.

2. The location is published to User 1's channel in Redis Pub/Sub server.

3. Redis Pub/Sub server broadcasts the location update to all subscribers. In this case, subscribers are WebSocket connection handlers (User 1's friends).

4. If the distance between the user sending the location (User 1) and the subscriber (User 2) doesn't exceed the search radius, the new location is sent to the client (User 2).

This computation is repeated for every subscriber to the channel. Since there are 400 friends on average, and we assume that 10% of those friends are online and nearby, there are about 40 location updates to forward for each user's location update.

API design

Now that we have created a high-level design, let's list APIs needed.

WebSocket: Users send and receive location updates through the WebSocket protocol. At the minimum, we need the following APIs.

1. Periodic location update
Request: Client sends latitude, longitude, and timestamp.
Response: Nothing.

2. Client receives location updates
Data sent: Friend location data and timestamp.

3. WebSocket initialization
Request: Client sends latitude, longitude, and timestamp.
Response: Client receives friends' location data.

4. Subscribe to a new friend
Request: WebSocket server sends friend ID.
Response: Friend's latest latitude, longitude, and timestamp.

5. Unsubscribe a friend
Request: WebSocket server sends friend ID.
Response. Nothing.

HTTP requests: the API servers handle tasks like adding/removing friends, updating user profiles, etc. These are very common and we will not go into detail here.

Data model

Another important element to discuss is the data model. We already talked about the User DB in the high-level design, so let's focus on the location cache and location history database.

Location cache

The location cache stores the latest locations of all active users who have had the nearby friends feature turned on. We use Redis for this cache. The key/value of the cache is shown in Table 2.1.

key	value
user_id	{latitude, longitude, timestamp}

Table 2.1: Location cache

Why don't we use a database to store location data?

The "nearby friends" feature only cares about the **current** location of a user. Therefore, we only need to store one location per user. Redis is an excellent choice because it provides super-fast read and write operations. It supports TTL, which we use to auto-purge users from the cache who are no longer active. The current locations do not need to be durably stored. If the Redis instance goes down, we could replace it with an empty new instance and let the cache be filled as new location updates stream in. The active users could miss location updates from friends for an update cycle or two while the new cache warms. It is an acceptable tradeoff. In the deep dive section, we will discuss ways to lessen the impact on users when the cache gets replaced.

Location history database

The location history database stores users' historical location data and the schema looks like this:

user_id	latitude	longitude	timestamp

We need a database that handles the heavy-write workload well and can be horizontally scaled. Cassandra is a good candidate. We could also use a relational database. However, with a relational database, the historical data would not fit in a single instance so we need to shard that data. The most basic approach is to shard by user ID. This sharding scheme ensures that load is evenly distributed among all the shards, and operationally, it is easy to maintain.

Step 3 - Design Deep Dive

The high-level design we created in the previous section works in most cases, but it will likely break at our scale. In this section, we work together to uncover the bottlenecks as we increase the scale, and along the way work on solutions to eliminate those bottlenecks.

How well does each component scale?

API servers

The methods to scale the RESTful API tiers are well understood. These are stateless servers, and there are many ways to auto-scale the clusters based on CPU usage, load, or I/O. We will not go into detail here.

WebSocket servers

For the WebSocket cluster, it is not difficult to auto-scale based on usage. However, the WebSocket servers are stateful, so care must be taken when removing existing nodes. Before a node can be removed, all existing connections should be allowed to drain. To achieve that, we can mark a node as "draining" at the load balancer so that no new WebSocket connections will be routed to the draining server. Once all the existing connections are closed (or after a reasonably long wait), the server is then removed.

Releasing a new version of the application software on a WebSocket server requires the same level of care.

It is worth noting that effective auto-scaling of stateful servers is the job of a good load balancer. Most cloud load balancers handle this job very well.

Client initialization

The mobile client on startup establishes a persistent WebSocket connection with one of the WebSocket server instances. Each connection is long-running. Most modern languages are capable of maintaining many long-running connections with a reasonably small memory footprint.

When a WebSocket connection is initialized, the client sends the initial location of the user, and the server performs the following tasks in the WebSocket connection handler.

1. It updates the user's location in the location cache.
2. It saves the location in a variable of the connection handler for subsequent calculations.
3. It loads all the user's friends from the user database.
4. It makes a batched request to the location cache to fetch the locations for all the friends. Note that because we set a TTL on each entry in the location cache to match our inactivity timeout period, if a friend is inactive then their location will not be in the location cache.
5. For each location returned by the cache, the server computes the distance between the user and the friend at that location. If the distance is within the search radius, the friend's profile, location, and last updated timestamp are returned over the WebSocket connection to the client.
6. For each friend, the server subscribes to the friend's channel in the Redis Pub/Sub server. We will explain our use of Redis Pub/Sub shortly. Since creating a new channel is cheap, the user subscribes to all active and inactive friends. The inactive friends will take up a small amount of memory on the Redis Pub/Sub server, but they will not consume any CPU or I/O (since they do not publish updates) until they come online.
7. It sends the user's current location to the user's channel in the Redis Pub/Sub server.

User database

The user database holds two distinct sets of data: user profiles (user ID, username, profile URL, etc.) and friendships. These datasets at our design scale will likely not fit in a single relational database instance. The good news is that the data is horizontally scalable by sharding based on user ID. Relational database sharding is a very common technique.

As a side note, at the scale we are designing for, the user and friendship datasets will likely be managed by a dedicated team and be available via an internal API. In this scenario, the WebSocket servers will use the internal API instead of querying the database directly to fetch user and friendship-related data. Whether accessing via API or direct database queries, it does not make much difference in terms of functionality or performance.

Location cache

We choose Redis to cache the most recent locations of all the active users. As mentioned earlier, we also set a TTL on each key. The TTL is renewed upon every location update. This puts a cap on the maximum amount of memory used. With 10 million active users at peak, and with each location taking no more than 100 bytes, a single modern Redis server with many GBs of memory should be able to easily hold the location information for all users.

However, with 10 million active users roughly updating every 30 seconds, the Redis server will have to handle 334K updates per second. That is likely a little too high, even for a modern high-end server. Luckily, this cache data is easy to shard. The location data for each user is independent, and we can evenly spread the load among several Redis servers by sharding the location data based on user ID.

To improve availability, we could replicate the location data on each shard to a standby node. If the primary node goes down, the standby could be quickly promoted to minimize downtime.

Redis Pub/Sub server

The Pub/Sub server is used as a routing layer to direct messages (location updates) from one user to all the online friends. As mentioned earlier, we choose Redis Pub/Sub because it is very lightweight to create new channels. A new channel is created when someone subscribes to it. If a message is published to a channel that has no subscribers, the message is dropped, placing very little load on the server. When a channel is created, Redis uses a small amount of memory to maintain a hash table and a linked list [3] to track the subscribers. If there is no update on a channel when a user is offline, no CPU cycles are used after a channel is created. We take advantage of this in our design in the following ways:

1. We assign a unique channel to every user who uses the "nearby friends" feature. A user would, upon app initialization, subscribe to each friend's channel, whether the friend is online or not. This simplifies the design since the backend does not need to handle subscribing to a friend's channel when the friend becomes active, or handling unsubscribing when the friend becomes inactive.

2. The tradeoff is that the design would use more memory. As we will see later, memory use is unlikely to be the bottleneck. Trading higher memory use for a simpler architecture is worth it in this case.

How many Redis Pub/Sub servers do we need?

Let's do some math on memory and CPU usage.

Memory usage

Assuming a channel is allocated for each user who uses the nearby friends feature, we need 100 million channels (1 billion × 10%). Assuming that on average a user has 100 active friends using this feature (this includes friends who are nearby, or not), and it takes about 20 bytes of pointers in the internal hash table and linked list to track each subscriber, it will need about 200GB (100 million × 20 bytes × 100 friends / 10^9 = 200GB) to hold all the channels. For a modern server with 100GB of memory, we will need about 2 Redis Pub/Sub servers to hold all the channels.

CPU usage

As previously calculated, the Pub/Sub server pushes about 14 million updates per second to subscribers. Even though it is not easy to estimate with any accuracy how many messages a modern Redis server could push a second without actual benchmarking, it is safe to assume that a single Redis server will not be able to handle that load. Let's pick a conservative number and assume that a modern server with a gigabit network could handle about 100,000 subscriber pushes per second. Given how small our location update messages are, this number is likely to be conservative. Using this conservative estimate, we will need to distribute the load among 14 million / 100,000 = 140 Redis servers. Again, this number is likely too conservative, and the actual number of servers could be much lower.

From the math, we conclude that:

- The bottleneck of Redis Pub/Sub server is the CPU usage, not the memory usage.
- To support our scale, we need a distributed Redis Pub/Sub cluster.

Distributed Redis Pub/Sub server cluster

How do we distribute the channels to hundreds of Redis servers? The good news is that the channels are independent of each other. This makes it relatively easy to spread the channels among multiple Pub/Sub servers by sharding, based on the publisher's user ID. Practically speaking though, with hundreds of Pub/Sub servers, we should go into a bit more detail on how this is done so that operationally it is somewhat manageable, as servers inevitably go down from time to time.

Here, we introduce a service discovery component to our design. There are many service discovery packages available, with etcd [4] and ZooKeeper [5] among the most popular ones. Our need for the service discovery component is very basic. We need these two features:

1. The ability to keep a list of servers in the service discovery component, and a simple UI or API to update it. Fundamentally, service discovery is a small key-value store for holding configuration data. Using Figure 2.9 as an example, the key and value for the hash ring could look like this:

   ```
   Key: /config/pub_sub_ring
   Value: ["p_1", "p_2", "p_3", "p_4"]
   ```

2. The ability for clients (in this case, the WebSocket servers) to subscribe to any updates to the "Value" (Redis Pub/Sub servers).

Under the "Key" mentioned in point 1, we store a hash ring of all the active Redis Pub/Sub servers in the service discovery component (See the consistent hashing chapter in Volume 1 of the System Design Interview book or [6] on details of a hash ring). The hash ring is used by the publishers and subscribers of the Redis Pub/Sub servers to determine the Pub/Sub server to talk to for each channel. For example, channel 2 lives in Redis Pub/Sub server 1 in Figure 2.9.

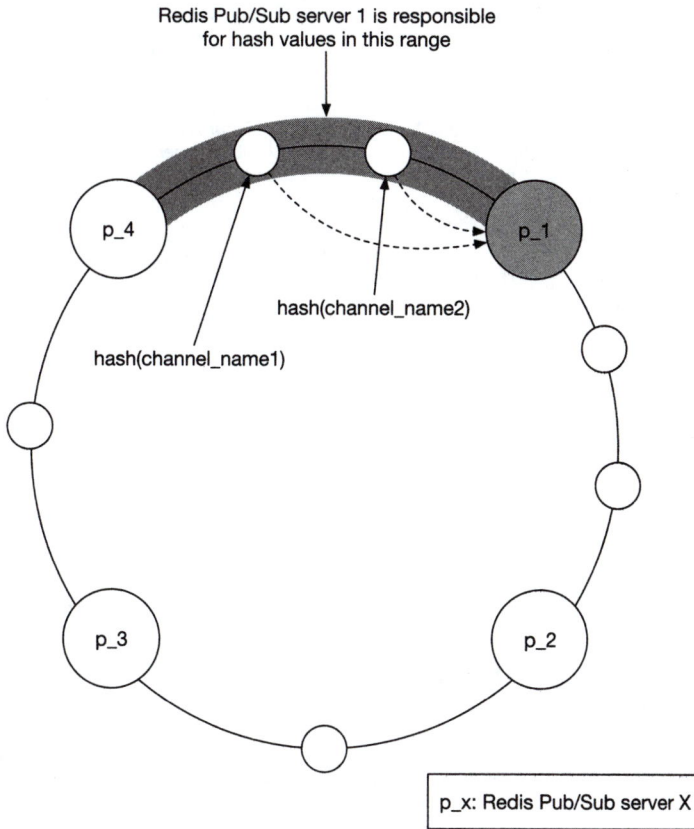

Figure 2.9: Consistent hashing

Figure 2.10 shows what happens when a WebSocket server publishes a location update to a user's channel.

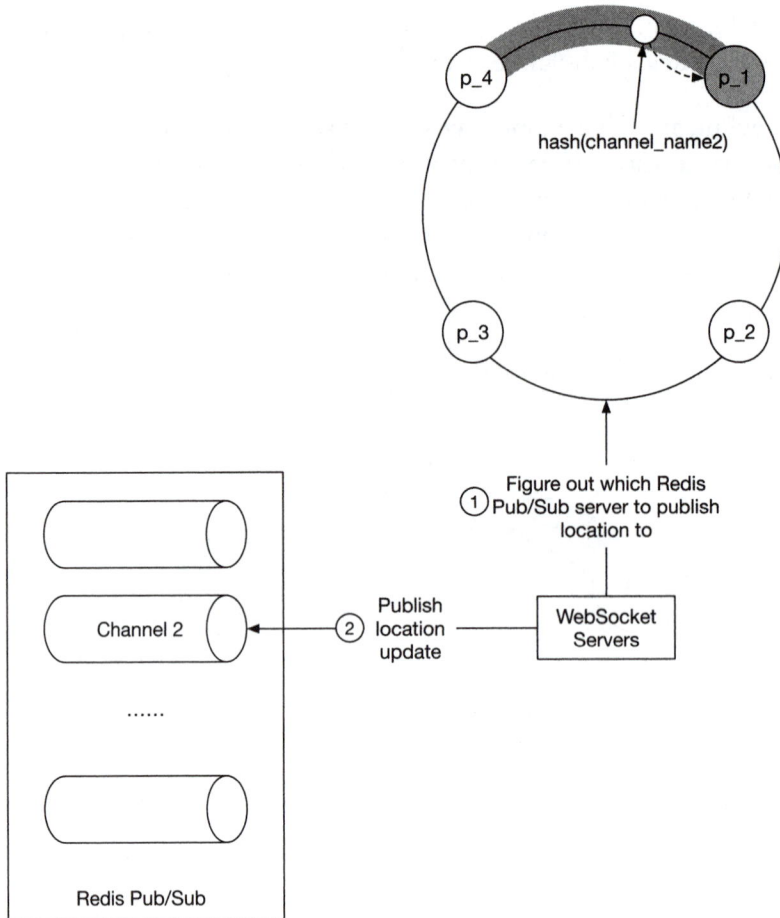

Figure 2.10: Figure out the correct Redis Pub/Sub server

1. The WebSocket server consults the hash ring to determine the Redis Pub/Sub server to write to. The source of truth is stored in service discovery, but for efficiency, a copy of the hash ring could be cached on each WebSocket server. The WebSocket server subscribes to any updates on the hash ring to keep its local in-memory copy up to date.

2. WebSocket server publishes the location update to the user's channel on that Redis Pub/Sub server.

Subscribing to a channel for location updates uses the same mechanism.

Scaling considerations for Redis Pub/Sub servers

How should we scale the Redis Pub/Sub server cluster? Should we scale it up and down daily, based on traffic patterns? This is a very common practice for stateless servers because it is low risk and saves costs. To answer these questions, let's examine some of the properties of the Redis Pub/Sub server cluster.

1. The messages sent on a Pub/Sub channel are not persisted in memory or on disk.

They are sent to all subscribers of the channel and removed immediately after. If there are no subscribers, the messages are just dropped. In this sense, the data going through the Pub/Sub channel is stateless.

2. However, there are indeed states stored in the Pub/Sub servers for the channels. Specifically, the subscriber list for each channel is a key piece of the states tracked by the Pub/Sub servers. If a channel is moved, which could happen when the channel's Pub/Sub server is replaced, or if a new server is added or an old server removed on the hash ring, then every subscriber to the moved channel must know about it, so they could unsubscribe from the channel on the old server and resubscribe to the replacement channel on the new server. In this sense, a Pub/Sub server is stateful, and coordination with all subscribers to the server must be orchestrated to minimize service interruptions.

For these reasons, we should treat the Redis Pub/Sub cluster more like a stateful cluster, similar to how we would handle a storage cluster. With stateful clusters, scaling up or down has some operational overhead and risks, so it should be done with careful planning. The cluster is normally over-provisioned to make sure it can handle daily peak traffic with some comfortable headroom to avoid unnecessary resizing of the cluster.

When we inevitably have to scale, be mindful of these potential issues:

- When we resize a cluster, many channels will be moved to different servers on the hash ring. When the service discovery component notifies all the WebSocket servers of the hash ring update, there will be a ton of resubscription requests.

- During these mass resubscription events, some location updates might be missed by the clients. Although occasional misses are acceptable for our design, we should minimize the occurrences.

- Because of the potential interruptions, resizing should be done when usage is at its lowest in the day.

How is resizing actually done? It is quite simple. Follow these steps:

- Determine the new ring size, and if scaling up, provision enough new servers.
- Update the keys of the hash ring with the new content.
- Monitor your dashboard. There should be some spike in CPU usage in the WebSocket cluster.

Using the hash ring from Figure 2.9 above, if we were to add 2 new nodes, say, p_5, and p_6, the hash ring would be updated like this:

```
Old: ["p_1", "p_2", "p_3", "p_4"]
New: ["p_1", "p_2", "p_3", "p_4", "p_5", "p_6"]
```

Operational considerations for Redis Pub/Sub servers

The operational risk of replacing an existing Redis Pub/Sub server is much, much lower. It does not cause a large number of channels to be moved. Only the channels on the server being replaced will need to be handled. This is good because servers inevitably go down and need to be replaced regularly.

When a Pub/Sub server goes down, the monitoring software should alert the on-call operator. Precisely how the monitoring software monitors the health of a Pub/Sub server is beyond the scope of this chapter, so it is not covered. The on-call operator updates the hash ring key in service discovery to replace the dead node with a fresh standby node. The WebSocket servers are notified about the update and each one then notifies its connection handlers to re-subscribe to the channels on the new Pub/Sub server. Each WebSocket handler keeps a list of all channels it has subscribed to, and upon receiving the notification from the server, it checks each channel against the hash ring to determine if a channel needs to be re-subscribed on a new server.

Using the hash ring from Figure 2.9 above, if p_1 went down, and we replace it with p1_new, the hash ring would be updated like so:

Old: ["p_1", "p_2", "p_3", "p_4"]

New: ["p_1_new", "p_2", "p_3", "p_4"]

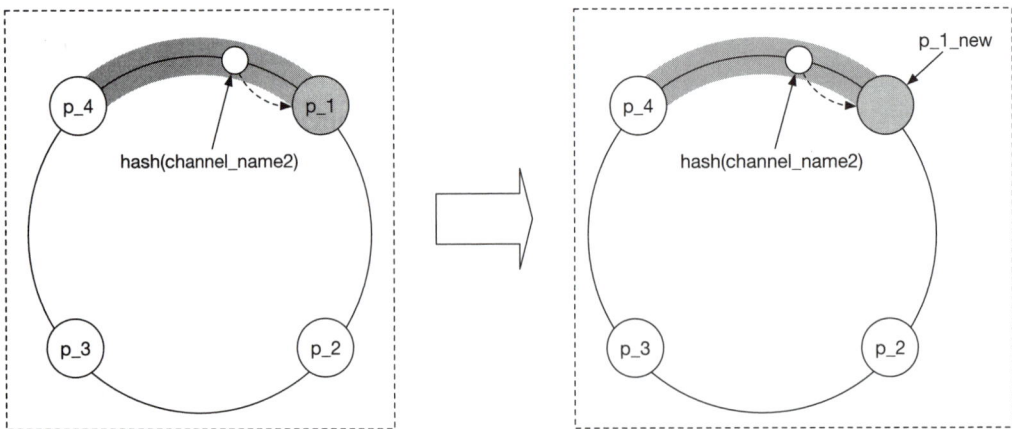

Figure 2.11: Replace Pub/Sub serverver

Adding/removing friends

What should the client do when the user adds or removes a friend? When a new friend is added, the client's WebSocket connection handler on the server needs to be notified, so it can subscribe to the new friend's Pub/Sub channel.

Since the "nearby friends" feature is within the ecosystem of a larger app, we can assume that the "nearby friends" feature could register a callback on the mobile client whenever a new friend is added. The callback, upon invocation, sends a message to the WebSocket server to subscribe to the new friend's Pub/Sub channel. The WebSocket server also returns a message containing the new friend's latest location and timestamp, if they are active.

Likewise, the client could register a callback in the application whenever a friend is removed. The callback would send a message to the WebSocket server to unsubscribe from the friend's Pub/Sub channel.

This subscribe/unsubscribe callback could also be used whenever a friend has opted in or out of the location update.

Users with many friends

It is worth discussing whether a user with many friends could cause performance hotspots in our design. We assume here that there is a hard cap on the number of friends. (Facebook has a cap of 5,000 friends, for example). Friendships are bi-directional. We are not talking about a follower model in which a celebrity could have millions of followers.

In a scenario with thousands of friends, the Pub/Sub subscribers will be scattered among the many WebSocket servers in the cluster. The update load would be spread among them and it's unlikely to cause any hotspots.

The user would place a bit more load on the Pub/Sub server where their channel lives. Since there are over 100 Pub/Sub servers, these "whale" users would be spread out among the Pub/Sub servers and the incremental load should not overwhelm any single one.

Nearby random person

You might call this section an extra credit, as it's not in the initial functional requirements. What if the interviewer wants to update the design to show random people who opted-in to location-sharing?

One way to do this while leveraging our design is to add a pool of Pub/Sub channels by geohash. (See Chapter 1 Proximity Service for details on geohash). As shown in Figure 2.12, an area is divided into four geohash grids and a channel is created for each grid.

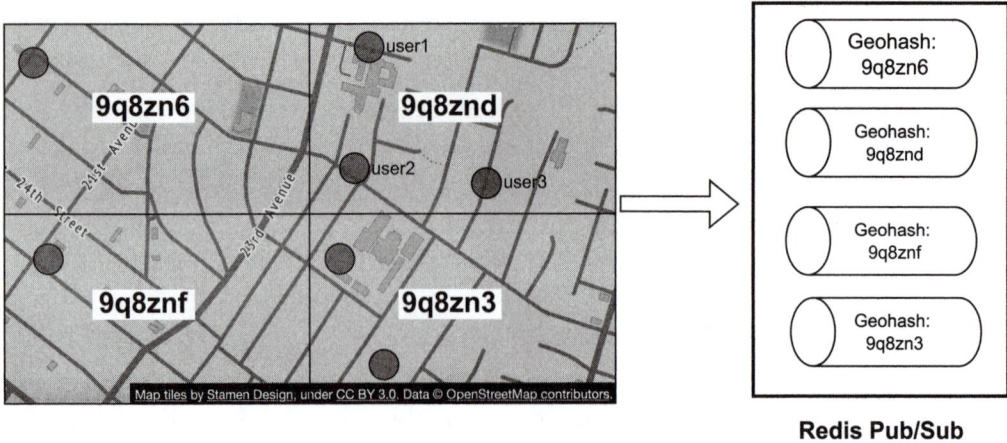

Figure 2.12: Redis Pub/Sub channels

Anyone within the grid subscribes to the same channel. Let's take grid 9q8znd for example as shown in Figure 2.13.

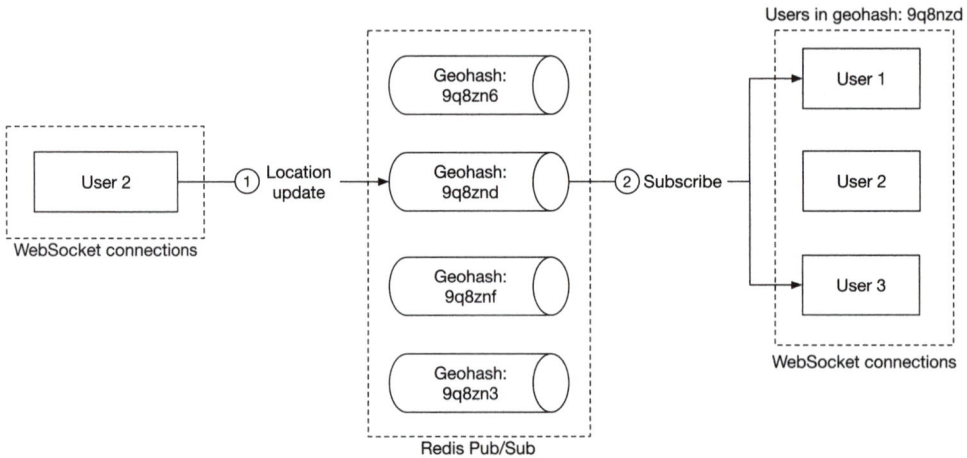

Figure 2.13: Publish location update to random nearby person

1. Here, when user 2 updates their location, the WebSocket connection handler computes the user's geohash ID and sends the location to the channel for that geohash.

2. Anyone nearby who subscribes to the channel (exclude the sender) will receive a location update message.

To handle people who are close to the border of a geohash grid, every client could subscribe to the geohash the user is in and the eight surrounding geohash grids. An example with all 9 geohash grids highlighted is shown in Figure 2.14.

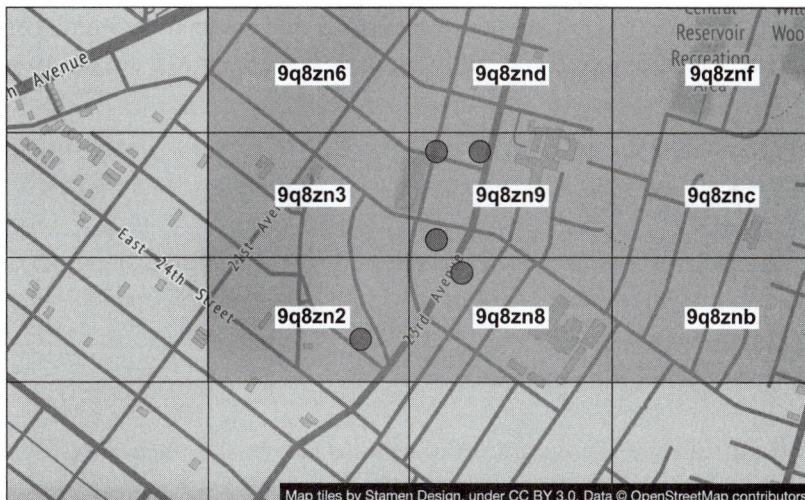

Figure 2.14: Nine geohash grids

Alternative to Redis Pub/Sub

Is there any good alternative to using Redis Pub/Sub as the routing layer? The answer is a resounding yes. Erlang [7] is a great solution for this particular problem. We would argue that Erlang is a better solution than the Redis Pub/Sub proposed above. However, Erlang is quite a niche, and hiring good Erlang programmers is hard. But if your team has Erlang expertise, this is a great option.

So, why Erlang? Erlang is a general programming language and runtime environment built for highly distributed and concurrent applications. When we say Erlang here, we specifically talk about the Erlang ecosystem itself. This includes the language component (Erlang or Elixir [8]) and the runtime environment and libraries (the Erlang virtual machine called BEAM [9] and the Erlang runtime libraries called OTP [10]).

The power of Erlang lies in its lightweight processes. An Erlang process is an entity running on the BEAM VM. It is several orders of magnitude cheaper to create than a Linux process. A minimal Erlang process takes about 300 bytes, and we can have millions of these processes on a single modern server. If there is no work to do in an Erlang process, it just sits there without using any CPU cycles at all. In other words, it is extremely cheap to model each of the 10 million active users in our design as an individual Erlang process.

Erlang is also very easy to distribute among many Erlang servers. The operational overhead is very low, and there are great tools to support debugging live production issues, safely. The deployment tools are also very strong.

How would we use Erlang in our design? We would implement the WebSocket service in Erlang, and also replace the entire cluster of Redis Pub/Sub with a distributed Erlang application. In this application, each user is modeled as an Erlang process. The user process would receive updates from the WebSocket server when a user's location is updated by the client. The user process also subscribes to updates from the Erlang processes of the user's friends. Subscription is native in Erlang/OTP and it's easy to build. This forms a mesh of connections that would efficiently route location updates from one user to many friends.

Step 4 - Wrap Up

In this chapter, we presented a design that supports a nearby friends feature. Conceptually, we want to design a system that can efficiently pass location updates from one user to their friends.

Some of the core components include:

- WebSocket: real-time communication between clients and the server.
- Redis: fast read and write of location data.
- Redis Pub/Sub: routing layer to direct location updates from one user to all the online friends.

We first came up with a high-level design at a lower scale and then discussed challenges that arise as the scale increases. We explored how to scale the following:

- RESTful API servers
- WebSocket servers
- Data layer
- Redis Pub/Sub servers
- Alternative to Redis Pub/Sub

Finally, we discussed potential bottlenecks when a user has many friends and we proposed a design for the "nearby random person" feature.

Congratulations on getting this far! Now give yourself a pat on the back. Good job!

Chapter Summary

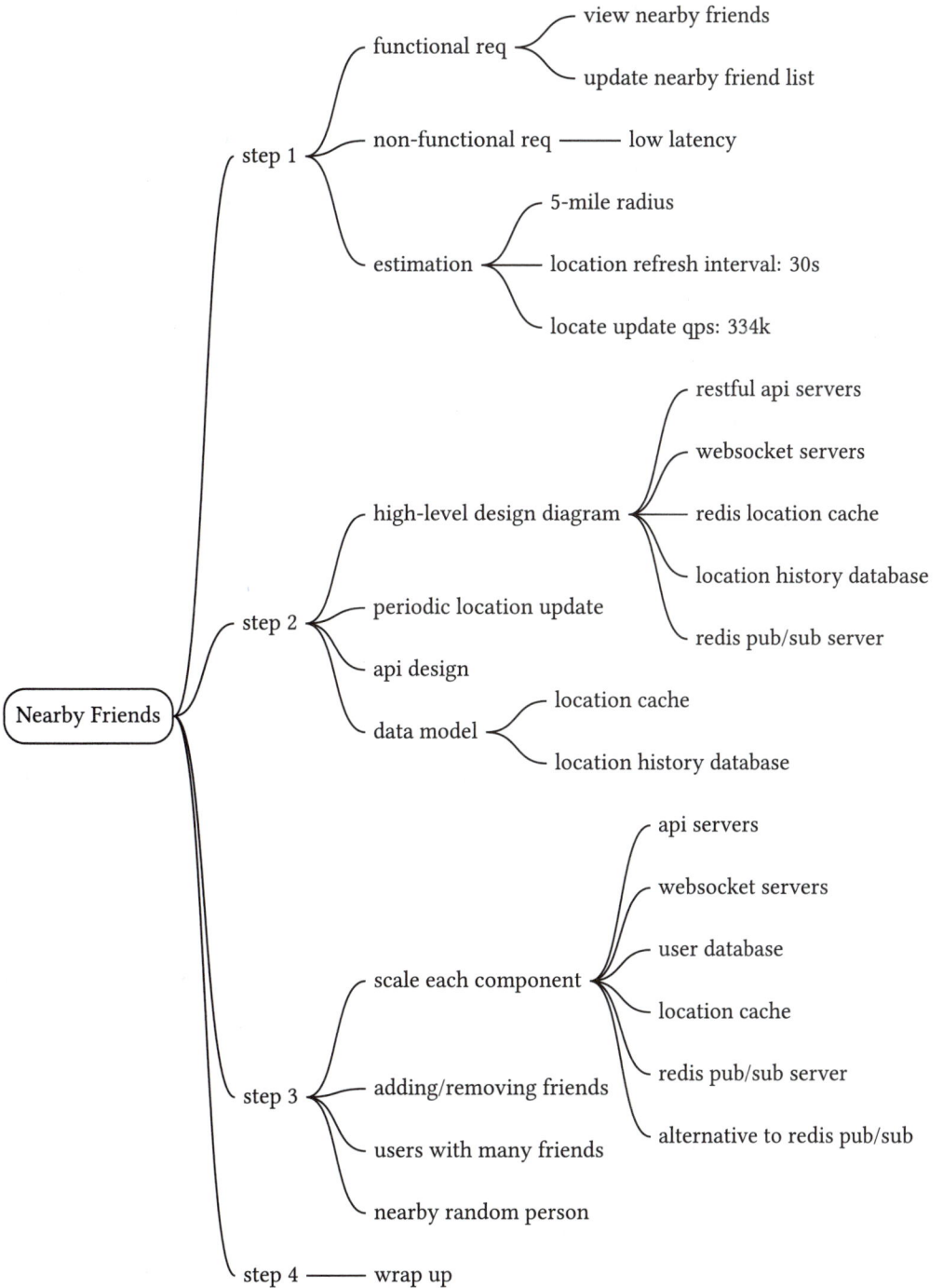

Nearby Friends

- step 1
  - functional req
    - view nearby friends
    - update nearby friend list
  - non-functional req —— low latency
  - estimation
    - 5-mile radius
    - location refresh interval: 30s
    - locate update qps: 334k
- step 2
  - high-level design diagram
    - restful api servers
    - websocket servers
    - redis location cache
    - location history database
    - redis pub/sub server
  - periodic location update
  - api design
  - data model
    - location cache
    - location history database
- step 3
  - scale each component
    - api servers
    - websocket servers
    - user database
    - location cache
    - redis pub/sub server
    - alternative to redis pub/sub
  - adding/removing friends
  - users with many friends
  - nearby random person
- step 4 —— wrap up

Reference Material

[1] Facebook Launches "Nearby Friends". https://techcrunch.com/2014/04/17/facebo ok-nearby-friends/.

[2] Redis Pub/Sub. https://redis.io/topics/pubsub.

[3] Redis Pub/Sub under the hood. https://making.pusher.com/redis-pubsub-under-t he-hood/.

[4] etcd. https://etcd.io/.

[5] ZooKeeper. https://zookeeper.apache.org/.

[6] Consistent hashingones. https://www.toptal.com/big-data/consistent-hashing.

[7] Erlang. https://www.erlang.org/.

[8] Elixir. https://elixir-lang.org/.

[9] A brief introduction to BEAM. https://www.erlang.org/blog/a-brief-beam-primer/.

[10] OTP. https://www.erlang.org/doc/design_principles/des_princ.html.

3   Google Maps

In this chapter, we design a simple version of Google Maps. Before we proceed to the system design, let's learn a bit about Google Maps. Google started Project Google Maps in 2005 and developed a web mapping service. It provides many services such as satellite imagery, street maps, real-time traffic conditions, and route planning [1].

Google Maps helps users find directions and navigate to their destination. As of March 2021, Google Maps had one billion daily active users, 99% coverage of the world, and 25 million updates daily of accurate and real-time location information [2]. Given the enormous complexity of Google Maps, it is important to nail down which features our version of it supports.

Step 1 - Understand the Problem and Establish Design Scope

The interaction between the interviewer and the candidate could look like this:

Candidate: How many daily active users are we expecting?
Interviewer: 1 billion DAU.

Candidate: Which features should we focus on? Direction, navigation, and estimated time of arrival (ETA)?
Interviewer: Let's focus on location update, navigation, ETA, and map rendering.

Candidate: How large is the road data? Can we assume we have access to it?
Interviewer: Great questions. Yes, let's assume we obtained the road data from different sources. It is terabytes (TBs) of raw data.

Candidate: Should our system take traffic conditions into consideration?
Interviewer: Yes, traffic conditions are very important for accurate time estimation.

Candidate: How about different travel modes such as driving, walking, bus, etc?
Interviewer: We should be able to support different travel modes.

Candidate: Should it support multi-stop directions?
Interviewer: It is good to allow a user to define multiple stops, but let's not focus on it.

Candidate: How about business places and photos? How many photos are we expecting?
Interviewer: I am happy you asked and considered these. We do not need to design those.

In the rest of the chapter, we focus on three key features. The main devices that we need to support are mobile phones.

- User location update.
- Navigation service, including ETA service.
- Map rendering.

Non-functional requirements and constraints

- Accuracy: Users should not be given the wrong directions.
- Smooth navigation: On the client-side, users should experience very smooth map rendering.
- Data and battery usage: The client should use as little data and battery as possible. This is very important for mobile devices.
- General availability and scalability requirements.

Before jumping into the design, we will briefly introduce some basic concepts and terminologies that are helpful in designing Google Maps.

Map 101

Positioning system

The world is a sphere that rotates on its axis. At the very top, there is the north pole, and the very bottom is the south pole.

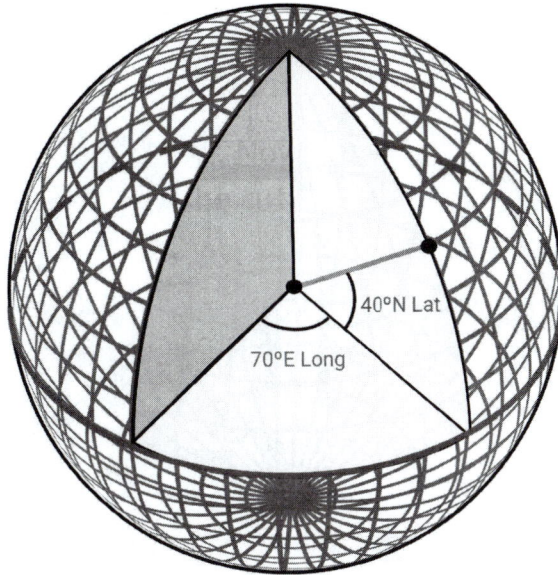

Figure 3.1: Latitude and longitude (source: [3])

Lat (Latitude): denotes how far north or south we are

Long (Longitude): denotes how far east or west we are

Going from 3D to 2D

The process of translating the points from a 3D globe to a 2D plane is called "Map Projection".

There are different ways to do map projection, and each comes with its own strengths and limitations. Almost all of them distort the actual geometry. Below we can see some examples.

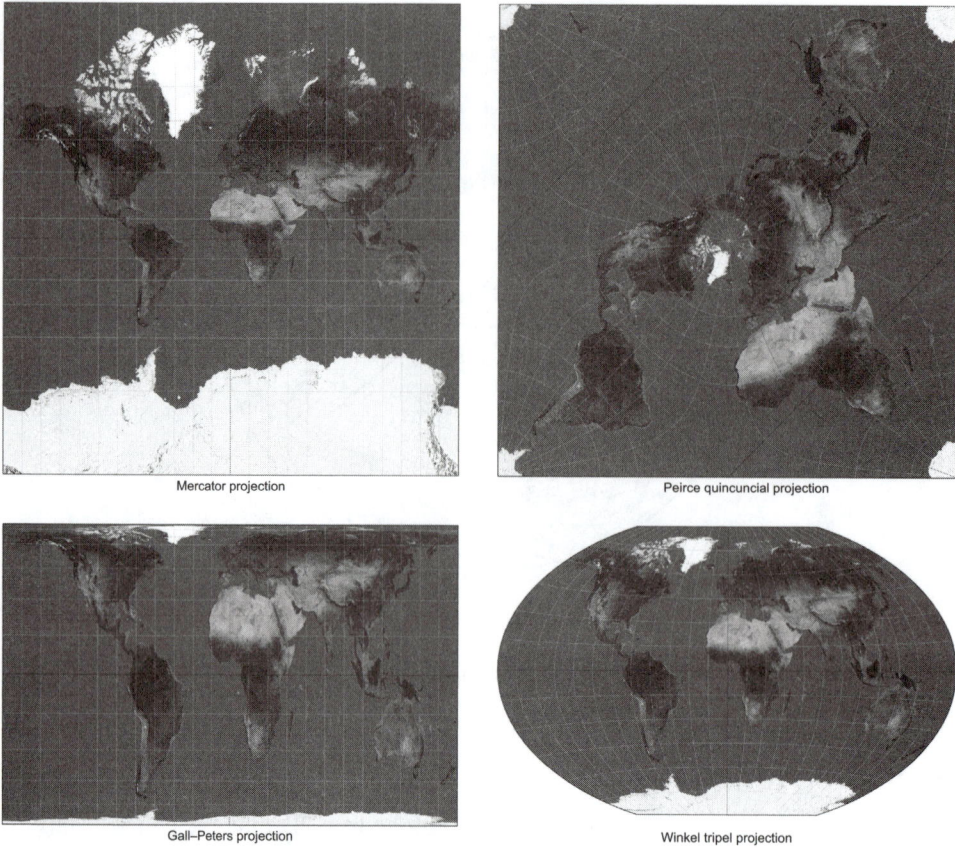

Figure 3.2: Map projections (source: Wikipedia [4] [5] [6] [7])

Google Maps selected a modified version of Mercator projection called Web Mercator. For more details on positioning systems and projections, please refer to [3].

Geocoding

Geocoding is the process of converting addresses to geographic coordinates. For instance, "1600 Amphitheatre Parkway, Mountain View, CA" is geocoded to a latitude/longitude pair of (latitude 37.423021, longitude -122.083739).

In the other direction, the conversion from the latitude/longitude pair to the actual human-readable address is called reverse geocoding.

One way to geocode is interpolation [8]. This method leverages the data from different sources such as geographic information systems (GIS) where the street network is mapped to the geographic coordinate space.

Geohashing

Geohashing is an encoding system that encodes a geographic area into a short string of letters and digits. At its core, it depicts the earth as a flattened surface and recursively divides the grids into sub-grids, which can be square or rectangular. We represent each grid with a string of numbers between 0 to 3 that are created recursively.

Let's assume the initial flattened surface is of size 20,000km × 10,000km. After the first division, we would have 4 grids of size 10,000km × 5,000km. We represent them as 00, 01, 10, and 11 as shown in Figure 3.3. We further divide each grid into 4 grids and use the same naming strategy. Each sub-grid is now of size 5,000km × 2,500km. We recursively divide the grids until each grid reaches a certain size threshold.

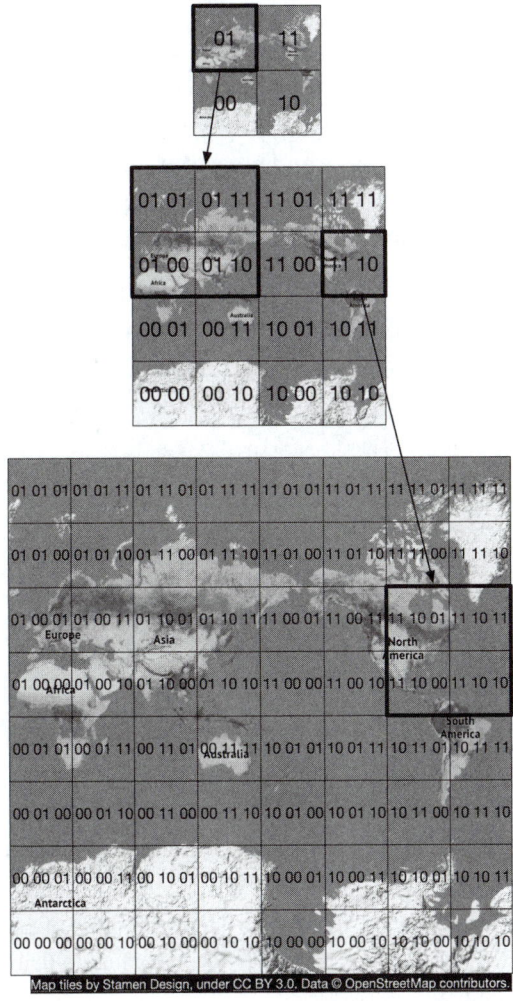

Figure 3.3: Geohashing

Geohashing has many uses. In our design, we use geohashing for map tiling. For more details on geohashing and its benefits, please refer to [9].

Map rendering

We won't go into a lot of detail about map rendering here, but it is worth mentioning the basics. One foundational concept in map rendering is tiling. Instead of rendering the entire map as one large custom image, the world is broken up into smaller tiles. The client only downloads the relevant tiles for the area the user is in and stitches them together like a mosaic for display.

There are distinct sets of tiles at different zoom levels. The client chooses the set of tiles appropriate for the zoom level of the map viewport on the client. This provides the right level of map details without consuming excess bandwidth. To illustrate with an extreme example, when the client is zoomed all the way out to show the entire world, we don't want to have to download hundreds of thousands of tiles for a very high zoom level. All the details would go to waste. Instead, the client would download one tile at the lowest zoom level, which represents the entire world with a single 256×256 pixel image.

Road data processing for navigation algorithms

Most routing algorithms are variations of Dijkstra's or A* pathfinding algorithms. The exact algorithm choice is a complex topic and we won't go into much detail in this chapter. What is important to note is that all these algorithms operate on a graph data structure, where intersections are nodes and roads are edges of the graph. See Figure 3.4 for an example:

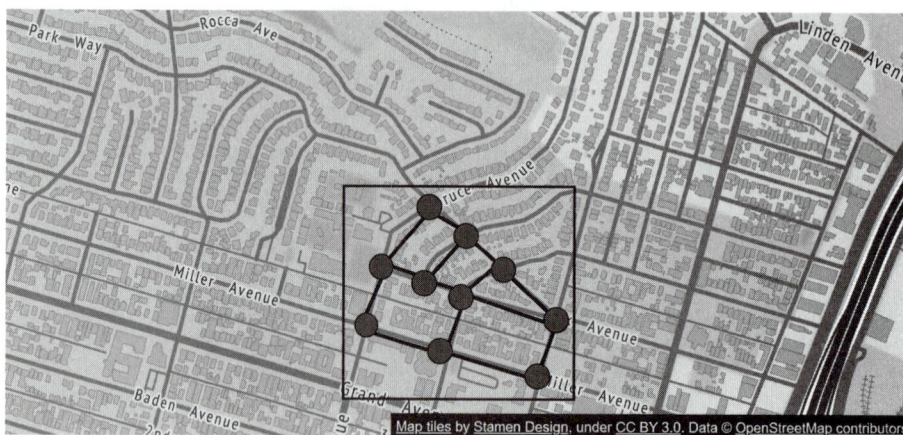

Figure 3.4: Map as a graph

The pathfinding performance for most of these algorithms is extremely sensitive to the size of the graph. Representing the entire world of road networks as a single graph would consume too much memory and is likely too large for any of these algorithms to run efficiently. The graph needs to be broken up into manageable units for these algorithms to work at our design scale.

One way to break up road networks around the world is very similar to the tiling concept we discussed for map rendering. By employing a similar subdivision technique as geohashing, we divide the world into small grids. For each grid, we convert the roads within the grid into a small graph data structure that consists of the nodes (intersections) and edges (roads) inside the geographical area covered by the grid. We call these grids routing tiles. Each routing tile holds references to all the other tiles it connects to. This is how the routing algorithms can stitch together a bigger road graph as it traverses these interconnected routing tiles.

By breaking up road networks into routing tiles that can be loaded on demand, the routing algorithms can significantly reduce memory consumption and improve pathfinding performance by only consuming a small subset of the routing tiles at a time, and only loading additional tiles as needed.

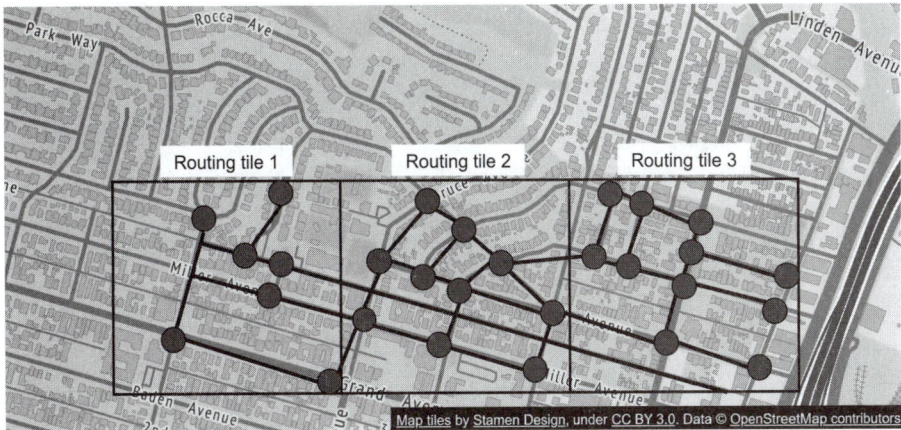

Figure 3.5: Routing tiles

Reminder
In Figure 3.5, we call these grids routing tiles. Routing tiles are similar to map tiles in that both are grids covering certain geographical areas. Map tiles are PNG images, while routing tiles are binary files of road data for the area covered by the tiles.

Hierarchical routing tiles

Efficient navigation routing also requires having road data at the right level of detail. For example, for cross country routing, it would be slow to run the routing algorithm against a highly detailed set of street-level routing tiles. The graph stitched together from these detailed routing tiles would likely be too large and consume too much memory.

There are typically three sets of routing tiles with different levels of detail. At the most detailed level, the routing tiles are small and contain only local roads. At the next level, the tiles are bigger and contain only arterial roads connecting districts together. At the lowest level of detail, the tiles cover large areas and contain only major highways connecting cities and states together. At each level, there could be edges connecting to tiles at a different zoom level. For example, for a freeway entrance from local street A to freeway F, there would be a reference from the node (street A) in the small tile to the node (freeway F) in the big tile. See Figure 3.6 for an example of routing tiles of varying sizes.

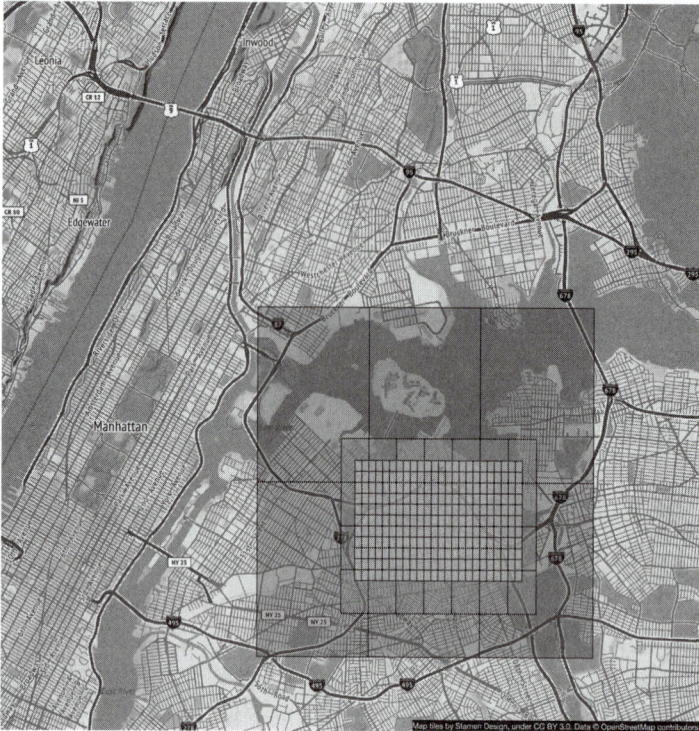

Figure 3.6: Routing tiles of varying sizes

Back-of-the-envelope estimation

Now that we understand the basics, let's do a back-of-the-envelope estimation. Since the focus of the design is mobile, data usage and battery consumption are two important factors to consider.

Before we dive into the estimation, here are some imperial/metric conversions for reference.

- 1 foot = 0.3048 meters
- 1 kilometer (km) = 0.6214 miles
- 1 km = 1,000 meters

Storage usage

We need to store three types of data.

- Map of the world: A detailed calculation is shown below.

- Metadata: Given that the metadata for each map tile could be negligible in size, we can skip the metadata in our computation.

- Road info: The interviewer told us there are TBs of road data from external sources. We transform this dataset into routing tiles, which are also likely to be terabytes in size.

Map of the world

We discussed the concept of map tiling in the "Map 101" section on page 60. There are many sets of map tiles, with one at each zoom level. To get an idea of the storage requirement for the entire collection of map tile images, it would be informative to estimate the size of the largest tile set at the highest zoom level first. At zoom level 21, there are about 4.3 trillion tiles (Table 3.1). Let's assume that each tile is a 256×256 pixel compressed PNG image, with the image size of about 100KB. The entire set at the highest zoom level would need about 4.4 trillion $\times$ 100KB = 440PB.

In Table 3.1, we show the progression of tile counts at every zoom level.

Zoom	Number of Tiles
0	1
1	4
2	16
3	64
4	256
5	1 024
6	4 096
7	16 384
8	65 536
9	262 144
10	1 048 576
11	4 194 304
12	16 777 216
13	67 108 864
14	268 435 456
15	1 073 741 824
16	4 294 967 296
17	17 179 869 184
18	68 719 476 736
19	274 877 906 944
20	1 099 511 627 776
21	4 398 046 511 104

Table 3.1: Zoom levels

However, keep in mind that about 90% of the world's surface is natural and mostly uninhabited areas like oceans, deserts, lakes, and mountains. Since these areas are highly compressible as images, we could conservatively reduce the storage estimate by 80 $\sim$ 90%. That would reduce the storage size to a range of 44 to 88PB. Let's pick a simple round number of 50PB.

Next, let's estimate how much storage each subsequent lower zoom level would take. At each lower zoom level, the number of tiles for both north-south and east-west directions drops by half. This results in a total reduction of the number of tiles by 4x, which drops the storage size for the zoom level also by 4x. With the storage size reduced by 4x at each lower zoom level, the math for the total size is a series: $50 + \frac{50}{4} + \frac{50}{16} + \frac{50}{64} + \cdots = \sim 67\text{PB}$. This is just a rough estimate. It is good enough to know that we need roughly about 100PB to store all the map tiles at varying levels of detail.

Server throughput

To estimate the server throughput, let's review the types of requests we need to support. There are two main types of requests. The first is navigation requests. These are sent by the clients to initiate a navigation session. The second is location update requests. These are sent by the client as the user moves around during a navigation session. The location data is used by downstream services in many different ways. For example, location data is one of the inputs for live traffic data. We will cover the use cases of location data in the design deep dive section.

Now we can analyze the server throughput for navigation requests. Let's assume we have 1 billion DAU, and each user on average uses navigation for a total of 35 minutes per week. This translates to 35 billion minutes per week or 5 billion minutes per day.

One simple approach would be to send GPS coordinates every second, which results in 300 billion (5 billion minutes × 60) requests per day, or 3 million QPS $\left(\frac{300 \text{ billion requests}}{10^5} = 3 \text{ million} \right)$. However, the client may not need to send a GPS update every second. We can batch these on the client and send them at a much lower frequency (for example, every 15 seconds or 30 seconds) to reduce the write QPS. The actual frequency could depend on factors such as how fast the user moves. If they are stuck in traffic, a client can slow down the GPS updates. In our design, we assume GPS updates are batched and then sent to the server every 15 seconds. With this batched approach, the QPS is reduced to 200,000 $\left(\frac{3 \text{ million}}{15} \right)$.

Assume peak QPS is five times the average. Peak QPS for location updates = 200,000 × 5 = 1 million.

Step 2 - Propose High-level Design and Get Buy-in

Now that we have more knowledge about Google Maps, we are ready to propose a high-level design (Figure 3.7).

High-level design

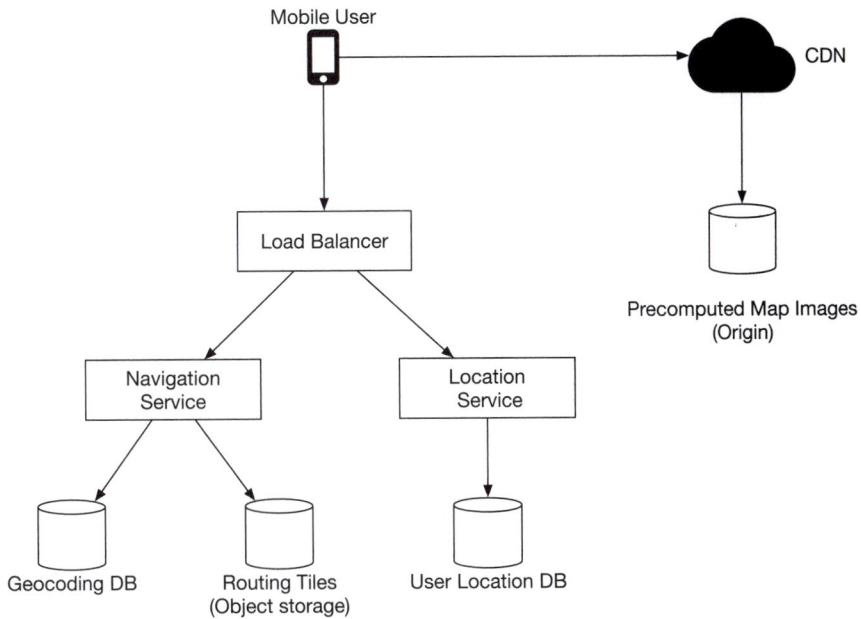

Figure 3.7: High-level design

The high-level design supports three features. Let's take a look at them one by one.

1. Location service
2. Navigation service
3. Map rendering

Location service

The location service is responsible for recording a user's location update. The architecture is shown in Figure 3.8.

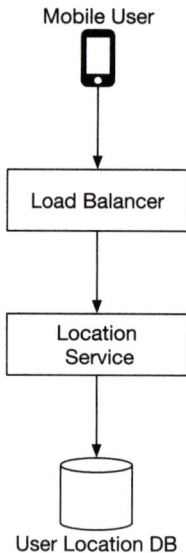

Figure 3.8: Location service

The basic design calls for the clients to send location updates every t seconds, where t is a configurable interval. The periodic updates have several benefits. First, we can leverage the streams of location data to improve our system over time. We can use the data to monitor live traffic, detect new or closed roads, and analyze user behavior to enable personalization, for example. Second, we can leverage the location data in near real-time to provide more accurate ETA estimates to the users and to reroute around traffic, if necessary.

But do we really need to send every location update to the server immediately? The answer is probably no. Location history can be buffered on the client and sent in batch to the server at a much lower frequency. For example, as shown in Figure 3.9, the location updates are recorded every second, but are only sent to the server as part of a batch every 15 seconds. This significantly reduces the total update traffic sent by all the clients.

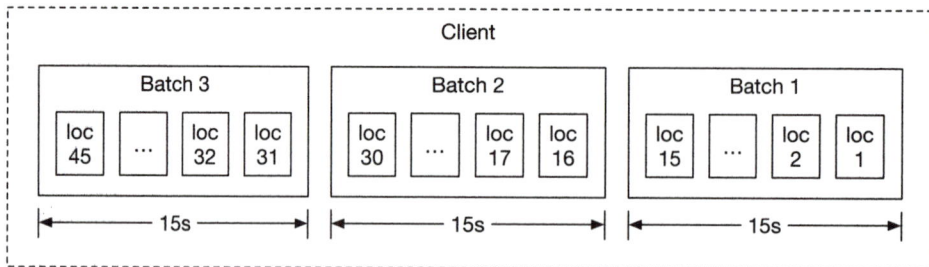

Figure 3.9: Batch requests

For a system like Google Maps, even when location updates are batched, the write volume is still very high. We need a database that is optimized for high write volume and is highly scalable, such as Cassandra. We may also need to log location data using a stream processing engine such as Kafka for further processing. We discuss this in detail in the deep dive section.

What communication protocol might be a good fit here? HTTP with the keep-alive option [10] is a good choice because it is very efficient. The HTTP request might look like this:

```
POST /v1/locations
Parameters
locs: JSON encoded array of (latitude, longitude, timestamp)
  tuples.
```

Navigation service

This component is responsible for finding a reasonably fast route from point A to point B. We can tolerate a little bit of latency. The calculated route does not have to be the fastest, but accuracy is critical.

As shown in Figure 3.8, the user sends an HTTP request to the navigation service through a load balancer. The request includes origin and destination as the parameters. The API might look like this:

```
GET /v1/nav?origin=1355+market+street,SF&destination=
Disneyland
```

Here is an example of what the navigation result could look like:

```
{
  'distance': {'text':'0.2 mi', 'value': 259},
  'duration': {'text': '1 min', 'value': 83},
  'end_location': {'lat': 37.4038943, 'lng': -121.9410454},
  'html_instructions': 'Head <b>northeast</b> on <b>Brandon St
      </b> toward <b>Lumin Way</b><div style="font-size:0.9em">
      Restricted usage road</div>',
  'polyline': {'points': '_fhcFjbhgVuAwDsCal'},
  'start_location': {'lat': 37.4027165, 'lng': -121.9435809},
  'geocoded_waypoints': [
  {
    "geocoder_status" : "OK",
    "partial_match" : true,
    "place_id" : "ChIJwZNMti1fawwRO2aVVVX2yKg",
    "types" : [ "locality", "political" ]
  },
  {
    "geocoder_status" : "OK",
    "partial_match" : true,
    "place_id" : "ChIJ3aPgQGtXawwRLYeiBMUi7bM",
    "types" : [ "locality", "political" ]
  }
  ],
  'travel_mode': 'DRIVING'
}
```

Please refer to [11] for more details on Google Maps' official APIs.

So far we have not taken reroute and traffic changes into consideration. Those problems are tackled by the Adaptive ETA service in the deep dive section.

Map rendering

As we discussed in the back-of-the-envelope estimation, the entire collection of map tiles at various zoom levels is about a hundred petabytes in size. It is not practical to hold the entire dataset on the client. The map tiles must be fetched on-demand from the server based on the client's location and the zoom level of the client viewport.

When should the client fetch new map tiles from the server? Here are some scenarios:

- The user is zooming and panning the map viewpoint on the client to explore their surroundings.
- During navigation, the user moves out of the current map tile into a nearby tile.

We are dealing with a lot of data. Let's see how we could serve these map tiles from the server efficiently.

Option 1

The server builds the map tiles on the fly, based on the client location and zoom level of the client viewport. Considering that there is an infinite number of location and zoom level combinations, generating map tiles dynamically has a few severe disadvantages:

- It puts a huge load on the server cluster to generate every map tile dynamically.
- Since the map tiles are dynamically generated, it is hard to take advantage of caching.

Option 2

Another option is to serve a pre-generated set of map tiles at each zoom level. The map tiles are static, with each tile covering a fixed rectangular grid using a subdivision scheme like geohashing. Each tile is therefore represented by its geohash. In other words, there is a unique geohash associated with each grid. When a client needs a map tile, it first determines the map tile collection to use based on its zoom level. It then computes the map tile URL by converting its location to the geohash at the appropriate zoom level.

These static, pre-generated images are served by a CDN as shown in Figure 3.10.

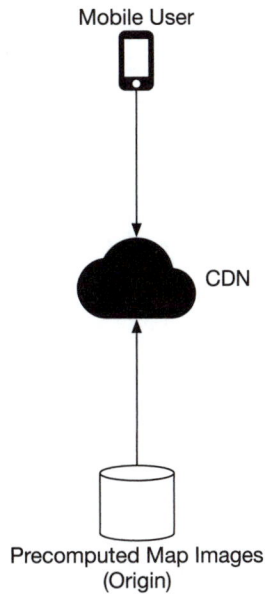

Figure 3.10: Pre-generated images are served by a CDN

In the diagram above, the mobile user makes an HTTP request to fetch a tile from the CDN. If the CDN has not yet served that specific tile before, it fetches a copy from the origin server, caches it locally, and returns it to the user. On subsequent requests, even if those requests are from different users, the CDN returns a cached copy without contacting the origin server.

This approach is more scalable and performant because the map tiles are served from the nearest point of presence (POP) to the client, as shown in Figure 3.11. The static nature of the map tiles makes them highly cacheable.

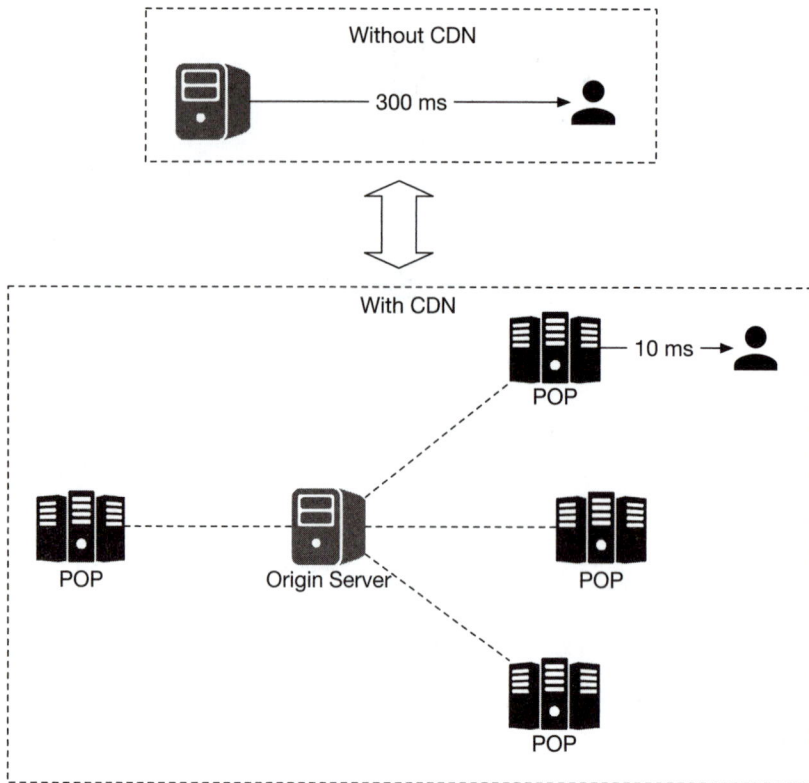

Figure 3.11: Without CDN vs with CDN

It is important to keep mobile data usage low. Let's calculate the amount of data the client needs to load during a typical navigation session. Note the following calculations don't take client-side caching into consideration. Since the routes a user takes could be similar each day, the data usage is likely to be a lot lower with client-side caching.

Data usage
Let's assume a user moves at 30km/h, and at a zoom level where each image covers a block of 200m × 200m (a block can be represented by a 256-pixel by 256-pixel image and the average image size is 100KB). For an area of 1km × 1km, we need 25 images or 2.5MB (25 × 100KB) of data. Therefore, if the speed is 30km/h, we need 75MB (30 × 2.5MB) of data per hour or 1.25MB of data per minute.

Next, we estimate the CDN data usage. At our scale, the cost is an important factor to consider.

As mentioned earlier, we serve 5 billion minutes of navigation per day. This translates to 5 billion $\times$ 1.25MB = 6.25 billion MB per day. Hence, we serve 62,500MB $\left(\frac{6.25 \text{ billion}}{10^5 \text{ seconds in a day}} \right)$ of map data per second. With a CDN, these map images are going to be served from the POPs all over the world. Let's assume there are 200 POPs. Each POP would only need to serve a few hundred MBs $\left(\frac{62,500}{200} \right)$ per second.

There is one final detail in the map rendering design we have only briefly touched on. How does the client know which URLs to use to fetch the map tiles from the CDN? Keep in mind that we are using option 2 as discussed above. With that option, the map tiles are static and pre-generated based on fixed sets of grids, with each set representing a discrete zoom level.

Since we encode the grids in geohash, and there is one unique geohash per grid, computationally it is very efficient to go from the client's location (in latitude and longitude) and zoom level to the geohash, for the map tile. This calculation can be done on the client and we can fetch any static image tile from the CDN. For example, the URL for the image tile of Google headquarter could look like this: `https://cdn.map-provider.com/tiles/9q9hvu.png`

Refer to Chapter 1 Proximity Service on page 10 for a more detailed discussion of geohash encoding.

Calculating geohash on the client should work well. However, keep in mind that this algorithm is hardcoded in all the clients on all different platforms. Shipping changes to mobile apps is a time-consuming and somewhat risky process. We have to be sure that geohashing is the method we plan to use long-term to encode the collection of map tiles and that it is unlikely to change. If we need to switch to another encoding method for some reason, it will take a lot of effort and the risk is not low.

Here is another option worth considering. Instead of using a hardcoded client-side algorithm to convert a latitude/longitude (lat/lng) pair and zoom level to a tile URL, we could introduce a service as an intermediary whose job is to construct the tile URLs based on the same inputs mentioned above. This is a very simple service. The added operational flexibility might be worth it. This is a very interesting tradeoff discussion we could have with the interviewer. The alternative map rendering flow is shown in Figure 3.12.

When a user moves to a new location or to a new zoom level, the map tile service determines which tiles are needed and translates that information into a set of tile URLs to retrieve.

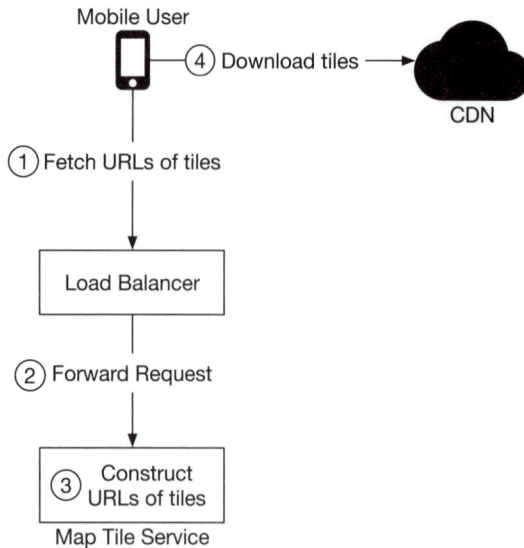

Figure 3.12: Map rendering

1. A mobile user calls the map tile service to fetch the tile URLs. The request is sent to the load balancer.

2. The load balancer forwards the request to the map tile service.

3. The map tile service takes the client's location and zoom level as inputs and returns 9 URLs of the tiles to the client. These tiles include the tile to render and the eight surrounding tiles.

4. The mobile client downloads the tiles from the CDN.

We will go into more detail on the precomputed map tiles in the design deep dive section.

Step 3 - Design Deep Dive

In this section, we first have a discussion about the data model. Then we talk about location service, navigation service, and map rendering in more detail.

Data model

We are dealing with four types of data: routing tiles, user location data, geocoding data, and precomputed map tiles of the world.

Routing tiles

As mentioned previously, the initial road dataset is obtained from different sources and authorities. It contains terabytes of data. The dataset is improved over time by the location data the application continuously collects from the users as they use the application.

This dataset contains a large number of roads and associated metadata such as names, county, longitude, and latitude. This data is not organized as graph data structures and is not usable by most routing algorithms. We run a periodic offline processing pipeline, called routing tile processing service, to transform this dataset into the routing tiles we introduced. The service runs periodically to capture new changes to the road data.

The output of the routing tile processing service is routing tiles. There are three sets of these tiles at different resolutions, as described in the "Map 101" section on page 60. Each tile contains a list of graph nodes and edges representing the intersections and roads within the area covered by the tile. It also contains references to other tiles its roads connect to. These tiles together form an interconnected network of roads that the routing algorithms can consume incrementally.

Where should the routing tile processing service store these tiles? Most graph data is represented as adjacency lists [12] in memory. There are too many tiles to keep the entire set of adjacency lists in memory. We could store the nodes and edges as rows in a database, but we would only be using the database as storage, and it seems an expensive way to store bits of data. We also don't need any database features for routing tiles.

The more efficient way to store these tiles is in object storage like S3 and cache it aggressively on the routing service that uses those tiles. There are many high-performance software packages we could use to serialize the adjacency lists to a binary file. We could organize these tiles by their geohashes in object storage. This provides a fast lookup mechanism to locate a tile by lat/lng pair.

We discuss how the shortest path service uses these routing tiles shortly.

User location data

User location data is valuable. We use it to update our road data and routing tiles. We also use it to build a database of live and historical traffic data. This location data is also consumed by multiple data stream processing services to update the map data.

For user location data, we need a database that can handle the write-heavy workload well and can be horizontally scaled. Cassandra could be a good candidate.

Here is what a single row could look like:

user_id	timestamp	user_mode	driving_mode	location
101	1635740977	active	driving	(20.0, 30.5)

Table 3.2: Location table

Geocoding database

This database stores places and their corresponding lat/lng pair. We can use a key-value database such as Redis for fast reads, since we have frequent reads and infrequent writes. We use it to convert an origin or destination to a lat/lng pair before passing it to the route planner service.

Precomputed images of the world map

When a device asks for a map of a particular area, we need to get nearby roads and compute an image that represents that area with all the roads and related details. These computations would be heavy and redundant, so it could be helpful to compute them once and then cache the images. We precompute images at different zoom levels and store them on a CDN, which is backed by cloud storage such as Amazon S3. Here is an example of such an image:

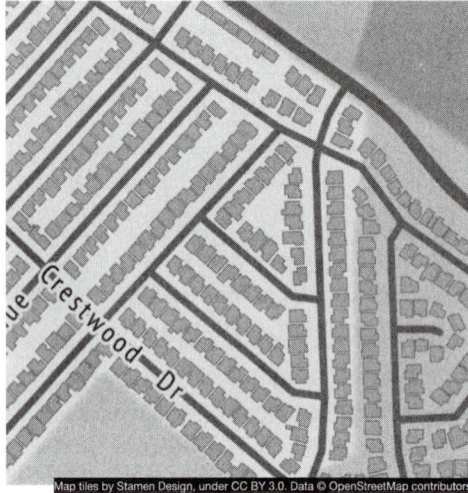

Figure 3.13: Precomputed tiles

Services

Now that we have discussed the data model, let's take a close look at some of the most important services: location service, map rendering service, and navigation service.

Location service

In the high-level design, we discussed how location service works. In this section, we focus on the database design for this service and also how user location is used in detail.

In Figure 3.14, the key-value store is used to store user location data. Let's take a close look.

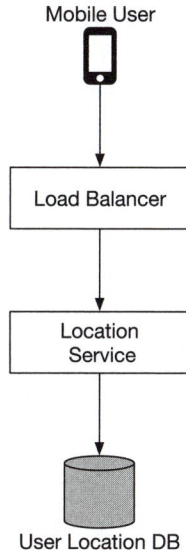

Figure 3.14: User location database

Given the fact we have 1 million location updates every second, we need to have a database that supports fast writes. A NoSQL key-value database or column-oriented database would be a good choice here. In addition, a user's location is continuously changing and becomes stale as soon as a new update arrives. Therefore, we can prioritize availability over consistency. The CAP theorem [13] states that we could choose two attributes among consistency, availability, and partition tolerance. Given our constraints, we would go with availability and partition tolerance. One database that is a good fit is Cassandra. It can handle our scale with a strong availability guarantee.

The key is the combination of (user_id, timestamp) and the value is a lat/lng pair. In this setup, user_id is the primary key and timestamp is the clustering key. The advantage of using user_id as the partition key is that we can quickly read the latest position of a specific user. All the data with the same partition key are stored together, sorted by timestamp. With this arrangement, the retrieval of the location data for a specific user within a time range is very efficient.

Below is an example of what the table may look like.

key (user_id)	timestamp	lat	long	user_mode	navigation_mode
51	132053000	21.9	89.8	active	driving

Table 3.3: Location data

How do we use the user location data?

User location data is essential. It supports many use cases. We use the data to detect new and recently closed roads. We use it as one of the inputs to improve the accuracy of our map over time. It is also an input for live traffic data.

To support these use cases, in addition to writing current user locations in our database, we log this information into a message queue, such as Kafka. Kafka is a unified low-latency, high-throughput data streaming platform designed for real-time data feeds. Figure 3.15 shows how Kafka is used in the improved design.

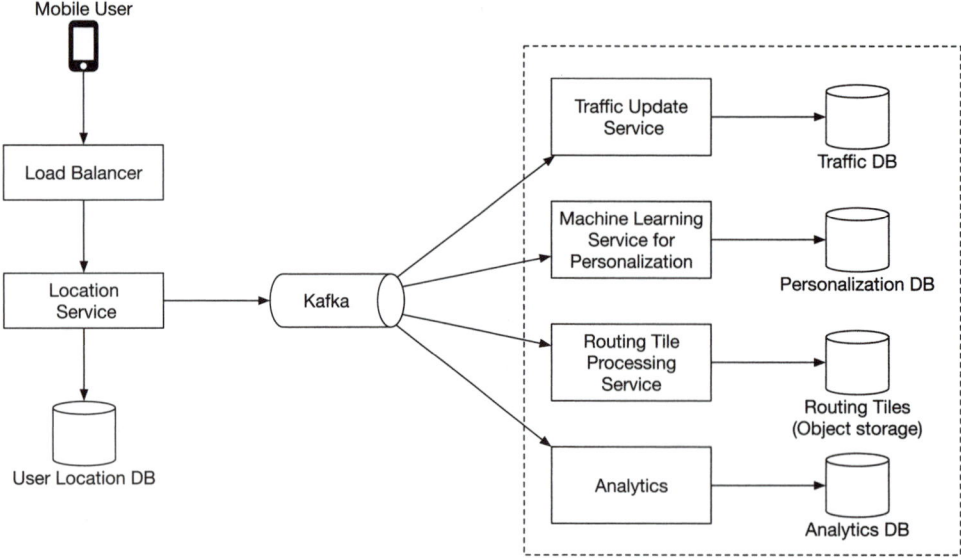

Figure 3.15: Location data is used by other services

Other services consume the location data stream from Kafka for various use cases. For instance, the live traffic service digests the output stream and updates the live traffic database. The routing tile processing service improves the map of the world by detecting new or closed roads and updating the affected routing tiles in object storage. Other services can also tap into the stream for different purposes.

Rendering map

In this section, we dive deep into precomputed map tiles and map rendering optimization. They are primarily inspired by the work of Google Design [3].

Precomputed tiles

As mentioned previously, there are different sets of precomputed map tiles at various distinct zoom levels to provide the appropriate level of map detail to the user, based on the client's viewport size and zoom level. Google Maps uses 21 zoom levels (Table 3.1). This is what we use, as well.

Level 0 is the most zoomed-out level. The entire map is represented by a single tile of size 256×256 pixels.

With each increment of the zoom level, the number of map tiles doubles in both north-south and east-west directions, while each tile stays at 256×256 pixels. As shown in Figure 3.16, at zoom level 1, there are 2×2 tiles, with a total combined resolution of 512×512 pixels. At zoom level 2, there are 4×4 tiles, with a total combined resolution of 1024×1024 pixels. With each increment, the entire set of tiles has 4x as many pixels as the previous level. The increased pixel count provides an increasing level of detail to the user. This allows the client to render the map at the best granularities depending on the client's zoom level, without consuming excessive bandwidth to download tiles in excessive detail.

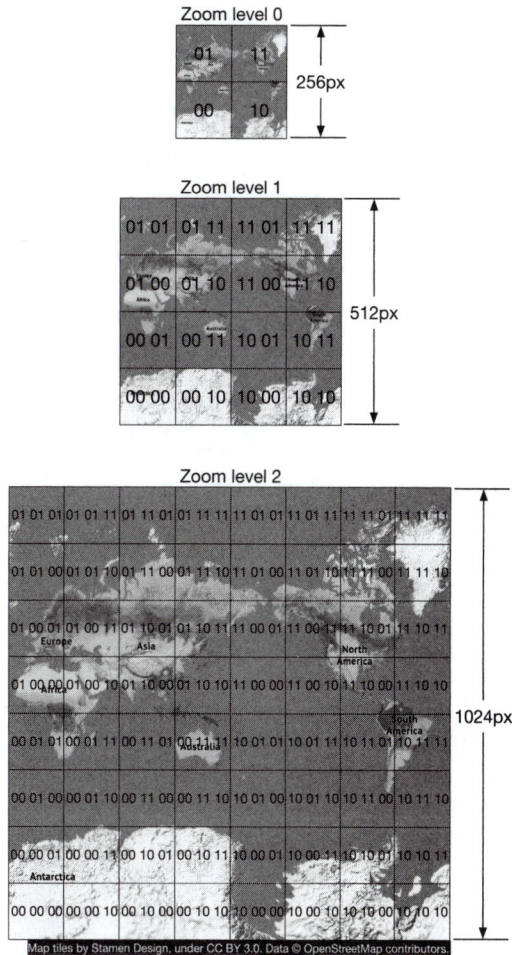

Figure 3.16: Zoom levels

Optimization: use vectors

With the development and implementation of WebGL, one potential improvement is to change the design from sending the images over the network, to sending the vector information (paths and polygons) instead. The client draws the paths and polygons from the vector information.

One obvious advantage of vector tiles is that vector data compresses much better than images do. The bandwidth saving is substantial.

A less obvious benefit is that vector tiles provide a much better zooming experience. With rasterized images, as the client zooms in from one level to another, everything gets stretched and looks pixelated. The visual effect is pretty jarring. With vectorized images, the client can scale each element appropriately, providing a much smoother zooming experience.

Navigation service

Next, let's deep dive into the navigation service. This service is responsible for finding the fastest routes. The design diagram is shown in Figure 3.17.

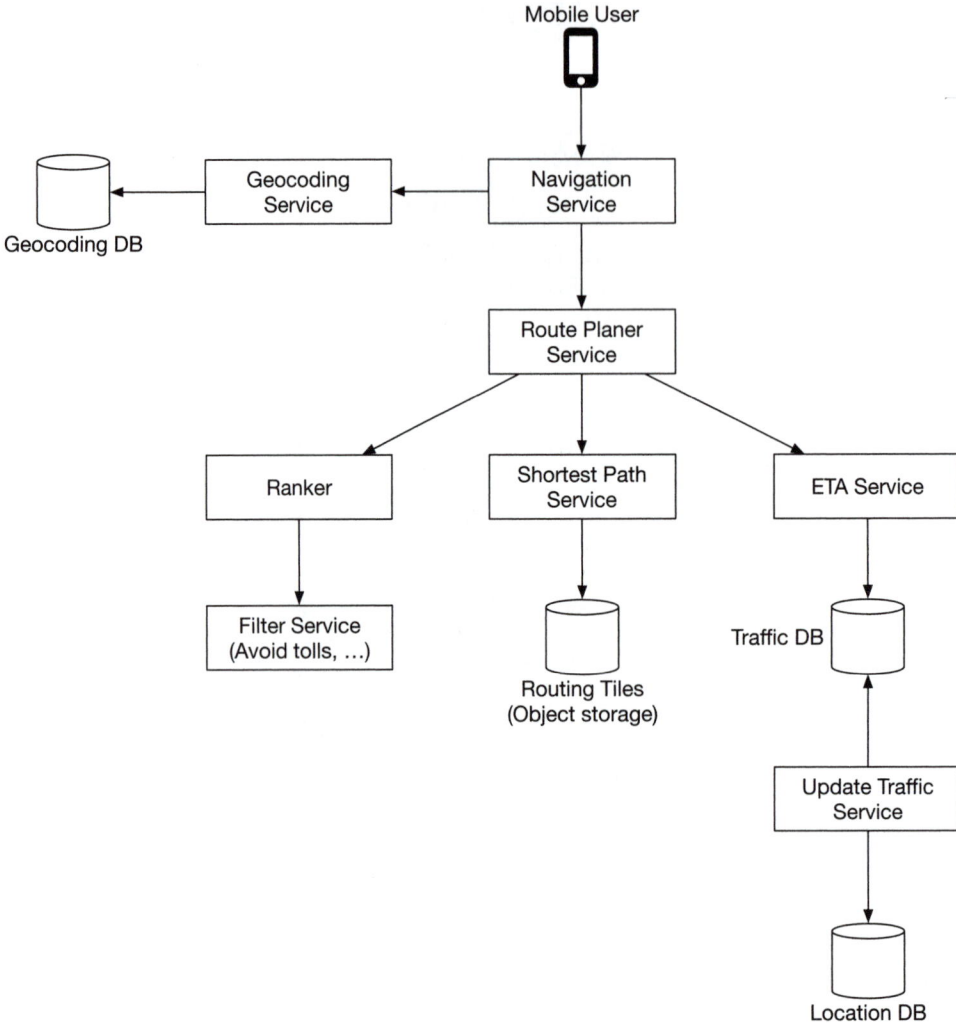

Figure 3.17: Navigation service

Let's go over each component in the system.

Geocoding service

First, we need to have a service to resolve an address to a location of a latitude and longitude pair. An address could be in different formats, for example, it could be the name of a place or a textual address.

Here is an example request and response from Google's geocoding API.

Request:

```
https://maps.googleapis.com/maps/api/geocode/json?address=1600+
    Amphitheatre+Parkway,+Mountain+View,+CA
```

JSON response:

```json
{
  "results" : [
  {
    "formatted_address" : "1600 Amphitheatre Parkway, Mountain
        View, CA 94043, USA",
    "geometry" : {
      "location" : {
        "lat" : 37.4224764,
        "lng" : -122.0842499
      },
      "location_type" : "ROOFTOP",
      "viewport" : {
        "northeast" : {
          "lat" : 37.4238253802915,
          "lng" : -122.0829009197085
        },
        "southwest" : {
          "lat" : 37.4211274197085,
          "lng" : -122.0855988802915
        }
      }
    },
    "place_id" : "ChIJ2eUgeAK6j4ARbn5u_wAGqWA",
    "plus_code": {
      "compound_code": "CWC8+W5 Mountain View, California,
          United States",
      "global_code": "849VCWC8+W5"
    },
    "types" : [ "street_address" ]
  }
  ],
  "status" : "OK"
}
```

The navigation service calls this service to geocode the origin and the destination before passing the latitude/longitude pairs downstream to find the routes.

Route planner service

This service computes a suggested route that is optimized for travel time according to current traffic and road conditions. It interacts with several services which are discussed next.

Shortest-path service

The shortest-path service receives the origin and the destination in lat/lng pairs and returns the top-k shortest paths without considering traffic or current conditions. This computation only depends on the structure of the roads. Here, caching the routes could be beneficial because the graph rarely changes.

The shortest-path service runs a variation of A* pathfinding algorithms against the routing tiles in object storage. Here is an overview:

- The algorithm receives the origin and destination in lat/lng pairs. The lat/lng pairs are converted to geohashes which are then used to load the start and end-points of routing tiles.

- The algorithm starts from the origin routing tile, traverses the graph data structure, and hydrates additional neighboring tiles from object storage (or its local cache if it has loaded it before) as it expands the search area. It's worth noting that there are connections from one level of tile to another covering the same area. This is how the algorithm could "enter" the bigger tiles containing only highways, for example. The algorithm continues to expand its search by hydrating more neighboring tiles (or tiles at different resolutions) as needed until a set of best routes is found.

Figure 3.18 (based on [14]) gives a conceptual overview of the tiles used in the graph traversal.

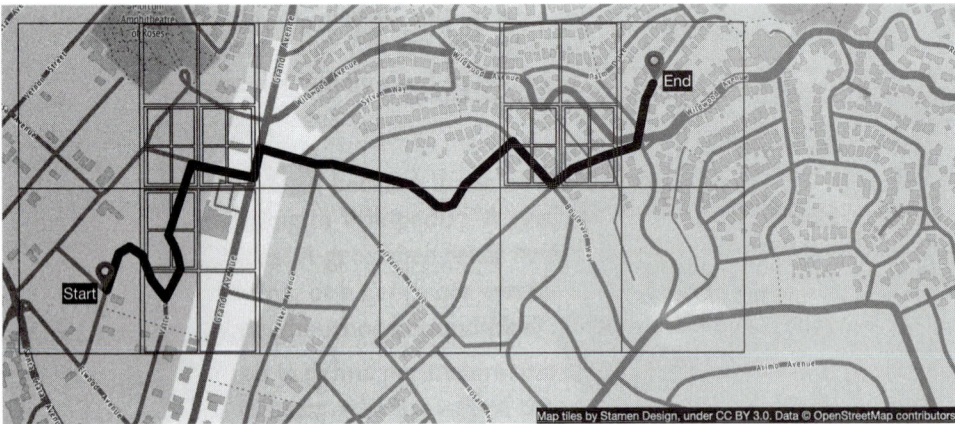

Figure 3.18: Graph traversal

ETA service

Once the route planner receives a list of possible shortest paths, it calls the ETA service for each possible route and gets a time estimate. For this, the ETA service uses machine learning to predict the ETAs based on the current traffic and historical data.

One of the challenges here is that we not only need to have real-time traffic data but also to predict how the traffic will look like in 10 or 20 minutes. These kinds of challenges need to be addressed at an algorithmic level and will not be discussed in this section. If you are interested, refer to [15] and [16].

Ranker service

Finally, after the route planner obtains the ETA predictions, it passes this info to the ranker to apply possible filters as defined by the user. Some example filters include options to avoid toll roads or to avoid freeways. The ranker service then ranks the possible routes from fastest to slowest and returns top-k results to the navigation service.

Updater services

These services tap into the Kafka location update stream and asynchronously update some of the important databases to keep them up-to-date. The traffic database and the routing tiles are some examples.

The routing tile processing service is responsible for transforming the road dataset with newly found roads and road closures into a continuously updated set of routing tiles. This helps the shortest path service to be more accurate.

The traffic update service extracts traffic conditions from the streams of location updates sent by the active users. This insight is fed into the live traffic database. This enables the ETA service to provide more accurate estimates.

Improvement: adaptive ETA and rerouting

The current design does not support adaptive ETA and rerouting. To address this, the server needs to keep track of all the active navigating users and update them on ETA continuously, whenever traffic conditions change. Here we need to answer a few important questions:

- How do we track actively navigating users?
- How do we store the data, so that we can efficiently locate the users affected by traffic changes among millions of navigation routes?

Let's start with a naive solution. In Figure 3.19, user_1's navigation route is represented by routing tiles r_1, r_2, r_3, ..., r_7.

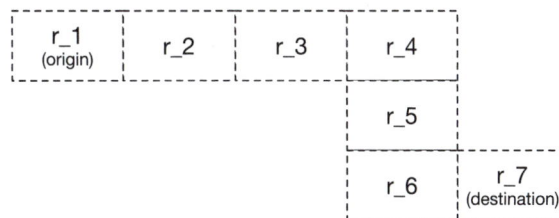

Figure 3.19: Navigation route

The database stores actively navigating users and routes information which might look like this:

user_1: r_1, r_2, r_3, ..., r_k

user_2: r_4, r_6, r_9, ..., r_n

---

user_3: r_2, r_8, r_9, …, r_m

…

user_n: r_2, r_10, r_21, ..., r_1

Let's say there is a traffic incident in routing tile 2 (r_2). To figure out which users are affected, we scan through each row and check if routing tile 2 is in our list of routing tiles (see example below).

user_1: r_1, r_2, r_3, …, r_k

user_2: r_4, r_6, r_9, …, r_n

user_3: r_2, r_8, r_9, …, r_m

…

user_n: r_2, r_10, r_21, ..., r_1

Assume the number of rows in the table is n and the average length of the navigation route is m. The time complexity to find all users affected by the traffic change is $O(n \times m)$.

Can we make this process faster? Let's explore a different approach. For each actively navigating user, we keep the current routing tile, the routing tile at the next resolution level that contains it, and recursively find the routing tile at the next resolution level until we find the user's destination in the tile as well (Figure 3.20). By doing this, we can get a row of the database table like this.

user_1, r_1, super(r_1), super(super(r_1)), …

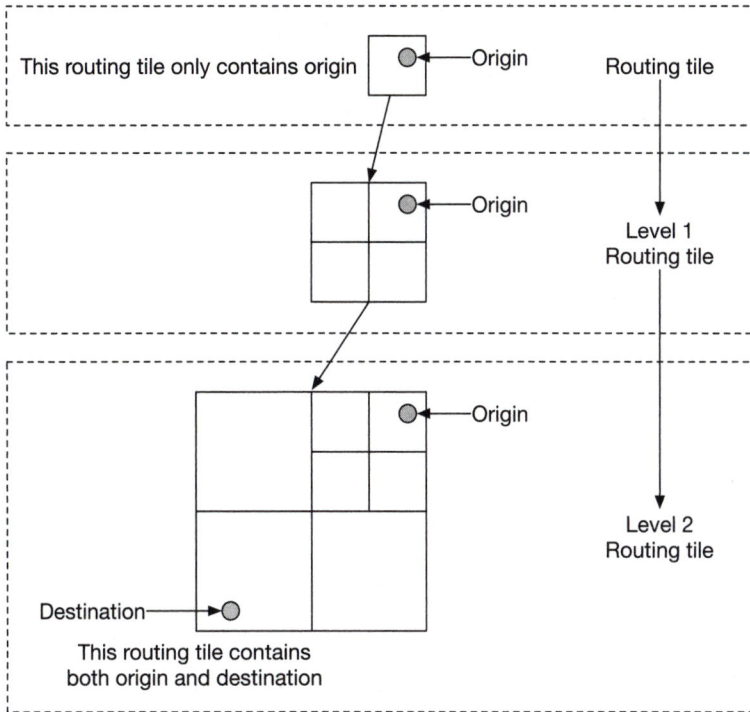

Figure 3.20: Build routing tiles

To find out if a user is affected by the traffic change, we need only check if a routing tile is inside the last routing tile of a row in the database. If not, the user is not impacted. If it is, the user is affected. By doing this, we can quickly filter out many users.

This approach doesn't specify what happens when traffic clears. For example, if routing tile 2 clears and users can go back to the old route, how do users know rerouting is available? One idea is to keep track of all possible routes for a navigating user, recalculate the ETAs regularly and notify the user if a new route with a shorter ETA is found.

Delivery protocols

It is a reality that during navigation, route conditions can change and the server needs a reliable way to push data to mobile clients. For delivery protocol from the server to the client, our options include mobile push notification, long polling, WebSocket, and Server-Sent Events (SSE).

- Mobile push notification is not a great option because the payload size is very limited (4,096 bytes for iOS) and it doesn't support web applications.

- WebSocket is generally considered to be a better option than long polling because it has a very light footprint on servers.

- Since we have ruled out the mobile push notification and long polling, the choice is mainly between WebSocket and SSE. Even though both can work, we lean towards WebSocket because it supports bi-directional communication and features such as last-mile delivery might require bi-directional real-time communication.

For more details about ETA and rerouting, please refer to [15].

Now we have every piece of the design together. Please see the updated design in Figure 3.21.

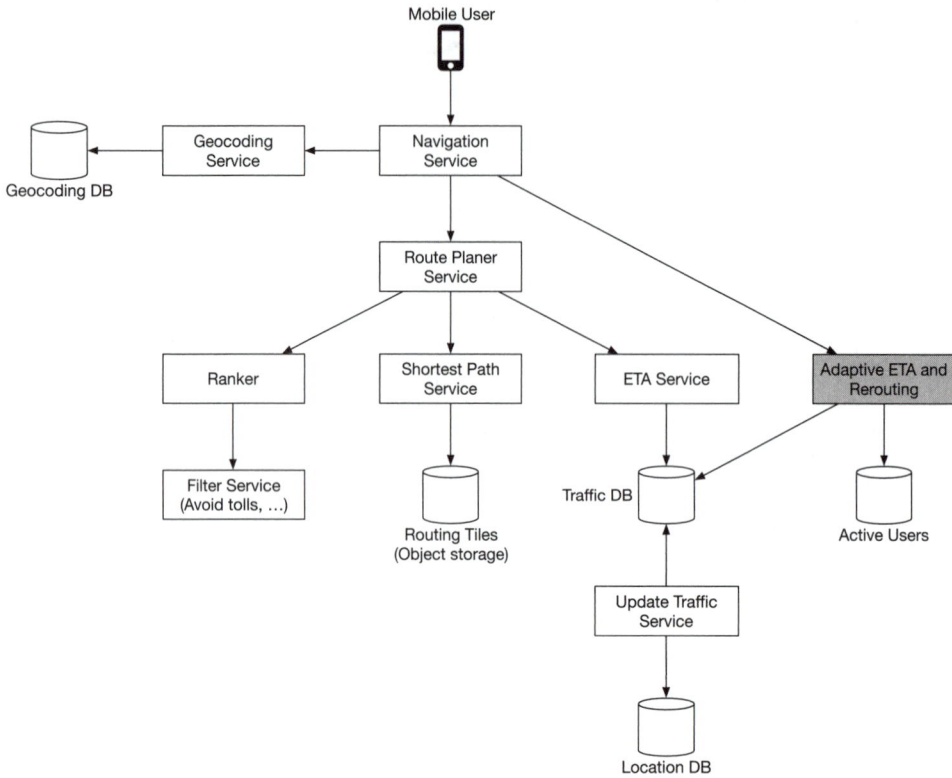

Figure 3.21: Final design

Step 4 - Wrap Up

In this chapter, we designed a simplified Google Maps application with key features such as location update, ETAs, route planning, and map rendering. If you are interested in expanding the system, one potential improvement would be to provide multi-stop navigation capability for enterprise customers. For example, for a given set of destinations, we have to find the optimal order in which to visit them all and provide proper navigation, based on live traffic conditions. This could be helpful for delivery services such as DoorDash, Uber, Lyft, etc.

Congratulations on getting this far! Now give yourself a pat on the back. Good job!

Chapter Summary

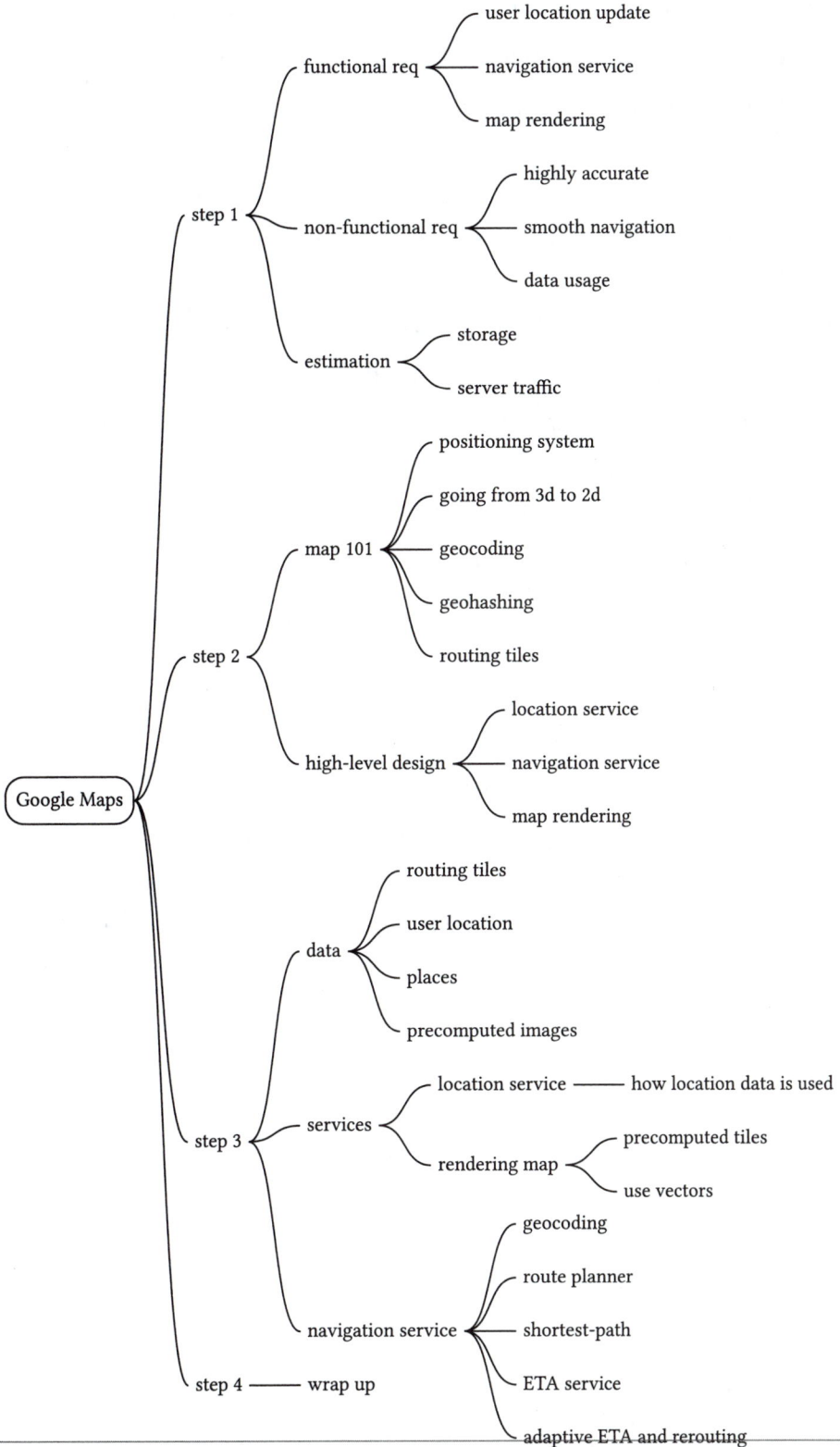

- **Google Maps**
  - **step 1**
    - functional req
      - user location update
      - navigation service
      - map rendering
    - non-functional req
      - highly accurate
      - smooth navigation
      - data usage
    - estimation
      - storage
      - server traffic
  - **step 2**
    - map 101
      - positioning system
      - going from 3d to 2d
      - geocoding
      - geohashing
      - routing tiles
    - high-level design
      - location service
      - navigation service
      - map rendering
  - **step 3**
    - data
      - routing tiles
      - user location
      - places
      - precomputed images
    - services
      - location service —— how location data is used
      - rendering map
        - precomputed tiles
        - use vectors
    - navigation service
      - geocoding
      - route planner
      - shortest-path
      - ETA service
      - adaptive ETA and rerouting
  - **step 4** —— wrap up

Reference Material

[1] Google Maps. https://developers.google.com/maps?hl=en_US.

[2] Google Maps Platform. https://cloud.google.com/maps-platform/.

[3] Prototyping a Smoother Map. https://medium.com/google-design/google-maps-cb0326d165f5.

[4] Mercator projection. https://en.wikipedia.org/wiki/Mercator_projection.

[5] Peirce quincuncial projection. https://en.wikipedia.org/wiki/Peirce_quincuncial_projection.

[6] Gall–Peters projection. https://en.wikipedia.org/wiki/Gall–Peters_projection.

[7] Winkel tripel projection. https://en.wikipedia.org/wiki/Winkel_tripel_projection.

[8] Address geocoding. https://en.wikipedia.org/wiki/Address_geocoding.

[9] Geohashing. https://kousiknath.medium.com/system-design-design-a-geo-spatial-index-for-real-time-location-search-10968fe62b9c.

[10] HTTP keep-alive. https://en.wikipedia.org/wiki/HTTP_persistent_connection.

[11] Directions API. https://developers.google.com/maps/documentation/directions/start?hl=en_US.

[12] Adjacency list. https://en.wikipedia.org/wiki/Adjacency_list.

[13] CAP theorem. https://en.wikipedia.org/wiki/CAP_theorem.

[14] Routing Tiles. https://valhalla.readthedocs.io/en/latest/mjolnir/why_tiles/.

[15] ETAs with GNNs. https://deepmind.com/blog/article/traffic-prediction-with-advanced-graph-neural-networks.

[16] Google Maps 101: How AI helps predict traffic and determine routes. https://blog.google/products/maps/google-maps-101-how-ai-helps-predict-traffic-and-determine-routes/.

4   Distributed Message Queue

In this chapter, we explore a popular question in system design interviews: design a distributed message queue. In modern architecture, systems are broken up into small and independent building blocks with well-defined interfaces between them. Message queues provide communication and coordination for those building blocks. What benefits do message queues bring?

- Decoupling. Message queues eliminate the tight coupling between components so they can be updated independently.
- Improved scalability. We can scale producers and consumers independently based on traffic load. For example, during peak hours, more consumers can be added to handle the increased traffic.
- Increased availability. If one part of the system goes offline, the other components can continue to interact with the queue.
- Better performance. Message queues make asynchronous communication easy. Producers can add messages to a queue without waiting for the response and consumers consume messages whenever they are available. They don't need to wait for each other.

Figure 4.1 shows some of the most popular distributed message queues on the market.

Figure 4.1: Popular distributed message queues

Message queues vs event streaming platforms

Strictly speaking, Apache Kafka and Pulsar are not message queues as they are event streaming platforms. However, there is a convergence of features that starts to blur the distinction between message queues (RocketMQ, ActiveMQ, RabbitMQ, ZeroMQ, etc.) and event streaming platforms (Kafka, Pulsar). For example, RabbitMQ, which is a typical message queue, added an optional streams feature to allow repeated message consumption and long message retention, and its implementation uses an append-only log, much like an event streaming platform would. Apache Pulsar is primarily a Kafka competitor, but it is also flexible and performant enough to be used as a typical distributed message queue.

In this chapter, we will design a distributed message queue with **additional features, such as long data retention, repeated consumption of messages, etc.**, that are typically only available on event streaming platforms. These additional features make the design more complicated. Throughout the chapter, we will highlight places where the design could be simplified if the focus of your interview centers around the more traditional distributed message queues.

Step 1 - Understand the Problem and Establish Design Scope

In a nutshell, the basic functionality of a message queue is straightforward: producers send messages to a queue, and consumers consume messages from it. Beyond this basic functionality, there are other considerations including performance, message delivery semantics, data detention, etc. The following set of questions will help clarify requirements and narrow down the scope.

Candidate: What's the format and average size of messages? Is it text only? Is multimedia allowed?
Interviewer: Text messages only. Messages are generally measured in the range of kilobytes (KBs).

Candidate: Can messages be repeatedly consumed?
Interviewer: Yes, messages can be repeatedly consumed by different consumers. Note that this is an added feature. A traditional distributed message queue does not retain a message once it has been successfully delivered to a consumer. Therefore, a message cannot be repeatedly consumed in a traditional message queue.

Candidate: Are messages consumed in the same order they were produced?
Interviewer: Yes, messages should be consumed in the same order they were produced. Note that this is an added feature. A traditional distributed message queue does not usually guarantee delivery orders.

Candidate: Does data need to be persisted and what is the data retention?

Interviewer: Yes, let's assume data retention is two weeks. This is an added feature. A traditional distributed message queue does not retain messages.

Candidate: How many producers and consumers are we going to support?
Interviewer: The more the better.

Candidate: What's the data delivery semantic we need to support? For example, at-most-once, at-least-once, and exactly once.
Interviewer: We definitely want to support at-least-once. Ideally, we should support all of them and make them configurable.

Candidate: What's the target throughput and end-to-end latency?
Interviewer: It should support high throughput for use cases like log aggregation. It should also support low latency delivery for more traditional message queue use cases.

With the above conversation, let's assume we have the following functional requirements:

- Producers send messages to a message queue.
- Consumers consume messages from a message queue.
- Messages can be consumed repeatedly or only once.
- Historical data can be truncated.
- Message size is in the kilobyte range.
- Ability to deliver messages to consumers in the order they were added to the queue.
- Data delivery semantics (at-least once, at-most once, or exactly once) can be configured by users.

Non-functional requirements

- High throughput or low latency, configurable based on use cases.
- Scalable. The system should be distributed in nature. It should be able to support a sudden surge in message volume.
- Persistent and durable. Data should be persisted on disk and replicated across multiple nodes.

Adjustments for traditional message queues

Traditional message queues like RabbitMQ do not have as strong a retention requirement as event streaming platforms. Traditional queues retain messages in memory just long enough for them to be consumed. They provide on-disk overflow capacity [1] which is several orders of magnitude smaller than the capacity required for event streaming platforms. Traditional message queues do not typically maintain message ordering. The messages can be consumed in a different order than they were produced. These differences greatly simplify the design which we will discuss where appropriate.

Step 2 - Propose High-level Design and Get Buy-in

First, let's discuss the basic functionalities of a message queue.

Figure 4.2 shows the key components of a message queue and the simplified interactions between these components.

Figure 4.2: Key components in a message queue

- Producer sends messages to a message queue.
- Consumer subscribes to a queue and consumes the subscribed messages.
- Message queue is a service in the middle that decouples the producers from the consumers, allowing each of them to operate and scale independently.
- Both producer and consumer are clients in the client/server model, while the message queue is the server. The clients and servers communicate over the network.

Messaging models

The most popular messaging models are point-to-point and publish-subscribe.

Point-to-point

This model is commonly found in traditional message queues. In a point-to-point model, a message is sent to a queue and consumed by one and only one consumer. There can be multiple consumers waiting to consume messages in the queue, but each message can only be consumed by a single consumer. In Figure 4.3, message A is only consumed by consumer 1.

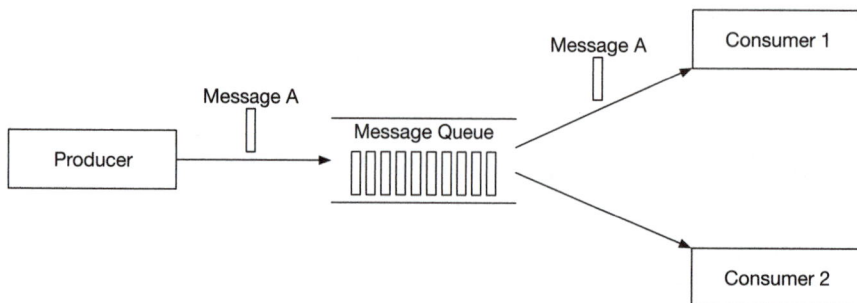

Figure 4.3: Point-to-point model

Once the consumer acknowledges that a message is consumed, it is removed from the queue. There is no data retention in the point-to-point model. In contrast, our design includes a persistence layer that keeps the messages for two weeks, which allows messages to be repeatedly consumed.

While our design could simulate a point-to-point model, its capabilities map more naturally to the publish-subscribe model.

Publish-subscribe

First, let's introduce a new concept, the topic. Topics are the categories used to organize messages. Each topic has a name that is unique across the entire message queue service. Messages are sent to and read from a specific topic.

In the publish-subscribe model, a message is sent to a topic and received by the consumers subscribing to this topic. As shown in Figure 4.4, message A is consumed by both consumer 1 and consumer 2.

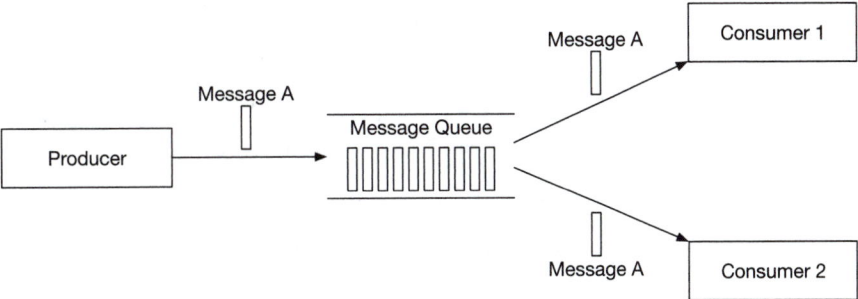

Figure 4.4: Publish-subscribe model

Our distributed message queue supports both models. The publish-subscribe model is implemented by **topics**, and the point-to-point model can be simulated by the concept of the **consumer group**, which will be introduced in the consumer group section.

Topics, partitions, and brokers

As mentioned earlier, messages are persisted by topics. What if the data volume in a topic is too large for a single server to handle?

One approach to solve this problem is called **partition (sharding)**. As Figure 4.5 shows, we divide a topic into partitions and deliver messages evenly across partitions. Think of a partition as a small subset of the messages for a topic. Partitions are evenly distributed across the servers in the message queue cluster. These servers that hold partitions are called **brokers**. The distribution of partitions among brokers is the key element to support high scalability. We can scale the topic capacity by expanding the number of partitions.

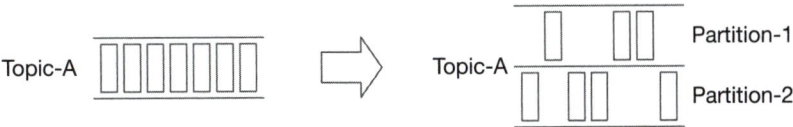

Figure 4.5: Partitions

Each topic partition operates in the form of a queue with the FIFO (first in, first out) mechanism. This means we can keep the order of messages inside a partition. The position of a message in the partition is called an **offset**.

When a message is sent by a producer, it is actually sent to one of the partitions for the topic. Each message has an optional message key (for example, a user's ID), and all messages for the same message key are sent to the same partition. If the message key is absent, the message is randomly sent to one of the partitions.

When a consumer subscribes to a topic, it pulls data from one or more of these partitions. When there are multiple consumers subscribing to a topic, each consumer is responsible for a subset of the partitions for the topic. The consumers form a **consumer group** for a topic.

The message queue cluster with brokers and partitions is represented in Figure 4.6.

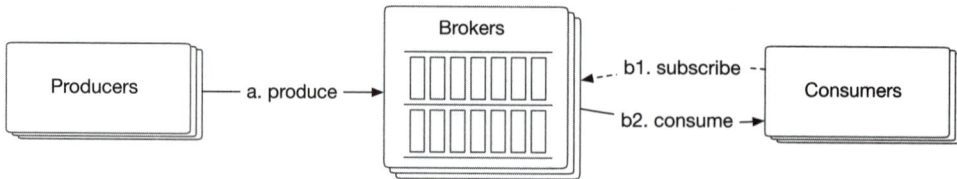

Figure 4.6: Message queue cluster

Consumer group

As mentioned earlier, we need to support both point-to-point and subscribe-publish models. **A consumer group** is a set of consumers, working together to consume messages from topics.

Consumers can be organized into groups. Each consumer group can subscribe to multiple topics and maintain its own consuming offsets. For example, we can group consumers by use cases, one group for billing and the other for accounting.

The instances in the same group can consume traffic in parallel, as in Figure 4.7.

- Consumer group 1 subscribes to topic A.
- Consumer group 2 subscribes to both topics A and B.
- Topic A is subscribed by both consumer groups-1 and group-2, which means the same message is consumed by multiple consumers. This pattern supports the subscribe/publish model.

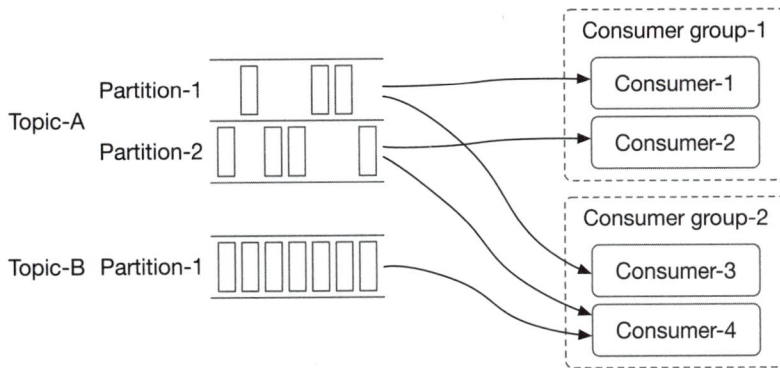

Figure 4.7: Consumer groups

However, there is one problem. Reading data in parallel improves the throughput, but the consumption order of messages in the same partition cannot be guaranteed. For example, if Consumer-1 and Consumer-2 both read from Partition-1, we will not be able to guarantee the message consumption order in Partition-1.

The good news is we can fix this by adding a constraint, that a single partition can only be consumed by one consumer in the same group. If the number of consumers of a group is larger than the number of partitions of a topic, some consumers will not get data from this topic. For example, in Figure 4.7, Consumer-3 in Consumer group-2 cannot consume messages from topic B because it is consumed by Consumer-4 in the same consumer group, already.

With this constraint, if we put all consumers in the same consumer group, then messages in the same partition are consumed by only one consumer, which is equivalent to the point-to-point model. Since a partition is the smallest storage unit, we can allocate enough partitions in advance to avoid the need to dynamically increase the number of partitions. To handle high scale, we just need to add consumers.

High-level architecture

Figure 4.8 shows the updated high-level design.

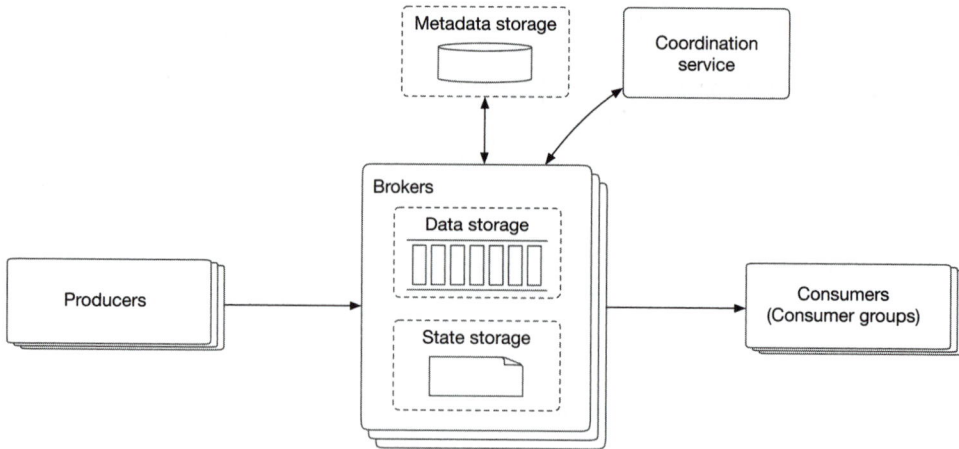

Figure 4.8: High-level design

Clients

- Producer: pushes messages to specific topics.
- Consumer group: subscribes to topics and consumes messages.

Core service and storage

- Broker: holds multiple partitions. A partition holds a subset of messages for a topic.
- Storage:
    - Data storage: messages are persisted in data storage in partitions.
    - State storage: consumer states are managed by state storage.
    - Metadata storage: configuration and properties of topics are persisted in metadata storage.
- Coordination service:
    - Service discovery: which brokers are alive.
    - Leader election: one of the brokers is selected as the active controller. There is only one active controller in the cluster. The active controller is responsible for assigning partitions.
    - Apache ZooKeeper [2] or etcd [3] are commonly used to elect a controller.

Step 3 - Design Deep Dive

To achieve high throughput while satisfying the high data retention requirement, we made three important design choices, which we explain in detail now.

- We chose an on-disk data structure that takes advantage of the great sequential access performance of rotational disks and the aggressive disk caching strategy of modern operating systems.

- We designed the message data structure to allow a message to be passed from the producer to the queue and finally to the consumer, with no modifications. This minimizes the need for copying which is very expensive in a high volume and high traffic system.

- We designed the system to favor batching. Small I/O is an enemy of high throughput. So, wherever possible, our design encourages batching. The producers send messages in batches. The message queue persists messages in even larger batches. The consumers fetch messages in batches when possible, too.

Data storage

Now let's explore the options to persist messages in more detail. In order to find the best choice, let's consider the traffic pattern of a message queue.

- Write-heavy, read-heavy.
- No update or delete operations. As a side note, a traditional message queue does not persist messages unless the queue falls behind, in which case there will be "delete" operations when the queue catches up. What we are talking about here is the persistence of a data streaming platform.
- Predominantly sequential read/write access.

Option 1: Database

The first option is to use a database.

- Relational database: create a topic table and write messages to the table as rows.
- NoSQL database: create a collection as a topic and write messages as documents.

Databases can handle the storage requirement, but they are not ideal because it is hard to design a database that supports both write-heavy and read-heavy access patterns at a large scale. The database solution does not fit our specific data usage patterns very well.

This means a database is not the best choice and could become a bottleneck of the system.

Option 2: Write-ahead log (WAL)

The second option is write-ahead log (WAL). WAL is just a plain file where new entries are appended to an append-only log. WAL is used in many systems, such as the redo log in MySQL [4] and the WAL in ZooKeeper.

We recommend persisting messages as WAL log files on disk. WAL has a pure sequential read/write access pattern. The disk performance of sequential access is very good [5]. Also, rotational disks have large capacity and they are pretty affordable.

As shown in Figure 4.9, a new message is appended to the tail of a partition, with a monotonically increasing offset. The easiest option is to use the line number of the log file as the offset. However, a file cannot grow infinitely, so it is a good idea to divide it into segments.

With segments, new messages are appended only to the active segment file. When the active segment reaches a certain size, a new active segment is created to receive new messages, and the currently active segment becomes inactive, like the rest of the non-active segments. Non-active segments only serve read requests. Old non-active segment files can be truncated if they exceed the retention or capacity limit.

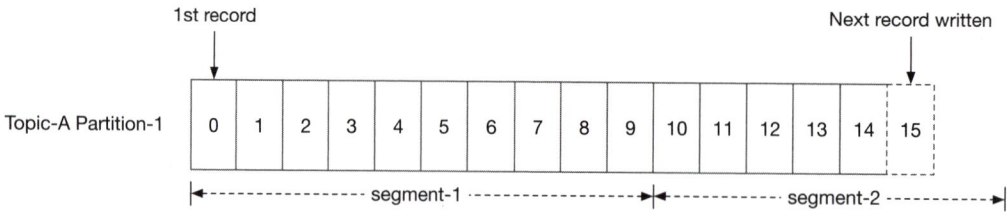

Figure 4.9: Append new messages

Segment files of the same partition are organized in a folder named `Partition-{:parti tion_id}`. The structure is shown in Figure 4.10.

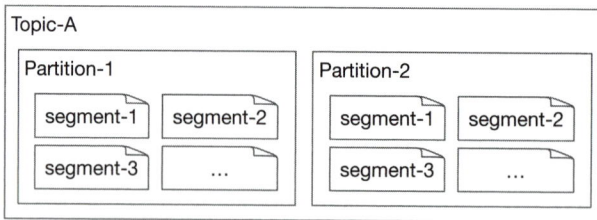

Figure 4.10: Data segment file distribution in topic partitions

A note on disk performance

To meet the high data retention requirement, our design relies heavily on disk drives to hold a large amount of data. There is a common misconception that rotational disks are slow, but this is really only the case for random access. For our workload, as long as we design our on-disk data structure to take advantage of the sequential access pattern, the modern disk drives in a RAID configuration (i.e., with disks striped together for higher performance) could comfortably achieve several hundred MB/sec of read and write speed. This is more than enough for our needs, and the cost structure is favorable.

Also, a modern operating system caches disk data in main memory very aggressively, so much so that it would happily use all available free memory to cache disk data. The WAL takes advantage of the heavy OS disk caching, too, as we described above.

Message data structure

The data structure of a message is key to high throughput. It defines the contract between the producers, message queue, and consumers. Our design achieves high performance by eliminating unnecessary data copying while the messages are in transit from the producers to the queue and finally to the consumers. If any parts of the system disagree on this contract, messages will need to be mutated which involves expensive copying. It could seriously hurt the performance of the system.

Below is a sample schema of the message data structure:

Field Name	Data Type
key	byte[]
value	byte[]
topic	string
partition	integer
offset	long
timestamp	long
size	integer
crc	integer

Table 4.1: Data schema of a message

Message key

The key of the message is used to determine the partition of the message. If the key is not defined, the partition is randomly chosen. Otherwise, the partition is chosen by hash(key) % numPartitions. If we need more flexibility, the producer can define its own mapping algorithm to choose partitions. Please note that the key is not equivalent to the partition number.

The key can be a string or a number. It usually carries some business information. The partition number is a concept in the message queue, which should not be explicitly exposed to clients.

With a proper mapping algorithm, if the number of partitions changes, messages can still be evenly sent to all the partitions.

Message value

The message value is the payload of a message. It can be plain text or a compressed binary block.

Reminder
The key and value of a message are different from the key-value pair in a key-value (KV) store. In the KV store, keys are unique, and we can find the value by key. In a message, keys do not need to be unique. Sometimes they are not even mandatory, and we don't need to find a value by key.

Other fields of a message

- Topic: the name of the topic that the message belongs to.
- Partition: the ID of the partition that the message belongs to.

- Offset: the position of the message in the partition. We can find a message via the combination of three fields: topic, partition, offset.
- Timestamp: the timestamp of when this message is stored.
- Size: the size of this message.
- CRC: Cyclic redundancy check (CRC) is used to ensure the integrity of raw data.

To support additional features, some optional fields can be added on demand. For example, messages can be filtered by tags, if tags are part of the optional fields.

Batching

Batching is pervasive in this design. We batch messages in the producer, the consumer, and the message queue itself. Batching is critical to the performance of the system. In this section, we focus primarily on batching in the message queue. We discuss batching for producer and consumer in more detail, shortly.

Batching is critical to improving performance because:

- It allows the operating system to group messages together in a single network request and amortizes the cost of expensive network round trips.
- The broker writes messages to the append logs in large chunks, which leads to larger blocks of sequential writes and larger contiguous blocks of disk cache, maintained by the operating system. Both lead to much greater sequential disk access throughput.

There is a tradeoff between throughput and latency. If the system is deployed as a traditional message queue where latency might be more important, the system could be tuned to use a smaller batch size. Disk performance will suffer a little bit in this use case. If tuned for throughput, there might need to be a higher number of partitions per topic, to make up for the slower sequential disk write throughput.

So far, we've covered the main disk storage subsystem and its associated on-disk data structure. Now, let's switch gears and discuss the producer and consumer flows. Then we will come back and finish the deep dive into the rest of the message queue.

Producer flow

If a producer wants to send messages to a partition, which broker should it connect to? The first option is to introduce a routing layer. All messages sent to the routing layer are routed to the "correct" broker. If the brokers are replicated, the "correct" broker is the leader replica. We will cover replication later.

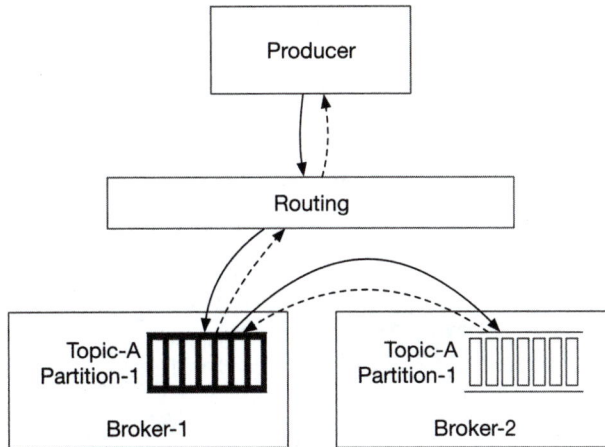

Figure 4.11: Routing layer

As shown in Figure 4.11, the producer tries to send messages to Partition-1 of Topic-A.

1. The producer sends messages to the routing layer.
2. The routing layer reads the replica distribution plan[1] from the metadata storage and caches it locally. When a message arrives, it routes the message to the leader replica of Partition-1, which is stored in Broker-1.
3. The leader replica receives the message and follower replicas pull data from the leader.
4. When "enough" replicas have synchronized the message, the leader commits the data (persisted on disk), which means the data can be consumed. Then it responds to the producer.

You might be wondering why we need both leader and follower replicas. The reason is fault tolerance. We dive deep into this process in the "In-sync replicas" section on page 113.

This approach works, but it has a few drawbacks:

- A new routing layer means additional network latency caused by overhead and additional network hops.
- Request batching is one of the big drivers of efficiency. This design doesn't take that into consideration.

Figure 4.12 shows the improved design.

---

[1]The distribution of replicas for each partition is called a replica distribution plan

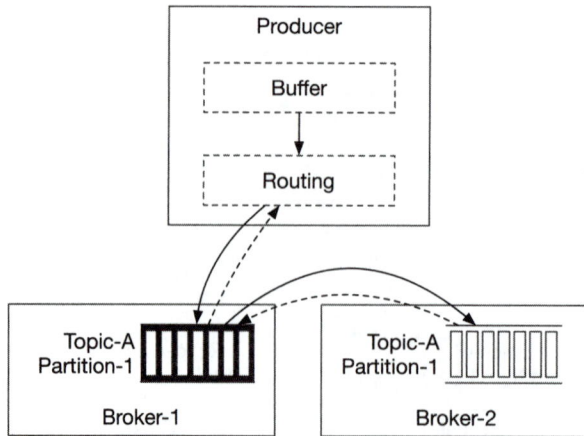

Figure 4.12: Producer with buffer and routing

The routing layer is wrapped into the producer and a buffer component is added to the producer. Both can be installed in the producer as part of the producer client library. This change brings several benefits:

- Fewer network hops mean lower latency.
- Producers can have their own logic to determine which partition the message should be sent to.
- Batching buffers messages in memory and sends out larger batches in a single request. This increases throughput.

The choice of the batch size is a classic tradeoff between throughput and latency (Figure 4.13). With a large batch size, the throughput increases but latency is higher, due to a longer wait time to accumulate the batch. With a small batch size, requests are sent sooner so the latency is lower, but throughput suffers. Producers can tune the batch size based on use cases.

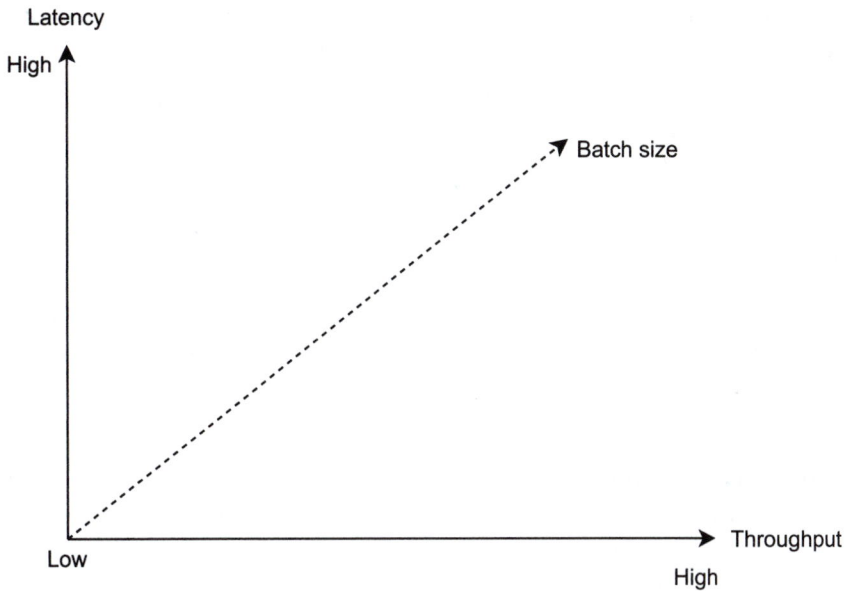

Figure 4.13: The choice of the batch size

Consumer flow

The consumer specifies its offset in a partition and receives back a chunk of events beginning from that position. An example is shown in Figure 4.14.

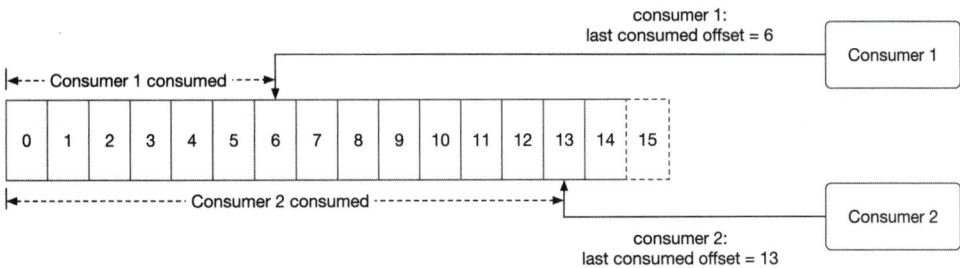

Figure 4.14: Consumer flow

Push vs pull

An important question to answer is whether brokers should push data to consumers, or if consumers should pull data from the brokers.

Push model

Pros:

- Low latency. The broker can push messages to the consumer immediately upon receiving them.

Cons:

- If the rate of consumption falls below the rate of production, consumers could be overwhelmed.
- It is difficult to deal with consumers with diverse processing power because the brokers control the rate at which data is transferred.

Pull model

Pros:

- Consumers control the consumption rate. We can have one set of consumers process messages in real-time and another set of consumers process messages in batch mode.
- If the rate of consumption falls below the rate of production, we can scale out the consumers, or simply catch up when it can.
- The pull model is more suitable for batch processing. In the push model, the broker has no knowledge of whether consumers will be able to process messages immediately. If the broker sends one message at a time to the consumer and the consumer is backed up, new messages will end up waiting in the buffer. A pull model pulls all available messages after the consumer's current position in the log (or up to the configurable max size). It is suitable for aggressive batching of data.

Cons:

- When there is no message in the broker, a consumer might still keep pulling data, wasting resources. To overcome this issue, many message queues support long polling mode, which allows pulls to wait a specified amount of time for new messages [6].

Based on these considerations, most message queues choose the pull model.

Figure 4.15 shows the workflow of the consumer pull model.

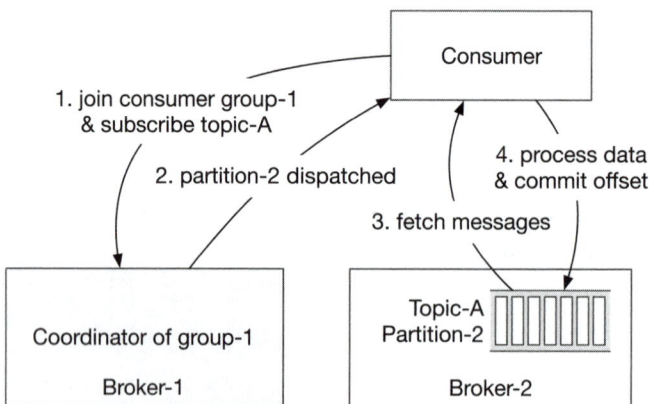

Figure 4.15: Pull model

1. A new consumer wants to join group-1 and subscribes to Topic-A. It finds the corre-

sponding broker node by hashing the group name. By doing so, all the consumers in the same group connect to the same broker, which is also called the coordinator of this consumer group. Despite the naming similarity, the consumer group coordinator is different from the coordination service mentioned in Figure 4.8. This coordinator coordinates the consumer group, while the coordination service mentioned earlier coordinates the broker cluster.

2. The coordinator confirms that the consumer has joined the group and assigns Partition-2 to the consumer. There are different partition assignment strategies including round-robin, range, etc. [7]

3. Consumer fetches messages from the last consumed offset, which is managed by the state storage.

4. Consumer processes messages and commits the offset to the broker. The order of data processing and offset committing affects the message delivery semantics, which will be discussed shortly.

Consumer rebalancing

Consumer rebalancing decides which consumer is responsible for which subset of partitions. The process could occur when a consumer joins, when a consumer leaves, when a consumer crashes, or when partitions are adjusted.

When consumer rebalancing occurs, the coordinator plays an important role. Let's first take a look at what a coordinator is. The coordinator is one of the brokers responsible for communicating with consumers to achieve consumer rebalancing. The coordinator receives heartbeat from consumers and manages their offset on the partitions.

Let's use an example to understand how the coordinator and the consumers work together.

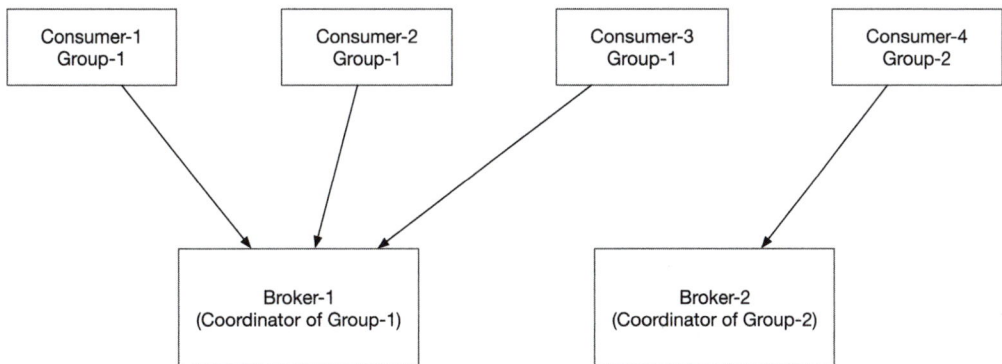

Figure 4.16: Coordinator of consumer groups

- As shown in Figure 4.16, each consumer belongs to a group. It finds the dedicated coordinator by hashing the group name. All consumers from the same group are connected to the same coordinator.

- The coordinator maintains a joined consumer list. When the list changes, the coordinator elects a new leader of the group.

- As the new leader of the consumer group, it generates a new partition dispatch plan and reports it back to the coordinator. The coordinator will broadcast the plan to the other consumers in the group.

In a distributed system, consumers might encounter all sorts of issues including network issues, crashes, restarts, etc. From the coordinator's perspective, they will no longer have heartbeats. When this happens, the coordinator will trigger a rebalance process to re-dispatch the partitions as illustrated in Figure 4.17.

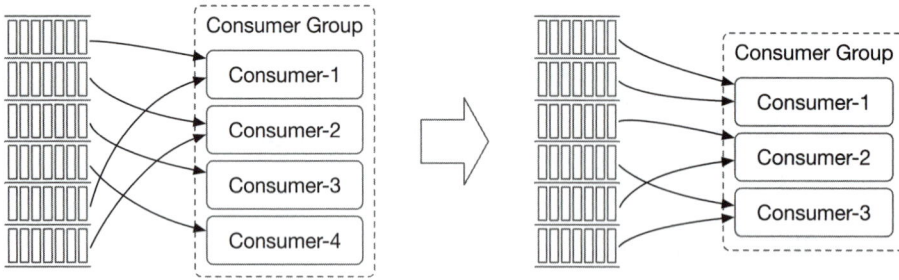

Figure 4.17: Consumer rebalance

Let's simulate a few rebalance scenarios. Assume there are 2 consumers in the group, and 4 partitions in the subscribed topic. Figure 4.18 shows the flow when a new Consumer B joins the group.

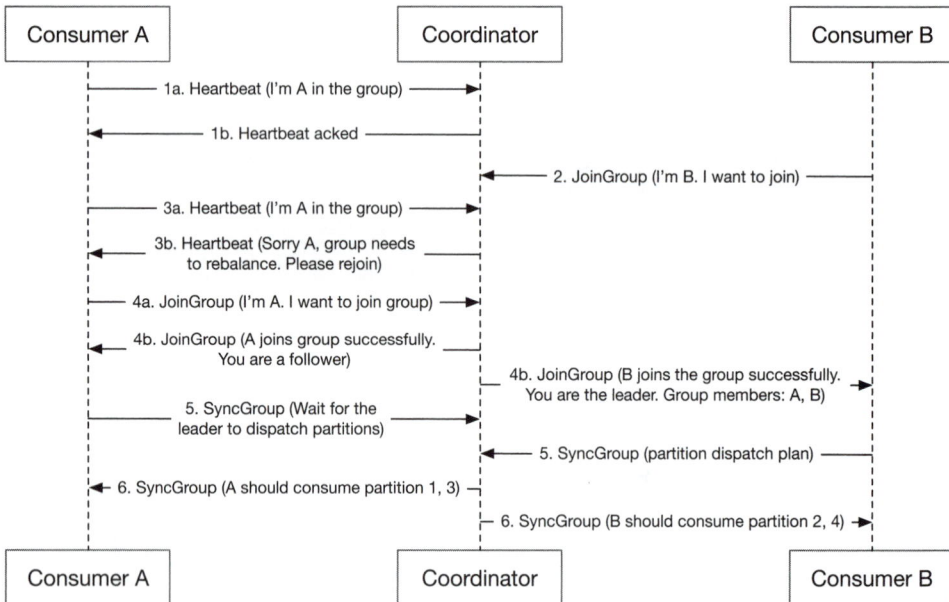

Figure 4.18: New consumer joins

1. Initially, only Consumer A is in the group. It consumes all the partitions and keeps the heartbeat with the coordinator.

2. Consumer B sends a request to join the group.

3. The coordinator knows it's time to rebalance, so it notifies all the consumers in the group in a passive way. When Consumer A's heartbeat is received by the coordinator, it asks Consumer A to rejoin the group.

4. Once all the consumers have rejoined the group, the coordinator chooses one of them as the leader and informs all the consumers about the election result.

5. The leader consumer generates the partition dispatch plan and sends it to the coordinator. Follower consumers ask the coordinator about the partition dispatch plan.

6. Consumers start consuming messages from newly assigned partitions.

Figure 4.19 shows the flow when an existing Consumer A leaves the group.

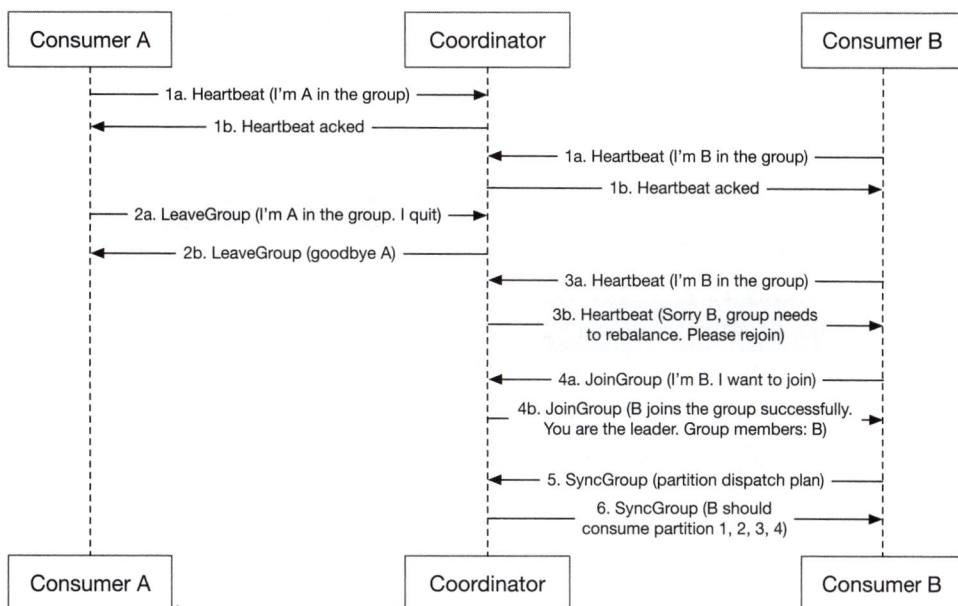

Figure 4.19: Existing consumer leaves

1. Consumer A and B are in the same consumer group.

2. Consumer A needs to be shut down, so it requests to leave the group.

3. The coordinator knows it's time to rebalance. When Consumer B's heartbeat is received by the coordinator, it asks Consumer B to rejoin the group.

4. The remaining steps are the same as the ones shown in Figure 4.18.

Figure 4.20 shows the flow when an existing Consumer A crashes.

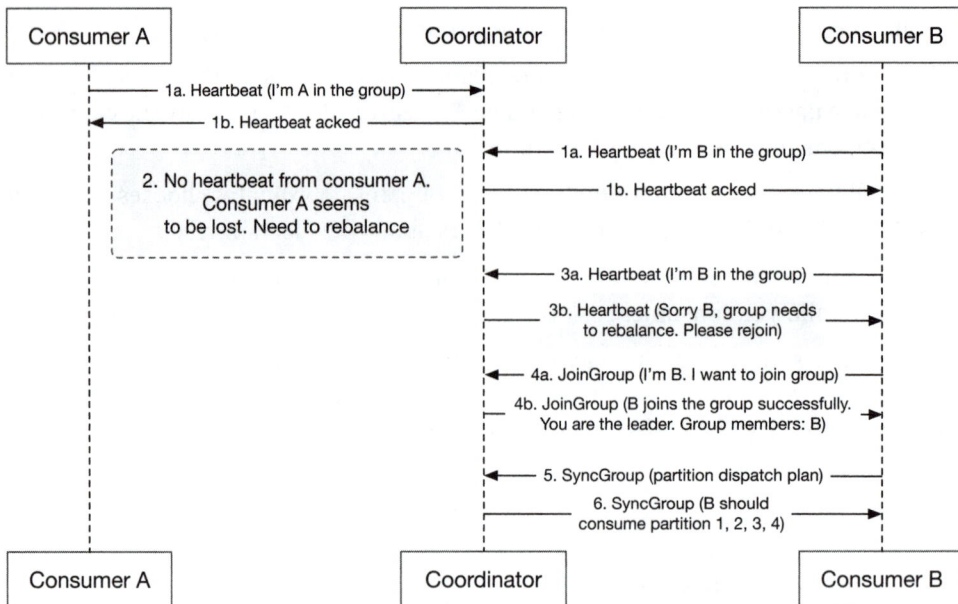

Figure 4.20: Existing consumer crashes

1. Consumer A and B keep heartbeats with the coordinator.

2. Consumer A crashes, so there is no heartbeat sent from Consumer A to the coordinator. Since the coordinator doesn't get any heartbeat signal within a specified amount of time from Consumer A, it marks the consumer as dead.

3. The coordinator triggers the rebalance process.

4. The following steps are the same as the ones in the previous scenario.

Now that we finished the detour on producer and consumer flows, let's come back and finish the deep dive on the rest of the message queue broker.

State storage

In the message queue broker, the state storage stores:

- The mapping between partitions and consumers.

- The last consumed offsets of consumer groups for each partition. As shown in Figure 4.21, the last consumed offset for consumer group-1 is 6 and the offset for consumer group-2 is 13.

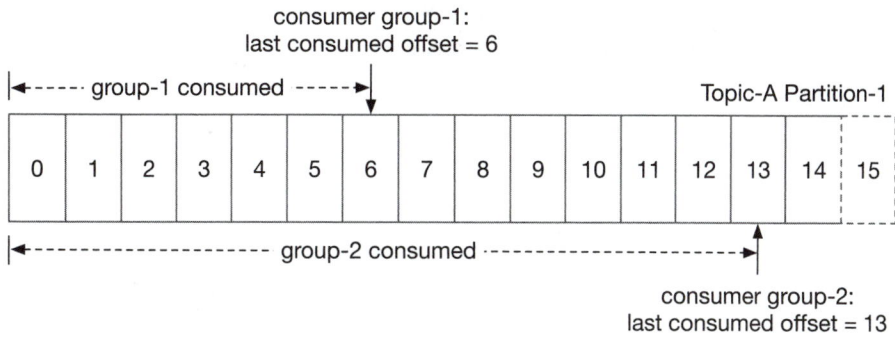

Figure 4.21: Last consumed offset of consumer groups

For example, as shown in Figure 4.21, a consumer in group-1 consumes messages from the partition in sequence and commits the consumed offset 6. This means all the messages before and at offset 6 are already consumed. If the consumer crashes, another new consumer in the same group will resume consumption by reading the last consumed offset from the state storage.

The data access patterns for consumer states are:

- Frequent read and write operations but the volume is not high.
- Data is updated frequently and is rarely deleted.
- Random read and write operations.
- Data consistency is important.

Lots of storage solutions can be used for storing the consumer state data. Considering the data consistency and fast read/write requirements, a KV store like ZooKeeper is a great choice. Kafka has moved the offset storage from ZooKeeper to Kafka brokers. Interested readers can read the reference material [8] to learn more.

Metadata storage

The metadata storage stores the configuration and properties of topics, including a number of partitions, retention period, and distribution of replicas.

Metadata does not change frequently and the data volume is small, but it has a high consistency requirement. ZooKeeper is a good choice for storing metadata.

ZooKeeper

By reading previous sections, you probably have already sensed that ZooKeeper is very helpful for designing a distributed message queue. If you are not familiar with it, ZooKeeper is an essential service for distributed systems offering a hierarchical key-value store. It is commonly used to provide a distributed configuration service, synchronization service, and naming registry [2].

ZooKeeper is used to simplify our design as shown in Figure 4.22.

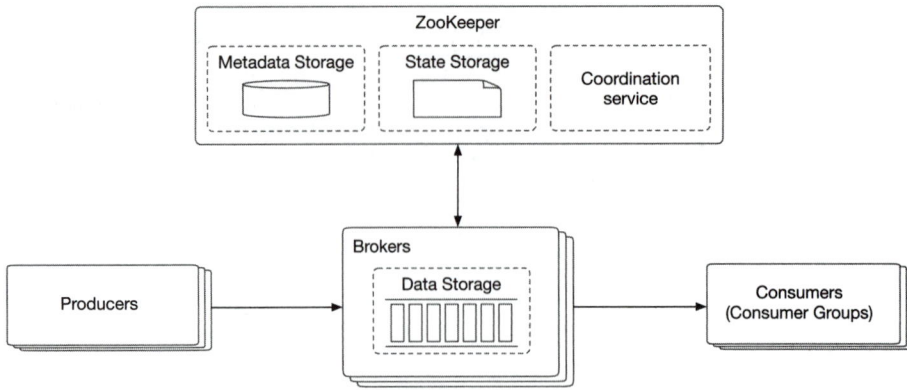

Figure 4.22: ZooKeeper

Let's briefly go over the change.

- Metadata and state storage are moved to ZooKeeper.
- The broker now only needs to maintain the data storage for messages.
- ZooKeeper helps with the leader election of the broker cluster.

Replication

In distributed systems, hardware issues are common and cannot be ignored. Data gets lost when a disk is damaged or fails permanently. Replication is the classic solution to achieve high availability.

As in Figure 4.23, each partition has 3 replicas, distributed across different broker nodes.

For each partition, the highlighted replicas are the leaders and the others are followers. Producers only send messages to the leader replica. The follower replicas keep pulling new messages from the leader. Once messages are synchronized to enough replicas, the leader returns an acknowledgment to the producer. We will go into detail about how to define "enough" in the In-sync Replicas section on page 113.

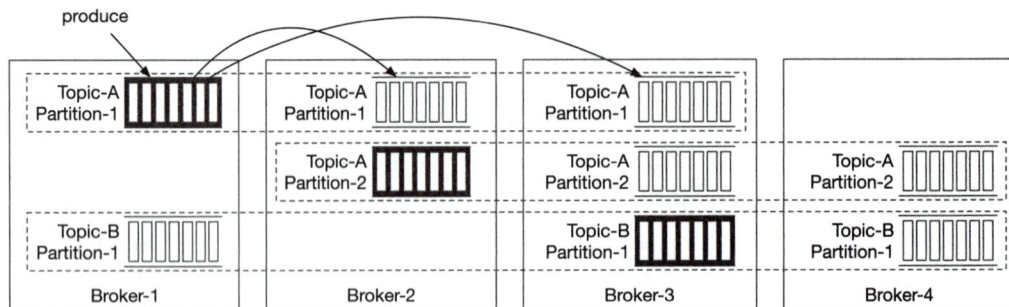

Figure 4.23: Replication

The distribution of replicas for each partition is called a replica distribution plan. For example, the replica distribution plan in Figure 4.23 can be described as:

- Partition-1 of Topic-A: 3 replicas, leader in Broker-1, followers in Broker-2 and 3;
- Partition-2 of Topic-A: 3 replicas, leader in Broker-2, followers in Broker-3 and 4;
- Partition-1 of Topic-B: 3 replicas, leader in Broker-3, followers in Broker-4 and 1.

Who makes the replica distribution plan? It works as follows; with the help of the coordination service, one of the broker nodes is elected as the leader. It generates the replica distribution plan and persists the plan in metadata storage. All the brokers now can work according to the plan.

If you are interested in knowing more about replications, check out "Chapter 5. Replication" of the book "Design Data-Intensive Applications" [9].

In-sync replicas

We mentioned that messages are persisted in multiple partitions to avoid single node failure, and each partition has multiple replicas. Messages are only written to the leader, and followers synchronize data from the leader. One problem we need to solve is keeping them in sync.

In-sync replicas (ISR) refer to replicas that are "in-sync" with the leader. The definition of "in-sync" depends on the topic configuration. For example, if the value of replica.lag.max.messages is 4, it means that as long as the follower is behind the leader by no more than 3 messages, it will not be removed from ISR [10]. The leader is an ISR by default.

Let's use an example as shown in Figure 4.24 to shows how ISR works.

- The committed offset in the leader replica is 13. Two new messages are written to the leader, but not committed yet. Committed offset means that all messages before and at this offset are already synchronized to all the replicas in ISR.
- Replica-2 and replica-3 have fully caught up with the leader, so they are in ISR and can fetch new messages.
- Replica-4 did not fully catch up with the leader within the configured lag time, so it is not in ISR. When it catches up again, it can be added to ISR.

replica-2 (follower)

10	11	12	13	14

fetch

replica-1 (leader)

10	11	12	13	14	15

replica-3 (follower)

10	11	12	13

fetch

not caught up

committed offset = 13

replica-4 (follower)

10	11

ISR: {replica-1, replica-2, replica-3}

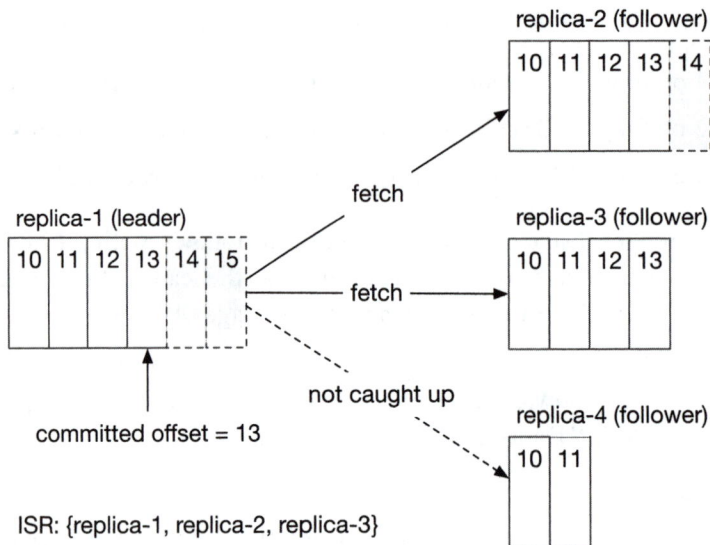

Figure 4.24: How ISR works

Why do we need ISR? The reason is that ISR reflects the trade-off between performance and durability. If producers don't want to lose any messages, the safest way to do that is to ensure all replicas are already in sync before sending an acknowledgment. But a slow replica will cause the whole partition to become slow or unavailable.

Now that we've discussed ISR, let's take a look at acknowledgment settings. Producers can choose to receive acknowledgments until the k number of ISRs has received the message, where k is configurable.

ACK=all

Figure 4.25 illustrates the case with ACK=all. With ACK=all, the producer gets an ACK when all ISRs have received the message. This means it takes a longer time to send a message because we need to wait for the slowest ISR, but it gives the strongest message durability.

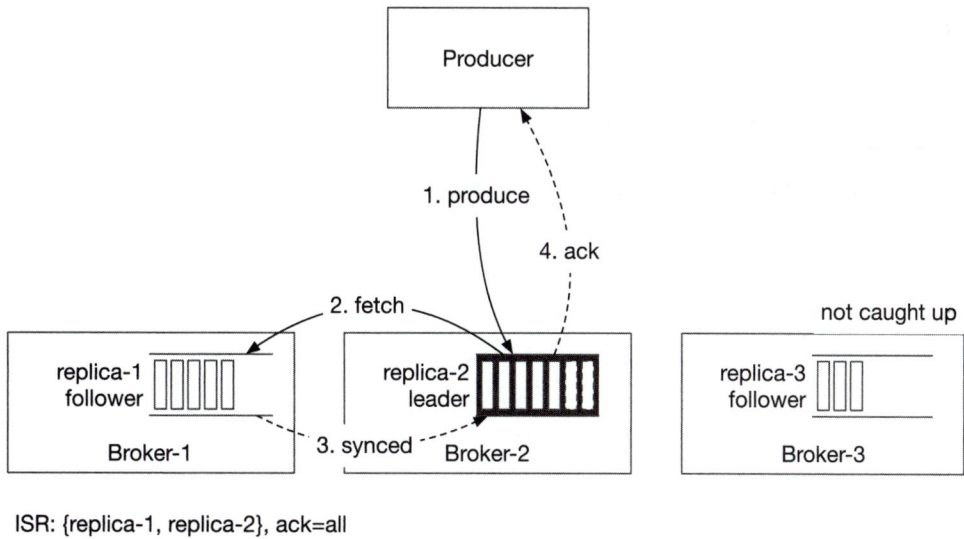

Figure 4.25: ACK=all

ACK=1

With ACK=1, the producer receives an ACK once the leader persists the message. The latency is improved by not waiting for data synchronization. If the leader fails immediately after a message is acknowledged but before it is replicated by follower nodes, then the message is lost. This setting is suitable for low latency systems where occasional data loss is acceptable.

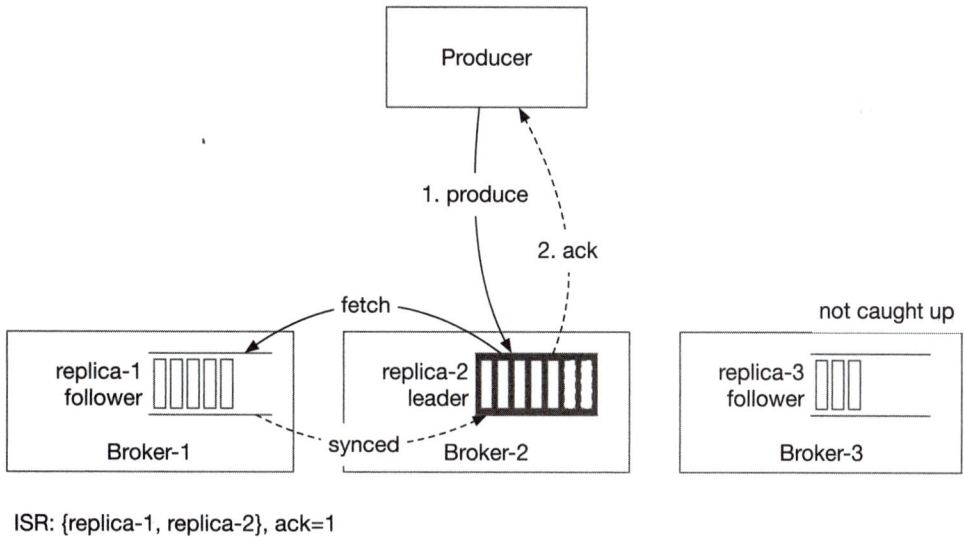

Figure 4.26: ACK=1

ACK=0

The producer keeps sending messages to the leader without waiting for any acknowledgment, and it never retries. This method provides the lowest latency at the cost of potential message loss. This setting might be good for use cases like collecting metrics or logging data since data volume is high and occasional data loss is acceptable.

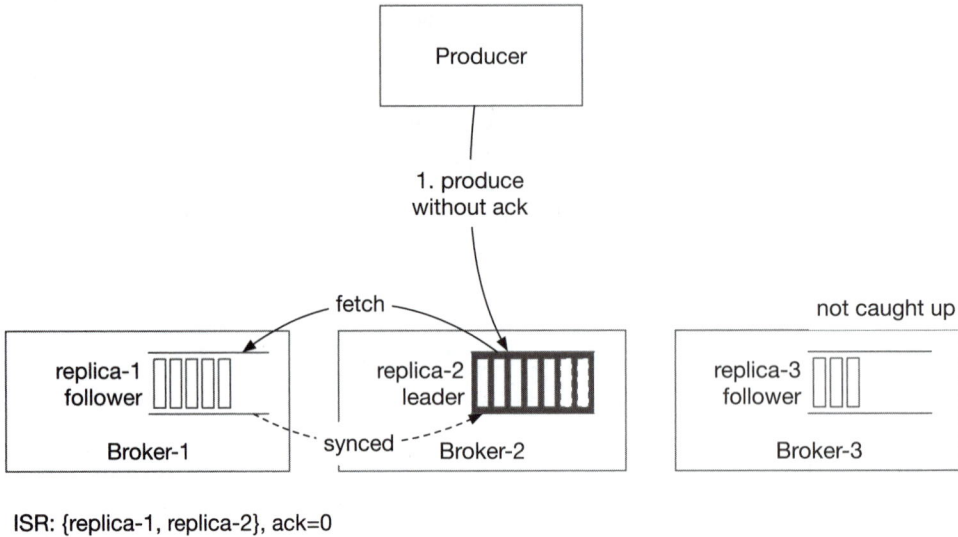

ISR: {replica-1, replica-2}, ack=0

Figure 4.27: ACK=0

Configurable ACK allows us to trade durability for performance.

Now let's look at the consumer side. The easiest setup is to let consumers connect to a leader replica to consume messages.

You might be wondering if the leader replica would be overwhelmed by this design and why messages are not read from ISRs. The reasons are:

- Design and operational simplicity.
- Since messages in one partition are dispatched to only one consumer within a consumer group, this limits the number of connections to the leader replica.
- The number of connections to the leader replicas is usually not large as long as a topic is not super hot.
- If a topic is hot, we can scale by expanding the number of partitions and consumers.

In some scenarios, reading from the leader replica might not be the best option. For example, if a consumer is located in a different data center from the leader replica, the read performance suffers. In this case, it is worthwhile to enable consumers to read from the closest ISRs. Interested readers can check out the reference material about this [11].

ISR is very important. How does it determine if a replica is ISR or not? Usually, the leader for every partition tracks the ISR list by computing the lag of every replica from itself. If you are interested in detailed algorithms, you can find the implementations in reference materials [12] [13].

Scalability

By now we have made great progress designing the distributed message queue system. In the next step, let's evaluate the scalability of different system components:

- Producers
- Consumers
- Brokers
- Partitions

Producer

The producer is conceptually much simpler than the consumer because it doesn't need group coordination. The scalability of producers can easily be achieved by adding or removing producer instances.

Consumer

Consumer groups are isolated from each other, so it is easy to add or remove a consumer group. Inside a consumer group, the rebalancing mechanism helps to handle the cases where a consumer gets added or removed, or when it crashes. With consumer groups and the rebalance mechanism, the scalability and fault tolerance of consumers can be achieved.

Broker

Before discussing scalability on the broker side, let's first consider the failure recovery of brokers.

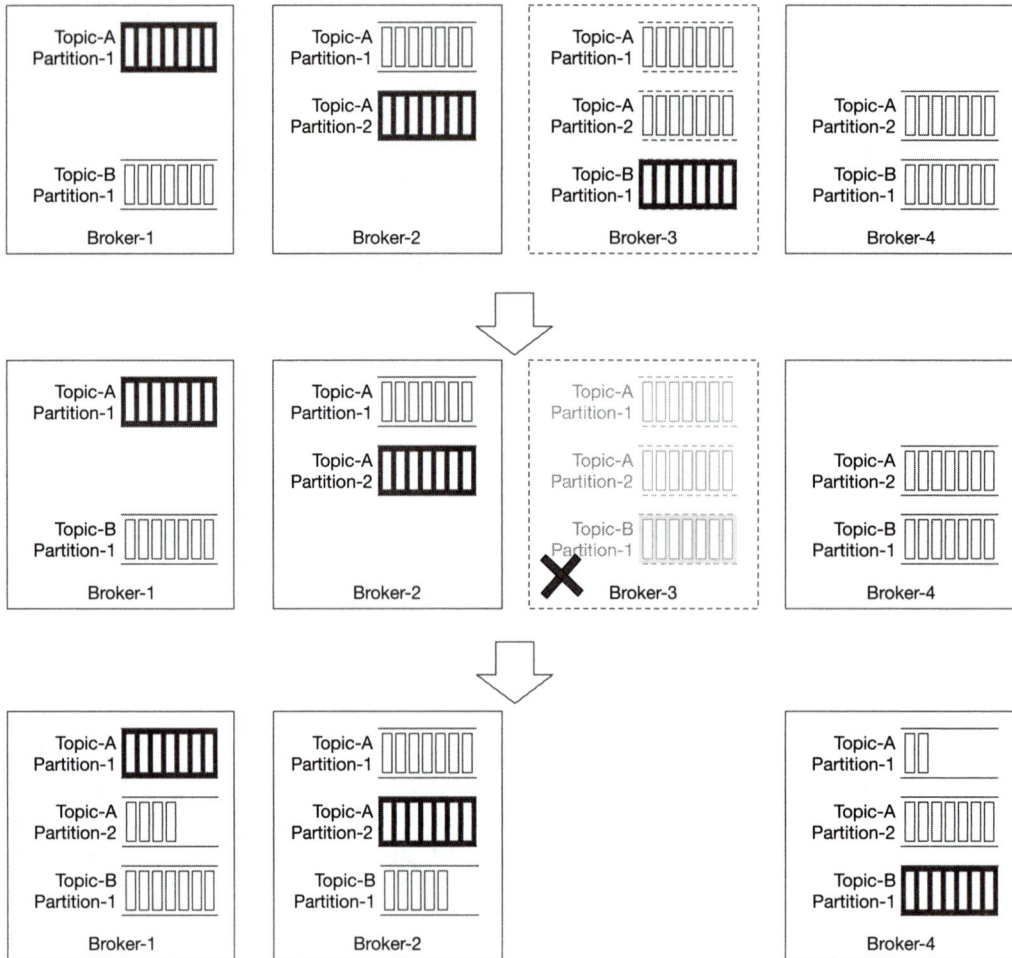

Figure 4.28: Broker node crashes

Let's use an example in Figure 4.28 to explain how failure recovery works.

1. Assume there are 4 brokers and the partition (replica) distribution plan is shown below:

   - Partition-1 of topic A: replicas in Broker-1 (leader), 2, and 3.
   - Partition-2 of topic A: replicas in Broker-2 (leader), 3, and 4.
   - Partition-1 of topic B: replicas in Broker-3 (leader), 4, and 1.

2. Broker-3 crashes, which means all the partitions on the node are lost. The partition distribution plan is changed to:

   - Partition-1 of topic A: replicas in Broker-1 (leader) and 2.
   - Partition-2 of topic A: replicas in Broker-2 (leader) and 4.
   - Partition-1 of topic B: replicas in Broker-4 and 1.

3. The broker controller detects Broker-3 is down and generates a new partition distri-

bution plan for the remaining broker nodes:

- Partition-1 of topic A: replicas in Broker-1 (leader), 2, and 4 (new).
- Partition-2 of topic A: replicas in Broker-2 (leader), 4, and 1 (new).
- Partition-1 of topic B: replicas in Broker-4 (leader), 1, and 2 (new).

4. The new replicas work as followers and catch up with the leader.

To make the broker fault-tolerant, here are additional considerations:

- The minimum number of ISRs specifies how many replicas the producer must receive before a message is considered to be successfully committed. The higher the number, the safer. But on the other hand, we need to balance latency and safety.
- If all replicas of a partition are in the same broker node, then we cannot tolerate the failure of this node. It is also a waste of resources to replicate data in the same node. Therefore, replicas should not be in the same node.
- If all the replicas of a partition crash, the data for that partition is lost forever. When choosing the number of replicas and replica locations, there's a trade-off between data safety, resource cost, and latency. It is safer to distribute replicas across data centers, but this will incur much more latency and cost, to synchronize data between replicas. As a workaround, data mirroring can help to copy data across data centers, but this is out of scope. The reference material [14] covers this topic.

Now let's get back to discussing the scalability of brokers. The simplest solution would be to redistribute the replicas when broker nodes are added or removed.

However, there is a better approach. The broker controller can temporarily allow more replicas in the system than the number of replicas in the config file. When the newly added broker catches up, we can remove the ones that are no longer needed. Let's use an example as shown in Figure 4.29 to understand the approach.

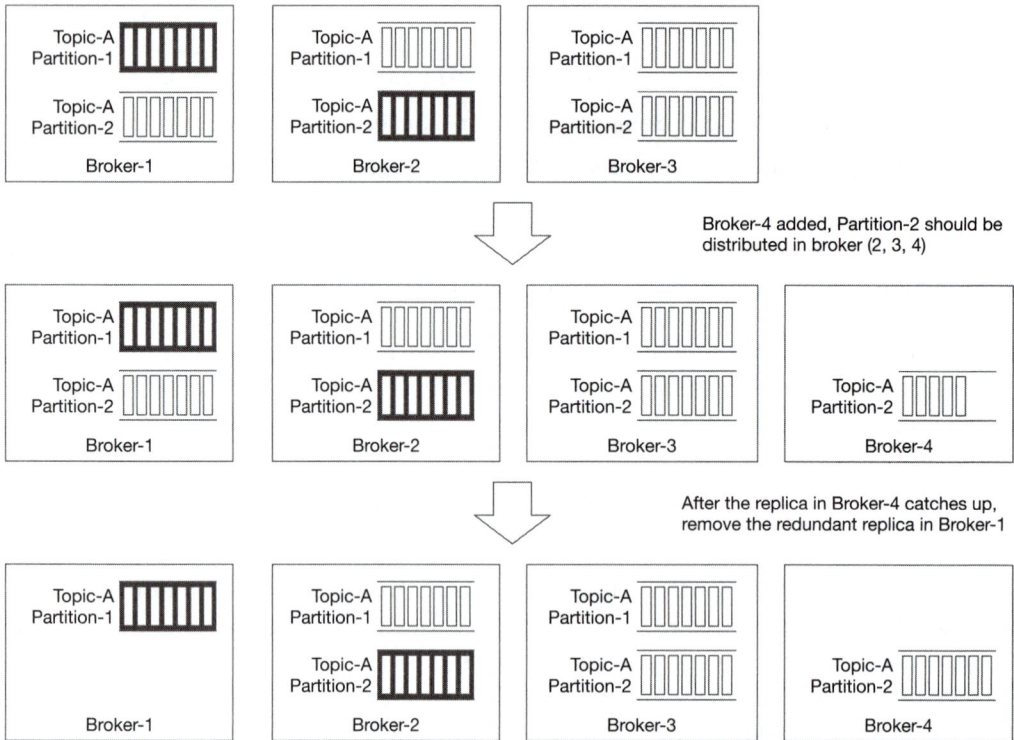

Figure 4.29: Add new broker node

1. The initial setup: 3 brokers, 2 partitions, and 3 replicas for each partition.

2. New Broker-4 is added. Assume the broker controller changes the replica distribution of Partition-2 to the broker (2, 3, 4). The new replica in Broker-4 starts to copy data from leader Broker-2. Now the number of replicas for Partition-2 is temporarily more than 3.

3. After the replica in Broker-4 catches up, the redundant partition in Broker-1 is gracefully removed.

By following this process, data loss while adding brokers can be avoided. A similar process can be applied to remove brokers safely.

Partition

For various operational reasons, such as scaling the topic, throughput tuning, balancing availability/ throughput, etc., we may change the number of partitions. When the number of partitions changes, the producer will be notified after it communicates with any broker, and the consumer will trigger consumer rebalancing. Therefore, it is safe for both the producer and consumer.

Now let's consider the data storage layer when the number of partitions changes. As in Figure 4.30, we have added a partition to the topic.

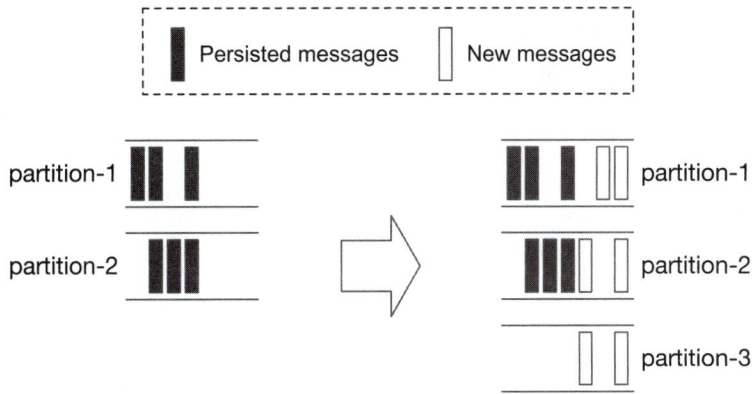

Figure 4.30: Partition increase

- Persisted messages are still in the old partitions, so there's no data migration.
- After the new partition (partition-3) is added, new messages will be persisted in all 3 partitions.

So it is straightforward to scale the topic by increasing partitions.

Decrease the number of partitions

Decreasing partitions is more complicated, as illustrated in Figure 4.31.

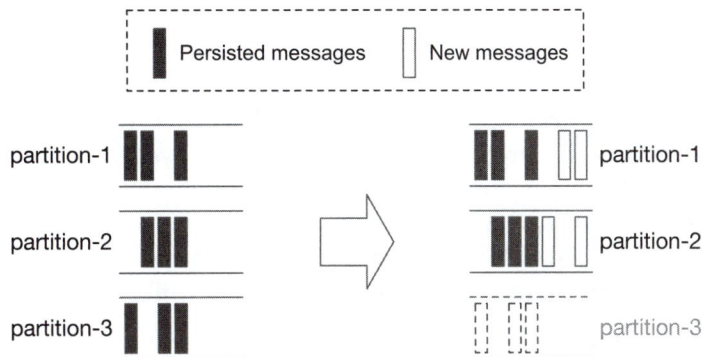

Figure 4.31: Partition decrease

- Partition-3 is decommissioned so new messages are only received by the remaining partitions (partition-1 and partition-2).
- The decommissioned partition (partition-3) cannot be removed immediately because data might be currently consumed by consumers for a certain amount of time. Only after the configured retention period passes, data can be truncated and storage space is freed up. Reducing partitions is not a shortcut to reclaiming data space.
- During this transitional period (while partition-3 is decommissioned), producers only send messages to the remaining 2 partitions, but consumers can still consume from all 3 partitions. After the retention period of the decommissioned partition expires, consumer groups need rebalancing.

Data delivery semantics

Now that we understand the different components of a distributed message queue, let's discuss different delivery semantics: at-most once, at-least once, and exactly once.

At-most once

As the name suggests, at-most once means a message will be delivered not more than once. Messages may be lost but are not redelivered. This is how at-most once delivery works at the high level.

- The producer sends a message asynchronously to a topic without waiting for an acknowledgment (ACK=0). If message delivery fails, there is no retry.

- Consumer fetches the message and commits the offset before the data is processed. If the consumer crashes just after offset commit, the message will not be re-consumed.

Figure 4.32: At-most once

It is suitable for use cases like monitoring metrics, where a small amount of data loss is acceptable.

At-least once

With this data delivery semantic, it's acceptable to deliver a message more than once, but no message should be lost. Here is how it works at a high level.

- Producer sends a message synchronously or asynchronously with a response callback, setting ACK=1 or ACK=all, to make sure messages are delivered to the broker. If the message delivery fails or timeouts, the producer will keep retrying.

- Consumer fetches the message and commits the offset only after the data is successfully processed. If the consumer fails to process the message, it will re-consume the message so there won't be data loss. On the other hand, if a consumer processes the message but fails to commit the offset to the broker, the message will be re-consumed when the consumer restarts, resulting in duplicates.

- A message might be delivered more than once to the brokers and consumers.

Figure 4.33: At-least once

Use cases: With at-least once, messages won't be lost but the same message might be delivered multiple times. While not ideal from a user perspective, at-least once delivery semantics are usually good enough for use cases where data duplication is not a big issue or deduplication is possible on the consumer side. For example, with a unique key in each message, a message can be rejected when writing duplicate data to the database.

Exactly once

Exactly once is the most difficult delivery semantic to implement. It is friendly to users, but it has a high cost for the system's performance and complexity.

Figure 4.34: Exactly once

Use cases: Financial-related use cases (payment, trading, accounting, etc.). Exactly once is especially important when duplication is not acceptable and the downstream service or third party doesn't support idempotency.

Advanced features

In this section, we talk briefly about some advanced features, such as message filtering, delayed messages, and scheduled messages.

Message filtering

A topic is a logical abstraction that contains messages of the same type. However, some consumer groups may only want to consume messages of certain subtypes. For example, the ordering system sends all the activities about the order to a topic, but the payment system only cares about messages related to checkout and refund.

One option is to build a dedicated topic for the payment system and another topic for the ordering system. This method is simple, but it might raise some concerns.

- What if other systems ask for different subtypes of messages? Do we need to build dedicated topics for every single consumer request?
- It is a waste of resources to save the same messages on different topics.
- The producer needs to change every time a new consumer requirement comes, as the producer and consumer are now tightly coupled.

Therefore, we need to resolve this requirement using a different approach. Luckily, message filtering comes to the rescue.

A naive solution for message filtering is that the consumer fetches the full set of messages and filters out unnecessary messages during processing time. This approach is flexible but introduces unnecessary traffic that will affect system performance.

A better solution is to filter messages on the broker side so that consumers will only get messages they care about. Implementing this requires some careful consideration. If data filtering requires data decryption or deserialization, it will degrade the performance of the brokers. Additionally, if messages contain sensitive data, they should not be readable in the message queue.

Therefore, the filtering logic in the broker should not extract the message payload. It is better to put data used for filtering into the metadata of a message, which can be efficiently read by the broker. For example, we can attach a tag to each message. With a message tag, a broker can filter messages in that dimension. If more tags are attached, the messages can be filtered in multiple dimensions. Therefore, a list of tags can support most of the filtering requirements. To support more complex logic such as mathematical formulae, the broker will need a grammar parser or a script executor, which might be too heavyweight for the message queue.

With tags attached to each message, a consumer can subscribe to messages based on the specified tag, as shown in Figure 4.35. Interested readers can refer to the reference material [15].

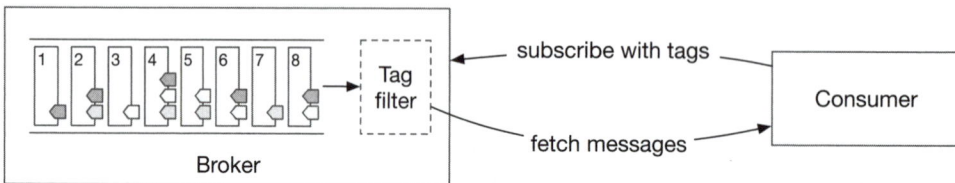

Figure 4.35: Message filtering by tags

Delayed messages & scheduled messages

Sometimes you want to delay the delivery of messages to a consumer for a specified period of time. For example, an order should be closed if not paid within 30 minutes after the order is created. A delayed verification message (check if the payment is completed) is sent immediately but is delivered to the consumer 30 minutes later. When the consumer receives the message, it checks the payment status. If the payment is not completed, the order will be closed. Otherwise, the message will be ignored.

Different from sending instant messages, we can send delayed messages to temporary storage on the broker side instead of to the topics immediately, and then deliver them to the topics when time's up. The high-level design for this is shown in Figure 4.36.

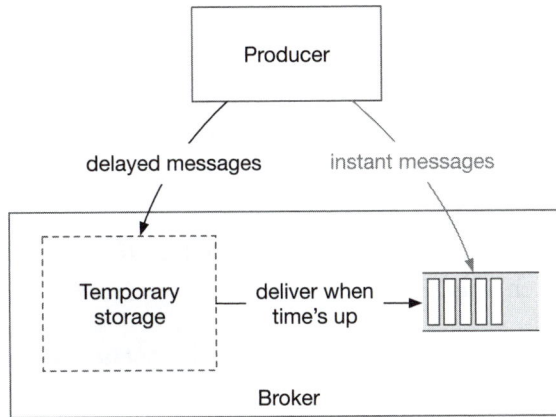

Figure 4.36: Delayed messages

Core components of the system include the temporary storage and the timing function.

- The temporary storage can be one or more special message topics.
- The timing function is out of scope, but here are 2 popular solutions:
  - Dedicated delay queues with predefined delay levels [16]. For example, RocketMQ doesn't support delayed messages with arbitrary time precision, but delayed messages with specific levels are supported. Message delay levels are 1s, 5s, 10s, 30s, 1m, 2m, 3m, 4m, 6m, 8m, 9m, 10m, 20m, 30m, 1h, and 2h.
  - Hierarchical time wheel [17].

A scheduled message means a message should be delivered to the consumer at the scheduled time. The overall design is very similar to delayed messages.

Step 4 - Wrap Up

In this chapter, we have presented the design of a distributed message queue with some advanced features commonly found in data streaming platforms. If there is extra time at the end of the interview, here are some additional talking points:

- Protocol: it defines rules, syntax, and APIs on how to exchange information and transfer data between different nodes. In a distributed message queue, the protocol should be able to:
  - Cover all the activities such as production, consumption, heartbeat, etc.
  - Effectively transport data with large volumes.
  - Verify the integrity and correctness of the data.

  Some popular protocols include Advanced Message Queuing Protocol (AMQP) [18] and Kafka protocol [19].

- Retry consumption. If some messages cannot be consumed successfully, we need to retry the operation. In order not to block incoming messages, how can we retry the operation after a certain time period? One idea is to send failed messages to a dedicated retry topic, so they can be consumed later.

- Historical data archive. Assume there is a time-based or capacity-based log retention mechanism. If a consumer needs to replay some historical messages that are already truncated, how can we do it? One possible solution is to use storage systems with large capacities, such as HDFS [20] or object storage, to store historical data.

Congratulations on getting this far! Now give yourself a pat on the back. Good job!

Chapter summary

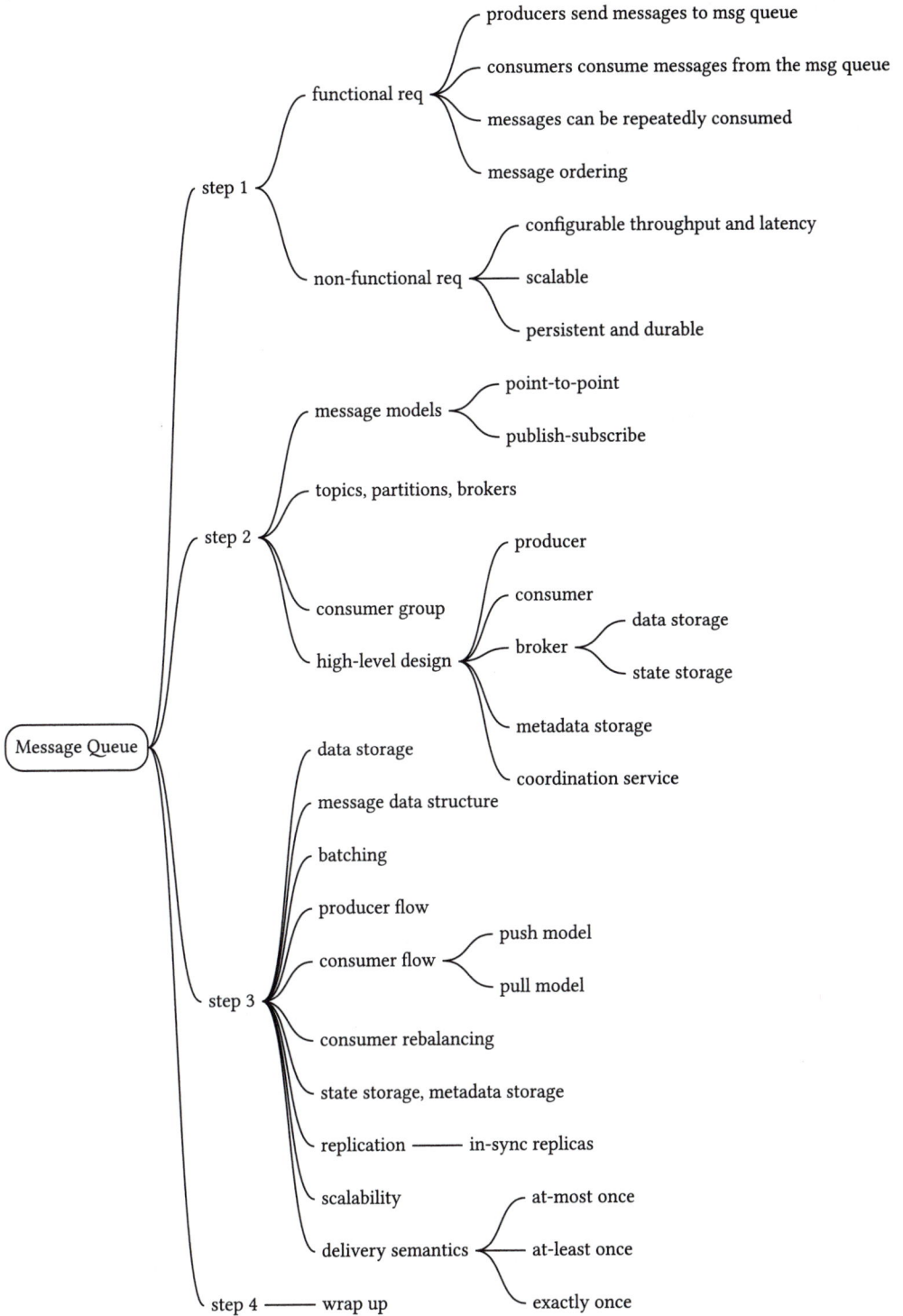

- **Message Queue**
  - **step 1**
    - functional req
      - producers send messages to msg queue
      - consumers consume messages from the msg queue
      - messages can be repeatedly consumed
      - message ordering
    - non-functional req
      - configurable throughput and latency
      - scalable
      - persistent and durable
  - **step 2**
    - message models
      - point-to-point
      - publish-subscribe
    - topics, partitions, brokers
    - consumer group
    - high-level design
      - producer
      - consumer
      - broker
        - data storage
        - state storage
      - metadata storage
      - coordination service
  - **step 3**
    - data storage
    - message data structure
    - batching
    - producer flow
    - consumer flow
      - push model
      - pull model
    - consumer rebalancing
    - state storage, metadata storage
    - replication —— in-sync replicas
    - scalability
    - delivery semantics
      - at-most once
      - at-least once
      - exactly once
  - **step 4** —— wrap up

Reference Material

[1] Queue Length Limit. https://www.rabbitmq.com/maxlength.html.

[2] Apache ZooKeeper - Wikipedia. https://en.wikipedia.org/wiki/Apache_ZooKeeper.

[3] etcd. https://etcd.io/.

[4] MySQL. https://www.mysql.com/.

[5] Comparison of disk and memory performance. https://deliveryimages.acm.org/10.1145/1570000/1563874/jacobs3.jpg.

[6] Push vs. pull. https://kafka.apache.org/documentation/#design_pull.

[7] Kafka 2.0 Documentation. https://kafka.apache.org/20/documentation.html#consumerconfigs.

[8] Kafka No Longer Requires ZooKeeper. https://towardsdatascience.com/kafka-no-longer-requires-zookeeper-ebfbf3862104.

[9] Martin Kleppmann. Replication. In *Designing Data-Intensive Applications*, pages 151–197. O'Reilly Media, 2017.

[10] ISR in Apache Kafka. https://www.cloudkarafka.com/blog/what-does-in-sync-in-apache-kafka-really-mean.html.

[11] Global map in a geographic Coordinate Reference System. https://cwiki.apache.org/confluence/display/KAFKA/KIP-392%3A+Allow+consumers+to+fetch+from+closest+replica.

[12] Hands-free Kafka Replication. https://www.confluent.io/blog/hands-free-kafka-replication-a-lesson-in-operational-simplicity/.

[13] Kafka high watermark. https://rongxinblog.wordpress.com/2016/07/29/kafka-high-watermark/.

[14] Kafka mirroring. https://cwiki.apache.org/confluence/pages/viewpage.action?pageId=27846330.

[15] Message filtering in RocketMQdtree. https://partners-intl.aliyun.com/help/doc-detail/29543.htm.

[16] Scheduled messages and delayed messages in Apache RocketMQ. https://partners-intl.aliyun.com/help/doc-detail/43349.htm.

[17] Hashed and hierarchical timing wheels. http://www.cs.columbia.edu/~nahum/w6998/papers/sosp87-timing-wheels.pdf.

[18] Advanced Message Queuing Protocol. https://en.wikipedia.org/wiki/Advanced_Message_Queuing_Protocol.

[19] Kafka protocol guide. https://kafka.apache.org/protocol.

[20] HDFS. https://hadoop.apache.org/docs/r1.2.1/hdfs_design.html.

5   Metrics Monitoring and Alerting System

In this chapter, we explore the design of a scalable metrics monitoring and alerting system. A well-designed monitoring and alerting system plays a key role in providing clear visibility into the health of the infrastructure to ensure high availability and reliability.

Figure 5.1 shows some of the most popular metrics monitoring and alerting services in the marketplace. In this chapter, we design a similar service that can be used internally by a large company.

Figure 5.1: Popular metrics monitoring and alerting services

Step 1 - Understand the Problem and Establish Design Scope

A metrics monitoring and alerting system can mean many different things to different companies, so it is essential to nail down the exact requirements first with the interviewer. For example, you do not want to design a system that focuses on logs such as web server error or access logs if the interviewer has only infrastructure metrics in mind.

Let's first fully understand the problem and establish the scope of the design before diving into the details.

Candidate: Who are we building the system for? Are we building an in-house system for a large corporation like Facebook or Google, or are we designing a SaaS service like Datadog [1], Splunk [2], etc?
Interviewer: That's a great question. We are building it for internal use only.

Candidate: Which metrics do we want to collect?
Interviewer: We want to collect operational system metrics. These can be low-level usage data of the operating system, such as CPU load, memory usage, and disk space consumption. They can also be high-level concepts such as requests per second of a service or the running server count of a web pool. Business metrics are not in the scope of this design.

Candidate: What is the scale of the infrastructure we are monitoring with this system?
Interviewer: 100 million daily active users, 1,000 server pools, and 100 machines per pool.

Candidate: How long should we keep the data?
Interviewer: Let's assume we want 1 year retention.

Candidate: May we reduce the resolution of the metrics data for long-term storage?
Interviewer: That's a great question. We would like to be able to keep newly received data for 7 days. After 7 days, you may roll them up to a 1 minute resolution for 30 days. After 30 days, you may further roll them up at a 1 hour resolution.

Candidate: What are the supported alert channels?
Interviewer: Email, phone, PagerDuty [3], or webhooks (HTTP endpoints).

Candidate: Do we need to collect logs, such as error log or access log?
Interviewer: No.

Candidate: Do we need to support distributed system tracing?
Interviewer: No.

High-level requirements and assumptions

Now you have finished gathering requirements from the interviewer and have a clear scope of the design. The requirements are:

- The infrastructure being monitored is large-scale.
  - 100 million daily active users
  - Assume we have 1,000 server pools, 100 machines per pool, 100 metrics per machine $\Rightarrow \sim$ 10 million metrics
  - 1 year data retention
  - Data retention policy: raw form for 7 days, 1 minute resolution for 30 days, 1 hour resolution for 1 year.

- A variety of metrics can be monitored, for example:
    - CPU usage
    - Request count
    - Memory usage
    - Message count in message queues

Non-functional requirements

- Scalability. The system should be scalable to accommodate growing metrics and alert volume.
- Low latency. The system needs to have low query latency for dashboards and alerts.
- Reliability. The system should be highly reliable to avoid missing critical alerts.
- Flexibility. Technology keeps changing, so the pipeline should be flexible enough to easily integrate new technologies in the future.

Which requirements are out of scope?

- Log monitoring. The Elasticsearch, Logstash, Kibana (ELK) stack is very popular for collecting and monitoring logs [4].
- Distributed system tracing [5] [6]. Distributed tracing refers to a tracing solution that tracks service requests as they flow through distributed systems. It collects data as requests go from one service to another.

Step 2 - Propose High-level Design and Get Buy-in

In this section, we discuss some fundamentals of building the system, the data model, and the high-level design.

Fundamentals

A metrics monitoring and alerting system generally contains five components, as illustrated in Figure 5.2.

- Data collection: collect metric data from different sources.
- Data transmission: transfer data from sources to the metrics monitoring system.
- Data storage: organize and store incoming data.
- Alerting: analyze incoming data, detect anomalies, and generate alerts. The system must be able to send alerts to different communication channels.
- Visualization: present data in graphs, charts, etc. Engineers are better at identifying patterns, trends, or problems when data is presented visually, so we need visualization functionality.

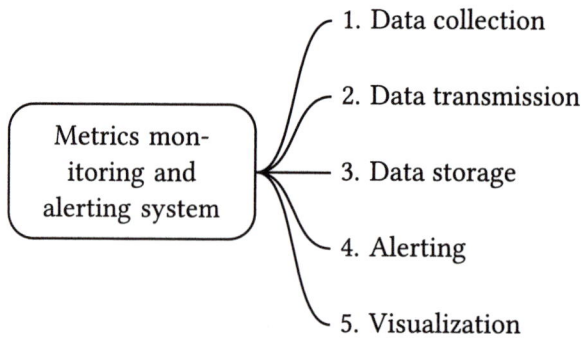

Figure 5.2: Five components of the system

Data model

Metrics data is usually recorded as a time series that contains a set of values with their associated timestamps. The series itself can be uniquely identified by its name, and optionally by a set of labels.

Let's take a look at two examples.

Example 1:

What is the CPU load on production server instance i631 at 20:00?

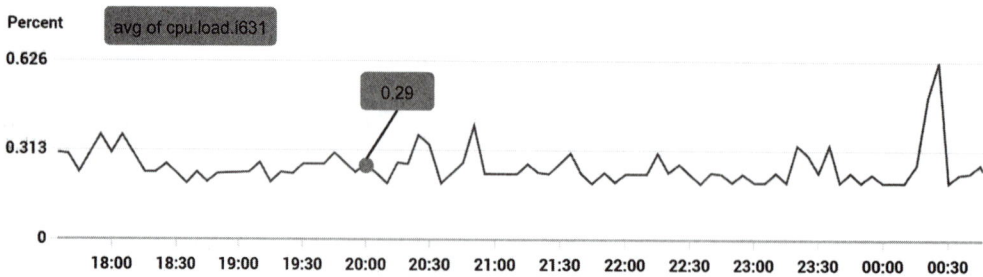

Figure 5.3: Popular metrics monitoring and alerting services

The data point highlighted in Figure 5.3 can be represented by Table 5.1.

metric_name	cpu.load
labels	host:i631,env:prod
timestamp	1613707265
value	0.29

Table 5.1: The data point represented by a table

In this example, the time series is represented by the metric name, the labels (host:i631,env:prod), and a single point value at a specific time.

Example 2:

What is the average CPU load across all web servers in the us-west region for the last 10 minutes? Conceptually, we would pull up something like this from storage where the metric name is CPU.load and the region label is us-west:

```
CPU.load host=webserver01,region=us-west 1613707265 50
CPU.load host=webserver01,region=us-west 1613707265 62
CPU.load host=webserver02,region=us-west 1613707265 43
CPU.load host=webserver02,region=us-west 1613707265 53
...
CPU.load host=webserver01,region=us-west 1613707265 76
CPU.load host=webserver01,region=us-west 1613707265 83
```

The average CPU load could be computed by averaging the values at the end of each line. The format of the lines in the above example is called the line protocol. It is a common input format for many monitoring software in the market. Prometheus [7] and OpenTSDB [8] are two examples.

Every time series consists of the following [9]:

Name	Type
A metric name	String
A set of tags/labels	List of <key:value> pairs
An array of values and their timestamps	An array of <value, timestamp> pairs

Table 5.2: Time series

Data access pattern

In Figure 5.4, each label on the y-axis represents a time series (uniquely identified by the names and labels) while the x-axis represents time.

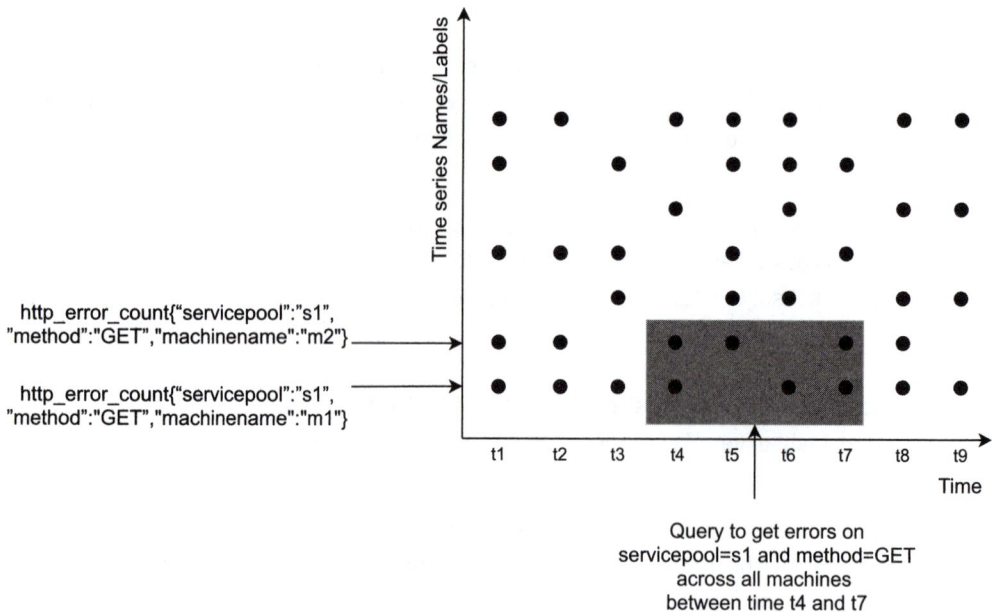

Figure 5.4: Data access pattern

The write load is heavy. As you can see, there can be many time-series data points written at any moment. As we mentioned in the "High-level requirements" section on page 132, about 10 million operational metrics are written per day, and many metrics are collected at high frequency, so the traffic is undoubtedly write-heavy.

At the same time, the read load is spiky. Both visualization and alerting services send queries to the database, and depending on the access patterns of the graphs and alerts, the read volume could be bursty.

In other words, the system is under constant heavy write load, while the read load is spiky.

Data storage system

The data storage system is the heart of the design. It's not recommended to build your own storage system or use a general-purpose storage system (for example, MySQL [10]) for this job.

A general-purpose database, in theory, could support time-series data, but it would require expert-level tuning to make it work at our scale. Specifically, a relational database is not optimized for operations you would commonly perform against time-series data. For example, computing the moving average in a rolling time window requires complicated SQL that is difficult to read (there is an example of this in the deep dive section). Besides, to support tagging/labeling data, we need to add an index for each tag. Moreover, a general-purpose relational database does not perform well under constant heavy write load. At our scale, we would need to expend significant effort in tuning the database, and even then, it might not perform well.

How about NoSQL? In theory, a few NoSQL databases on the market could handle time-series data effectively. For example, Cassandra and Bigtable [11] can both be used for time series data. However, this would require deep knowledge of the internal workings of each NoSQL to devise a scalable schema for effectively storing and querying time-series data. With industrial-scale time-series databases readily available, using a general-purpose NoSQL database is not appealing.

There are many storage systems available that are optimized for time-series data. The optimization lets us use far fewer servers to handle the same volume of data. Many of these databases also have custom query interfaces specially designed for the analysis of time-series data that are much easier to use than SQL. Some even provide features to manage data retention and data aggregation. Here are a few examples of time-series databases.

OpenTSDB is a distributed time-series database, but since it is based on Hadoop and HBase, running a Hadoop/HBase cluster adds complexity. Twitter uses MetricsDB [12], and Amazon offers Timestream as a time-series database [13]. According to DB-engines [14], the two most popular time-series databases are InfluxDB [15] and Prometheus, which are designed to store large volumes of time-series data and quickly perform real-time analysis on that data. Both of them primarily rely on an in-memory cache and on-disk storage. And they both handle durability and performance quite well. As shown in Figure 5.5, an InfluxDB with 8 cores and 32GB RAM can handle over 250,000 writes per second.

vCPU or CPU	RAM	IOPS	Writes per second	Queries* per second	Unique series
2-4 cores	2-4 GB	500	< 5,000	< 5	< 100,000
4-6 cores	8-32 GB	500-1000	< 250,000	< 25	< 1,000,000
8+ cores	32+ GB	1000+	> 250,000	> 25	> 1,000,000

Figure 5.5: InfluxDb benchmarking

Since a time-series database is a specialized database, you are not expected to understand the internals in an interview unless you explicitly mentioned it in your resume. For the purpose of an interview, it's important to understand the metrics data are time-series in nature and we can select time-series databases such as InfluxDB for storage to store them.

Another feature of a strong time-series database is efficient aggregation and analysis of a large amount of time-series data by labels, also known as tags in some databases. For example, InfluxDB builds indexes on labels to facilitate the fast lookup of time-series by labels [15]. It provides clear best-practice guidelines on how to use labels, without overloading the database. The key is to make sure each label is of low cardinality (having a small set of possible values). This feature is critical for visualization, and it would take a lot of effort to build this with a general-purpose database.

High-level design

The high-level design diagram is shown in Figure 5.6.

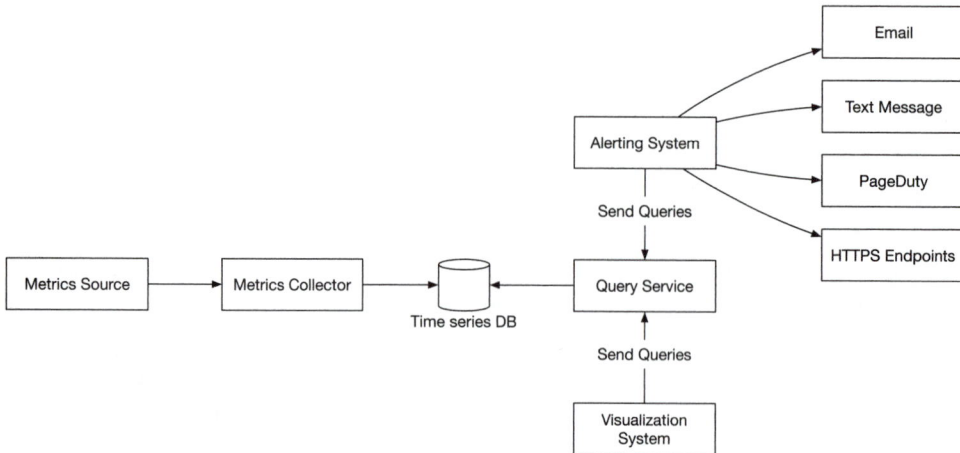

Figure 5.6: High-level design

- **Metrics source.** This can be application servers, SQL databases, message queues, etc.

- **Metrics collector.** It gathers metrics data and writes data into the time-series database.

- **Time-series database.** This stores metrics data as time series. It usually provides a custom query interface for analyzing and summarizing a large amount of time-series data. It maintains indexes on labels to facilitate the fast lookup of time-series data by labels.

- **Query service.** The query service makes it easy to query and retrieve data from the time-series database. This should be a very thin wrapper if we choose a good time-series database. It could also be entirely replaced by the time-series database's own query interface.

- **Alerting system.** This sends alert notifications to various alerting destinations.

- **Visualization system.** This shows metrics in the form of various graphs/charts.

Step 3 - Design Deep Dive

In a system design interview, candidates are expected to dive deep into a few key components or flows. In this section, we investigate the following topics in detail:

- Metrics collection

- Scaling the metrics transmission pipeline
- Query service
- Storage layer
- Alerting system
- Visualization system

Metrics collection

For metrics collection like counters or CPU usage, occasional data loss is not the end of the world. It's acceptable for clients to fire and forget. Now let's take a look at the metrics collection flow. This part of the system is inside the dashed box (Figure 5.7).

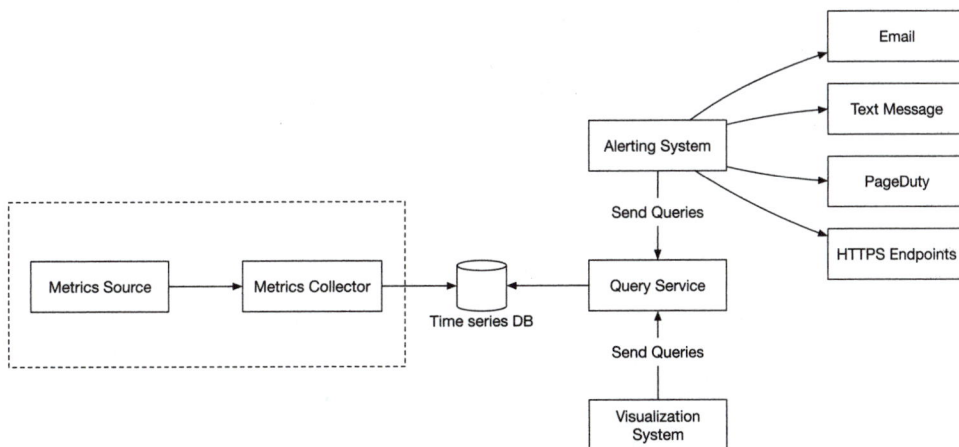

Figure 5.7: Metrics collection flow

Pull vs push models

There are two ways metrics data can be collected, pull or push. It is a routine debate as to which one is better and there is no clear answer. Let's take a close look.

Pull model

Figure 5.8 shows data collection with a pull model over HTTP. We have dedicated metric collectors which pull metrics values from the running applications periodically.

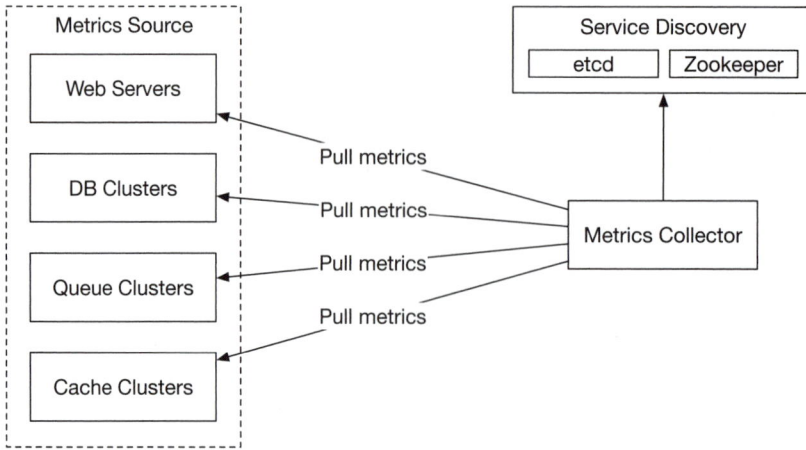

Figure 5.8: Pull model

In this approach, the metrics collector needs to know the complete list of service endpoints to pull data from. One naive approach is to use a file to hold DNS/IP information for every service endpoint on the "metric collector" servers. While the idea is simple, this approach is hard to maintain in a large-scale environment where servers are added or removed frequently, and we want to ensure that metric collectors don't miss out on collecting metrics from any new servers. The good news is that we have a reliable, scalable, and maintainable solution available through Service Discovery, provided by etcd [16], ZooKeeper [17], etc., wherein services register their availability and the metrics collector can be notified by the Service Discovery component whenever the list of service endpoints changes.

Service discovery contains configuration rules about when and where to collect metrics as shown in Figure 5.9.

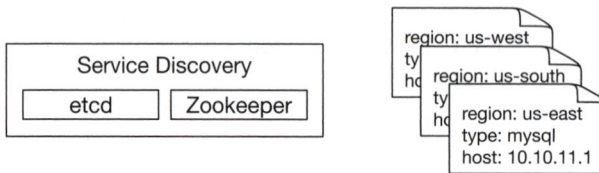

Figure 5.9: Service discovery

Figure 5.10 explains the pull model in detail.

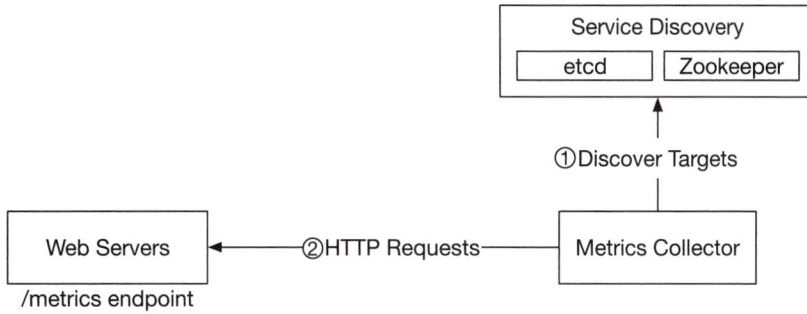

Figure 5.10: Pull model in detail

1. The metrics collector fetches configuration metadata of service endpoints from Service Discovery. Metadata include pulling interval, IP addresses, timeout and retry parameters, etc.

2. The metrics collector pulls metrics data via a pre-defined HTTP endpoint (for example, /metrics). To expose the endpoint, a client library usually needs to be added to the service. In Figure 5.10, the service is Web Servers.

3. Optionally, the metrics collector registers a change event notification with Service Discovery to receive an update whenever the service endpoints change. Alternatively, the metrics collector can poll for endpoint changes periodically.

At our scale, a single metrics collector will not be able to handle thousands of servers. We must use a pool of metrics collectors to handle the demand. One common problem when there are multiple collectors is that multiple instances might try to pull data from the same resource and produce duplicate data. There must exist some coordination scheme among the instances to avoid this.

One potential approach is to designate each collector to a range in a consistent hash ring, and then map every single server being monitored by its unique name in the hash ring. This ensures one metrics source server is handled by one collector only. Let's take a look at an example.

As shown in Figure 5.11, there are four collectors and six metrics source servers. Each collector is responsible for collecting metrics from a distinct set of servers. Collector 2 is responsible for collecting metrics from Server 1 and Server 5.

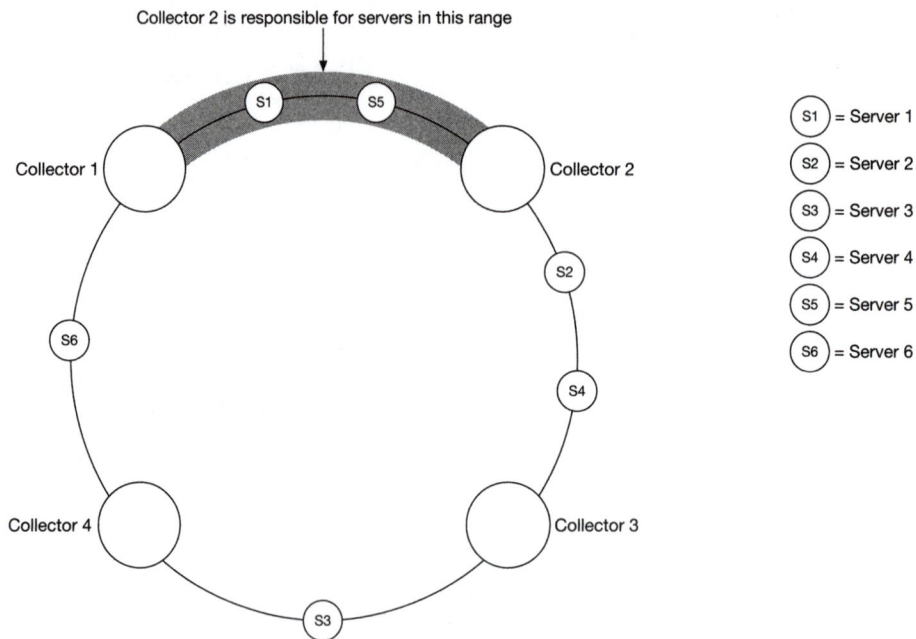

Figure 5.11: Consistent hashing

Push model

As shown in Figure 5.12, in a push model various metrics sources, such as web servers, database servers, etc., directly send metrics to the metrics collector.

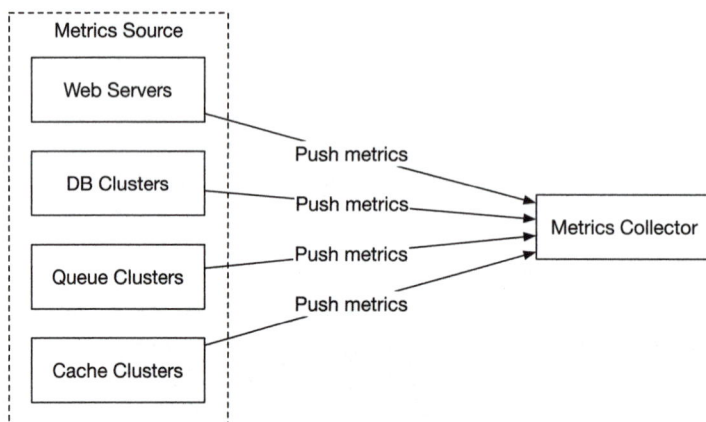

Figure 5.12: Push model

In a push model, a collection agent is commonly installed on every server being monitored. A collection agent is a piece of long-running software that collects metrics from the services running on the server and pushes those metrics periodically to the metrics collector. The collection agent may also aggregate metrics (especially a simple counter) locally, before sending them to metric collectors.

Aggregation is an effective way to reduce the volume of data sent to the metrics collector.

If the push traffic is high and the metrics collector rejects the push with an error, the agent could keep a small buffer of data locally (possibly by storing them locally on disk), and resend them later. However, if the servers are in an auto-scaling group where they are rotated out frequently, then holding data locally (even temporarily) might result in data loss when the metrics collector falls behind.

To prevent the metrics collector from falling behind in a push model, the metrics collector should be in an auto-scaling cluster with a load balancer in front of it (Figure 5.13). The cluster should scale up and down based on the CPU load of the metric collector servers.

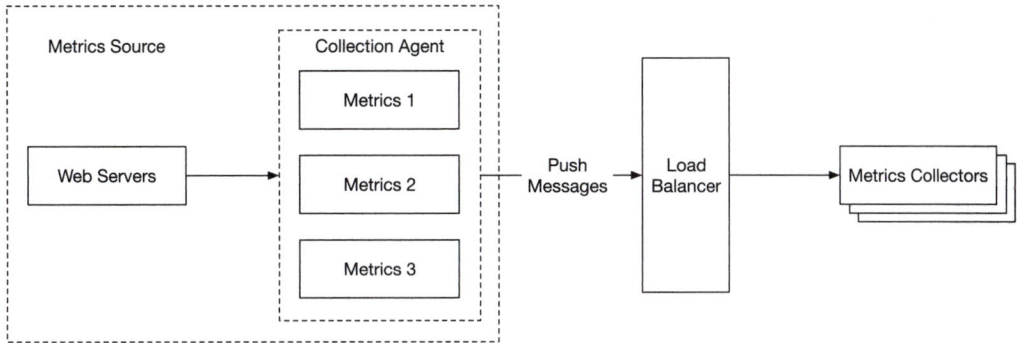

Figure 5.13: Load balancer

Pull or push?

So, which one is the better choice for us? Just like many things in life, there is no clear answer. Both sides have widely adopted real-world use cases.

- Examples of pull architectures include Prometheus.
- Examples of push architectures include Amazon CloudWatch [18] and Graphite [19].

Knowing the advantages and disadvantages of each approach is more important than picking a winner during an interview. Table 5.3 compares the pros and cons of push and pull architectures [20] [21] [22] [23].

	Pull	Push
Easy debugging	The /metrics endpoint on application servers used for pulling metrics can be used to view metrics at any time. You can even do this on your laptop. **Pull wins.**	
Health check	If an application server doesn't respond to the pull, you can quickly figure out if an application server is down. **Pull wins.**	If the metrics collector doesn't receive metrics, the problem might be caused by network issues.
Short-lived jobs		Some of the batch jobs might be short-lived and don't last long enough to be pulled. **Push wins.** This can be fixed by introducing push gateways for the pull model [24].
Firewall or complicated network setups	Having servers pulling metrics requires all metric endpoints to be reachable. This is potentially problematic in multiple data center setups. It might require a more elaborate network infrastructure.	If the metrics collector is set up with a load balancer and an auto-scaling group, it is possible to receive data from anywhere. **Push wins.**

Performance	Pull methods typically use TCP.	Push methods typically use UDP. This means the push method provides lower-latency transports of metrics. The counterargument here is that the effort of establishing a TCP connection is small compared to sending the metrics payload.
Data authenticity	Application servers to collect metrics from are defined in config files in advance. Metrics gathered from those servers are guaranteed to be authentic.	Any kind of client can push metrics to the metrics collector. This can be fixed by whitelisting servers from which to accept metrics, or by requiring authentication.

Table 5.3: Pull vs push

As mentioned above, pull vs push is a routine debate topic and there is no clear answer. A large organization probably needs to support both, especially with the popularity of serverless [25] these days. There might not be a way to install an agent from which to push data in the first place.

Scale the metrics transmission pipeline

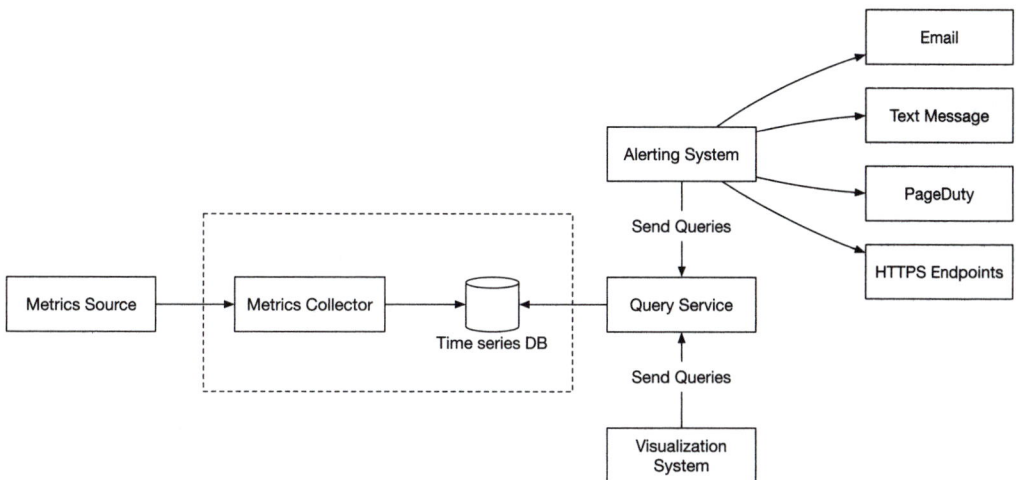

Figure 5.14: Metrics transmission pipeline

Let's zoom in on the metrics collector and time-series databases. Whether you use the push or pull model, the metrics collector is a cluster of servers, and the cluster receives enormous amounts of data. For either push or pull, the metrics collector cluster is set up for auto-scaling, to ensure that there are an adequate number of collector instances to handle the demand.

However, there is a risk of data loss if the time-series database is unavailable. To mitigate this problem, we introduce a queueing component as shown in Figure 5.15.

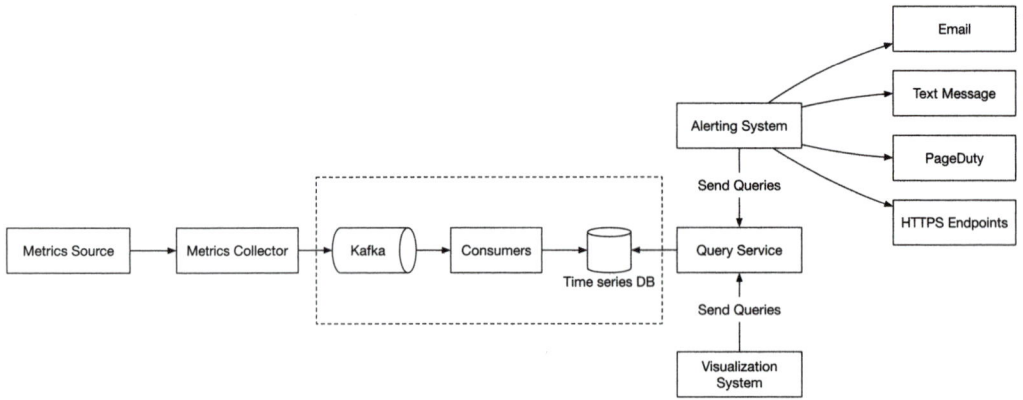

Figure 5.15: Add queues

In this design, the metrics collector sends metrics data to queuing systems like Kafka. Then consumers or streaming processing services such as Apache Storm, Flink, and Spark, process and push data to the time-series database. This approach has several advantages:

- Kafka is used as a highly reliable and scalable distributed messaging platform.
- It decouples the data collection and data processing services from each other.
- It can easily prevent data loss when the database is unavailable, by retaining the data in Kafka.

Scale through Kafka

There are a couple of ways that we can leverage Kafka's built-in partition mechanism to scale our system.

- Configure the number of partitions based on throughput requirements.
- Partition metrics data by metric names, so consumers can aggregate data by metrics names.
- Further partition metrics data with tags/labels.
- Categorize and prioritize metrics so that important metrics can be processed first.

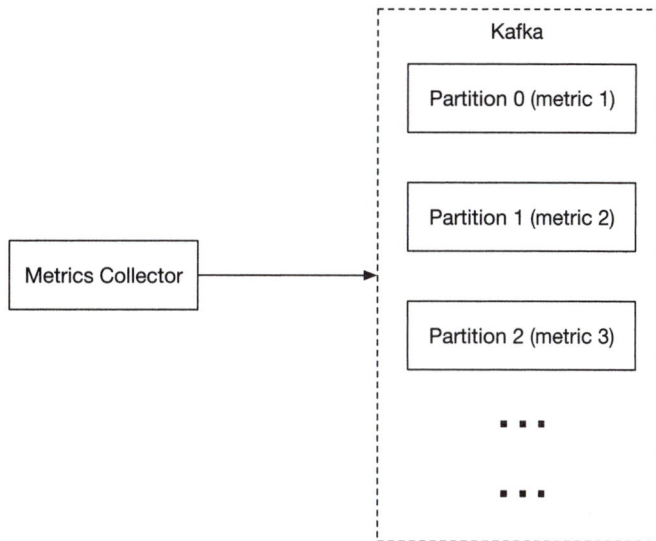

Figure 5.16: Kafka partition

Alternative to Kafka

Maintaining a production-scale Kafka system is no small undertaking. You might get pushback from the interviewer about this. There are large-scale monitoring ingestion systems in use without using an intermediate queue. Facebook's Gorilla [26] in-memory time-series database is a prime example; it is designed to remain highly available for writes, even when there is a partial network failure. It could be argued that such a design is as reliable as having an intermediate queue like Kafka.

Where aggregations can happen

Metrics can be aggregated in different places; in the collection agent (on the client-side), the ingestion pipeline (before writing to storage), and the query side (after writing to storage). Let's take a closer look at each of them.

Collection agent. The collection agent installed on the client-side only supports simple aggregation logic. For example, aggregate a counter every minute before it is sent to the metrics collector.

Ingestion pipeline. To aggregate data before writing to the storage, we usually need stream processing engines such as Flink. The write volume will be significantly reduced since only the calculated result is written to the database. However, handling late-arriving events could be a challenge and another downside is that we lose data precision and some flexibility because we no longer store the raw data.

Query side. Raw data can be aggregated over a given time period at query time. There is no data loss with this approach, but the query speed might be slower because the query result is computed at query time and is run against the whole dataset.

Query service

The query service comprises a cluster of query servers, which access the time-series databases and handle requests from the visualization or alerting systems. Having a dedicated set of query servers decouples time-series databases from the clients (visualization and alerting systems). And this gives us the flexibility to change the time-series database or the visualization and alerting systems, whenever needed.

Cache layer

To reduce the load of the time-series database and make query service more performant, cache servers are added to store query results, as shown in Figure 5.17.

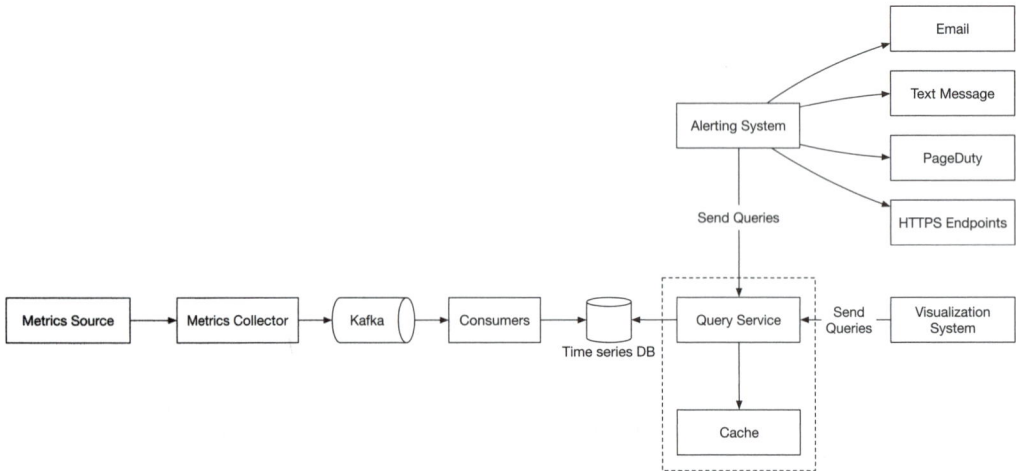

Figure 5.17: Cache layer

The case against query service

There might not be a pressing need to introduce our own abstraction (a query service) because most industrial-scale visual and alerting systems have powerful plugins to interface with well-known time-series databases on the market. And with a well-chosen time-series database, there is no need to add our own caching, either.

Time-series database query language

Most popular metrics monitoring systems like Prometheus and InfluxDB don't use SQL and have their own query languages. One major reason for this is that it is hard to build SQL queries to query time-series data. For example, as mentioned here [27], computing an exponential moving average might look like this in SQL:

```
select id,
       temp,
       avg(temp) over (partition by group_nr order by
time_read)
       as rolling_avg
from (
    select id,
           temp,
           time_read,
           interval_group,
           id - row_number() over (partition by interval_group
order
           by time_read) as group_nr
    from (
        select id,
           time_read,
           "epoch"::timestamp + "900 seconds"::interval * (
extract(epoch from time_read)::int4 / 900) as interval_group,
           temp
           from readings
    ) t1
) t2
order by time_read;
```

While in Flux, a language that's optimized for time-series analysis (used in InfluxDB), it looks like this. As you can see, it's much easier to understand.

```
from(db:"telegraf")
    |> range(start:-1h)
    |> filter(fn: (r) => r._measurement == "foo")
    |> exponentialMovingAverage(size:-10s)
```

Storage layer

Now let's dive into the storage layer.

Choose a time-series database carefully

According to a research paper published by Facebook [26], at least 85% of all queries to the operational data store were for data collected in the past 26 hours. If we use a time-series database that harnesses this property, it could have a significant impact on overall system performance. If you are interested in the design of the storage engine, please refer to the design document of the InfluxDB storage engine [28].

Space optimization

As explained in high-level requirements, the amount of metric data to store is enormous. Here are a few strategies for tackling this.

Data encoding and compression

Data encoding and compression can significantly reduce the size of data. Those features are usually built into a good time-series database. Here is a simple example.

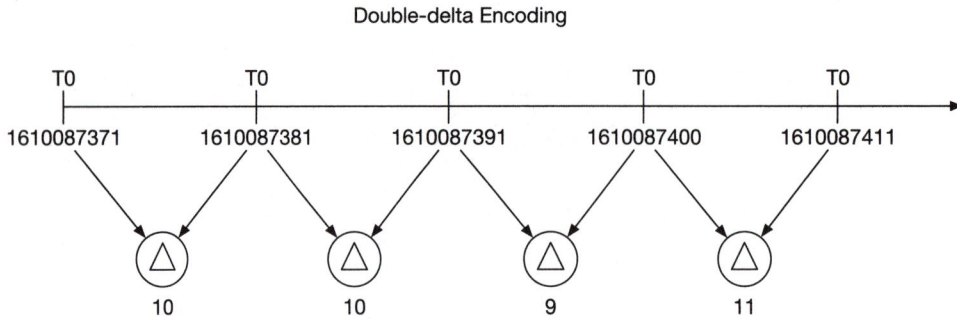

Figure 5.18: Data encoding

As you can see in the image above, 1610087371 and 1610087381 differ by only 10 seconds, which takes only 4 bits to represent, instead of the full timestamp of 32 bits. So, rather than storing absolute values, the delta of the values can be stored along with one base value like: 1610087371, 10, 10, 9, 11.

Downsampling

Downsampling is the process of converting high-resolution data to low-resolution to reduce overall disk usage. Since our data retention is 1 year, we can downsample old data. For example, we can let engineers and data scientists define rules for different metrics. Here is an example:

- Retention: 7 days, no sampling
- Retention: 30 days, downsample to 1 minute resolution
- Retention: 1 year, downsample to 1 hour resolution

Let's take a look at another concrete example. It aggregates 10-second resolution data to 30-second resolution data.

metric	timestamp	hostname	metric_value
cpu	2021-10-24T19:00:00Z	host-a	10
cpu	2021-10-24T19:00:10Z	host-a	16
cpu	2021-10-24T19:00:20Z	host-a	20
cpu	2021-10-24T19:00:30Z	host-a	30
cpu	2021-10-24T19:00:40Z	host-a	20
cpu	2021-10-24T19:00:50Z	host-a	30

Table 5.4: 10-second resolution data

Rollup from 10 second resolution data to 30 second resolution data.

metric	timestamp	hostname	Metric_value (avg)
cpu	2021-10-24T19:00:00Z	host-a	19
cpu	2021-10-24T19:00:30Z	host-a	25

Table 5.5: 30-second resolution data

Cold storage

Cold storage is the storage of inactive data that is rarely used. The financial cost for cold storage is much lower.

In a nutshell, we should probably use third-party visualization and alerting systems, instead of building our own.

Alerting system

For the purpose of the interview, let's look at the alerting system, shown in Figure 5.19 below.

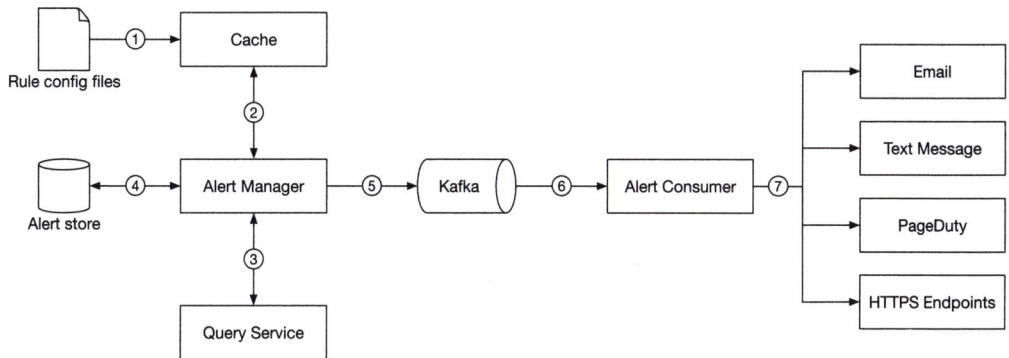

Figure 5.19: Alerting system

The alert flow works as follows:

1. Load config files to cache servers. Rules are defined as config files on the disk. YAML [29] is a commonly used format to define rules. Here is an example of alert rules:

```
- name: instance_down
rules:

# Alert for any instance that is unreachable for >5
minutes.
- alert: instance_down
    expr: up == 0
    for: 5m
    labels:
    severity: page
```

2. The alert manager fetches alert configs from the cache.

3. Based on config rules, the alert manager calls the query service at a predefined interval. If the value violates the threshold, an alert event is created. The alert manager is responsible for the following:

   - Filter, merge, and dedupe alerts. Here is an example of merging alerts that are triggered within one instance within a short amount of time (instance 1) (Figure 5.20).

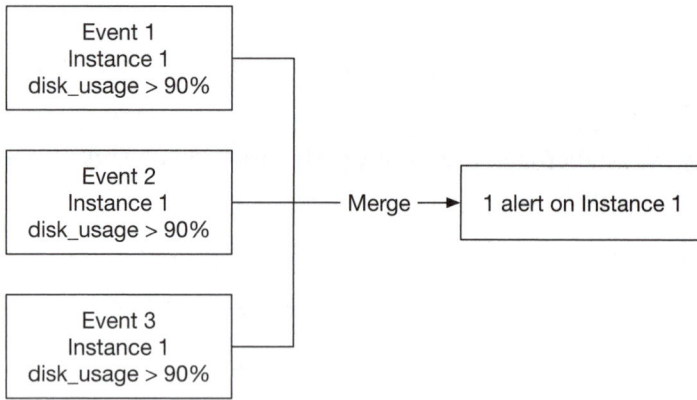

Figure 5.20: Merge alerts

- Access control. To avoid human error and keep the system secure, it is essential to restrict access to certain alert management operations to authorized individuals only.

- Retry. The alert manager checks alert states and ensures a notification is sent at least once.

4. The alert store is a key-value database, such as Cassandra, that keeps the state (inactive, pending, firing, resolved) of all alerts. It ensures a notification is sent at least once.

5. Eligible alerts are inserted into Kafka.

6. Alert consumers pull alert events from Kafka.

7. Alert consumers process alert events from Kafka and send notifications over to different channels such as email, text message, PagerDuty, or HTTP endpoints.

Alerting system - build vs buy

There are many industrial-scale alerting systems available off-the-shelf, and most provide tight integration with the popular time-series databases. Many of these alerting systems integrate well with existing notification channels, such as email and PagerDuty. In the real world, it is a tough call to justify building your own alerting system. In interview settings, especially for a senior position, be ready to justify your decision.

Visualization system

Visualization is built on top of the data layer. Metrics can be shown on the metrics dashboard over various time scales and alerts can be shown on the alerts dashboard. Figure 5.21 shows a dashboard that displays some of the metrics like the current server requests, memory/CPU utilization, page load time, traffic, and login information [30].

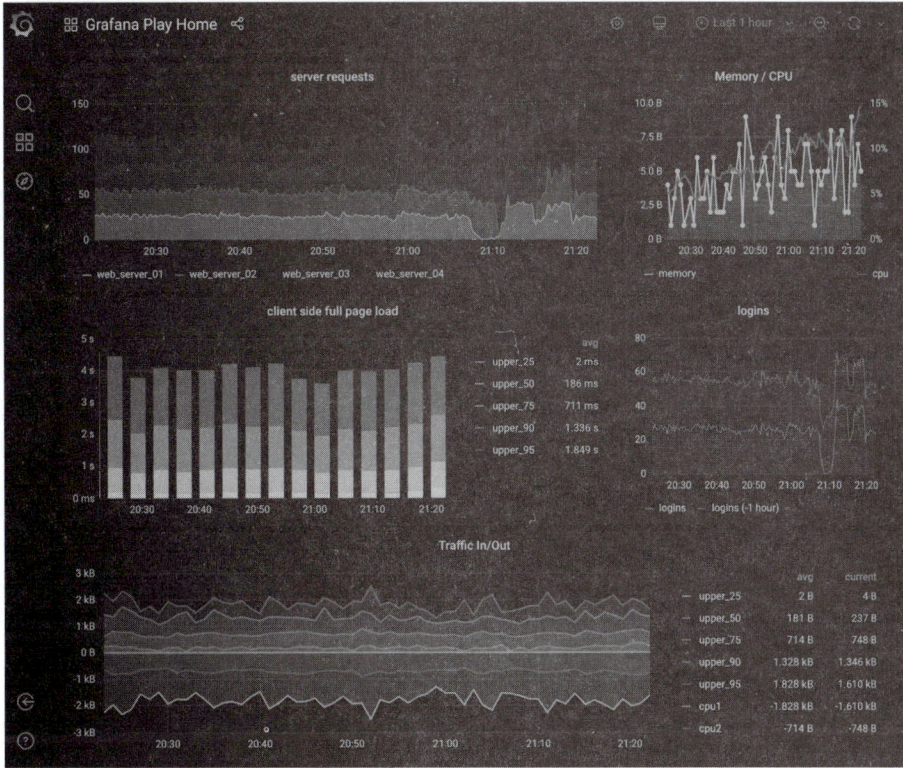

Figure 5.21: Grafana UI

A high-quality visualization system is hard to build. The argument for using an off-the-shelf system is very strong. For example, Grafana can be a very good system for this purpose. It integrates well with many popular time-series databases which you can buy.

Step 4 - Wrap Up

In this chapter, we presented the design for a metrics monitoring and alerting system. At a high level, we talked about data collection, time-series database, alerts, and visualization. Then we went in-depth into some of the most important techniques/components:

- Pull vs pull model for collecting metrics data.
- Utilize Kafka to scale the system.
- Choose the right time-series database.
- Use downsampling to reduce data size.
- Build vs buy options for alerting and visualization systems.

We went through a few iterations to refine the design, and our final design looks like this:

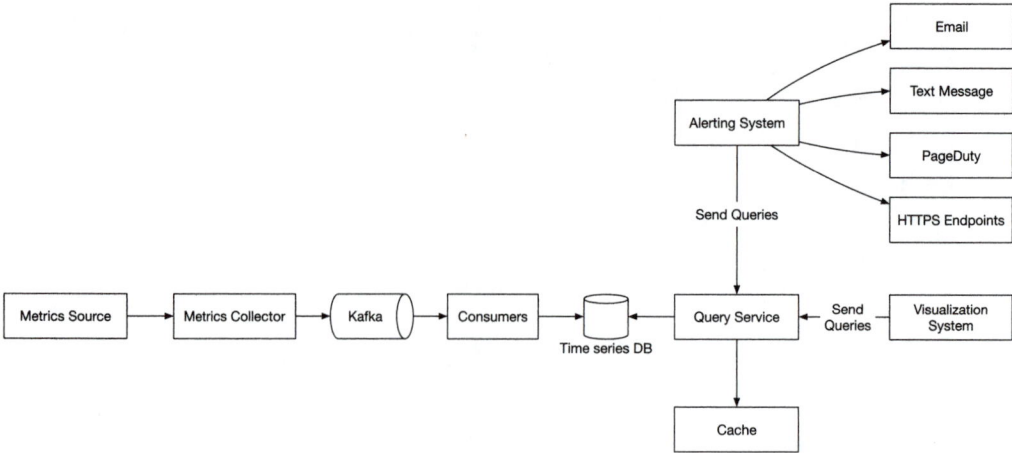

Figure 5.22: Final design

Congratulations on getting this far! Now give yourself a pat on the back. Good job!

Chapter Summary

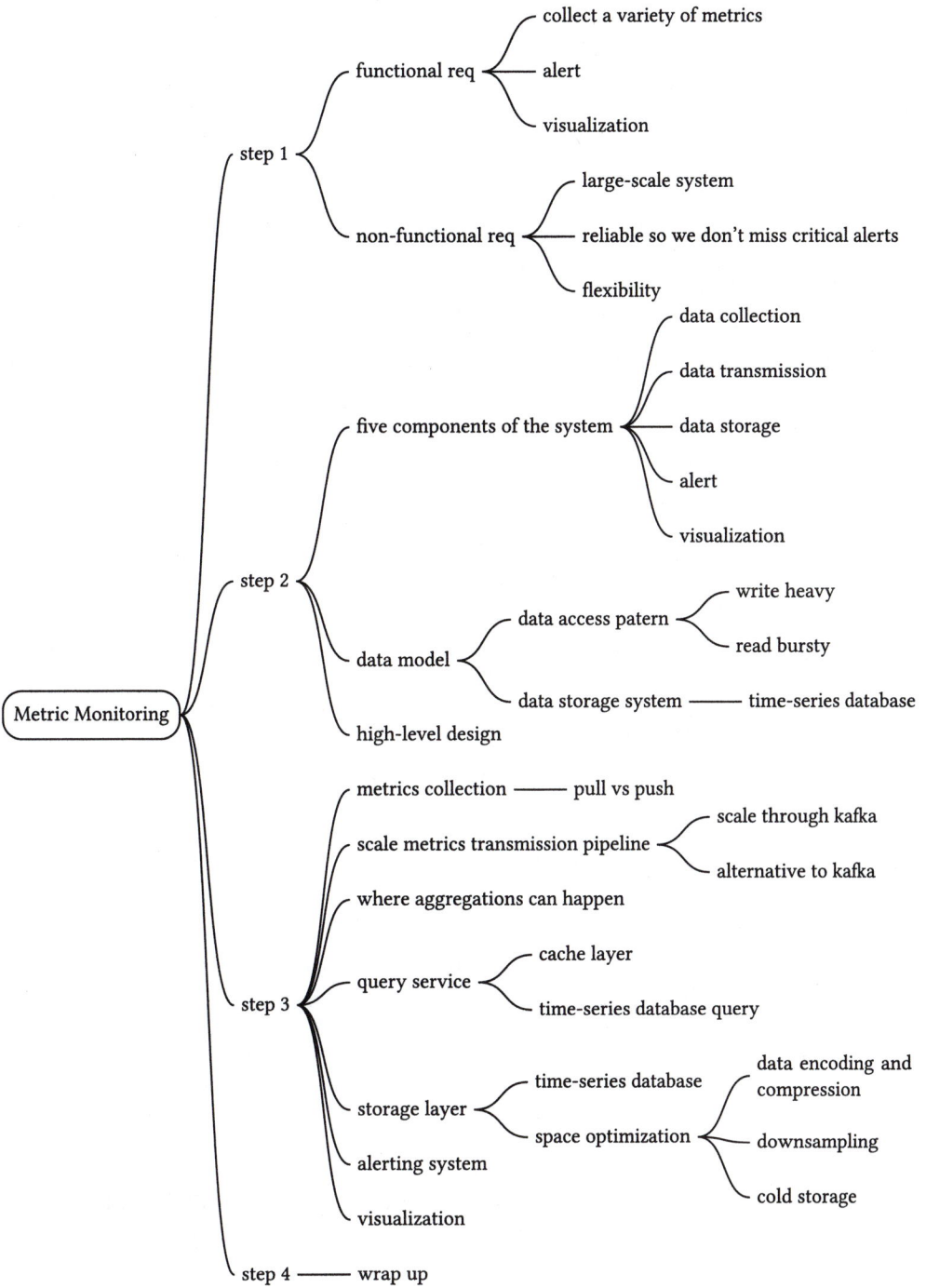

- Metric Monitoring
  - step 1
    - functional req
      - collect a variety of metrics
      - alert
      - visualization
    - non-functional req
      - large-scale system
      - reliable so we don't miss critical alerts
      - flexibility
  - step 2
    - five components of the system
      - data collection
      - data transmission
      - data storage
      - alert
      - visualization
    - data model
      - data access patern
        - write heavy
        - read bursty
      - data storage system —— time-series database
    - high-level design
  - step 3
    - metrics collection —— pull vs push
    - scale metrics transmission pipeline
      - scale through kafka
      - alternative to kafka
    - where aggregations can happen
    - query service
      - cache layer
      - time-series database query
    - storage layer
      - time-series database
      - space optimization
        - data encoding and compression
        - downsampling
        - cold storage
    - alerting system
    - visualization
  - step 4 —— wrap up

Reference Material

[1] Datadog. https://www.datadoghq.com/.

[2] Splunk. https://www.splunk.com/.

[3] PagerDuty. https://www.pagerduty.com/.

[4] Elastic stack. https://www.elastic.co/elastic-stack.

[5] Dapper, a Large-Scale Distributed Systems Tracing Infrastructure. https://research
.google/pubs/pub36356/.

[6] Distributed Systems Tracing with Zipkin. https://blog.twitter.com/engineering/e
n_us/a/2012/distributed-systems-tracing-with-zipkin.html.

[7] Prometheus. https://prometheus.io/docs/introduction/overview/.

[8] OpenTSDB - A Distributed, Scalable Monitoring System. http://opentsdb.net/.

[9] Data model. :https://prometheus.io/docs/concepts/data_model/.

[10] MySQL. https://www.mysql.com/.

[11] Schema design for time-series data | Cloud Bigtable Documentation. https://cloud.
google.com/bigtable/docs/schema-design-time-series.

[12] MetricsDB. TimeSeriesDatabaseforstoringmetricsatTwitter:https://blog.twitter.c
om/engineering/en_us/topics/infrastructure/2019/metricsdb.html.

[13] Amazon Timestream. https://aws.amazon.com/timestream/.

[14] DB-Engines Ranking of time-series DBMS. https://db-engines.com/en/ranking/ti
me+series+dbms.

[15] InfluxDB. https://www.influxdata.com/.

[16] etcd. https://etcd.io/.

[17] Service Discovery with ZooKeeper. https://cloud.spring.io/spring-cloud-zookeep
er/1.2.x/multi/multi_spring-cloud-zookeeper-discovery.html.

[18] Amazon CloudWatch. https://aws.amazon.com/cloudwatch/.

[19] Graphite. https://graphiteapp.org/.

[20] Push vs Pull. http://bit.ly/3aJEPxE.

[21] Pull doesn't scale - or does it? https://prometheus.io/blog/2016/07/23/pull-does-n
ot-scale-or-does-it/.

[22] Monitoring Architecture. https://developer.lightbend.com/guides/monitoring-at-s
cale/monitoring-architecture/architecture.html.

[23] Push vs Pull in Monitoring Systems. https://giedrius.blog/2019/05/11/push-vs-pul l-in-monitoring-systems/.

[24] Pushgateway. https://github.com/prometheus/pushgateway.

[25] Building Applications with Serverless Architectures. https://aws.amazon.com/lam bda/serverless-architectures-learn-more/.

[26] Gorilla. AFast,Scalable,In-MemoryTimeSeriesDatabase:http://www.vldb.org/pvl db/vol8/p1816-teller.pdf.

[27] Why We're Building Flux, a New Data Scripting and Query Language. https://ww w.influxdata.com/blog/why-were-building-flux-a-new-data-scripting-and-query -language/.

[28] InfluxDB storage engine. https://docs.influxdata.com/influxdb/v2.0/reference/inte rnals/storage-engine/.

[29] YAML. https://en.wikipedia.org/wiki/YAML.

[30] Grafana Demo. https://play.grafana.org/.

6   Ad Click Event Aggregation

With the rise of Facebook, YouTube, TikTok, and the online media economy, digital advertising is taking an ever-bigger share of the total advertising spending. As a result, tracking ad click events is very important. In this chapter, we explore how to design an ad click event aggregation system at Facebook or Google scale.

Before we dive into technical design, let's learn about the core concepts of online advertising to better understand this topic. One core benefit of online advertising is its measurability, as quantified by real-time data.

Digital advertising has a core process called Real-Time Bidding (RTB), in which digital advertising inventory is bought and sold. Figure 6.1 shows how the online advertising process works.

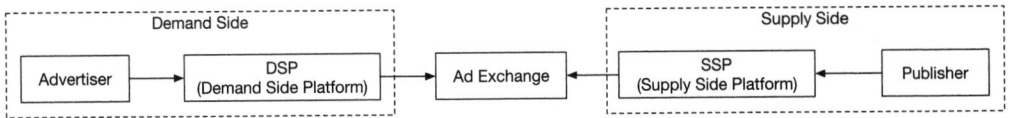

Figure 6.1: RTB process

The speed of the RTB process is important as it usually occurs in less than a second.

Data accuracy is also very important. Ad click event aggregation plays a critical role in measuring the effectiveness of online advertising, which essentially impacts how much money advertisers pay. Based on the click aggregation results, campaign managers can control the budget or adjust bidding strategies, such as changing targeted audience groups, keywords, etc. The key metrics used in online advertising, including click-through rate (CTR) [1] and conversion rate (CVR) [2], depend on aggregated ad click data.

Step 1 - Understand the Problem and Establish Design Scope

The following set of questions helps to clarify requirements and narrow down the scope.

Candidate: What is the format of the input data?
Interviewer: It's a log file located in different servers and the latest click events are appended to the end of the log file. The event has the following attributes: `ad_id`, `click_timestamp`, `user_id`, `ip`, and `country`.

Candidate: What's the data volume?
Interviewer: 1 billion ad clicks per day and 2 million ads in total. The number of ad click events grows 30% year-over-year.

Candidate: What are some of the most important queries to support?
Interviewer: The system needs to support the following 3 queries:

- Return the number of click events for a particular ad in the last M minutes.
- Return the top 100 most clicked ads in the past 1 minute. Both parameters should be configurable. Aggregation occurs every minute.
- Support data filtering by `ip`, `user_id`, or `country` for the above two queries.

Candidate: Do we need to worry about edge cases? I can think of the following:

- There might be events that arrive later than expected.
- There might be duplicated events.
- Different parts of the system might be down at any time, so we need to consider system recovery.

Interviewer: That's a good list. Yes, take these into consideration.

Candidate: What is the latency requirement?
Interviewer: A few minutes of end-to-end latency. Note that latency requirements for RTB and ad click aggregation are very different. While latency for RTB is usually less than one second due to the responsiveness requirement, a few minutes of latency is acceptable for ad click event aggregation because it is primarily used for ad billing and reporting.

With the information gathered above, we have both functional and non-functional requirements.

Functional requirements

- Aggregate the number of clicks of `ad_id` in the last M minutes.
- Return the top 100 most clicked `ad_id` every minute.
- Support aggregation filtering by different attributes.

- Dataset volume is at Facebook or Google scale (see the back-of-envelope estimation section below for detailed system scale requirements).

Non-functional requirements

- Correctness of the aggregation result is important as the data is used for RTB and ads billing.
- Properly handle delayed or duplicate events.
- Robustness. The system should be resilient to partial failures.
- Latency requirement. End-to-end latency should be a few minutes, at most.

Back-of-the-envelope estimation

Let's do an estimation to understand the scale of the system and the potential challenges we will need to address.

- 1 billion DAU (Daily Active Users).
- Assume on average each user clicks 1 ad per day. That's 1 billion ad click events per day.
- Ad click QPS $= \dfrac{10^9 \text{ events}}{10^5 \text{ seconds in a day}} = 10{,}000$
- Assume peak ad click QPS is 5 times the average number. Peak QPS $= 50{,}000$ QPS.
- Assume a single ad click event occupies 0.1KB storage. Daily storage requirement is: 0.1KB $\times$ 1 billion = 100GB. The monthly storage requirement is about 3TB.

Step 2 - Propose High-level Design and Get Buy-in

In this section, we discuss query API design, data model, and high-level design.

Query API design

The purpose of the API design is to have an agreement between the client and the server. In a consumer app, a client is usually the end-user who uses the product. In our case, however, a client is the dashboard user (data scientist, product manager, advertiser, etc.) who runs queries against the aggregation service.

Let's review the functional requirements so we can better design the APIs:

- Aggregate the number of clicks of ad_id in the last M minutes.
- Return the top N most clicked ad_ids in the last M minute.
- Support aggregation filtering by different attributes.

We only need two APIs to support those three use cases because filtering (the last requirement) can be supported by adding query parameters to the requests.

API 1: Aggregate the number of clicks of ad_id in the last M minutes.

API	Detail
GET /v1/ads/{:ad_id}/aggregated_count	Return aggregated event count for a given ad_id

Table 6.1: API for aggregating the number of clicks

Request parameters are:

Field	Description	Type
from	Start minute (default is now minus 1 minute)	long
to	End minute (default is now)	long
filter	An identifier for different filtering strategies. For example, filter = 001 filters out non-US clicks	long

Table 6.2: Request parameters for /v1/ads/{:ad_id}/aggregated_count

Response:

Field	Description	Type
ad_id	The identifier of the ad	string
count	The aggregated count between the start and end minutes	long

Table 6.3: Response for /v1/ads/{:ad_id}/aggregated_count

API 2: Return top N most clicked ad_ids in the last M minutes

API	Detail
GET /v1/ads/popular_ads	Return top N most clicked ads in the last M minutes

Table 6.4: API for /v1/ads/popular_ads

Request parameters are:

Field	Description	Type
count	Top N most clicked ads	integer
window	The aggregation window size (M) in minutes	integer
filter	An identifier for different filtering strategies	long

Table 6.5: Request parameters for /v1/ads/popular_ads

Response:

Field	Description	Type
ad_ids	A list of the most clicked ads	array

Table 6.6: Response for /v1/ads/popular_ads

Data model

There are two types of data in the system: raw data and aggregated data.

Raw data

Below shows what the raw data looks like in log files:

```
[AdClickEvent] ad001, 2021-01-01 00:00:01, user 1, 207.148.22.22, USA
```

Table 6.7 lists what the data fields look like in a structured way. Data is scattered on different application servers.

ad_id	click_timestamp	user_id	ip	country
ad001	2021-01-01 00:00:01	user1	207.148.22.22	USA
ad001	2021-01-01 00:00:02	user1	207.148.22.22	USA
ad002	2021-01-01 00:00:02	user2	209.153.56.11	USA

Table 6.7: Raw data

Aggregated data

Assume that ad click events are aggregated every minute. Table 6.8 shows the aggregated result.

ad_id	click_minute	count
ad001	202101010000	5
ad001	202101010001	7

Table 6.8: Aggregated data

To support ad filtering, we add an additional field called filter_id to the table. Records with the same ad_id and click_minute are grouped by filter_id as shown in Table 6.9, and filters are defined in Table 6.10.

ad_id	click_minute	filter_id	count
ad001	202101010000	0012	2
ad001	202101010000	0023	3
ad001	202101010001	0012	1
ad001	202101010001	0023	6

Table 6.9: Aggregated data with filters

filter_id	region	ip	user_id
0012	US	0012	*
0013	*	0023	123.1.2.3

Table 6.10: Filter table

To support the query to return the top N most clicked ads in the last M minutes, the following structure is used.

Most_clicked_ads		
window_size	integer	The aggregation window size (M) in minutes
update_time_minute	timestamp	Last updated timestamp (in 1-minute granularity)
most_clicked_ads	array	List of ad IDs in JSON format

Table 6.11: Support top N most clicked ads in the last M minutes

Comparison

The comparison between storing raw data and aggregated data is shown below:

	Raw data only	Aggregated data only
Pros	• Full data set • Support data filter and recalculation	• Smaller data set • Fast query
Cons	• Huge data storage • Slow query	• Data loss. This is derived data. For example, 10 entries might be aggregated to 1 entry

Table 6.12: Raw data vs aggregated data

Should we store raw data or aggregated data? Our recommendation is to store both. Let's take a look at why.

- It's a good idea to keep the raw data. If something goes wrong, we could use the raw data for debugging. If the aggregated data is corrupted due to a bad bug, we can recalculate the aggregated data from the raw data, after the bug is fixed.

- Aggregated data should be stored as well. The data size of the raw data is huge. The large size makes querying raw data directly very inefficient. To mitigate this problem, we run read queries on aggregated data.

- Raw data serves as backup data. We usually don't need to query raw data unless recalculation is needed. Old raw data could be moved to cold storage to reduce costs.

- Aggregated data serves as active data. It is tuned for query performance.

Choose the right database

When it comes to choosing the right database, we need to evaluate the following:

- What does the data look like? Is the data relational? Is it a document or a blob?

- Is the workflow read-heavy, write-heavy, or both?

- Is transaction support needed?

- Do the queries rely on many online analytical processing (OLAP) functions [3] like SUM, COUNT?

Let's examine the raw data first. Even though we don't need to query the raw data during normal operations, it is useful for data scientists or machine learning engineers to study user response prediction, behavioral targeting, relevance feedback, etc. [4].

As shown in the back of the envelope estimation, the average write QPS is 10,000, and the peak QPS can be 50,000, so the system is write-heavy. On the read side, raw data is used as backup and a source for recalculation, so in theory, the read volume is low.

Relational databases can do the job, but scaling the write can be challenging. NoSQL databases like Cassandra and InfluxDB are more suitable because they are optimized for write and time-range queries.

Another option is to store the data in Amazon S3 using one of the columnar data formats like ORC [5], Parquet [6], or AVRO [7]. We could put a cap on the size of each file (say, 10GB) and the stream processor responsible for writing the raw data could handle the file rotation when the size cap is reached. Since this setup may be unfamiliar for many, in this design we use Cassandra as an example.

For aggregated data, it is time-series in nature and the workflow is both read and write heavy. This is because, for each ad, we need to query the database every minute to display the latest aggregation count for customers. This feature is useful for auto-refreshing the dashboard or triggering alerts in a timely manner. Since there are two million ads in total, the workflow is read-heavy. Data is aggregated and written every minute by the aggregation service, so it's write-heavy as well. We could use the same type of database to store both raw data and aggregated data.

Now we have discussed query API design and data model, let's put together the high-level design.

High-level design

In real-time big data [8] processing, data usually flows into and out of the processing system as unbounded data streams. The aggregation service works in the same way; the input is the raw data (unbounded data streams), and the output is the aggregated results (see Figure 6.2).

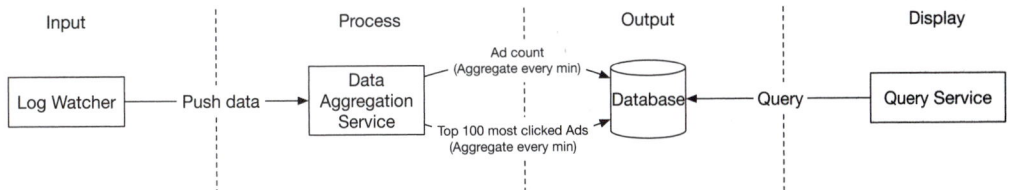

Figure 6.2: Aggregation workflow

Asynchronous processing

The design we currently have is synchronous. This is not good because the capacity of producers and consumers is not always equal. Consider the following case; if there is a sudden increase in traffic and the number of events produced is far beyond what consumers can handle, consumers might get out-of-memory errors or experience an unexpected shutdown. If one component in the synchronous link is down, the whole system stops working.

A common solution is to adopt a message queue (Kafka) to decouple producers and consumers. This makes the whole process asynchronous and producers/consumers can be scaled independently.

Putting everything we have discussed together, we come up with the high-level design as shown in Figure 6.3. Log watcher, aggregation service, and database are decoupled by two message queues. The database writer polls data from the message queue, transforms the data into the database format, and writes it to the database.

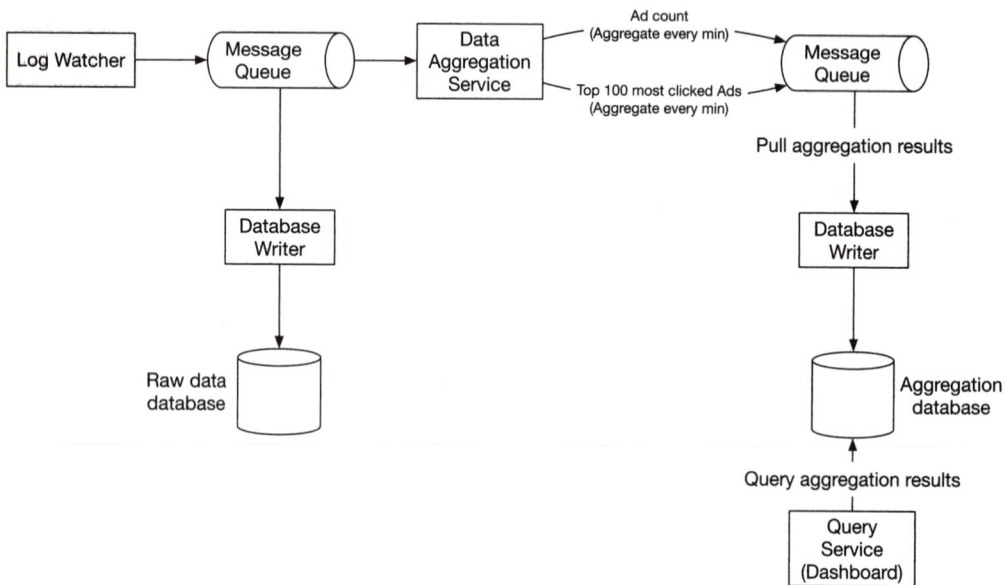

Figure 6.3: High-level design

What is stored in the first message queue? It contains ad click event data as shown in Table 6.13.

ad_id	click_timestamp	user_id	ip	country

Table 6.13: Data in the first message queue

What is stored in the second message queue? The second message queue contains two types of data:

1. Ad click counts aggregated at per-minute granularity.

ad_id	click_minute	count

Table 6.14: Data in the second message queue

2. Top N most clicked ads aggregated at per-minute granularity.

update_time_minute	most_clicked_ads

Table 6.15: Data in the second message queue

You might be wondering why we don't write the aggregated results to the database directly. The short answer is that we need the second message queue like Kafka to achieve end-to-end exactly once semantics (atomic commit) [9].

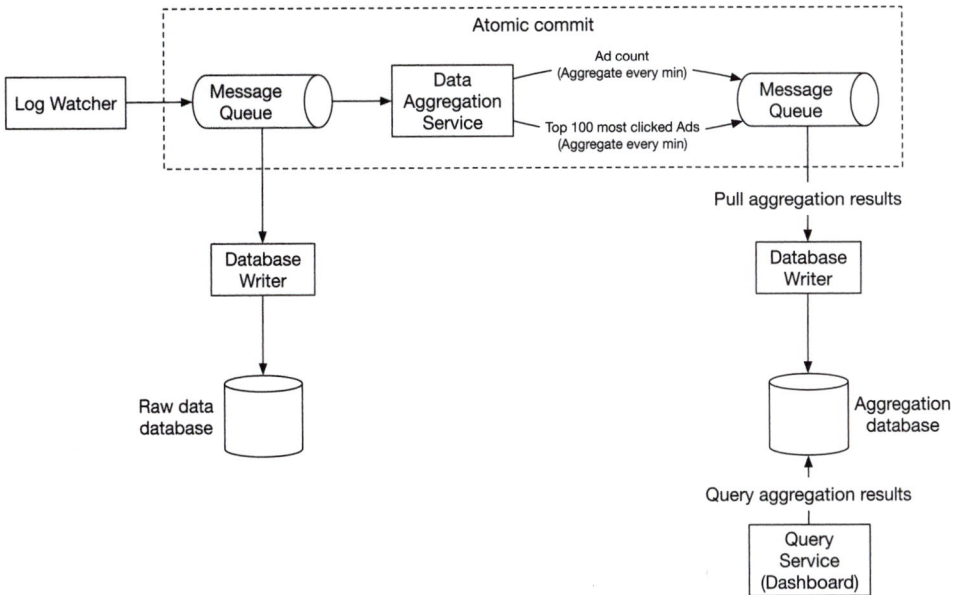

Figure 6.4: End-to-end exactly once

Next, let's dig into the details of the aggregation service.

Aggregation service

The MapReduce framework is a good option to aggregate ad click events. The directed acyclic graph (DAG) is a good model for it [10]. The key to the DAG model is to break down the system into small computing units, like the Map/Aggregate/Reduce nodes, as shown in Figure 6.5.

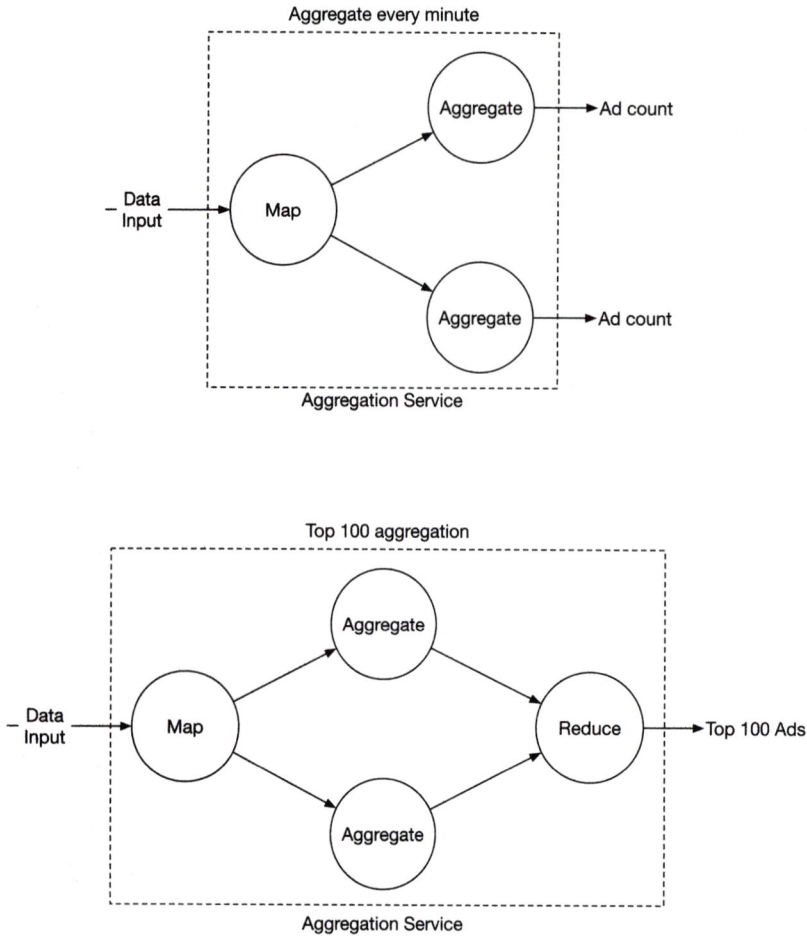

Figure 6.5: Aggregation service

Each node is responsible for one single task and it sends the processing result to its downstream nodes.

Map node

A Map node reads data from a data source, and then filters and transforms the data. For example, a Map node sends ads with ad_id %2 = 0 to node 1, and the other ads go to node 2, as shown in Figure 6.6.

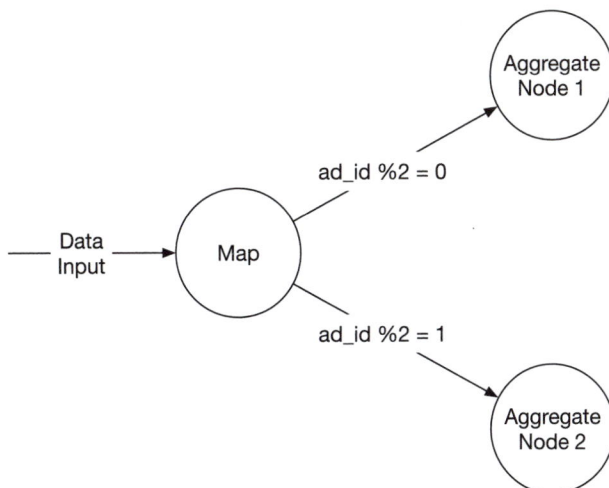

Figure 6.6: Map operation

You might be wondering why we need the Map node. An alternative option is to set up Kafka partitions or tags and let the aggregate nodes subscribe to Kafka directly. This works, but the input data may need to be cleaned or normalized, and these operations can be done by the Map node. Another reason is that we may not have control over how data is produced and therefore events with the same ad_id might land in different Kafka partitions.

Aggregate node

An Aggregate node counts ad click events by ad_id in memory every minute. In the MapReduce paradigm, the Aggregate node is part of the Reduce. So the map-aggregate-reduce process really means map-reduce-reduce.

Reduce node

A Reduce node reduces aggregated results from all "Aggregate" nodes to the final result. For example, as shown in Figure 6.7, there are three aggregation nodes and each contains the top 3 most clicked ads within the node. The Reduce node reduces the total number of most clicked ads to 3.

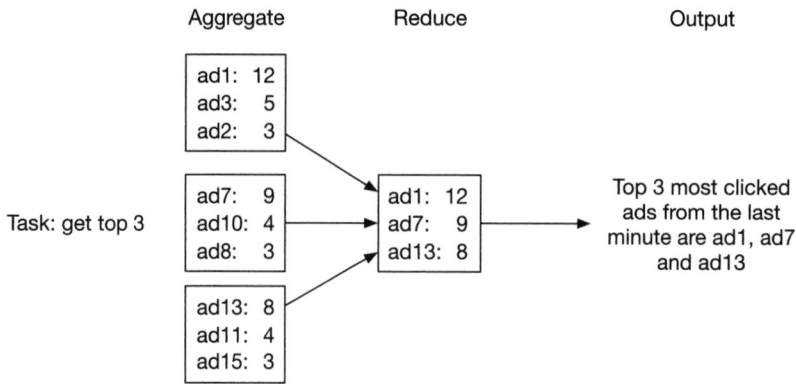

```
        Aggregate           Reduce              Output

       ┌──────────┐
       │ ad1:  12 │
       │ ad3:   5 │
       │ ad2:   3 │
       └──────────┘ \
                     \    ┌──────────┐
       ┌──────────┐   \   │ ad1:  12 │      Top 3 most clicked
       │ ad7:   9 │────────│ ad7:   9 │      ads from the last
Task: get top 3  ad10: 4  │ ad13:  8 │      minute are ad1, ad7
       │ ad8:   3 │   /   └──────────┘        and ad13
       └──────────┘  /
       ┌──────────┐ /
       │ ad13:  8 │
       │ ad11:  4 │
       │ ad15:  3 │
       └──────────┘
```

Figure 6.7: Reduce node

The DAG model represents the well-known MapReduce paradigm. It is designed to take big data and use parallel distributed computing to turn big data into little- or regular-sized data.

In the DAG model, intermediate data can be stored in memory and different nodes communicate with each other through either TCP (nodes running in different processes) or shared memory (nodes running in different threads).

Main use cases

Now that we understand how MapReduce works at the high level, let's take a look at how it can be utilized to support the main use cases:

- Aggregate the number of clicks of ad_id in the last M mins.
- Return top N most clicked ad_ids in the last M minutes.
- Data filtering.

Use case 1: aggregate the number of clicks

As shown in Figure 6.8, input events are partitioned by ad_id (ad_id %3) in Map nodes and are then aggregated by Aggregation nodes.

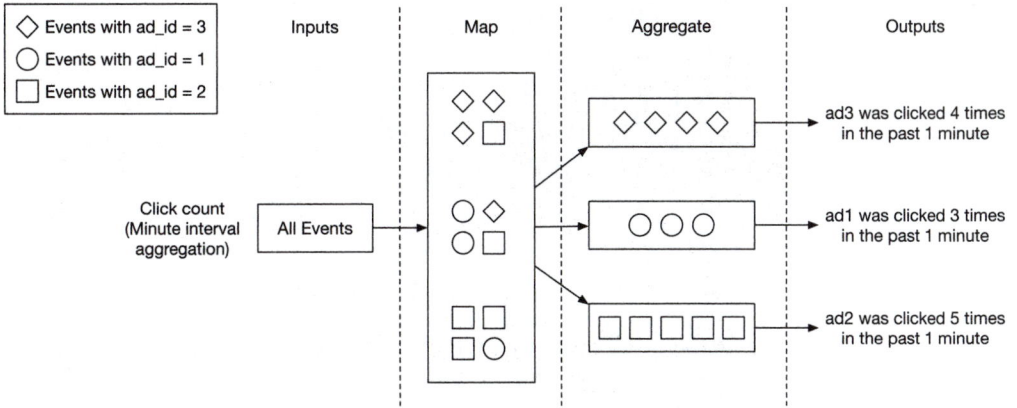

Figure 6.8: Aggregate the number of clicks

Use case 2: return top N most clicked ads

Figure 6.9 shows a simplified design of getting the top 3 most clicked ads, which can be extended to top N. Input events are mapped using ad_id and each Aggregate node maintains a heap data structure to get the top 3 ads within the node efficiently. In the last step, the Reduce node reduces 9 ads (top 3 from each aggregate node) to the top 3 most clicked ads every minute.

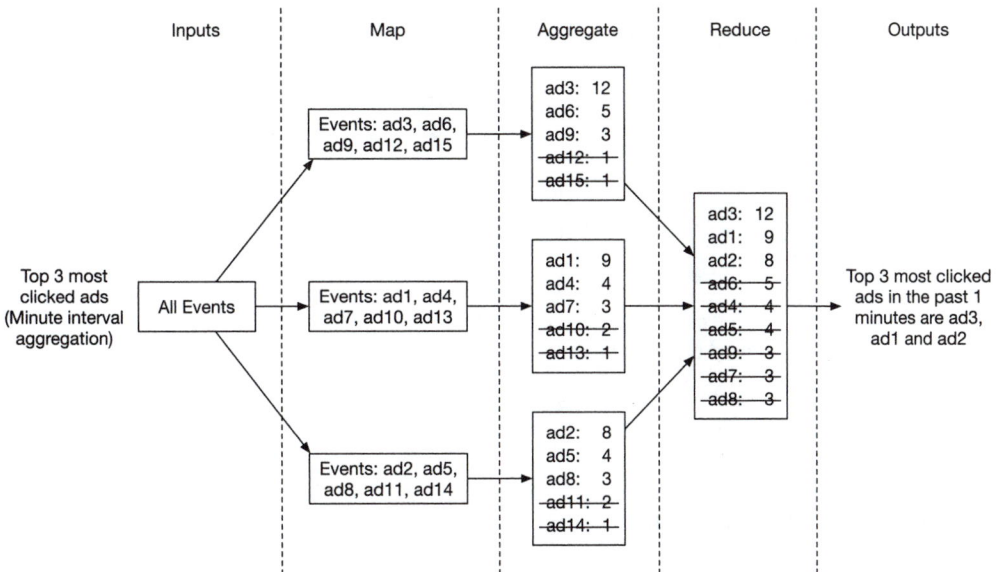

Figure 6.9: Return top N most clicked ads

Use case 3: data filtering

To support data filtering like "show me the aggregated click count for ad001 within the USA only", we can pre-define filtering criteria and aggregate based on them. For example, the aggregation results look like this for ad001 and ad002:

ad_id	click_minute	country	count
ad001	202101010001	USA	100
ad001	202101010001	GPB	200
ad001	202101010001	others	3000
ad002	202101010001	USA	10
ad002	202101010001	GPB	25
ad002	202101010001	others	12

Table 6.16: Aggregation results (filter by country)

This technique is called the star schema [11], which is widely used in data warehouses. The filtering fields are called dimensions. This approach has the following benefits:

- It is simple to understand and build.
- The current aggregation service can be reused to create more dimensions in the star schema. No additional component is needed.
- Accessing data based on filtering criteria is fast because the result is pre-calculated.

A limitation with this approach is that it creates many more buckets and records, especially when we have a lot of filtering criteria.

Step 3 - Design Deep Dive

In this section, we will dive deep into the following:

- Streaming vs batching
- Time and aggregation window
- Delivery guarantees
- Scale the system
- Data monitoring and correctness
- Final design diagram
- Fault tolerance

Streaming vs batching

The high-level architecture we proposed in Figure 6.3 is a type of stream processing system. Table 6.17 shows the comparison of three types of systems [12]:

	Services (Online system)	Batch system (offline system)	Streaming system (near real-time system)
Responsiveness	Respond to the client quickly	No response to the client needed	No response to the client needed
Input	User requests	Bounded input with finite size. A large amount of data	Input has no boundary (infinite streams)
Output	Responses to clients	Materialized views, aggregated metrics, etc.	Materialized views, aggregated metrics, etc.
Performance measurement	Availability, latency	Throughput	Throughput, latency
Example	Online shopping	MapReduce	Flink [13]

Table 6.17: Comparison of three types of systems

In our design, both stream processing and batch processing are used. We utilized stream processing to process data as it arrives and generates aggregated results in a near real-time fashion. We utilized batch processing for historical data backup.

For a system that contains two processing paths (batch and streaming) simultaneously, this architecture is called lambda [14]. A disadvantage of lambda architecture is that you have two processing paths, meaning there are two codebases to maintain. Kappa architecture [15], which combines the batch and streaming in one processing path, solves the problem. The key idea is to handle both real-time data processing and continuous data reprocessing using a single stream processing engine. Figure 6.10 shows a comparison of lambda and kappa architecture.

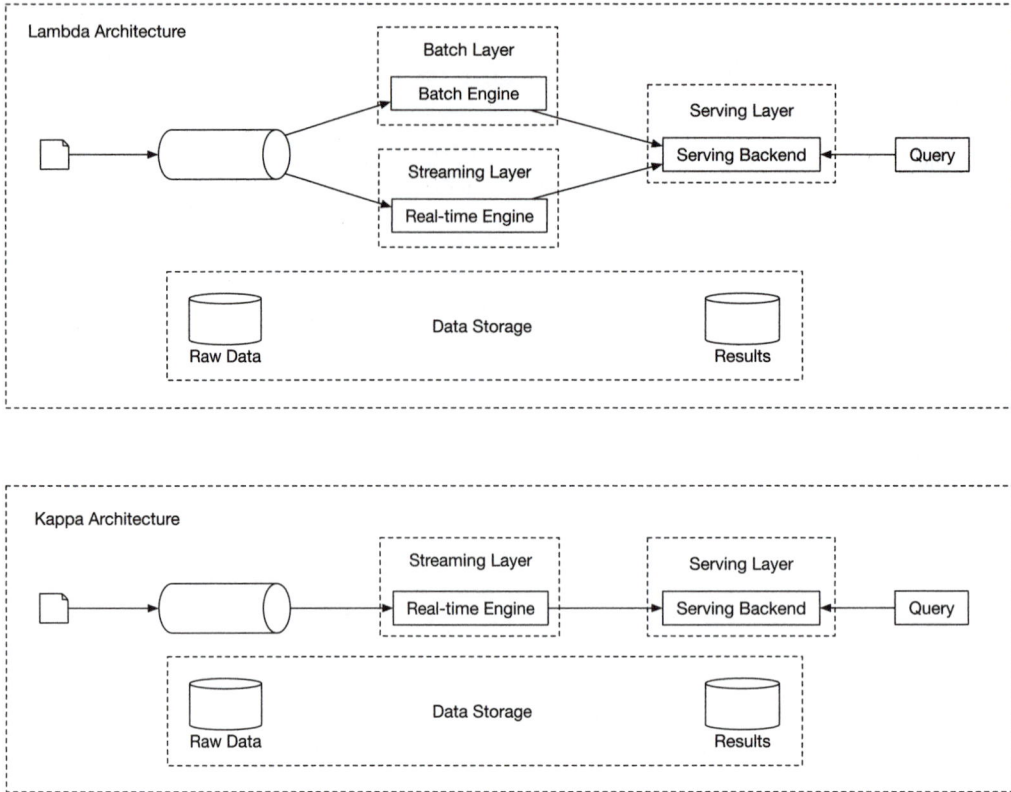

Figure 6.10: Lambda and Kappa architectures

Our high-level design uses Kappa architecture, where the reprocessing of historical data also goes through the real-time aggregation service. See the "Data recalculation" section below for details.

Data recalculation

Sometimes we have to recalculate the aggregated data, also called historical data replay. For example, if we discover a major bug in the aggregation service, we would need to recalculate the aggregated data from raw data starting at the point where the bug was introduced. Figure 6.11 shows the data recalculation flow:

1. The recalculation service retrieves data from raw data storage. This is a batched job.

2. Retrieved data is sent to a dedicated aggregation service so that the real-time processing is not impacted by historical data replay.

3. Aggregated results are sent to the second message queue, then updated in the aggregation database.

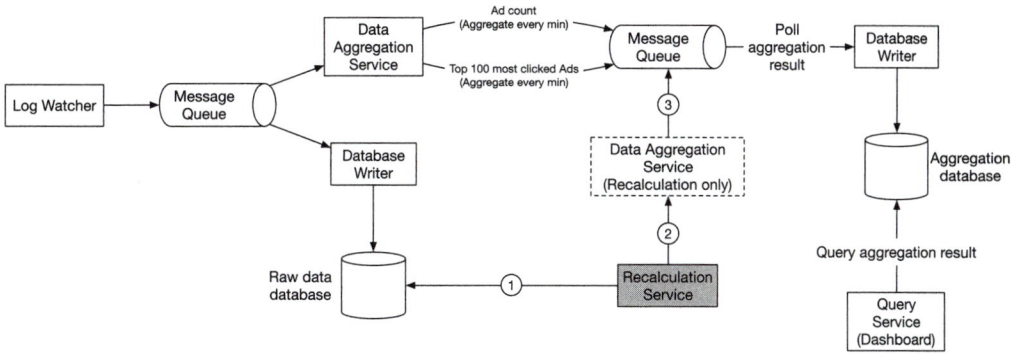

Figure 6.11: Recalculation service

The recalculation process reuses the data aggregation service but uses a different data source (the raw data).

Time

We need a timestamp to perform aggregation. The timestamp can be generated in two different places:

- Event time: when an ad click happens.
- Processing time: refers to the system time of the aggregation server that processes the click event.

Due to network delays and asynchronous environments (data go through a message queue), the gap between event time and processing time can be large. As shown in Figure 6.12, event 1 arrives at the aggregation service very late (5 hours later).

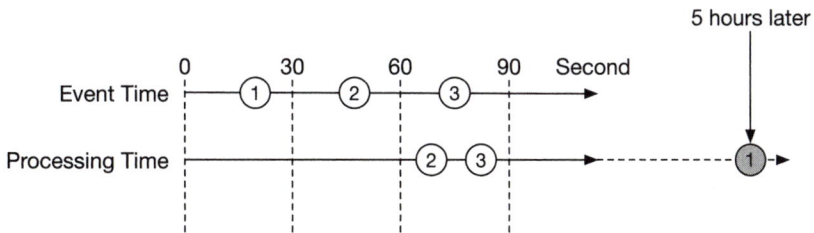

Figure 6.12: Late events

If event time is used for aggregation, we have to deal with delayed events. If processing time is used for aggregation, the aggregation result may not be accurate. There is no perfect solution, so we need to consider the trade-offs.

	Pros	Cons
Event time	Aggregation results are more accurate because the client knows exactly when an ad is clicked	It depends on the timestamp generated on the client-side. Clients might have the wrong time, or the timestamp might be generated by malicious users
Processing time	Server timestamp is more reliable	The timestamp is not accurate if an event reaches the system at a much later time

Table 6.18: Event time vs processing time

Since data accuracy is very important, we recommend using event time for aggregation. How do we properly process delayed events in this case? A technique called "watermark" is commonly utilized to handle slightly delayed events.

In Figure 6.13, ad click events are aggregated in the one-minute tumbling window (see the "Aggregation window" section on page 177 for more details). If event time is used to decide whether the event is in the window, window 1 misses event 2, and window 3 misses event 5 because they arrive slightly later than the end of their aggregation windows.

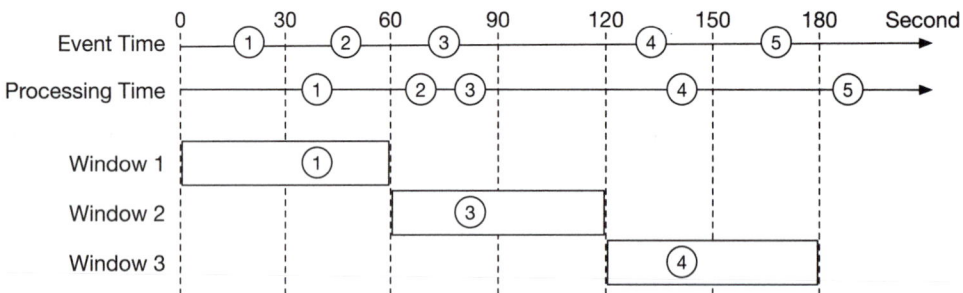

Figure 6.13: Miss events in an aggregation window

One way to mitigate this problem is to use "watermark" (the extended rectangles in Figure 6.14), which is regarded as an extension of an aggregation window. This improves the accuracy of the aggregation result. By extending an extra 15 second (adjustable) aggregation window, window 1 is able to include event 2, and window 3 is able to include event 5.

The value set for the watermark depends on the business requirement. A long watermark could catch events that arrive very late, but it adds more latency to the system. A short watermark means data is less accurate, but it adds less latency to the system.

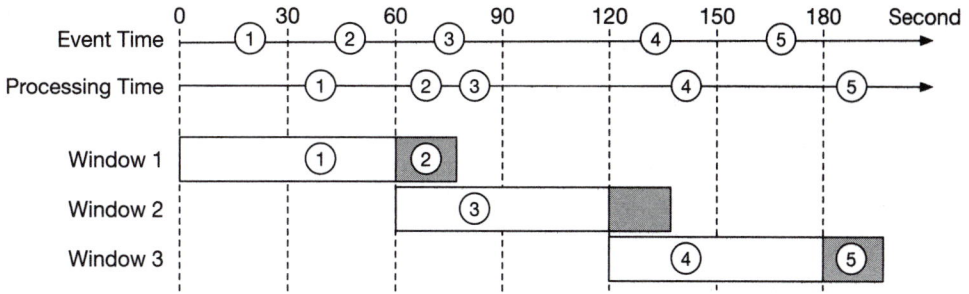

Figure 6.14: Watermark

Notice that the watermark technique does not handle events that have long delays. We can argue that it is not worth the return on investment (ROI) to have a complicated design for low probability events. We can always correct the tiny bit of inaccuracy with end-of-day reconciliation (see "Reconciliation" section on page 188). One trade-off to consider is that using watermark improves data accuracy but increases overall latency, due to extended wait time.

Aggregation window

According to the "Designing data-intensive applications" book by Martin Kleppmann [16], there are four types of window functions: tumbling window (also called fixed window), hopping window, sliding window, and session window. We will discuss the tumbling window and sliding window as they are most relevant to our system.

In the tumbling window (highlighted in Figure 6.15), time is partitioned into same-length, non-overlapping chunks. The tumbling window is a good fit for aggregating ad click events every minute (use case 1).

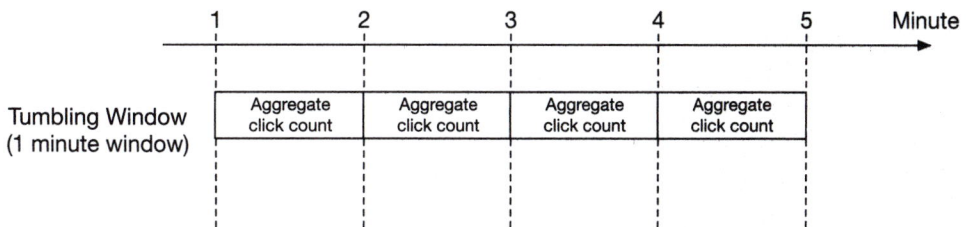

Figure 6.15: Tumbling window

In the sliding window (highlighted in Figure 6.16), events are grouped within a window that slides across the data stream, according to a specified interval. A sliding window can be an overlapping one. This is a good strategy to satisfy our second use case; to get the top N most clicked ads during the last M minutes.

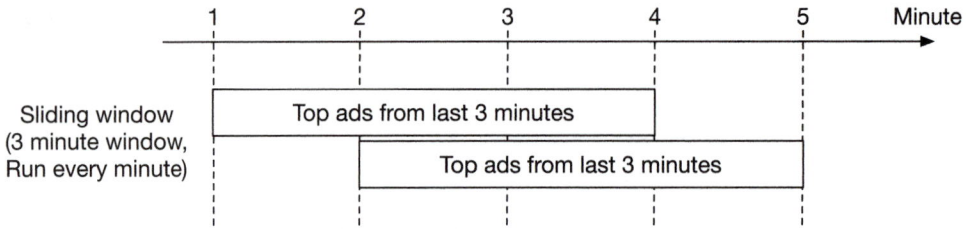

Figure 6.16: Sliding window

Delivery guarantees

Since the aggregation result is utilized for billing, data accuracy and completeness are very important. The system needs to be able to answer questions such as:

- How to avoid processing duplicate events?
- How to ensure all events are processed?

Message queues such as Kafka usually provide three delivery semantics: at-most once, at-least once, and exactly once.

Which delivery method should we choose?

In most circumstances, at-least once processing is good enough if a small percentage of duplicates are acceptable.

However, this is not the case for our system. Differences of a few percent in data points could result in discrepancies of millions of dollars. Therefore, we recommend exactly-once delivery for the system. If you are interested in learning more about a real-life ad aggregation system, take a look at how Yelp implements it [17].

Data deduplication

One of the most common data quality issues is duplicated data. Duplicated data can come from a wide range of sources and in this section, we discuss two common sources.

- Client-side. For example, a client might resend the same event multiple times. Duplicated events sent with malicious intent are best handled by ad fraud/risk control components. If this is of interest, please refer to the reference material [18].
- Server outage. If an aggregation service node goes down in the middle of aggregation and the upstream service hasn't yet received an acknowledgment, the same events might be sent and aggregated again. Let's take a closer look.

Figure 6.17 shows how the aggregation service node (Aggregator) outage introduces duplicate data. The Aggregator manages the status of data consumption by storing the offset in upstream Kafka.

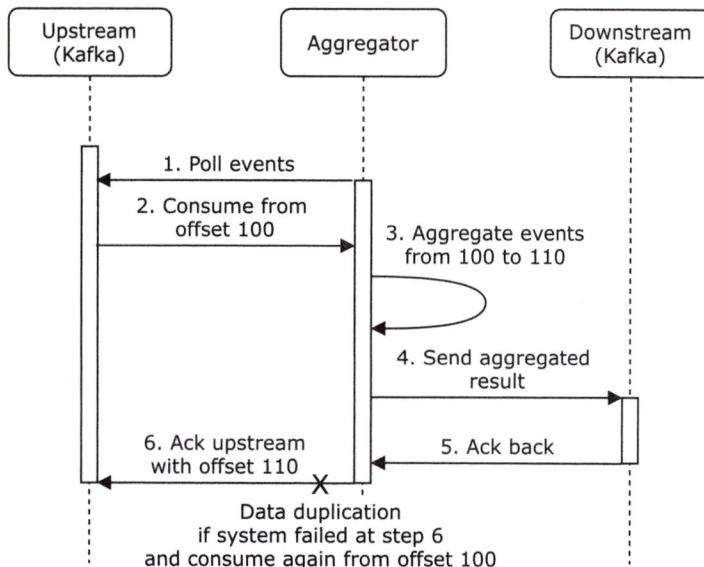

Figure 6.17: Duplicate data

If step 6 fails, perhaps due to Aggregator outage, events from 100 to 110 are already sent to the downstream, but the new offset 110 is not persisted in upstream Kafka. In this case, a new Aggregator would consume again from offset 100, even if those events are already processed, causing duplicate data.

The most straightforward solution (Figure 6.18) is to use external file storage, such as HDFS or S3, to record the offset. However, this solution has issues as well.

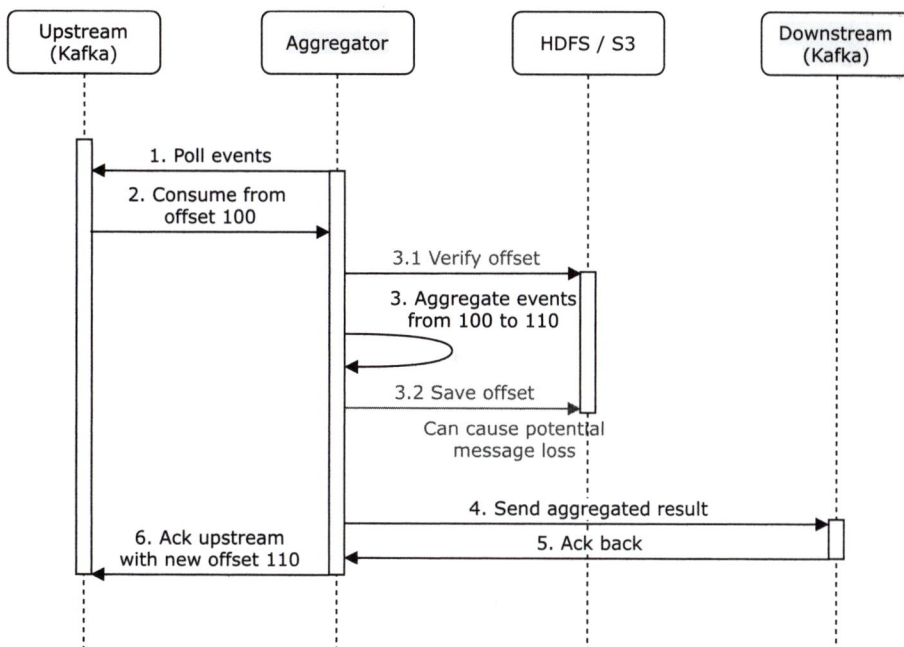

Figure 6.18: Record the offset

In step 3, the aggregator will process events from offset 100 to 110, only if the last offset stored in external storage is 100. If the offset stored in the storage is 110, the aggregator ignores events before offset 110.

But this design has a major problem: the offset is saved to HDFS or S3 (step 3.2) before the aggregation result is sent downstream. If step 4 fails due to Aggregator outage, events from 100 to 110 will never be processed by a newly brought up aggregator node, since the offset stored in external storage is 110.

To avoid data loss, we need to save the offset once we get an acknowledgment back from downstream. The updated design is shown in Figure 6.19.

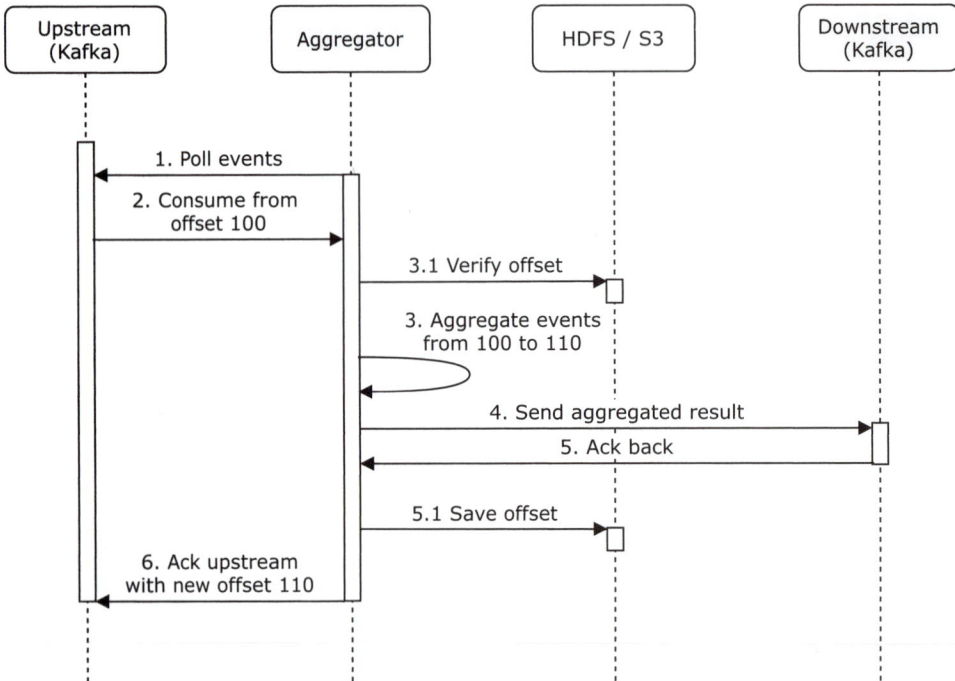

Figure 6.19: Save offset after receiving ack

In this design, if the Aggregator is down before step 5.1 is executed, events from 100 to 110 will be sent downstream again. To achieve exactly once processing, we need to put operations between step 4 to step 6 in one distributed transaction. A distributed transaction is a transaction that works across several nodes. If any of the operations fails, the whole transaction is rolled back.

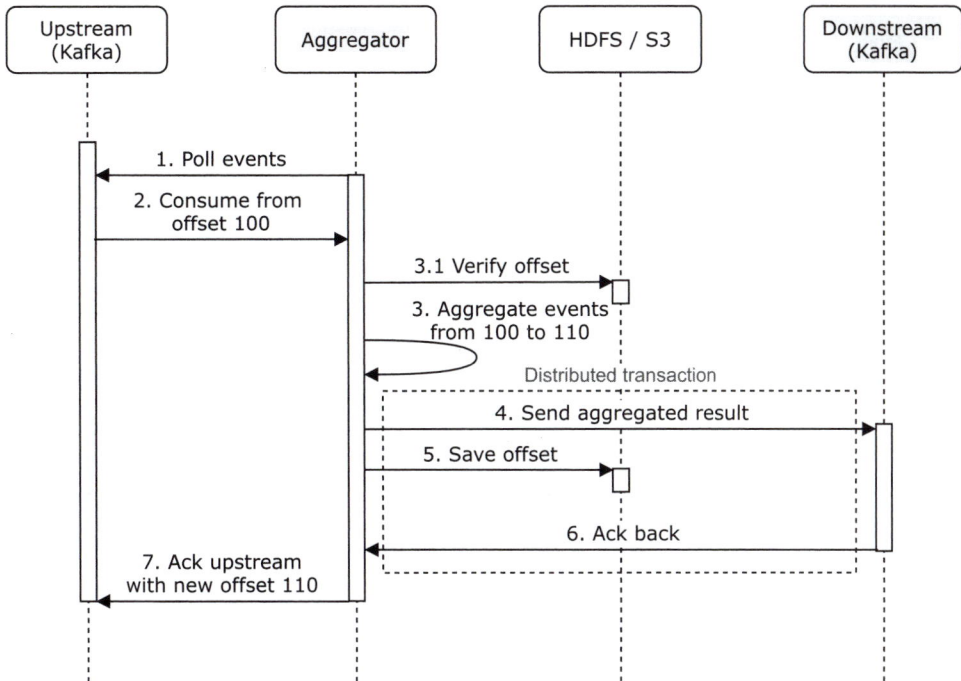

Figure 6.20: Distributed transaction

As you can see, it's not easy to dedupe data in large-scale systems. How to achieve exactly-once processing is an advanced topic. If you are interested in the details, please refer to reference material [9].

Scale the system

From the back-of-the-envelope estimation, we know the business grows 30% per year, which doubles traffic every 3 years. How do we handle this growth? Let's take a look.

Our system consists of three independent components: message queue, aggregation service, and database. Since these components are decoupled, we can scale each one independently.

Scale the message queue

We have already discussed how to scale the message queue extensively in the "Distributed Message Queue" chapter, so we'll only briefly touch on a few points.

Producers. We don't limit the number of producer instances, so the scalability of producers can be easily achieved.

Consumers. Inside a consumer group, the rebalancing mechanism helps to scale the consumers by adding or removing nodes. As shown in Figure 6.21, by adding two more consumers, each consumer only processes events from one partition.

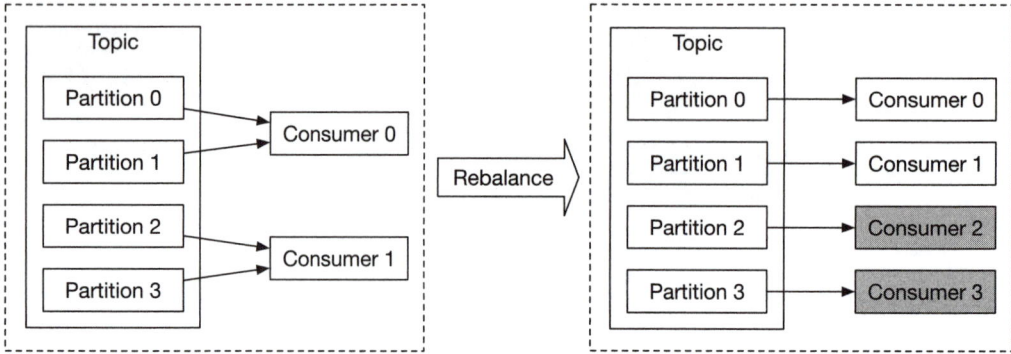

Figure 6.21: Add consumers

When there are hundreds of Kafka consumers in the system, consumer rebalance can be quite slow and could take a few minutes or even more. Therefore, if more consumers need to be added, try to do it during off-peak hours to minimize the impact.

Brokers

- **Hashing key**
  Using ad_id as hashing key for Kafka partition to store events from the same ad_id in the same Kafka partition. In this case, an aggregation service can subscribe to all events of the same ad_id from one single partition.

- **The number of partitions**
  If the number of partitions changes, events of the same ad_id might be mapped to a different partition. Therefore, it's recommended to pre-allocate enough partitions in advance, to avoid dynamically increasing the number of partitions in production.

- **Topic physical sharding**
  One single topic is usually not enough. We can split the data by geography (topic_north_america, topic_europe, topic_asia, etc.) or by business type (topic_web_ads, topic_mobile_ads, etc).

  - Pros: Slicing data to different topics can help increase the system throughput. With fewer consumers for a single topic, the time to rebalance consumer groups is reduced.

  - Cons: It introduces extra complexity and increases maintenance costs.

Scale the aggregation service

In the high-level design, we talked about the aggregation service being a map/reduce operation. Figure 6.22 shows how things are wired together.

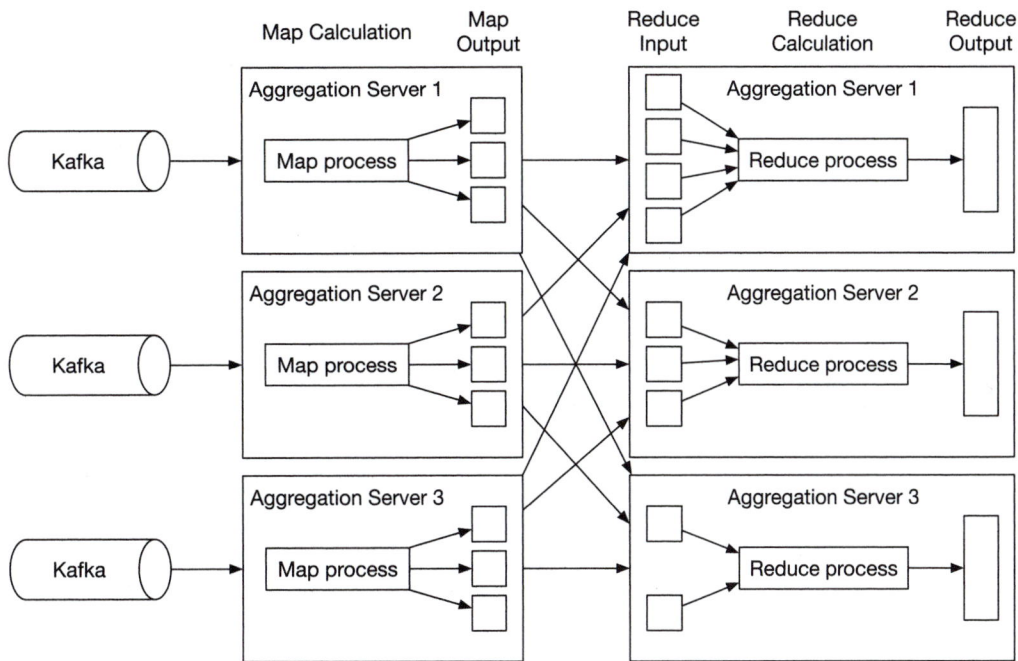

Figure 6.22: Aggregation service

If you are interested in the details, please refer to reference material [19]. Aggregation service is horizontally scalable by adding or removing nodes. Here is an interesting question; how do we increase the throughput of the aggregation service? There are two options.

Option 1: Allocate events with different ad_ids to different threads, as shown in Figure 6.23.

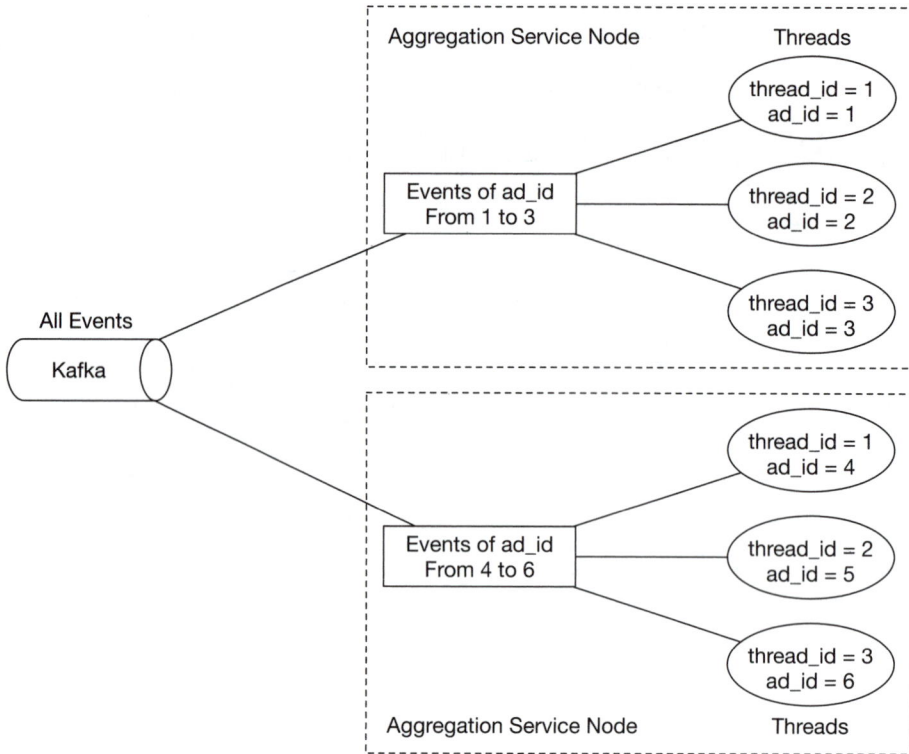

Figure 6.23: Multi-threading

Option 2: Deploy aggregation service nodes on resource providers like Apache Hadoop YARN [20]. You can think of this approach as utilizing multi-processing.

Option 1 is easier to implement and doesn't depend on resource providers. In reality, however, option 2 is more widely used because we can scale the system by adding more computing resources.

Scale the database

Cassandra natively supports horizontal scaling, in a way similar to consistent hashing.

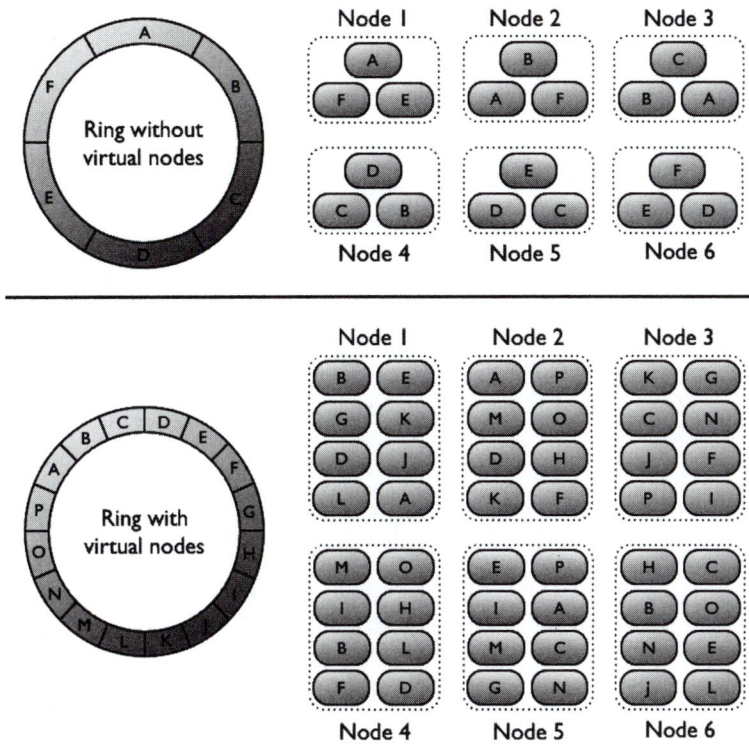

Figure 6.24: Virtual nodes [21]

Data is evenly distributed to every node with a proper replication factor. Each node saves its own part of the ring based on hashed value and also saves copies from other virtual nodes.

If we add a new node to the cluster, it automatically rebalances the virtual nodes among all nodes. No manual resharding is required. See Cassandra's official documentation for more details [21].

Hotspot issue

A shard or service that receives much more data than the others is called a hotspot. This occurs because major companies have advertising budgets in the millions of dollars and their ads are clicked more often. Since events are partitioned by ad_id, some aggregation service nodes might receive many more ad click events than others, potentially causing server overload.

This problem can be mitigated by allocating more aggregation nodes to process popular ads. Let's take a look at an example as shown in Figure 6.25. Assume each aggregation node can handle only 100 events.

1. Since there are 300 events in the aggregation node (beyond the capacity of a node can handle), it applies for extra resources through the resource manager.

2. The resource manager allocates more resources (for example, add two more aggregation nodes) so the original aggregation node isn't overloaded.

3. The original aggregation node split events into 3 groups and each aggregation node handles 100 events.

4. The result is written back to the original aggregate node.

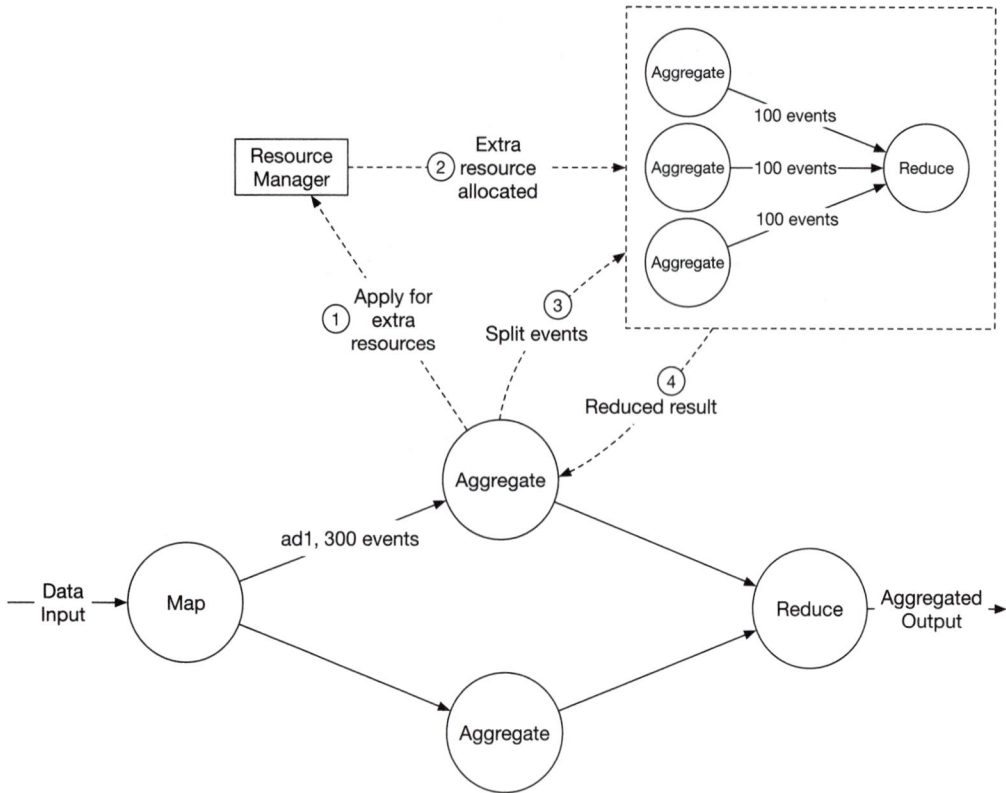

Figure 6.25: Allocate more aggregation nodes

There are more sophisticated ways to handle this problem, such as Global-Local Aggregation or Split Distinct Aggregation. For more information, please refer to [22].

Fault tolerance

Let's discuss the fault tolerance of the aggregation service. Since aggregation happens in memory, when an aggregation node goes down, the aggregated result is lost as well. We can rebuild the count by replaying events from upstream Kafka brokers.

Replaying data from the beginning of Kafka is slow. A good practice is to save the "system status" like upstream offset to a snapshot and recover from the last saved status. In our design, the "system status" is more than just the upstream offset because we need to store data like top N most clicked ads in the past M minutes.

Figure 6.26 shows a simple example of what the data looks like in a snapshot.

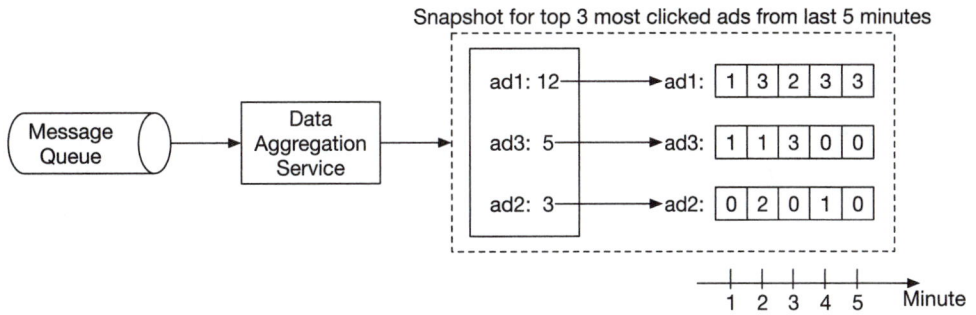

Figure 6.26: Data in a snapshot

With a snapshot, the failover process of the aggregation service is quite simple. If one aggregation service node fails, we bring up a new node and recover data from the latest snapshot (Figure 6.27). If there are new events that arrive after the last snapshot was taken, the new aggregation node will pull those data from the Kafka broker for replay.

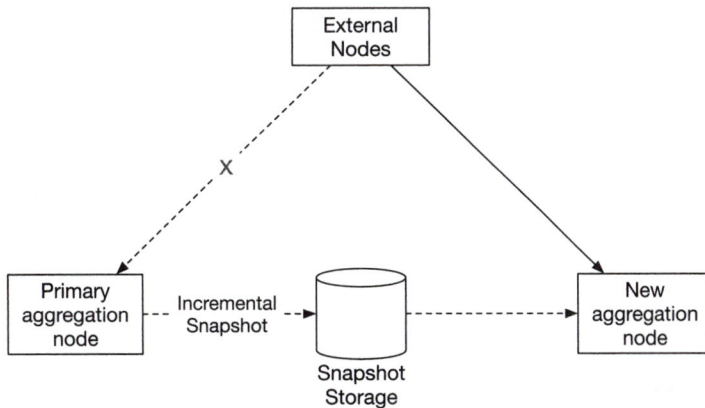

Figure 6.27: Aggregation node failover

Data monitoring and correctness

As mentioned earlier, aggregation results can be used for RTB and billing purposes. It's critical to monitor the system's health and to ensure correctness.

Continuous monitoring

Here are some metrics we might want to monitor:

- Latency. Since latency can be introduced at each stage, it's invaluable to track timestamps as events flow through different parts of the system. The differences between those timestamps can be exposed as latency metrics.

- Message queue size. If there is a sudden increase in queue size, we may need to add more aggregation nodes. Notice that Kafka is a message queue implemented as a distributed commit log, so we need to monitor the records-lag metrics instead.

- System resources on aggregation nodes: CPU, disk, JVM, etc.

Reconciliation

Reconciliation means comparing different sets of data in order to ensure data integrity. Unlike reconciliation in the banking industry, where you can compare your records with the bank's records, the result of ad click aggregation has no third-party result to reconcile with.

What we can do is to sort the ad click events by event time in every partition at the end of the day, by using a batch job and reconciling with the real-time aggregation result. If we have higher accuracy requirements, we can use a smaller aggregation window; for example, one hour. Please note, no matter which aggregation window is used, the result from the batch job might not match exactly with the real-time aggregation result, since some events might arrive late (see "Time" section on page 175).

Figure 6.28 shows the final design diagram with reconciliation support.

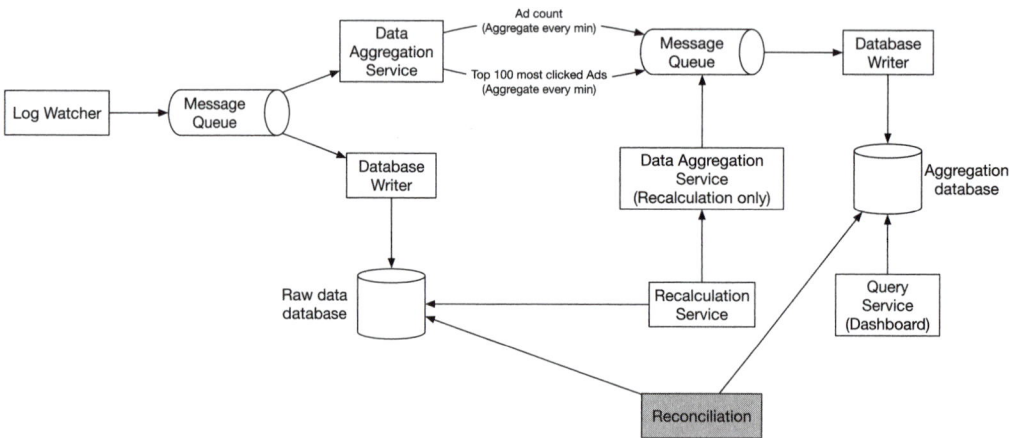

Figure 6.28: Final design

Alternative design

In a generalist system design interview, you are not expected to know the internals of different pieces of specialized software used in a big data pipeline. Explaining your thought process and discussing trade-offs is very important, which is why we propose a generic solution. Another option is to store ad click data in Hive, with an ElasticSearch layer built for faster queries. Aggregation is usually done in OLAP databases such as ClickHouse [23] or Druid [24]. Figure 6.29 shows the architecture.

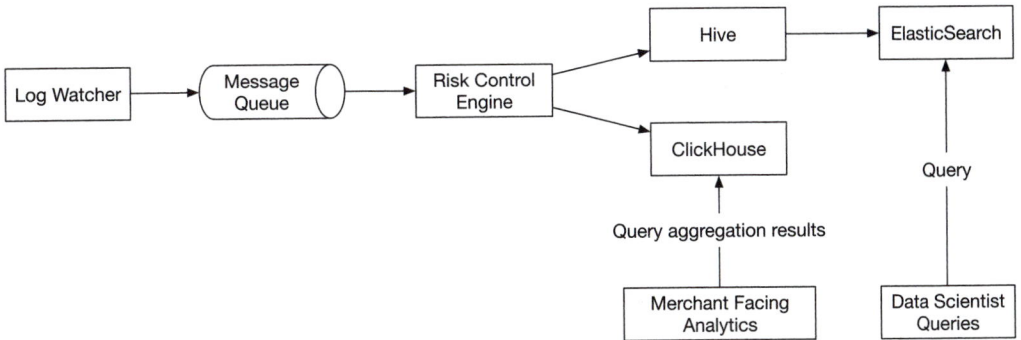

Figure 6.29: Alternative design

For more detail on this, please refer to reference material [25].

Step 4 - Wrap Up

In this chapter, we went through the process of designing an ad click event aggregation system at the scale of Facebook or Google. We covered:

- Data model and API design.
- Use MapReduce paradigm to aggregate ad click events.
- Scale the message queue, aggregation service, and database.
- Mitigate hotspot issue.
- Monitor the system continuously.
- Use reconciliation to ensure correctness.
- Fault tolerance.

The ad click event aggregation system is a typical big data processing system. It will be easier to understand and design if you have prior knowledge or experience with industry-standard solutions such as Apache Kafka, Apache Flink, or Apache Spark.

Congratulations on getting this far! Now give yourself a pat on the back. Good job!

Chapter Summary

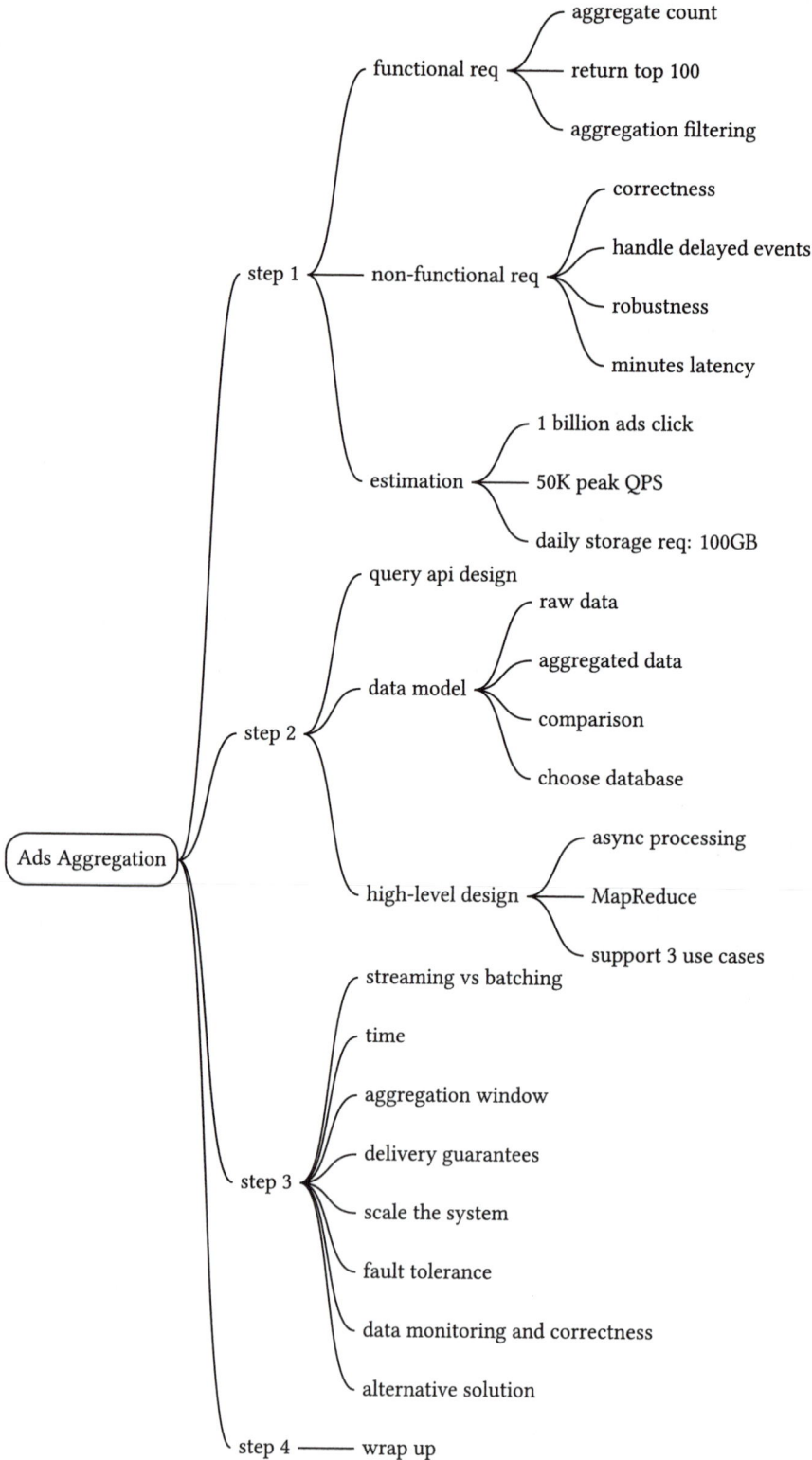

Ads Aggregation

- step 1
  - functional req
    - aggregate count
    - return top 100
    - aggregation filtering
  - non-functional req
    - correctness
    - handle delayed events
    - robustness
    - minutes latency
  - estimation
    - 1 billion ads click
    - 50K peak QPS
    - daily storage req: 100GB
- step 2
  - query api design
  - data model
    - raw data
    - aggregated data
    - comparison
    - choose database
  - high-level design
    - async processing
    - MapReduce
    - support 3 use cases
- step 3
  - streaming vs batching
  - time
  - aggregation window
  - delivery guarantees
  - scale the system
  - fault tolerance
  - data monitoring and correctness
  - alternative solution
- step 4 — wrap up

Reference Material

[1] Clickthrough rate (CTR): Definition. https://support.google.com/google-ads/answer/2615875?hl=en.

[2] Conversion rate: Definition. https://support.google.com/google-ads/answer/2684489?hl=en.

[3] OLAP functions. https://docs.oracle.com/database/121/OLAXS/olap_functions.htm#OLAXS169.

[4] Display Advertising with Real-Time Bidding (RTB) and Behavioural Targeting. https://arxiv.org/pdf/1610.03013.pdf.

[5] LanguageManual ORC. https://cwiki.apache.org/confluence/display/hive/languagemanual+orc.

[6] Parquet. https://databricks.com/glossary/what-is-parquet.

[7] What is avro. https://www.ibm.com/topics/avro.

[8] Big Data. https://www.datakwery.com/techniques/big-data/.

[9] An Overview of End-to-End Exactly-Once Processing in Apache Flink. https://flink.apache.org/features/2018/03/01/end-to-end-exactly-once-apache-flink.html.

[10] DAG model. https://en.wikipedia.org/wiki/Directed_acyclic_graph.

[11] Understand star schema and the importance for Power BI. https://docs.microsoft.com/en-us/power-bi/guidance/star-schema.

[12] Martin Kleppmann. *Designing Data-Intensive Applications.* O'Reilly Media, 2017.

[13] Apache Flink. https://flink.apache.org/.

[14] Lambda architecture. https://databricks.com/glossary/lambda-architecture.

[15] Kappa architecture. https://hazelcast.com/glossary/kappa-architecture/.

[16] Martin Kleppmann. Stream Processing. In *Designing Data-Intensive Applications.* O'Reilly Media, 2017.

[17] End-to-end Exactly-once Aggregation Over Ad Streams. https://www.youtube.com/watch?v=hzxytnPcAUM.

[18] Ad traffic quality. https://www.google.com/ads/adtrafficquality/.

[19] Understanding MapReduce in Hadoop. https://www.section.io/engineering-education/understanding-map-reduce-in-hadoop/.

[20] Flink on Apache Yarn. https://ci.apache.org/projects/flink/flink-docs-release-1.13/docs/deployment/resource-providers/yarn/.

[21] How data is distributed across a cluster (using virtual nodes). https://docs.datasta x.com/en/cassandra-oss/3.0/cassandra/architecture/archDataDistributeDistribute .html.

[22] Flink performance tuning. https://nightlies.apache.org/flink/flink-docs-master/do cs/dev/table/tuning/.

[23] ClickHouse. https://clickhouse.com/.

[24] Druid. https://druid.apache.org/.

[25] Real-Time Exactly-Once Ad Event Processing with Apache Flink, Kafka, and Pinot. https://eng.uber.com/real-time-exactly-once-ad-event-processing/.

7   Hotel Reservation System

In this chapter, we design a hotel reservation system for a hotel chain such as Marriott International. The design and techniques used in this chapter are also applicable to other popular booking-related interview topics:

- Design Airbnb
- Design a flight reservation system
- Design a movie ticket booking system

Step 1 - Understand the Problem and Establish Design Scope

The hotel reservation system is complicated and its components vary based on business use cases. Before diving into the design, we should ask the interviewer clarification questions to narrow down the scope.

Candidate: What is the scale of the system?
Interviewer: Let's assume we are building a website for a hotel chain that has 5,000 hotels and 1 million rooms in total.

Candidate: Do customers pay when they make reservations or when they arrive at the hotel?
Interviewer: For simplicity, they pay in full when they make reservations.

Candidate: Do customers book hotel rooms through the hotel's website only? Do we need to support other reservation options such as phone calls?
Interviewer: Let's assume people could book a hotel room through the hotel website or app.

Candidate: Can customers cancel their reservations?
Interviewer: Yes.

Candidate: Are there any other things we need to consider?

Interviewer: Yes, we allow 10% overbooking. In case you do not know, overbooking means the hotel will sell more rooms than they actually have. Hotels do this in anticipation that some customers will cancel their reservations.

Candidate: Since we have limited time, I assume the hotel room search is not in scope. We focus on the following features.

- Show the hotel-related page.
- Show the hotel room-related detail page.
- Reserve a room.
- Admin panel to add/remove/update hotel or room info.
- Support the overbooking feature.

Interviewer: Sounds good.

Interviewer: One more thing, hotel prices change dynamically. The price of a hotel room depends on how full the hotel is expected to be on a given day. For this interview, we can assume the price could be different each day.
Candidate: I'll keep this in mind.

Next, you might want to talk about the most important non-functional requirements.

Non-functional requirements

- Support high concurrency. During peak season or big events, some popular hotels may have a lot of customers trying to book the same room.
- Moderate latency. It's ideal to have a fast response time when a user makes the reservation, but it's acceptable if the system takes a few seconds to process a reservation request.

Back-of-the-envelope estimation

- 5,000 hotels and 1 million rooms in total.
- Assume 70% of the rooms are occupied and the average stay duration is 3 days.
- Estimated daily reservations: $\frac{1 \text{ million} \times 0.7}{3} = 233,333$ (rounding up to $\sim 240,000$)
- Reservations per second $= \frac{240,000}{10^5 \text{ seconds in a day}} =\sim 3$. As we can see, the average reservation transaction per second (TPS) is not high.

Next, let's do a rough calculation of the QPS of all pages in the system. There are three steps in a typical customer flow:

1. View hotel/room detail page. Users browse this page (query).

2. View the booking page. Users can confirm the booking details, such as dates, number of guests, payment information before booking (query).

3. Reserve a room. Users click on the "book" button to book the room and the room is reserved (transaction).

Let's assume around 10% of the users reach the next step and 90% of users drop off the flow before reaching the final step. We can also assume that no prefetching feature (prefetching the content before the user reaches the next step) is implemented. Figure 7.1 shows a rough estimation of what the QPS looks like for different steps. We know the final reservation TPS is 3 so we can work backward along the funnel. The QPS of the order confirmation page is 30 and the QPS for the detail page is 300.

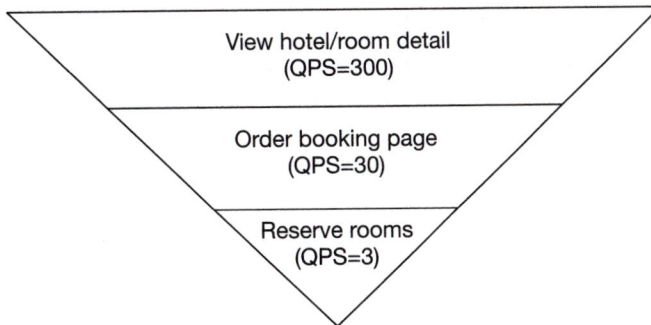

Figure 7.1: QPS distribution

Step 2 - Propose High-level Design and Get Buy-in

In this section, we'll discuss:

- API design
- Data models
- High-level design

API design

We explore the API design for the hotel reservation system. The most important APIs are listed below using the RESTful conventions.

Note that this chapter focuses on the design of a hotel reservation system. For a complete hotel website, the design needs to provide intuitive features for customers to search for rooms based on a large array of criteria. The APIs for these search features, while important, are not technically challenging. They are out of scope for this chapter.

Hotel-related APIs

API	Detail
GET /v1/hotels/ID	Get detailed information about a hotel.
POST /v1/hotels	Add a new hotel. This API is only available to hotel staff.
PUT /v1/hotels/ID	Update hotel information. This API is only available to hotel staff.
DELETE /v1/hotels/ID	Delete a hotel. This API is only available to hotel staff.

Table 7.1: Hotel-related APIs

Room-related APIs

API	Detail
GET /v1/hotels/ID/rooms/ID	Get detailed information about a room.
POST /v1/hotels/ID/rooms	Add a room. This API is only available to hotel staff.
PUT /v1/hotels/ID/rooms/ID	Update room information. This API is only available to hotel staff.
DELETE /v1/hotels/ID/rooms/ID	Delete a room. This API is only available to hotel staff.

Table 7.2: Hotel-related APIs

Reservation related APIs

API	Detail
GET /v1/reservations	Get the reservation history of the logged-in user.
GET /v1/reservations/ID	Get detailed information about a reservation.
POST /v1/reservations	Make a new reservation.
DELETE /v1/reservations/ID	Cancel a reservation.

Table 7.3: Reservation-related APIs

Making a new reservation is a very important feature. The request parameters of making a new reservation (POST /v1/reservations) could look like this.

```
{
    "startDate": "2021-04-28",
    "endDate":"2021-04-30",
    "hotelID":"245",
    "roomID":"U12354673389",
    "reservationID":"13422445"
}
```

Please note reservationID is used as the idempotency key to prevent double booking. Double booking means multiple reservations are made for the same room on the same day. The details are explained in the "Concurrency issue" section on page 204.

Data model

Before we decide which database to use, let's take a close look at the data access patterns. For the hotel reservation system, we need to support the following queries:

Query 1: View detailed information about a hotel.

Query 2: Find available types of rooms given a date range.

Query 3: Record a reservation.

Query 4: Look up a reservation or past history of reservations.

From the back-of-the-envelope estimation, we know the scale of the system is not large but we need to prepare for traffic surges during big events. With these requirements in mind, we choose a relational database because:

- A relational database works well with read-heavy and write less frequently workflow. This is because the number of users who visit the hotel website/apps is a few orders of magnitude higher than those who actually make reservations. NoSQL databases are generally optimized for writes and the relational database works well enough for read-heavy workflow.

- A relational database provides ACID (atomicity, consistency, isolation, durability) guarantees. ACID properties are important for a reservation system. Without those properties, it's not easy to prevent problems such as negative balance, double charge, double reservations, etc. ACID properties make application code a lot simpler and make the whole system easier to reason about. A relational database usually provides these guarantees.

- A relational database can easily model the data. The structure of the business data is very clear and the relationship between different entities (hotel, room, room_type, etc) is stable. This kind of data model is easily modeled by a relational database.

Now that we have chosen the relational database as our data store, let's explore the schema design. Figure 7.2 shows a straightforward schema design and it is the most natural way for many candidates to model the hotel reservation system.

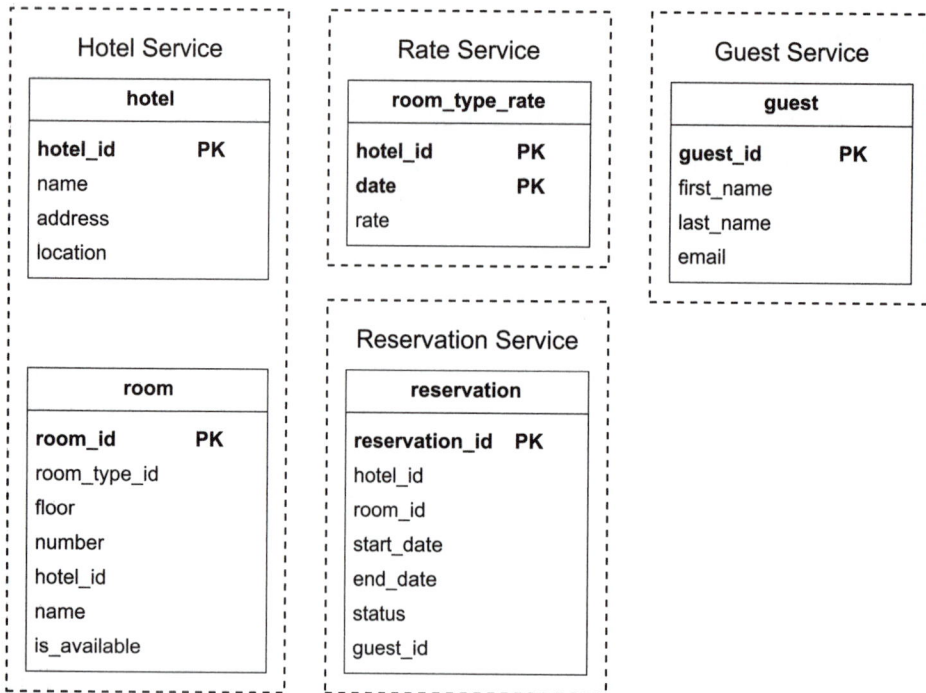

Figure 7.2: Database schema

Most attributes are self-explanatory and we will only explain the status field in the reservation table. The status field can be in one of these states: pending, paid, refunded, canceled, rejected. The state machine is shown in Figure 7.3.

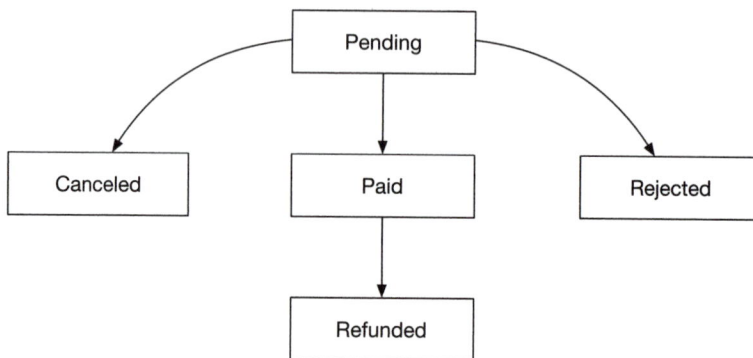

Figure 7.3: Reservation status

This schema design has a major issue. This data model works for companies like Airbnb as room_id (might be called listing_id) is given when users make reservations. However, this isn't the case for hotels. A user actually reserves **a type of room** in a given hotel instead of a specific room. For instance, a room type can be a standard room, king-size room, queen-size room with two queen beds, etc. Room numbers are given when the guest checks in and not at the time of the reservation. We need to update our data model to reflect this new requirement. See "Improved data model" in the deep dive section on page 201 for more details.

High-level design

We use the microservice architecture for this hotel reservation system. Over the past few years, microservice architecture has gained great popularity. Companies that use microservice include Amazon, Netflix, Uber, Airbnb, Twitter, etc. If you want to learn more about the benefits of a microservice architecture, you can check out some good resources [1] [2] .

Our design is modeled with the microservice architecture and the high-level design diagram is shown in Figure 7.4.

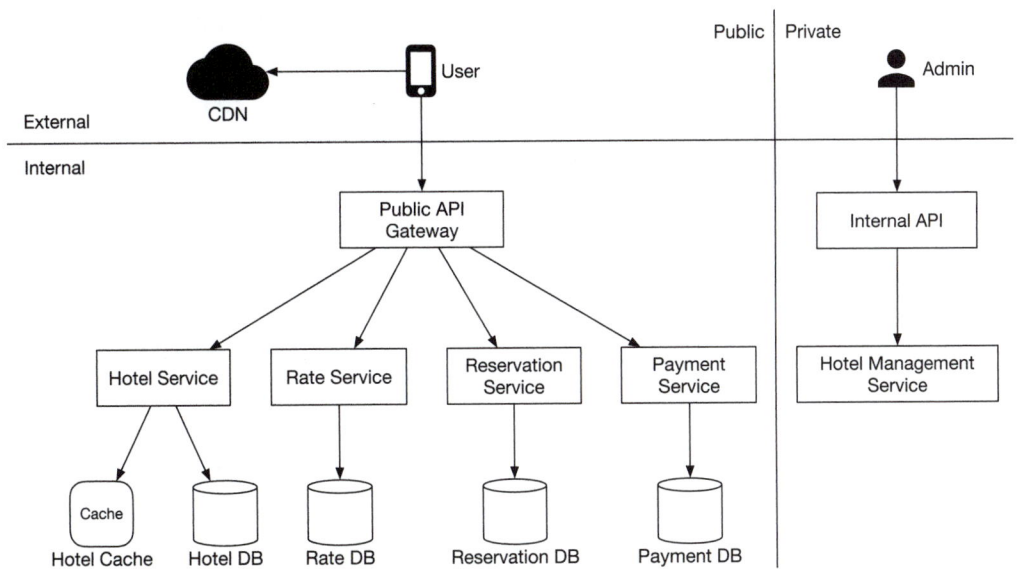

Figure 7.4: High-level design

We will briefly go over each component of the system from top to bottom.

- User: a user books a hotel room on their mobile phone or computer.

- Admin (hotel staff): authorized hotel staff perform administrative operations such as refunding a customer, canceling a reservation, updating room information, etc.

- CDN (content delivery network): for better load time, CDN is used to cache all static assets, including javascript bundles, images, videos, HTML, etc.

- Public API Gateway: this is a fully managed service that supports rate limiting, authentication, etc. The API gateway is configured to direct requests to specific services based on the endpoints. For example, requests to load the hotel homepage are directed to the hotel service and requests to book a hotel room are routed to the reservation service.

- Internal APIs: those APIs are only available for authorized hotel staff. They are accessible through internal software or websites. They are usually further protected by a VPN (virtual private network).

- Hotel Service: this provides detailed information on hotels and rooms. Hotel and room data are generally static, so can be easily cached.

- Rate Service: this provides room rates for different future dates. An interesting fact about the hotel industry is that the price of a room depends on how full the hotel is expected to be for a given day.

- Reservation Service: receives reservation requests and reserves the hotel rooms. This service also tracks room inventory as rooms are reserved or reservations are canceled.

- Payment Service: executes payment from a customer and updates the reservation status to paid once a payment transaction succeeds, or rejected if the transaction fails.

- Hotel Management Service: only available to authorized hotel staff. Hotel staff are eligible to use the following features: view the record of an upcoming reservation, reserve a room for a customer, cancel a reservation, etc.

For clarity, Figure 7.4 omits many arrows of interactions between microservices. For example, as shown in Figure 7.5, there should be an arrow between Reservation service and Rate service. Reservation service queries Rate service for room rates. This is used to compute the total room charge for a reservation. Another example is that there should be many arrows connecting the Hotel Management Service with most of the other services. When an admin makes changes via Hotel Management Service, the requests are forwarded to the actual service owning the data, to handle the changes.

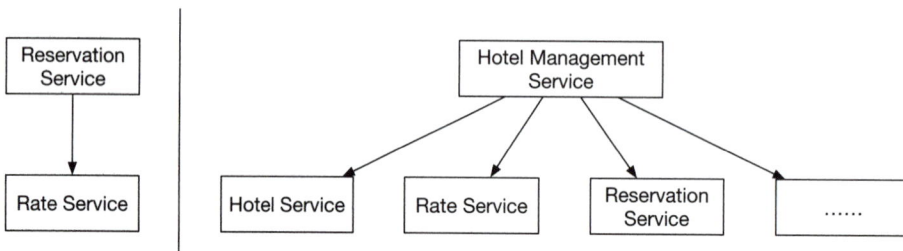

Figure 7.5: Connections between services

For production systems, inter-service communication often employs a modern and high-performance remote procedure call (RPC) framework like gPRC. There are many benefits to using such frameworks. To learn more about gPRC in particular, check out [3].

Step 3 - Design Deep Dive

Now we've talked about the high-level design, let's go deeper into the following.

- Improved data model
- Concurrency issues

- Scaling the system
- Resolving data inconsistency in the microservice architecture

Improved data model

As mentioned in the high-level design, when we reserve a hotel room, we actually reserve a type of room, as opposed to a specific room. What do we need to change about the API and schema to accommodate this?

For the reservation API, `roomID` is replaced by `roomTypeID` in the request parameter. The API to make a reservation looks like this:

`POST /v1/reservations`

Request parameters:

```
{
   "startDate": "2021-04-28",
   "endDate":"2021-04-30",
   "hotelID":"245",
   "roomTypeID":"12354673389",
   "reservationID":"13422445"
}
```

The updated schema is shown in Figure 7.6.

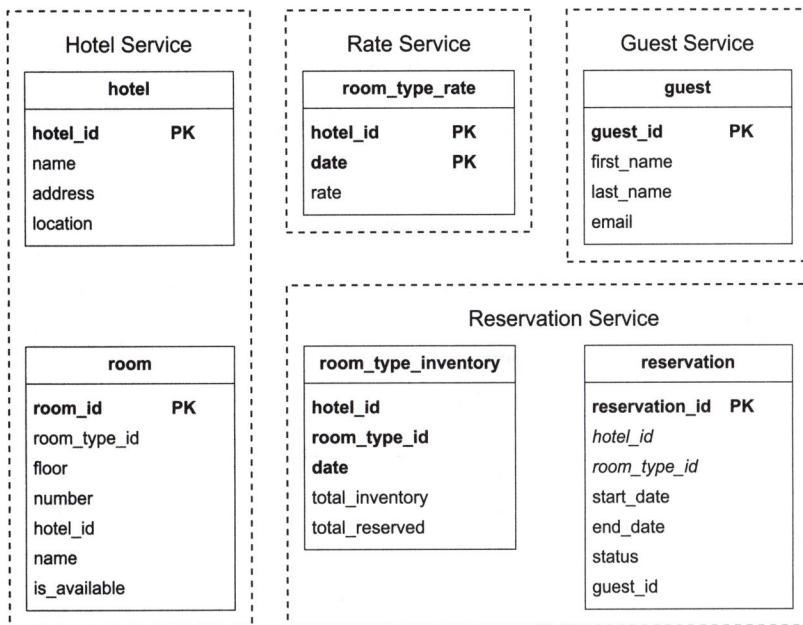

Figure 7.6: Updated schema

We'll briefly go over some of the most important tables.

`room`: contains information regarding a room.

`room_type_rate`: stores price data for a specific room type, for future dates.

reservation: records guest reservation data.

room_type_inventory: stores inventory data about hotel rooms. This table is very important for the reservation system, so let's take a close look at each column.

- hotel_id: ID of the hotel
- room_type_id: ID of a room type.
- date: a single date.
- total_inventory: the total number of rooms minus those that are temporarily taken off the inventory. Some rooms might be taken off from the market for maintenance.
- total_reserved: the total number of rooms booked for the specified hotel_id, room_type_id, and date.

There are other ways to design the room_type_inventory table, but having one row per date makes managing reservations within a date range and queries easy. As shown in Figure 7.6, (hotel_id, room_type_id, date) is the composite primary key. The rows of the table are pre-populated by querying the inventory data across all future dates within 2 years. We have a scheduled daily job that pre-populates inventory data when the dates advance further.

Now that we've finalized the schema design, let's do some estimation about the storage volume. As mentioned in the back-of-the-envelope estimation, we have 5,000 hotels. Assume each hotel has 20 types of rooms. That's (5,000 hotels $\times$ 20 types of rooms $\times$ 2 years $\times$ 365 days) = 73 million rows. 73 million is not a lot of data and a single database is enough to store the data. However, a single server means a single point of failure. To achieve high availability, we could set up database replications across multiple regions or availability zones.

Table 7.4 shows the sample data of the room_type_inventory table.

hotel_id	room_type_id	date	total_inventory	total_reserved
211	1001	2021-06-01	100	80
211	1001	2021-06-02	100	82
211	1001	2021-06-03	100	86
211	1001	...	...	
211	1001	2023-05-31	100	0
211	1002	2021-06-01	200	164
2210	101	2021-06-01	30	23
2210	101	2021-06-02	30	25

Table 7.4: Sample data of the room_type_inventory table

The room_type_inventory table is utilized to check if a customer can reserve a specific type of room or not. The input and output for a reservation might look like this:

- Input: startDate (2021-07-01), endDate (2021-07-03), roomTypeId, hotelId, numberOfRoomsToReserve

- Output: True if the specified type of room has inventory and users can book it. Otherwise, it returns False.

From the SQL perspective, it contains the following two steps:

1. Select rows within a date range

```
SELECT date, total_inventory, total_reserved
FROM room_type_inventory
WHERE room_type_id = ${roomTypeId} AND hotel_id = ${
hotelId}
AND date between ${startDate} and ${endDate}
```

This query returns data like this:

date	total_inventory	total_reserved
2021-07-01	100	97
2021-07-02	100	96
2021-07-03	100	95

Table 7.5: Hotel inventory

2. For each entry, the application checks the condition below:

```
if ((total_reserved + ${numberOfRoomsToReserve}) <=
total_inventory)
```

If the condition returns True for all entries, it means there are enough rooms for each date within the date range.

One of the requirements is to support 10% overbooking. With the new schema, it is easy to implement:

```
if ((total_reserved + ${numberOfRoomsToReserve}) <= 110% *
total_inventory)
```

At this point, the interviewer might ask a follow-up question: "if the reservation data is too large for a single database, what would you do?" There are a few strategies:

- Store only current and future reservation data. Reservation history is not frequently accessed. So they can be archived and some can even be moved to cold storage.
- Database sharding. The most frequent queries include making a reservation or looking up a reservation by name. In both queries, we need to choose the hotel first, meaning hotel_id is a good sharding key. The data can be sharded by hash(hotel_id) % number_of_servers.

Concurrency issues

Another important problem to look at is double booking. We need to solve two problems:

1. The same user clicks on the book button multiple times.

2. Multiple users try to book the same room at the same time.

Let's take a look at the first scenario. As shown in Figure 7.7, two reservations are made.

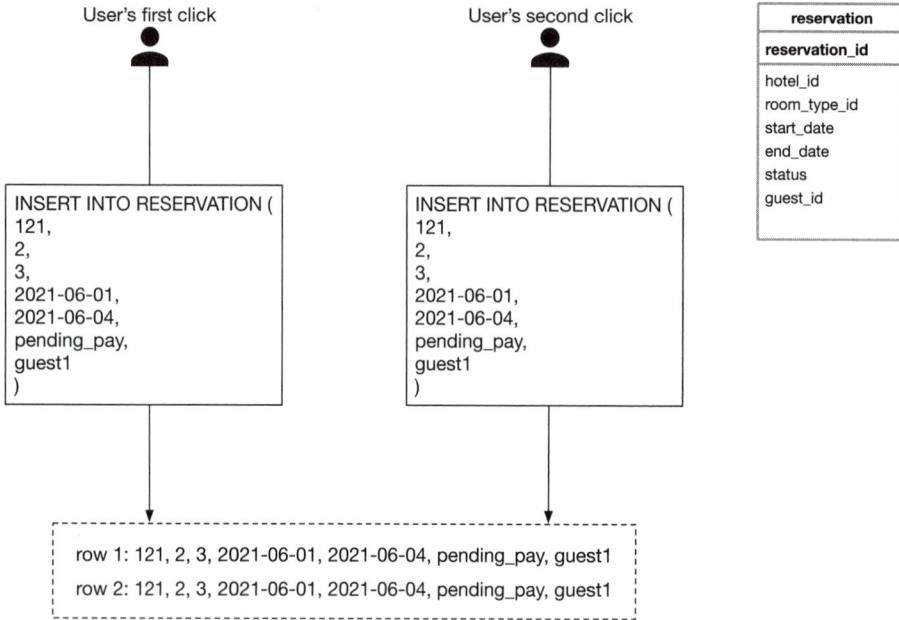

Figure 7.7: Two reservations are made

There are two common approaches to solve this problem:

- Client-side implementation. A client can gray out, hide or disable the "submit" button once a request is sent. This should prevent the double-clicking issue most of the time. However, this approach is not very reliable. For example, users can disable javascript, thereby bypassing the client check.

- Idempotent APIs. Add an idempotency key in the reservation API request. An API call is idempotent if it produces the same result no matter how many times it is called. Figure 7.8 shows how to use the idempotency key `reservation_id` to avoid the double-reservation issue. The detailed steps are explained below.

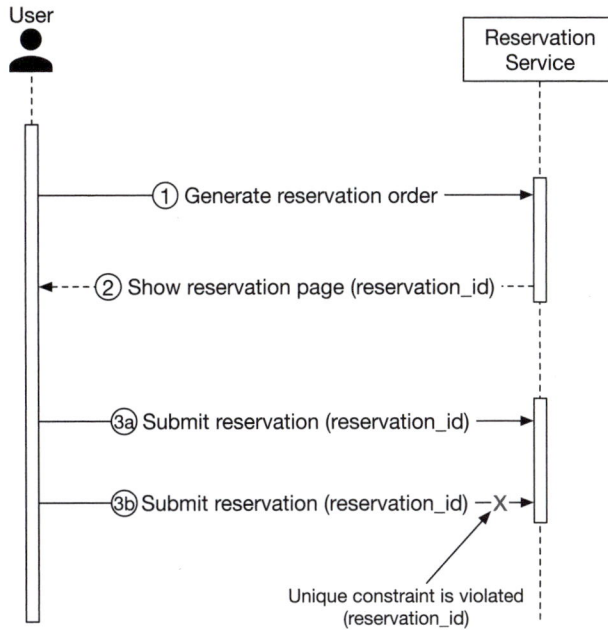

Figure 7.8: Unique constraint

1. Generate a reservation order. After a customer enters detailed information about the reservation (room type, check-in date, check-out date, etc) and clicks the "continue" button, a reservation order is generated by the reservation service.

2. The system generates a reservation order for the customer to review. The unique reservation_id is generated by a globally unique ID generator and returned as part of the API response. The UI of this step might look like this:

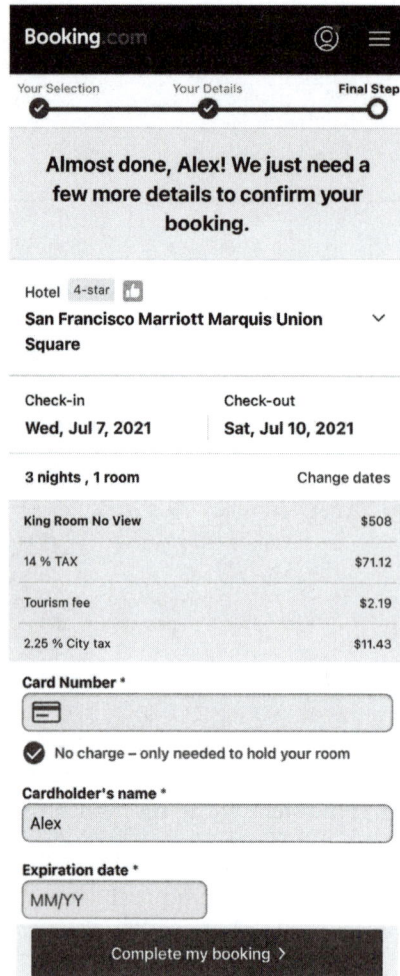

Figure 7.9: Confirmation page (Source: [4])

3a. Submit reservation 1. The reservation_id is included as part of the request. It is the primary key of the reservation table (Figure 7.6). Please note that the idempotency key doesn't have to be the reservation_id. We choose reservation_id because it already exists and works well for our design.

3b. If a user clicks the "Complete my booking" button a second time, reservation 2 is submitted. Because reservation_id is the primary key of the reservation table, we can rely on the unique constraint of the key to ensure no double reservation happens.

Figure 7.10 explains why double reservation can be avoided.

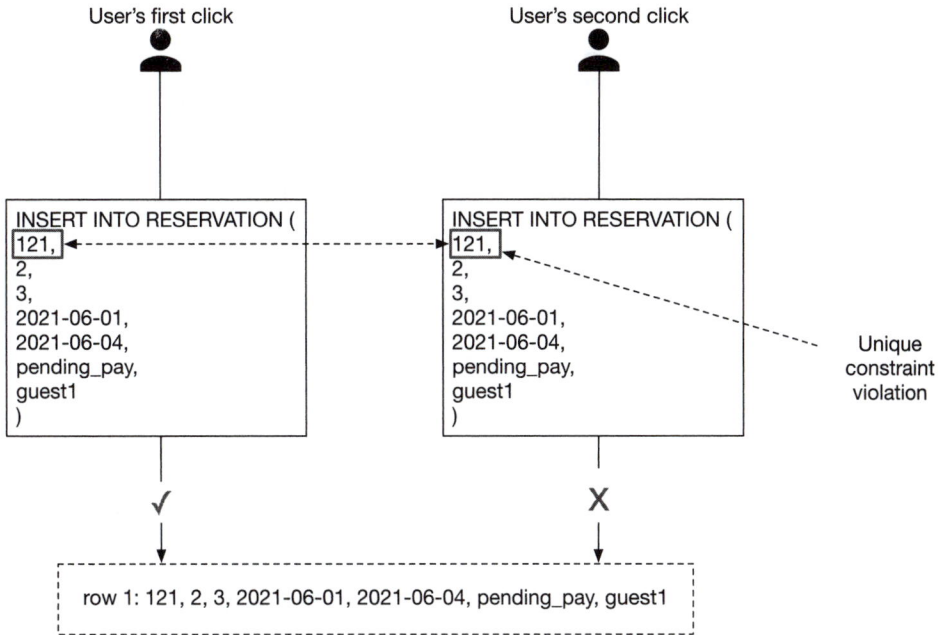

Figure 7.10: Unique constraint violation

Scenario 2: what happens if multiple users book the same type of room at the same time when there is only one room left? Let's consider the scenario as shown in Figure 7.11.

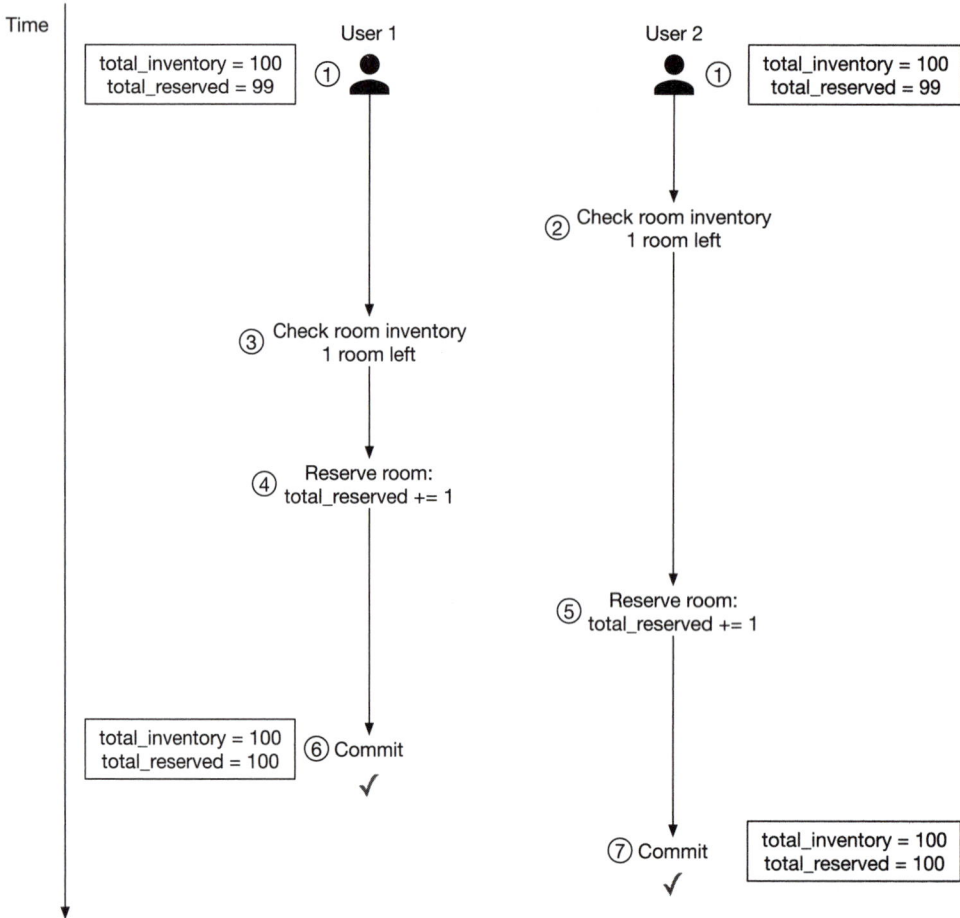

Figure 7.11: Race condition

1. Let's assume the database isolation level is not serializable [5]. User 1 and User 2 try to book the same type of room at the same time, but there is only 1 room left. Let's call User 1's execution transaction 1 and User 2's execution transaction 2. At this time, there are 100 rooms in the hotel and 99 of them are reserved.

2. Transaction 2 checks if there are enough rooms left by checking if (total_reserved + rooms_to_book) ≤ total_inventory. Since there is 1 more room left, it returns True.

3. Transaction 1 checks if there are enough rooms by checking if (total_reserved + rooms_to_book) ≤ total_inventory. Since there is 1 more room left, it returns True as well.

4. Transaction 1 reserves the room and updates the inventory: reserved_room becomes 100.

5. Then transaction 2 reserves the room. The **isolation** property in ACID means database transactions must complete their tasks independently from other transactions. So data changes made by transaction 1 are not visible to transaction 2 until transaction 1 is completed (committed). So transaction 2 still sees total_reserved

as 99 and reserves the room by updating the inventory: reserved_room becomes 100. This results in the system allowing both users to book a room, but there is only 1 room left.

6. Transaction 1 successfully commits the change.

7. Transaction 2 successfully commits the change.

The solution to this problem generally requires some form of locking mechanism. We explore the following techniques:

- Pessimistic locking
- Optimistic locking
- Database constraints

Before jumping into a fix, let's take a look at the SQL pseudo-code utilized to reserve a room. The SQL has two parts:

- Check room inventory
- Reserve a room

```
# step 1: check room inventory
SELECT date, total_inventory, total_reserved
FROM room_type_inventory
WHERE room_type_id = ${roomTypeId} AND hotel_id = ${hotelId}
AND date between ${startDate} and ${endDate}

# For every entry returned from step 1
if((total_reserved + ${numberOfRoomsToReserve}) > 110% *
  total_inventory) {
    Rollback
}

# step 2: reserve rooms
UPDATE room_type_inventory
SET total_reserved = total_reserved + ${numberOfRoomsToReserve}
WHERE room_type_id = ${roomTypeId}
AND date between ${startDate} and ${endDate}

Commit
```

Option 1: Pessimistic locking

The pessimistic locking [6], also called pessimistic concurrency control, prevents simultaneous updates by placing a lock on a record as soon as one user starts to update it. Other users who attempt to update the record have to wait until the first user has released the lock (committed the changes).

For MySQL, the "SELECT ... FOR UPDATE" statement works by locking the rows returned by a selection query. Let's assume a transaction is started by "transaction 1". Other transactions have to wait for transaction 1 to finish before beginning another transaction. A detailed explanation is shown in Figure 7.12.

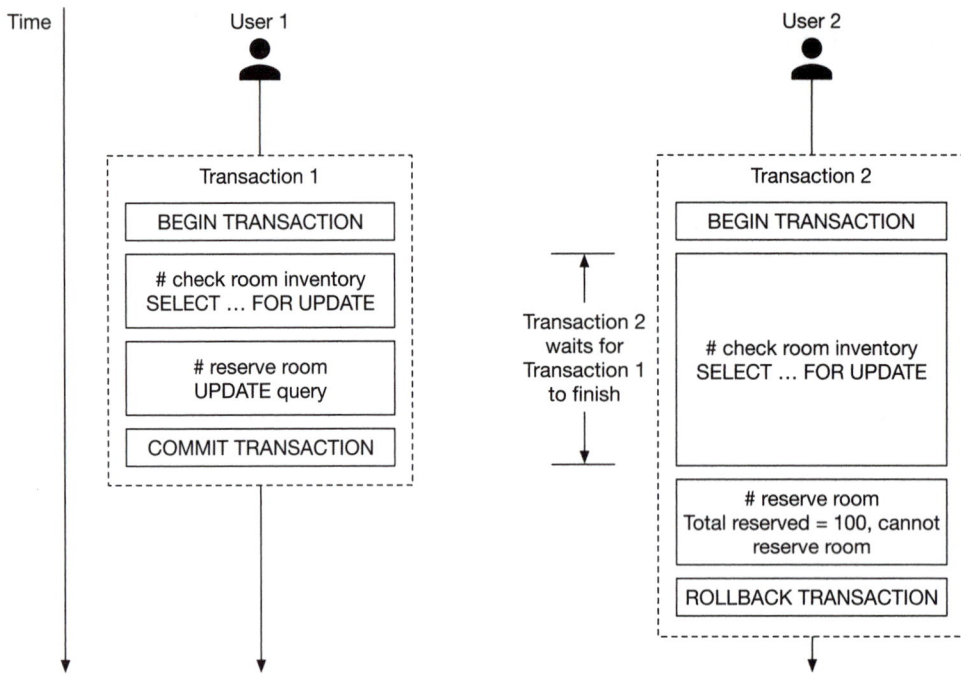

Figure 7.12: Pessimistic locking

In Figure 7.12, the "SELECT ... FOR UPDATE" statement of transaction 2 waits for transaction 1 to finish because transaction 1 locks the rows. After transaction 1 finishes, total_reserved becomes 100, which means there is no room for user 2 to book.

Pros:

- Prevents applications from updating data that is being or has been changed.

- It is easy to implement and it avoids conflict by serializing updates. Pessimistic locking is useful when data contention is heavy.

Cons:

- Deadlocks may occur when multiple resources are locked. Writing deadlock-free application code could be challenging.

- This approach is not scalable. If a transaction is locked for too long, other transactions cannot access the resource. This has a significant impact on database performance, especially when transactions are long-lived or involve a lot of entities.

Due to these limitations, we do not recommend pessimistic locking for the reservation system.

Option 2: Optimistic locking

Optimistic locking [7], also referred to as optimistic concurrency control, allows multiple concurrent users to attempt to update the same resource.

There are two common ways to implement optimistic locking: version number and timestamp. Version number is generally considered to be a better option because the server clock can be inaccurate over time. We explain how optimistic locking works with version number.

Figure 7.13 shows a successful case and a failure case.

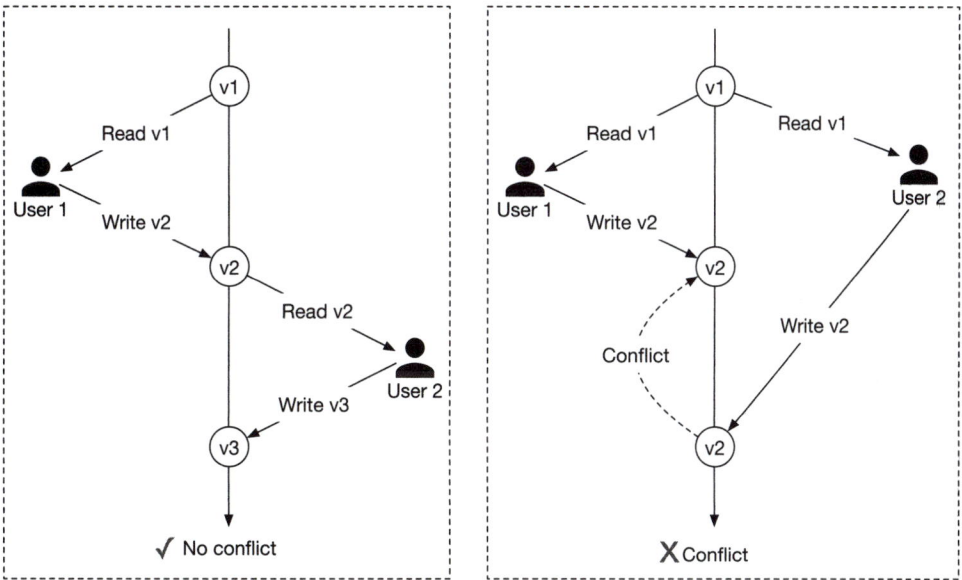

Figure 7.13: Optimistic locking

1. A new column called version is added to the database table.

2. Before a user modifies a database row, the application reads the version number of the row.

3. When the user updates the row, the application increases the version number by 1 and writes it back to the database.

4. A database validation check is put in place; the next version number should exceed the current version number by 1. The transaction aborts if the validation fails and the user tries again from step 2.

Optimistic locking is usually faster than pessimistic locking because we do not lock the database. However, the performance of optimistic locking drops dramatically when concurrency is high.

To understand why, consider the case when many clients try to reserve a hotel room at the same time. Because there is no limit on how many clients can read the available room count, all of them read back the same available room count and the current version number. When different clients make reservations and write back the results to the database, only one of them will succeed, and the rest of the clients receive a version check failure message. These clients have to retry. In the subsequent round of retries, there is only one successful client again, and the rest have to retry. Although the end result is correct, repeated retries cause a very unpleasant user experience.

Pros:

- It prevents applications from editing stale data.
- We don't need to lock the database resource. There's actually no locking from the database point of view. It's entirely up to the application to handle the logic with the version number.
- Optimistic locking is generally used when the data contention is low. When conflicts are rare, transactions can complete without the expense of managing locks.

Cons:

- Performance is poor when data contention is heavy.

Optimistic locking is a good option for a hotel reservation system since the QPS for reservations is usually not high.

Option 3: Database constraints

This approach is very similar to optimistic locking. Let's explore how it works. In the room_type_inventory table, add the following constraint:

```
CONSTRAINT `check_room_count` CHECK((`total_inventory - total_reserved
` >= 0))
```

Using the same example as shown in Figure 7.14, when user 2 tries to reserve a room, total_reserved becomes 101, which violates the total_inventory $(100)-$ total_reserved $(101) \geq 0$ constraint. The transaction is then rolled back.

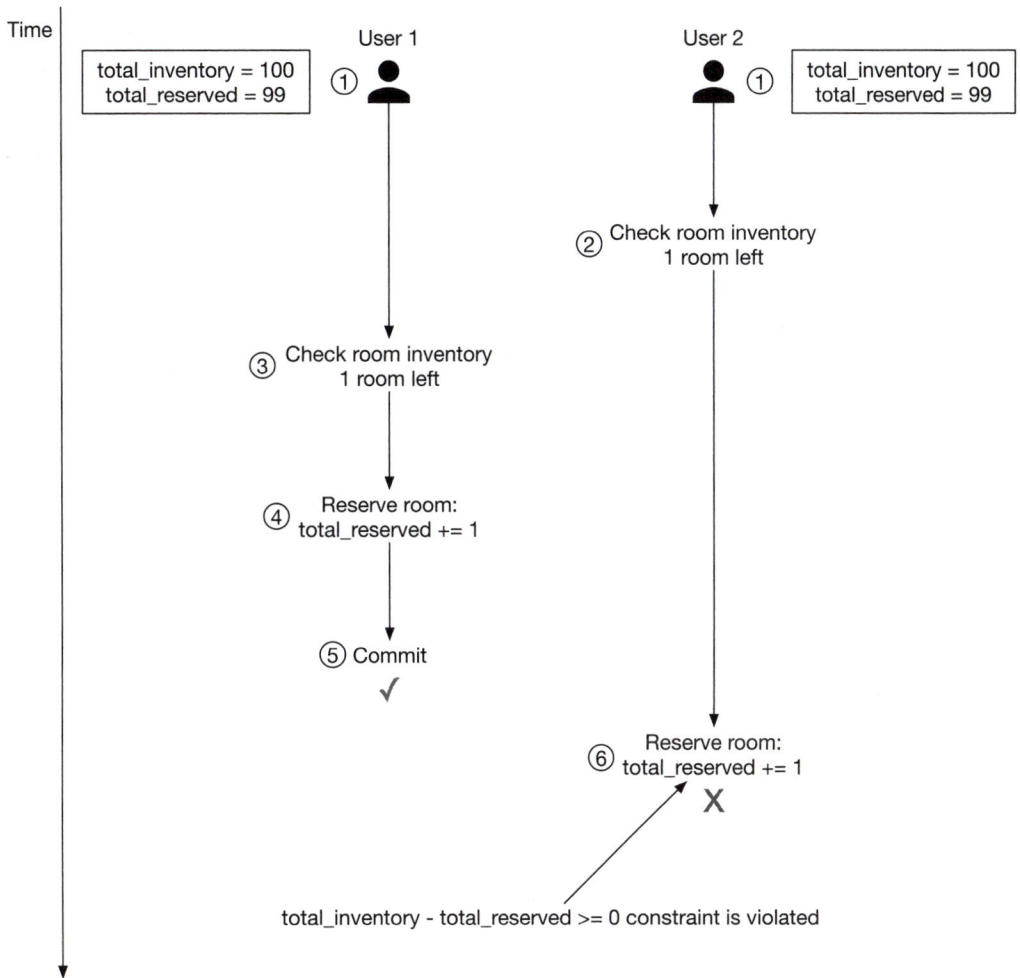

Figure 7.14: Database constraint

Pros

- Easy to implement.
- It works well when data contention is minimal.

Cons

- Similar to optimistic locking, when data contention is heavy, it can result in a high volume of failures. Users could see there are rooms available, but when they try to book one, they get the "no rooms available" response. The experience can be frustrating to users.
- The database constraints cannot be version-controlled easily like the application code.
- Not all databases support constraints. It might cause problems when we migrate from one database solution to another.

Since this approach is easy to implement and the data contention for a hotel reservation is usually not high (low QPS), it is another good option for the hotel reservation system.

Scalability

Usually, the load of the hotel reservation system is not high. However, the interviewer might have a follow-up question: "what if the hotel reservation system is used not just for a hotel chain but for a popular travel site such as booking.com or expedia.com?" In this case, the QPS could be 1,000 times higher.

When the system load is high, we need to understand what might become the bottleneck. All our services are stateless, so they can be easily expanded by adding more servers. The database, however, contains all the states and cannot be scaled up by simply adding more databases. Let's explore how to scale the database.

Database sharding

One way to scale the database is to apply database sharding. The idea is to split the data into multiple databases so that each of them only contains a portion of data.

When we shard a database, we need to consider how to distribute the data. As we can see from the data model section, most queries need to filter by hotel_id. So a natural conclusion is we shard data by hotel_id. In Figure 7.15, the load is spread among 16 shards. Assume the QPS is 30,000. After database sharding, each shard handles $\frac{30,000}{16} = 1,875$ QPS, which is within a single MySQL server's load capacity.

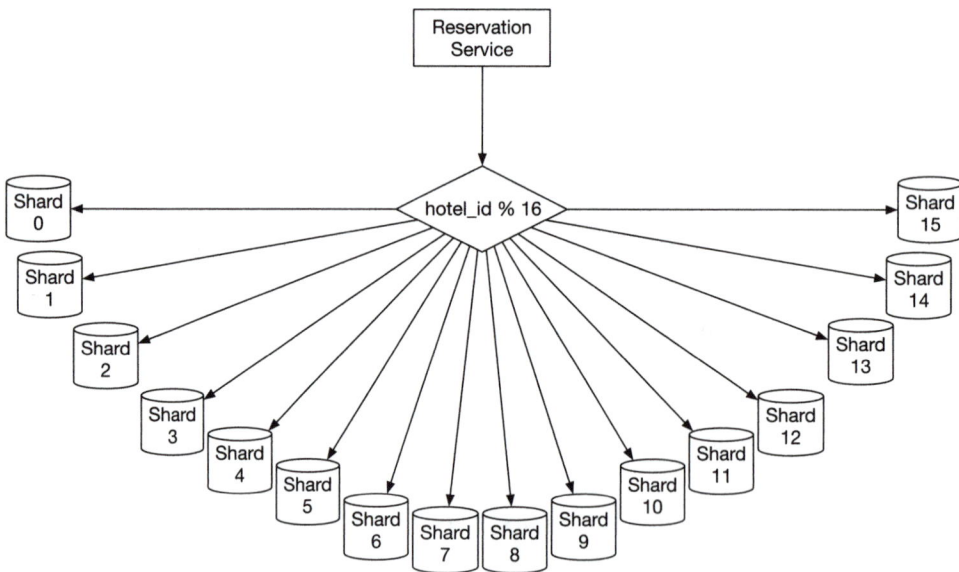

Figure 7.15: Database sharding

Caching

The hotel inventory data has an interesting characteristic; only current and future hotel inventory data are meaningful because customers can only book rooms in the near future.

So for the storage choice, ideally we want to have a time-to-live (TTL) mechanism to expire old data automatically. Historical data can be queried on a different database. Redis is a good choice because TTL and Least Recently Used (LRU) cache eviction policy help us make optimal use of memory.

If the loading speed and database scalability become an issue (for instance, we are designing at booking.com or Expedia's scale), we can add a cache layer on top of the database and move the check room inventory and reserve room logic to the cache layer, as shown in Figure 7.16. In this design, only a small percentage of the requests hit the inventory database as most ineligible requests are blocked by the inventory cache. One thing worth mentioning is that even when there is enough inventory shown in Redis, we still need to recheck the inventory at the database side as a precaution. The database is the source of truth for the inventory data.

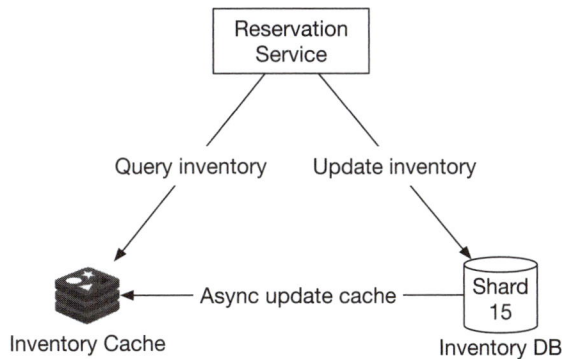

Figure 7.16: Caching

Let's first go over each component in this system.

Reservation service: supports the following inventory management APIs:

- Query the number of available rooms for a given hotel, room type, and date range.
- Reserve a room by executing total_reserved +1.
- Update inventory when a user cancels a reservation.

Inventory cache: all inventory management query operations are moved to the inventory cache (Redis) and we need to pre-populate inventory data to the cache. The cache is a key-value store with the following structure:

```
key: hotelID_roomTypeID_{date}
value: the number of available rooms for the given hotel ID,
   room type ID and date.
```

For a hotel reservation system, the volume of read operations (check room inventory) is an order of magnitude higher than write operations. Most of the read operations are answered by the cache.

Inventory DB: stores inventory data as the source of truth.

New challenges posed by the cache

Adding a cache layer significantly increases the system scalability and throughput, but it also introduces a new challenge: how to maintain data consistency between the database and the cache.

When a user books a room, two operations are executed in the happy path:

1. Query room inventory to find out if there are enough rooms left. The query runs on the Inventory cache.

2. Update inventory data. The inventory DB is updated first. The change is then propagated to the cache asynchronously. This asynchronous cache update could be invoked by the application code, which updates the inventory cache after data is saved to the database. It could also be propagated using change data capture (CDC) [8]. CDC is a mechanism that reads data changes from the database and applies the changes to another data system. One common solution is Debezium [9]. It uses a source connector to read changes from a database and applies them to cache solutions such as Redis [10].

Because the inventory data is updated on the database first, there is a possibility that the cache does not reflect the latest inventory data. For example, the cache may report there is still an empty room when the database says there is no room left or vice versa.

If you think carefully, you find that the inconsistency between inventory cache and database actually does not matter, as long as the database does the final inventory validation check.

Let's take a look at an example. Let's say the cache says there is still an empty room, but the database says no. In this case, when the user queries the room inventory, they find there is still room available, so they try to reserve it. When the request reaches the inventory database, the database does the validation and finds that there is no room left. In this case, the client receives an error, indicating someone else just booked the last room before them. When a user refreshes the website, they probably see there is no room left because the database has synchronized inventory data to the cache, before they click the refresh button.

Pros

- Reduced database load. Since read queries are answered by the cache layer, database load is significantly reduced.

- High performance. Read queries are very fast because results are fetched from memory.

Cons

- Maintaining data consistency between the database and cache is hard. We need to think carefully about how this inconsistency affects user experience.

Data consistency among services

In a traditional monolithic architecture [11], a shared relational database is used to ensure data consistency. In our microservice design, we chose a hybrid approach by having Reservation Service handle both reservation and inventory APIs so that the inventory and reservation database tables are stored in the same relational database. As explained in the "Concurrency issues" section on page 204, this arrangement allows us to leverage the ACID properties of the relational database to elegantly handle many concurrency issues that arise during the reservation flow.

However, if your interviewer is a microservice purist, they might challenge this hybrid approach. In their mind, for a microservice architecture, each microservice has its own databases as shown on the right in Figure 7.17.

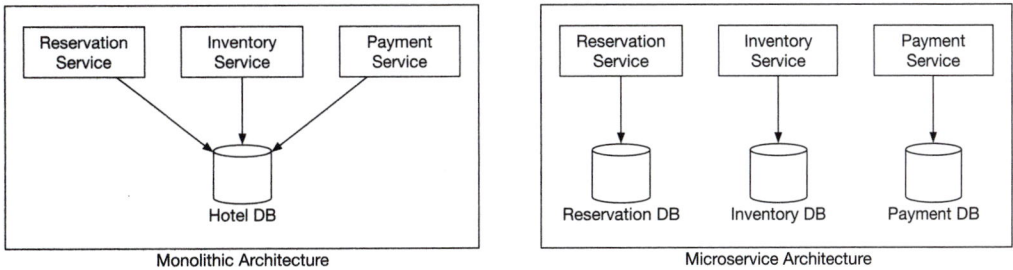

Figure 7.17: Monolithic vs microservice

This pure design introduces many data consistency issues. Since this is the first time we cover microservices, let's explain how and why it happens. To make it easier to understand, only two services are used in this discussion. In the real world, there could be hundreds of microservices within a company. In a monolithic architecture, as shown in Figure 7.18, different operations can be wrapped in a single transaction to ensure ACID properties.

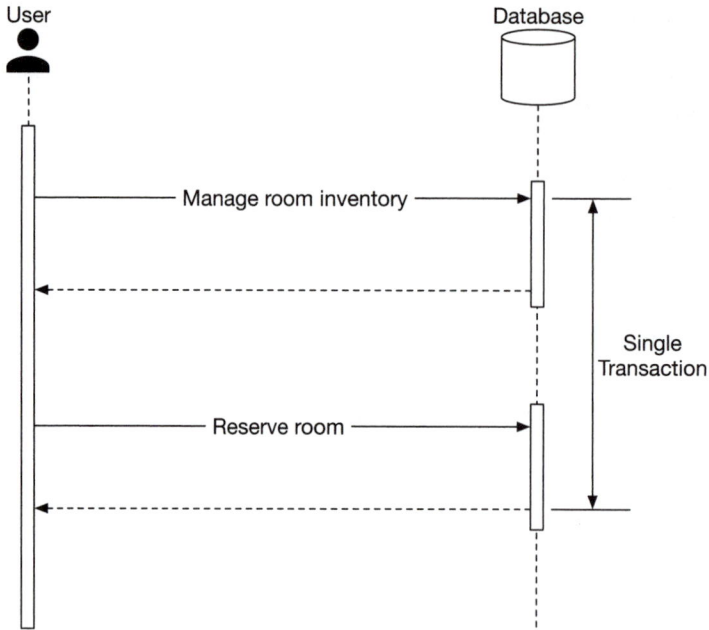

Figure 7.18: Monolithic architecture

However, in a microservice architecture, each service has its own database. One logically atomic operation can span multiple services. This means we cannot use a single transaction to ensure data consistency. As shown in Figure 7.19, if the update operation fails in the reservation database, we need to roll back the reserved room count in the inventory database. Generally, there is only one happy path, but many failure cases that could cause data inconsistency.

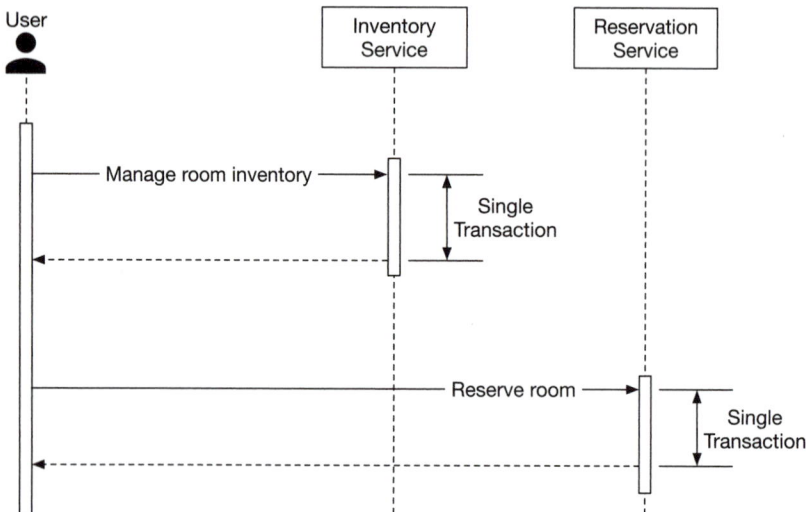

Figure 7.19: Microservice architecture

To address the data inconsistency, here is a high-level summary of industry-proven techniques. If you want to read the details, please refer to the reference materials.

- Two-phase commit (2PC) [12]. 2PC is a database protocol used to guarantee atomic transaction commit across multiple nodes, i.e., either all nodes succeeded or all nodes failed. Because 2PC is a blocking protocol, a single node failure blocks the progress until the node has recovered. It's not performant.
- Saga. A Saga is a sequence of local transactions. Each transaction updates and publishes a message to trigger the next transaction step. If a step fails, the saga executes compensating transactions to undo the changes that were made by preceding transactions [13]. 2PC works as a single commit to perform ACID transactions while Saga consists of multiple steps and relies on eventual consistency.

It is worth noting that addressing data inconsistency between microservices requires some complicated mechanisms that greatly increase the complexity of the overall design. It is up to you as an architect to decide if the added complexity is worth it. For this problem, we decided that it was not worth it and so went with the more pragmatic approach of storing reservation and inventory data under the same relational database.

Step 4 - Wrap Up

In this chapter, we presented a design for a hotel reservation system. We started by gathering requirements and calculating a back-of-the-envelope estimation to understand the scale. In the high-level design, we presented the API design, the first draft of the data model, and the system architecture diagram. In the deep dive, we explored alternative database schema design as we realized reservations should be made at the room type level, as opposed to specific rooms. We discussed race conditions in depth and proposed a few potential solutions:

- pessimistic locking
- optimistic locking
- database constraints

We then discussed different approaches to scale the system, including database sharding and using Redis cache. Lastly, we went through data consistency issues in microservice architecture and briefly went through a few solutions.

Congratulations on getting this far! Now give yourself a pat on the back. Good job!

Chapter Summary

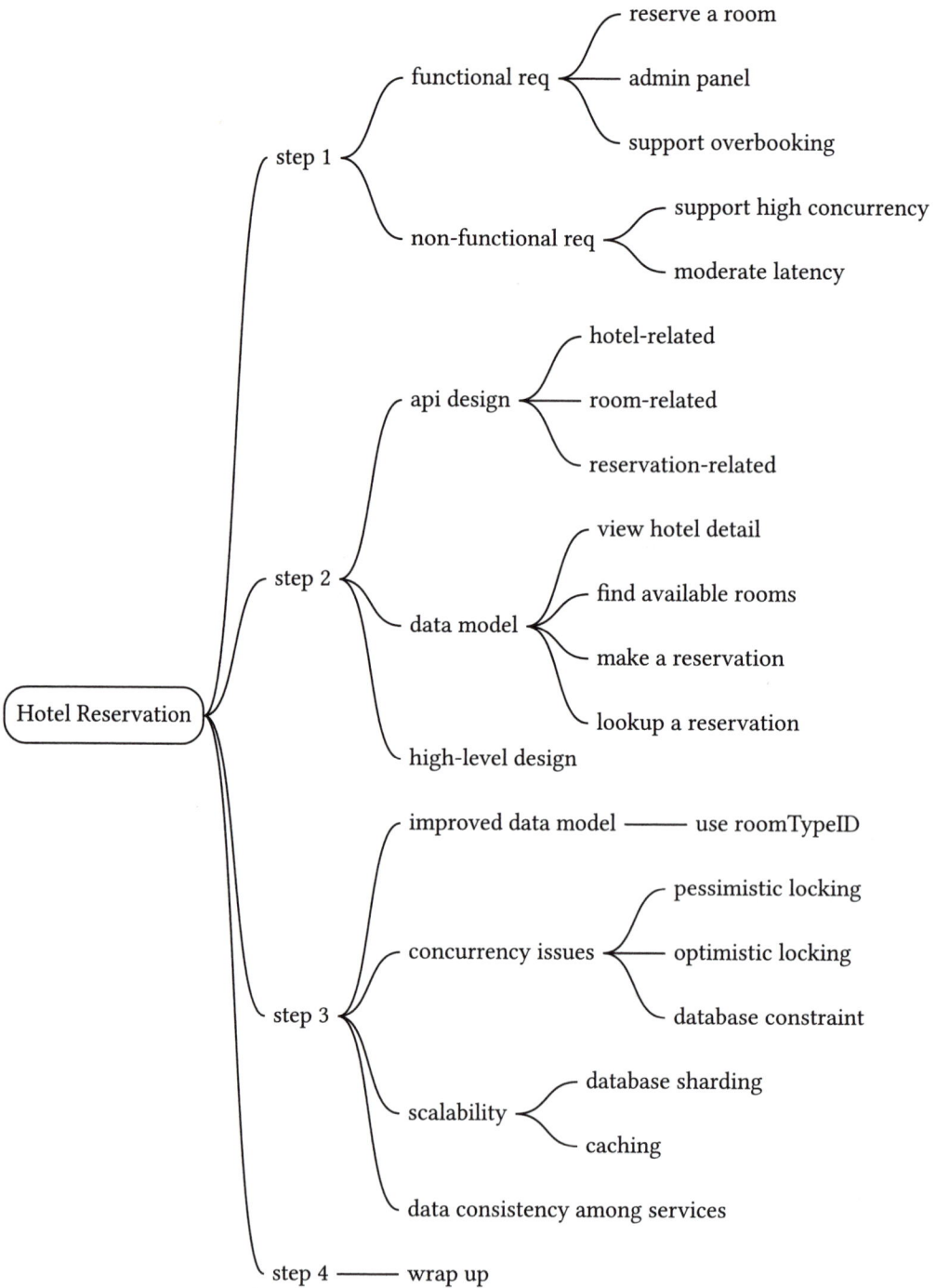

Hotel Reservation

- **step 1**
  - functional req
    - reserve a room
    - admin panel
    - support overbooking
  - non-functional req
    - support high concurrency
    - moderate latency
- **step 2**
  - api design
    - hotel-related
    - room-related
    - reservation-related
  - data model
    - view hotel detail
    - find available rooms
    - make a reservation
    - lookup a reservation
  - high-level design
- **step 3**
  - improved data model —— use roomTypeID
  - concurrency issues
    - pessimistic locking
    - optimistic locking
    - database constraint
  - scalability
    - database sharding
    - caching
  - data consistency among services
- **step 4** —— wrap up

Reference Material

[1] What Are The Benefits of Microservices Architecture? https://www.appdynamics.com/topics/benefits-of-microservices.

[2] Microservices. https://en.wikipedia.org/wiki/Microservices.

[3] gRPC. https://www.grpc.io/docs/what-is-grpc/introduction/.

[4] Booking.com iOS app.

[5] Serializability. https://en.wikipedia.org/wiki/Serializability.

[6] Optimistic and pessimistic record locking. https://ibm.co/3Eb293O.

[7] Optimistic concurrency control. https://en.wikipedia.org/wiki/Optimistic_concurrency_control.

[8] Change data capture. https://docs.oracle.com/cd/B10500_01/server.920/a96520/cdc.htm.

[9] Debizium. https://debezium.io/.

[10] Redis sink. https://bit.ly/3r3AEUD.

[11] Monolithic Architecture. https://microservices.io/patterns/monolithic.html.

[12] Two-phase commit protocol. https://en.wikipedia.org/wiki/Two-phase_commit_protocol.

[13] Saga. https://microservices.io/patterns/data/saga.html.

8   Distributed Email Service

In this chapter, we design a large-scale email service, such as Gmail, Outlook, or Yahoo Mail. The growth of the internet has led to an explosion in the volume of emails. In 2020, Gmail had over 1.8 billion active users and Outlook had over 400 million users worldwide [1] [2].

Figure 8.1: Popular email providers

Step 1 - Understand the Problem and Establish Design Scope

Over the years, email services have changed significantly in complexity and scale. A modern email service is a complex system with many features. There is no way we can design a real-world system in 45 minutes. So before jumping into the design, we definitely want to ask clarifying questions to narrow down the scope.

Candidate: How many people use the product?
Interviewer: One billion users.

Candidate: I think the following features are important:

- Authentication.
- Send and receive emails.
- Fetch all emails.
- Filter emails by read and unread status.
- Search emails by subject, sender, and body.
- Anti-spam and anti-virus.

Interviewer: That's a good list. We don't need to worry about authentication. Let's focus on the other features you mentioned.

Candidate: How do users connect with mail servers?

Interviewer: Traditionally, users connect with mail servers through native clients that use SMTP, POP, IMAP, and vendor-specific protocols. Those protocols are legacy to some extent, yet still very popular. For this interview, let's assume HTTP is used for client and server communication.

Candidate: Can emails have attachments?

Interviewer: Yes.

Non-functional requirements

Next, let's go over the most important non-functional requirements.

Reliability. We should not lose email data.

Availability. Email and user data should be automatically replicated across multiple nodes to ensure availability. Besides, the system should continue to function despite partial system failures.

Scalability. As the number of users grows, the system should be able to handle the increasing number of users and emails. The performance of the system should not degrade with more users or emails.

Flexibility and extensibility. A flexible/extensible system allows us to add new features or improve performance easily by adding new components. Traditional email protocols such as POP and IMAP have very limited functionality (more on this in high-level design). Therefore, we may need custom protocols to satisfy the flexibility and extensibility requirements.

Back-of-the-envelope estimation

Let's do a back-of-the-envelope calculation to determine the scale and to discover some challenges our solution will need to address. By design, emails are storage heavy applications.

- 1 billion users.

- Assume the average number of emails a person sends per day is 10. QPS for sending emails $= \dfrac{10^9 \times 10}{10^5} = 100,000$.
- Assume the average number of emails a person receives in a day is 40 [3] and the average size of email metadata is 50 KB. Metadata refers to everything related to an email, excluding attachment files.
- Assume metadata is stored in a database. Storage requirement for maintaining metadata in 1 year: 1 billion users × 40 emails/day × 365 days × 50 KB = 730 PB.
- Assume 20% of emails contain an attachment and the average attachment size is 500 KB.
- Storage for attachments in 1 year is: 1 billion users ×40 emails/day × 365 days × 20% × 500 KB = 1,460 PB

From this back-of-the-envelope calculation, it's clear we would deal with a lot of data. So, it's likely that we need a distributed database solution.

Step 2 - Propose High-level Design and Get Buy-in

In this section, we first discuss some basics about email servers and how email servers evolve over time. Then we look at the high-level design of distributed email servers. The content is structured as follows:

- Email knowledge 101
- Traditional mail servers
- Distributed mail servers

Email knowledge 101

There are various email protocols that are used to send and receive emails. Historically, most mail servers use email protocols such as POP, IMAP, and SMTP.

Email protocols

SMTP: Simple Mail Transfer Protocol (SMTP) is the standard protocol for **sending** emails from one mail server to another.

The most popular protocols for **retrieving** emails are known as Post Office Protocol (POP) and the Internet Mail Access Protocol (IMAP).

POP is a standard mail protocol to receive and download emails from a remote mail server to a local email client. Once emails are downloaded to your computer or phone, they are deleted from the email server, which means you can only access emails on one computer or phone. The details of POP are covered in RFC 1939 [4]. POP requires mail clients to download the entire email. This can take a long time if an email contains a large attachment.

IMAP is also a standard mail protocol for receiving emails for a local email client. When you read an email, you are connected to an external mail server, and data is transferred to your local device. IMAP only downloads a message when you click it, and emails are not deleted from mail servers, meaning that you can access emails from multiple devices. IMAP is the most widely used protocol for individual email accounts. It works well when the connection is slow because only the email header information is downloaded until opened.

HTTPS is not technically a mail protocol, but it can be used to access your mailbox, particularly for web-based email. For example, it's common for Microsoft Outlook to talk to mobile devices over HTTPS, on a custom-made protocol called ActiveSync [5].

Domain name service (DNS)

A DNS server is used to look up the mail exchanger record (MX record) for the recipient's domain. If you run DNS lookup for gmail.com from the command line, you may get MX records as shown in Figure 8.2.

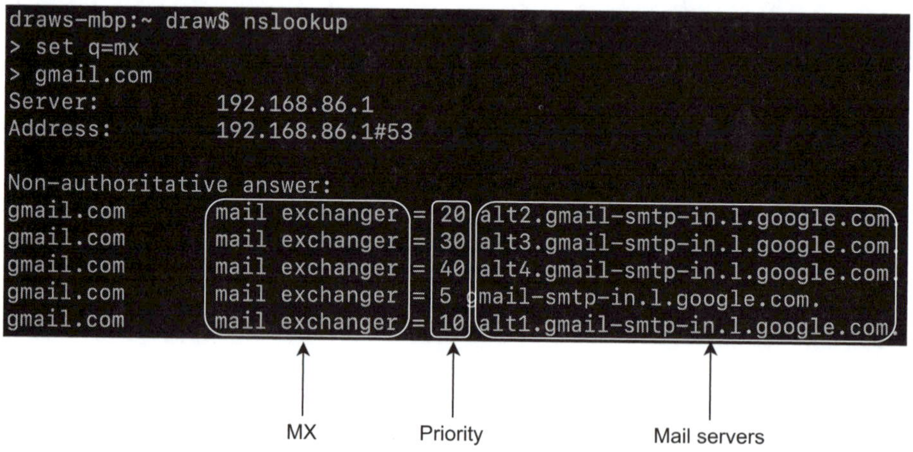

```
draws-mbp:~ draw$ nslookup
> set q=mx
> gmail.com
Server:         192.168.86.1
Address:        192.168.86.1#53

Non-authoritative answer:
gmail.com    mail exchanger = 20 alt2.gmail-smtp-in.l.google.com
gmail.com    mail exchanger = 30 alt3.gmail-smtp-in.l.google.com
gmail.com    mail exchanger = 40 alt4.gmail-smtp-in.l.google.com
gmail.com    mail exchanger = 5 gmail-smtp-in.l.google.com.
gmail.com    mail exchanger = 10 alt1.gmail-smtp-in.l.google.com
```

MX   Priority   Mail servers

Figure 8.2: MX records

The priority numbers indicate preferences, where the mail server with a lower priority number is more preferred. In Figure 8.2, `gmail-smtp-in.l.google.com` is used first (priority 5). A sending mail server will attempt to connect and send messages to this mail server first. If the connection fails, the sending mail server will attempt to connect to the mail server with the next lowest priority, which is `alt1.gmail-smtp-in.l.google.com` (priority 10).

Attachment

An email attachment is sent along with an email message, commonly with Base64 encoding [6]. There is usually a size limit for an email attachment. For example, Outlook and Gmail limit the size of attachments to 20MB and 25MB respectively as of June 2021. This number is highly configurable and varies from individual to corporate accounts. Multipurpose Internet Mail Extension (MIME) [7] is a specification that allows the attachment to be sent over the internet.

Traditional mail servers

Before we dive into distributed mail servers, let's dig a little bit through the history and
see how traditional mail servers work, as doing so provides good lessons about how to
scale an email server system. You can consider a traditional mail server as a system that
works when there are limited email users, usually on a single server.

Traditional mail server architecture

Figure 8.3 describes what happens when Alice sends an email to Bob, using traditional
email servers.

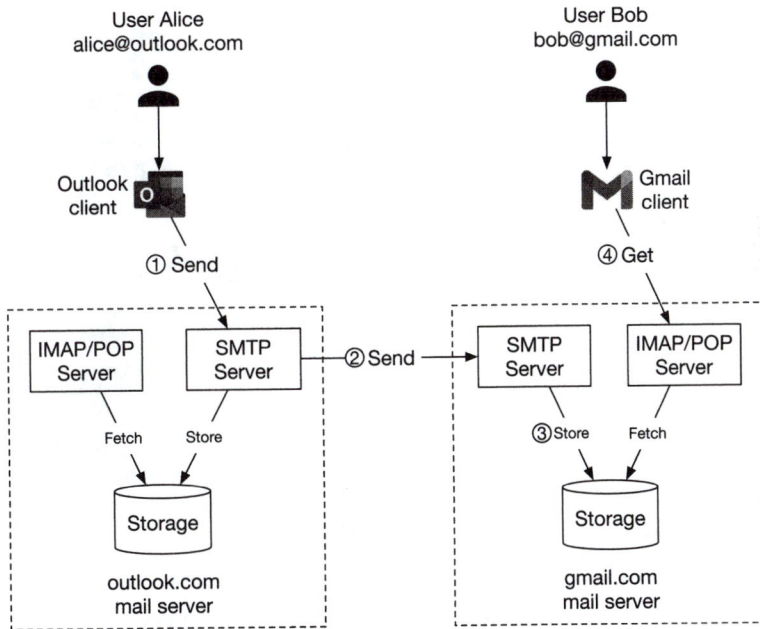

Figure 8.3: Traditional mail servers

The process consists of 4 steps:

1. Alice logs in to her Outlook client, composes an email, and presses the "send" button.
   The email is sent to the Outlook mail server. The communication protocol between
   the Outlook client and the mail server is SMTP.

2. Outlook mail server queries the DNS (not shown in the diagram) to find the address of
   the recipient's SMTP server. In this case, it is Gmail's SMTP server. Next, it transfers
   the email to the Gmail mail server. The communication protocol between the mail
   servers is SMTP.

3. The Gmail server stores the email and makes it available to Bob, the recipient.

4. Gmail client fetches new emails through the IMAP/POP server when Bob logs in to
   Gmail.

Storage

In a traditional mail server, emails were stored in local file directories and each email was stored in a separate file with a unique name. Each user maintained a user directory to store configuration data and mailboxes. Maildir was a popular way to store email messages on the mail server (Figure 8.4).

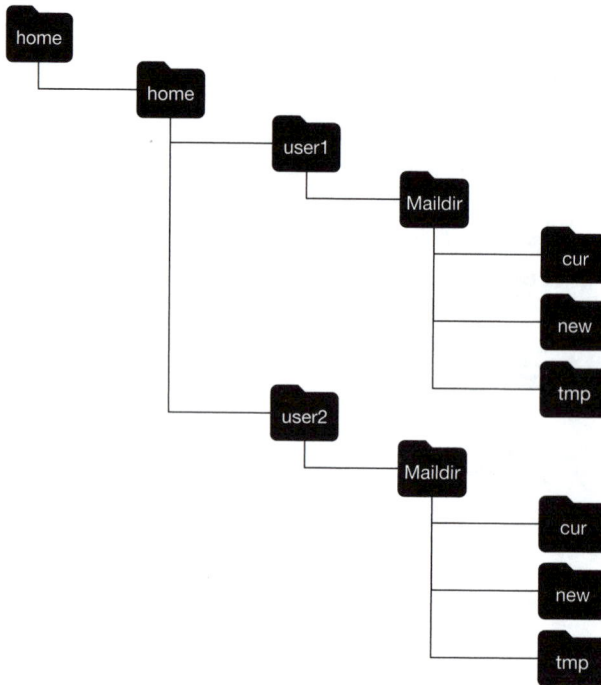

Figure 8.4: Maildir

File directories worked well when the user base was small, but it was challenging to retrieve and backup billions of emails. As the email volume grew and the file structure became more complex, disk I/O became a bottleneck. The local directories also don't satisfy our high availability and reliability requirements. The disk can be damaged and servers can go down. We need a more reliable distributed storage layer.

Email functionality has come a long way since it was invented in the 1960s, from text-based format to rich features such as multimedia, threading [8], search, labels, and more. But email protocols (POP, IMAP, and SMTP) were invented a long time ago and they were not designed to support these new features, nor were they scalable to support billions of users.

Distributed mail servers

Distributed mail servers are designed to support modern use cases and solve the problems of scale and resiliency. This section covers email APIs, distributed email server architecture, email sending, and email receiving flows.

Email APIs

Email APIs can mean very different things for different mail clients, or at different stages of an email's life cycle. For example;

- SMTP/POP/IMAP APIs for native mobile clients.
- SMTP communications between sender and receiver mail servers.
- RESTful API over HTTP for full-featured and interactive web-based email applications.

Due to the length limitations of this book, we cover only some of the most important APIs for webmail. A common way for webmail to communicate is through the HTTP protocol.

1. Endpoint: `POST /v1/messages`

Sends a message to the recipients in the To, Cc, and Bcc headers.

2. Endpoint: `GET /v1/folders`

Returns all folders of an email account.

Response:

```
[{id: string       Unique folder identifier.
  name: string     Name of the folder.
                   According to RFC6154 [9], the default folders can be one of
                   the following:
                   All, Archive, Drafts, Flagged, Junk, Sent, and Trash.
  user_id: string  Reference to the account owner
}]
```

3. Endpoint: `GET /v1/folders/{:folder_id}/messages`

Returns all messages under a folder. Keep in mind this is a highly simplified API. In reality, this needs to support pagination.

Response:

List of message objects.

4. Endpoint: `GET /v1/messages/{:message_id}`

Gets all information about a specific message. Messages are core building blocks for an email application, containing information about the sender, recipients, message subject, body, attachments, etc.

Response:

A message's object.

```
{
    user_id: string                          // Reference to the account owner.
    from: name: string, email: string        // <name, email> pair of the sender.
    to: [name: string, email: string]        // A list of <name, email> paris
    subject: string                          // Subject of an email
    body: string                             // Message body
    is_read: boolean                         // Indicate if a message is read or not.
}
```

Distributed mail server architecture

While it is easy to set up an email server that handles a small number of users, it is difficult to scale beyond one server. This is mainly because traditional email servers were designed to work with a single server only. Synchronizing data across servers can be difficult, and keeping emails from being misclassified as spam by recipients' mail servers is very challenging. In this section, we explore how to leverage cloud technologies to make it easier. The high-level design is shown in Figure 8.5.

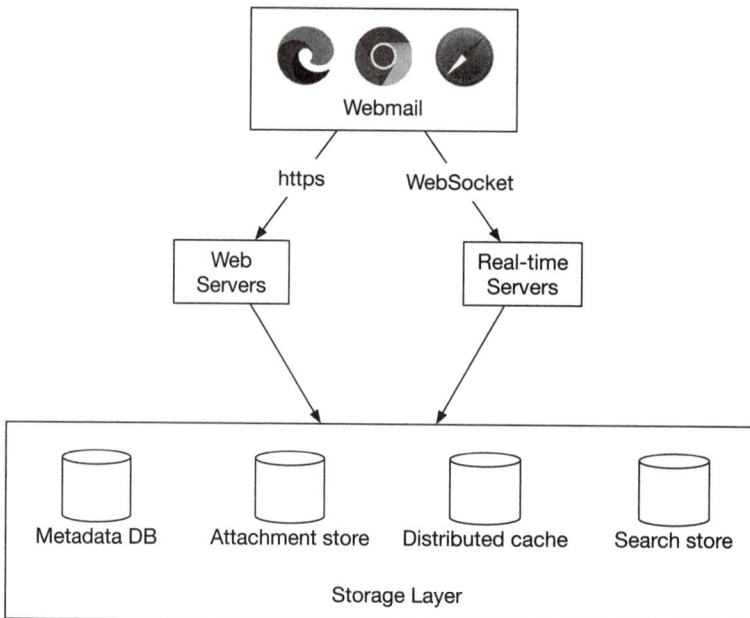

Figure 8.5: High-level design

Let us take a close look at each component.

Webmail. Users use web browsers to receive and send emails.

Web servers. Web servers are public-facing request/response services, used to manage features such as login, signup, user profile, etc. In our design, all email API requests, such as sending an email, loading mail folders, loading all mails in a folder, etc., go through web servers.

Real-time servers. Real-time servers are responsible for pushing new email updates to clients in real-time. Real-time servers are stateful servers because they need to maintain persistent connections. To support real-time communication, we have a few options, such as long polling and WebSocket. WebSocket is a more elegant solution but one drawback of it is browser compatibility. A possible solution is to establish a WebSocket connection whenever possible and to use long-polling as a fallback.

Here is an example of a real-world mail server (Apache James [10]) that implements the JSON Meta Application Protocol (JMAP) subprotocol over WebSocket [11].

Metadata database. This database stores mail metadata including mail subject, body, from user, to users, etc. We discuss the database choice in the deep dive section.

Attachment store. We choose object stores such as Amazon Simple Storage Service (S3) as the attachment store. S3 is a scalable storage infrastructure that's suitable for storing large files such as images, videos, files, etc. Attachments can take up to 25 MB in size. NoSQL column-family databases like Cassandra might not be a good fit for the following two reasons:

- Even though Cassandra supports blob data type and its maximum theoretical size for a blob is 2GB, the practical limit is less than 1MB [12].
- Another problem with putting attachments in Cassandra is that we can't use a row cache as attachments take too much memory space.

Distributed cache. Since the most recent emails are repeatedly loaded by a client, caching recent emails in memory significantly improves the load time. We can use Redis here because it offers rich features such as lists and it is easy to scale.

Search store. The search store is a distributed document store. It uses a data structure called inverted index [13] that supports very fast full-text searches. We will discuss this in more detail in the deep dive section.

Now that we have discussed some of the most important components to build distributed mail servers, let's assemble together two main workflows.

- Email sending flow.
- Email receiving flow.

Email sending flow

The email sending flow is shown in Figure 8.6.

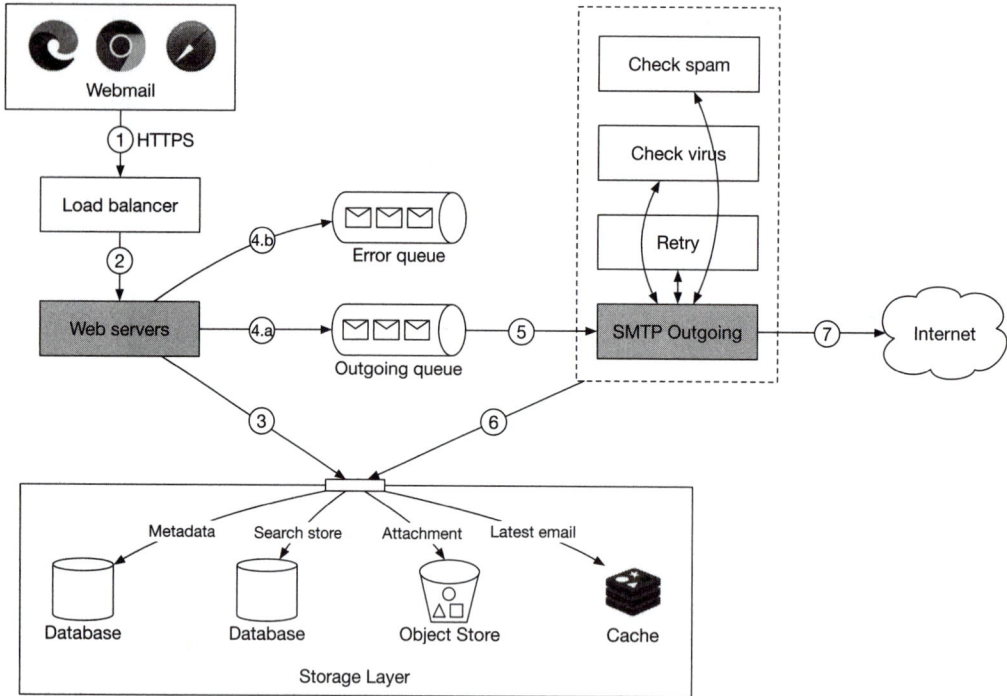

Figure 8.6: Email sending flow

1. A user writes an email on webmail and presses the send button. The request is sent to the load balancer.

2. The load balancer makes sure it doesn't exceed the rate limit and routes traffic to web servers.

3. Web servers are responsible for:

   - Basic email validation. Each incoming email is checked against pre-defined rules such as email size limit.

   - Checking if the domain of the recipient's email address is the same as the sender. If it is the same, the web server ensures the email data is spam and virus free. If so, email data is inserted into the sender's "Sent Folder" and recipient's "Inbox Folder". The recipient can fetch the email directly via the RESTful API. There is no need to go to step 4.

4. Message queues.

   4.1. If basic email validation succeeds, the email data is passed to the outgoing queue. If the attachment is too large to fit in the queue, we could store the attachment in the object store and save the object reference in the queued message.

   4.2. If basic email validation fails, the email is put in the error queue.

5. SMTP outgoing workers pull messages from the outgoing queue and make sure emails are spam and virus free.

6. The outgoing email is stored in the "Sent Folder" of the storage layer.

7. SMTP outgoing workers send the email to the recipient mail server.

Each message in the outgoing queue contains all the metadata required to create an email. A distributed message queue is a critical component that allows asynchronous mail processing. By decoupling SMTP outgoing workers from the web servers, we can scale SMTP outgoing workers independently.

We monitor the size of the outgoing queue very closely. If there are many emails stuck in the queue, we need to analyze the cause of the issue. Here are some possibilities:

- The recipient's mail server is unavailable. In this case, we need to retry sending the email at a later time. Exponential backoff [14] might be a good retry strategy.

- Not enough consumers to send emails. In this case, we may need more consumers to reduce the processing time.

Email receiving flow

The following diagram demonstrates the email receiving flow.

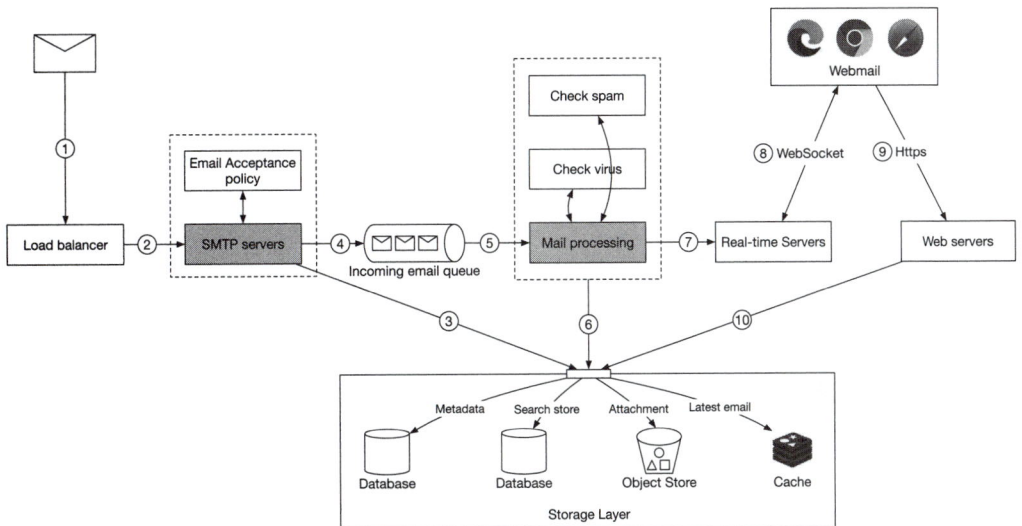

Figure 8.7: Email receiving flow

1. Incoming emails arrive at the SMTP load balancer.

2. The load balancer distributes traffic among SMTP servers. Email acceptance policy can be configured and applied at the SMTP-connection level. For example, invalid emails are bounced to avoid unnecessary email processing.

3. If the attachment of an email is too large to put into the queue, we can put it into the attachment store (S3).

4. Emails are put in the incoming email queue. The queue decouples mail processing workers from SMTP servers so they can be scaled independently. Moreover, the queue serves as a buffer in case the email volume surges.

5. Mail processing workers are responsible for a lot of tasks, including filtering out spam mails, stopping viruses, etc. The following steps assume an email passed the validation.

6. The email is stored in the mail storage, cache, and object data store.

7. If the receiver is currently online, the email is pushed to real-time servers.

8. Real-time servers are WebSocket servers that allow clients to receive new emails in real-time.

9. For offline users, emails are stored in the storage layer. When a user comes back online, the webmail client connects to web servers via RESTful API.

10. Web servers pull new emails from the storage layer and return them to the client.

Step 3 - Design Deep Dive

Now that we have talked about all the parts of the email server, let's go deeper into some key components and examine how to scale the system.

- Metadata database
- Search
- Deliverability
- Scalability

Metadata database

In this section, we discuss the characteristics of email metadata, choosing the right database, data model, and conversation threads (bonus point).

Characteristics of email metadata

- Email headers are usually small and frequently accessed.
- Email body sizes can range from small to big but are infrequently accessed. You normally only read an email once.
- Most of the mail operations, such as fetching mails, marking an email as read, and searching are isolated to an individual user. In other words, mails owned by a user are only accessible by that user and all the mail operations are performed by the same user.
- Data recency impacts data usage. Users usually only read the most recent emails. 82% of read queries are for data younger than 16 days [15].
- Data has high-reliability requirements. Data loss is not acceptable.

Choosing the right database

At Gmail or Outlook scale, the database system is usually custom-made to reduce input/output operations per second (IOPS) [16], as this can easily become a major constraint in the system. Choosing the right database is not easy. It is helpful to consider all the options we have on the table before deciding the most suitable one.

- Relational database. The main motivation behind this is to search through emails efficiently. We can build indexes for email header and body. With indexes, simple search queries are fast. However, relational databases are typically optimized for small chunks of data entries and are not ideal for large ones. A typical email is usually larger than a few KB and can easily be over 100KB when HTML is involved. You might argue that the BLOB data type is designed to support large data entries. However, search queries over unstructured BLOB data type are not efficient. So relational databases such as MySQL or PostgreSQL are not good fits.

- Distributed object storage. Another potential solution is to store raw emails in cloud storage such as Amazon S3, which can be a good option for backup storage, but it's hard to efficiently support features such as marking emails as read, searching emails based on keywords, threading emails, etc.

- NoSQL databases. Google Bigtable is used by Gmail, so it's definitely a viable solution. However, Bigtable is not open sourced and how email search is implemented remains a mystery. Cassandra might be a good option as well, but we haven't seen any large email providers use it yet.

Based on the above analysis, very few existing solutions seem to fit our needs perfectly. Large email service providers tend to build their own highly customized databases. However, in an interview setting, we won't have time to design a new distributed database, though it's important to explain the following characteristics that the database should have.

- A single column can be a single-digit of MB.
- Strong data consistency.
- Designed to reduce disk I/O.
- It should be highly available and fault-tolerant.
- It should be easy to create incremental backups.

Data model

One way to store the data is to use user_id as a partition key so data for one user is stored on a single shard. One limitation of this data model is that messages are not shared among multiple users. Since this is not a requirement for us in this interview, it's not something we need to worry about.

Now let us define the tables. The primary key contains two components, the partition key, and the clustering key.

- Partition key: responsible for distributing data across nodes. As a general rule, we want to spread the data evenly.

- Clustering key: responsible for sorting data within a partition.

At a high level, an email service needs to support the following queries at the data layer:

- The first query is to get all folders for a user.
- The second query is to display all emails for a specific folder.
- The third query is to create/delete/get a specific email.
- The fourth query is to fetch all read or unread emails.
- Bonus point: get conversation threads.

Let's take a look at them one by one.

Query 1: get all folders for a user.

As shown in Table 8.1, user_id is the partition key, so folders owned by the same user are located in one partition.

K	Partition Key
C↑	Clustering Key (ascending)
C↓	Clustering Key (descending)

folders_by_user		
user_id	UUID	K
folder_id	UUID	
folder_name	TEXT	

Table 8.1: Folders by user

Query 2: display all emails for a specific folder.

When a user loads their inbox, emails are usually sorted by timestamp, showing the most recent ones at the top. In order to store all emails for the same folder in one partition, composite partition key <user_id, folder_id> is used. Another column to note is email_id. Its data type is TIMEUUID [17], and it is the clustering key used to sort emails in chronological order.

emails_by_folder		
user_id	UUID	K
folder_id	UUID	K
email_id	TIMEUUID	C↓
from	TEXT	
subject	TEXT	
preview	TEXT	
is_read	BOOLEAN	

Table 8.2: Emails by folder

Query 3: create/delete/get an email

Due to space limitations, we only explain how to get detailed information about an email. The two tables in Table 8.3 are designed to support this query. The simple query looks like this:

```
SELECT * FROM emails_by_user WHERE email_id = 123;
```

An email can have multiple attachments, and these can be retrieved by the combination of email_id and filename fields.

emails_by_user		
user_id	UUID	K
email_id	TIMEUUID	C↓
from	TEXT	
to	LIST<TEXT>	
subject	TEXT	
body	TEXT	
attachments	LIST<filename|size>	

attachments		
email_id	TIMEUUID	C
filename	TEXT	K
url	TEXT	

Table 8.3: Emails by user

Query 4: fetch all read or unread emails

If our domain model was for a relational database, the query to fetch all read emails would look like this:

```
SELECT * FROM emails_by_folder
WHERE user_id = <user_id> and folder_id = <folder_id> and
  is_read = true
ORDER BY email_id;
```

The query to fetch all unread emails would look very similar. We just need to change is_read = true to is_read = false in the above query.

Our data model, however, is designed for NoSQL. A NoSQL database normally only supports queries on partition and cluster keys. Since is_read in the emails_by_folder table is neither of those, most NoSQL databases will reject this query.

One way to get around this limitation is to fetch the entire folder for a user and perform the filtering in the application. This could work for a small email service, but at our design scale, this does not work well.

This problem is commonly solved with denormalization in NoSQL. To support the read-/unread queries, we denormalize the emails_by_folder data into two tables as shown in Table 8.4.

- read_emails: it stores all emails that are in read status.
- unread_emails: it stores all emails that are in unread status.

To mark an UNREAD email as READ, the email is deleted from unread_emails and then inserted to read_emails.

To fetch all unread emails for a specific folder, we can run a query like this:

```
SELECT * FROM unread_emails
WHERE user_id = <user_id> and folder_id = <folder_id>
ORDER BY email_id;
```

read_emails		
user_id	UUID	K
folder_id	UUID	K
email_id	TIMEUUID	C↓
from	TEXT	
subject	TEXT	
preview	TEXT	

unread_emails		
user_id	UUID	K
folder_id	UUID	K
email_id	TIMEUUID	C↓
from	TEXT	
subject	TEXT	
preview	TEXT	

Table 8.4: Read and unread emails

Denormalization as shown above is a common practice. It makes the application code more complicated and harder to maintain, but it improves the read performance of these queries at scale.

Bonus point: conversation threads

Threads are a feature supported by many email clients. It groups email replies with their original message [8]. This allows users to retrieve all emails associated with one conversation. Traditionally, a thread is implemented using algorithms such as JWZ algorithm [18]. We will not go into detail about the algorithm, but just explain the core idea behind it. An email header generally contains the following three fields:

```
{
  "headers" {
    "Message-Id": "<7BA04B2A-430C-4D12-8B57-862103C34501@gmail.
      com>",
    "In-Reply-To": "<CAEWTXuPfN=LzECjDJtgY9Vu03kgFvJnJUSHTt6
      TW@gmail.com>",
    "References": ["<7BA04B2A-430C-4D12-8B57-862103C34501@gmail
      .com>"]
  }
}
```

Message-Id	The value of a message ID. It is generated by a client while sending a message.
In-Reply-To	The parent Message-Id to which the message replies.
References	A list of message IDs related to a thread.

Table 8.5: Email header

With these fields, an email client can reconstruct mail conversations from messages, if all messages in the reply chain are preloaded.

Consistency trade-off

Distributed databases that rely on replication for high availability must make a fundamental trade-off between consistency and availability. Correctness is very important for email systems, so by design, we want to have a single primary for any given mailbox. In the event of a failover, the mailbox isn't accessible by clients, so their sync/update operation is paused until failover ends. It trades availability in favor of consistency.

Email deliverability

It is easy to set up a mail server and start sending emails. The hard part is to get emails actually delivered to a user's inbox. If an email ends up in the spam folder, it means there is a very high chance a recipient won't read it. Email spam is a huge issue. According to research done by Statista [19], more than 50% of all emails sent are spam. If we set up a new mail server, most likely our emails will end up in the spam folder because a new email server has no reputation. There are a couple of factors to consider to improve email deliverability.

Dedicated IPs. It is recommended to have dedicated IP addresses for sending emails. Email providers are less likely to accept emails from new IP addresses that have no history.

Classify emails. Send different categories of emails from different IP addresses. For example, you may want to avoid sending marketing and other important emails from the same servers because it might make ISPs mark all emails as promotional.

Email sender reputation. Warm up new email server IP addresses slowly to build a good reputation, so big providers such as Office365, Gmail, Yahoo Mail, etc. are less likely to put our emails in the spam folder. According to Amazon Simple Email Service [20], it takes about 2 to 6 weeks to warm up a new IP address.

Ban spammers quickly. Spammers should be banned quickly before they have a significant impact on the server's reputation.

Feedback processing. It's very important to set up feedback loops with ISPs so we can keep the complaint rate low and ban spam accounts quickly. If an email fails to deliver or a user complains, one of the following outcomes occurs:

- Hard bounce. This means an email is rejected by ISP because the recipient's email address is invalid.

- Soft bounce. A soft bounce indicates an email failed to deliver due to temporary conditions, such as ISPs being too busy.

- Complaint. This means a recipient clicks the "report spam" button.

Figure 8.8 shows the process of collecting and processing bounces/complaints. We use separate queues for soft bounces, hard bounces, and complaints so they can be managed separately.

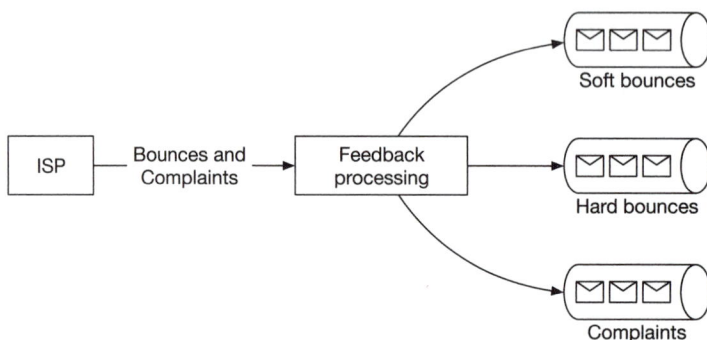

Figure 8.8: Handle feedback loop

Email authentication. According to the 2018 data breach investigation report provided by Verizon, phishing and pretexting represent 93% of breaches [21]. Some of the common techniques to combat phishing are: Sender Policy Framework (SPF) [22], DomainKeys Identified Mail (DKIM) [23], and Domain-based Message Authentication, Reporting and Conformance (DMARC) [24].

Figure 8.9 shows an example header of a Gmail message. As you can see, the sender @info6.citi.com is authenticated by SPF, DKIM, and DMARC.

Message ID		<617.3471674588.202105030141197779035.0039766680@info6.citi.com>	
Created at:		Sun, May 2, 2021 at 6:41 PM (Delivered after 17 seconds)	
From:		Citi Alerts <alerts@info6.citi.com> Using XyzMailer	
To:		▓▓▓▓▓▓▓▓▓▓▓@gmail.com>	
Subject:		Your Citi® account statement is ready	
SPF:		PASS with IP 63.239.204.146 Learn more	
DKIM:		'PASS' with domain info6.citi.com Learn more	
DMARC:		'PASS' Learn more	

Figure 8.9: An example of a Gmail header

You don't need to remember all those terms. The important thing to keep in mind is that getting emails to work as intended is hard. It requires not only domain knowledge, but good relationships with ISPs.

Search

Basic mail search refers to searching for emails that contain any of the entered keywords in the subject or body. More advanced features include filtering by "From", "Subject", "Unread", or other attributes. On one hand, whenever an email is sent, received, or deleted, we need to perform reindexing. On the other hand, a search query is only run when a user presses the search button. This means the search feature in email systems has a lot more writes than reads. By comparison with Google search, email search has quite different characteristics, as shown in Table 8.6.

	Scope	Sorting	Accuracy
Google search	The whole internet	Sort by relevance	Indexing generally takes time, so some items may not show in the search result immediately.
Email search	User's own email box	Sort by attributes such as time, has attachment, date within, is unread, etc.	Indexing should be near real-time, and the result has to be accurate.

Table 8.6: Google search vs email search

To support search functionality, we compare two approaches: Elasticsearch and native search embedded in the datastore.

Option 1: Elasticsearch

The high-level design for email search using Elasticsearch is shown in Figure 8.10. Because queries are mostly performed on the user's own email server, we can group underlying documents to the same node using user_id as the partition key.

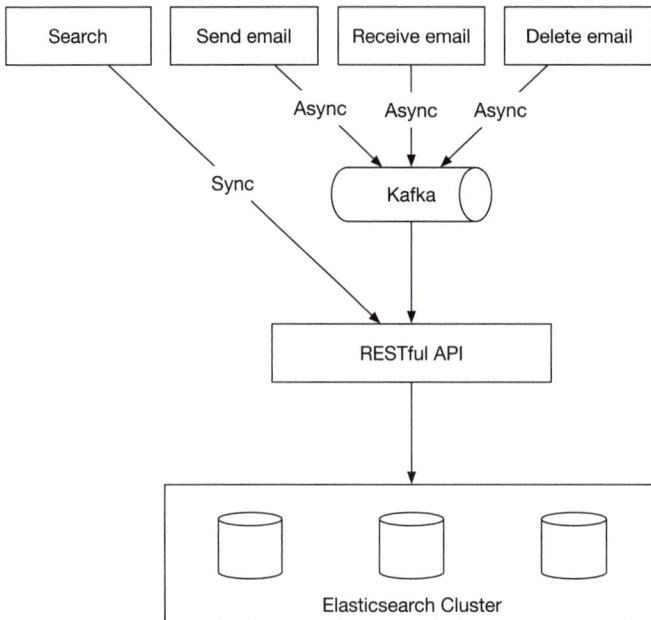

Figure 8.10: Elasticsearch

When a user clicks the search button, the user waits until the search response is received. A search request is synchronous. When events such as "send email", "receive email" or "delete email" are triggered, nothing related to search needs to be returned to the client. Reindexing is needed and it can be done with offline jobs. Kafka is used in the design to decouple services that trigger reindexing, from services that actually perform reindexing.

Elasticsearch is the most popular search-engine database as of June 2021 [25] and it supports full-text search of emails very well. One challenge of adding Elasticsearch is to keep our primary email store in sync with it.

Option 2: Custom search solution

Large-scale email providers usually develop their own custom search engines to meet their specific requirements. Designing an email search engine is a very complicated task and is out of the scope of this chapter. Here we only briefly touch on the disk I/O bottleneck, a primary challenge we will face for a custom search engine.

As shown in the back-of-the-envelope calculation, the size of the metadata and attachments added daily is at the petabyte (PB) level. Meanwhile, an email account can easily have over half a million emails. The main bottleneck of the index server is usually disk I/O.

Since the process of building the index is write-heavy, a good strategy might be to use Log-Structured Merge-Tree (LSM) [26] to structure the index data on disk (Figure 8.11). The write path is optimized by only performing sequential writes. LSM trees are the core data structure behind databases such as Bigtable, Cassandra, and RocksDB. When a new email arrives, it is first added to level 0 in-memory cache, and when data size in memory reaches the predefined threshold, data is merged to the next level. Another reason to use LSM is to separate data that change frequently from those that don't. For example, email data usually doesn't change, but folder information tends to change more often due to different filter rules. In this case, we can separate them into two different sections, so that if a request is related to a folder change, we change only the folder and leave the email data alone.

If you are interested in reading more about email search, it is highly recommended you take a look at how search works in Microsoft Exchange servers [27].

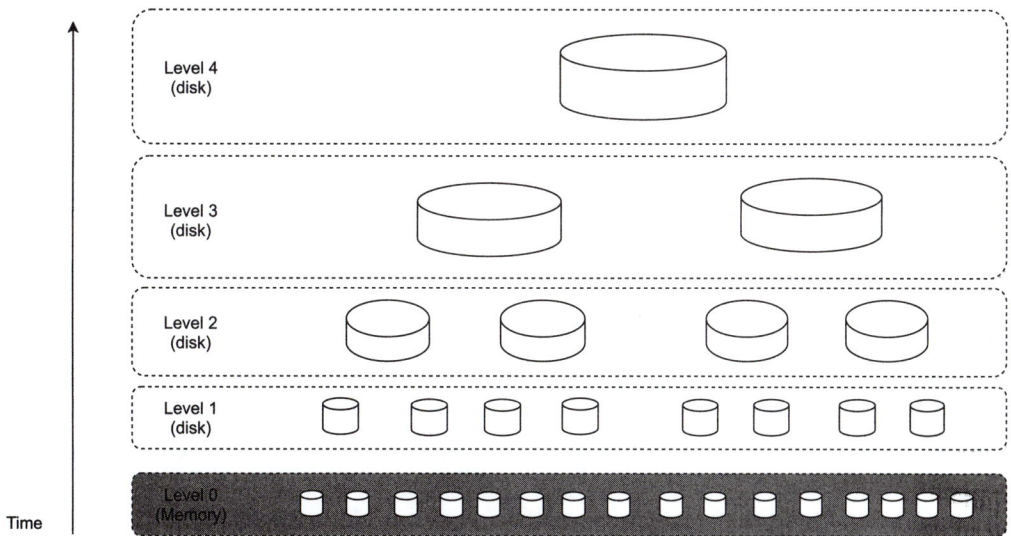

Figure 8.11: LSM tree

Each approach has pros and cons:

Feature	Elasticsearch	Custom search engine
Scalability	Scalable to some extent	Easier to scale as we can optimize the system for the email use case
System complexity	Need to maintain two different systems: datastore and Elasticsearch	One system
Data consistency	Two copies of data. One in the metadata datastore, and the other in Elasticsearch. Data consistency is hard to maintain	A single copy of data in the metadata datastore
Data loss possible	No. Can rebuild the Elasticsearch index from the primary storage, in case of failure	No
Development effort	Easy to integrate. To support large scale email search, a dedicated Elasticsearch team might be needed	Significant engineering effort is needed to develop a custom email search engine

Table 8.7: Elastic search vs custom search engine

A general rule of thumb is that for a smaller scale email system, Elasticsearch is a good option as it's easy to integrate and doesn't require significant engineering effort. For a larger scale, Elasticsearch might work, but we may need a dedicated team to develop and maintain the email search infrastructure. To support an email system at Gmail or Outlook scale, it might be a good idea to have a native search embedded in the database as opposed to the separate indexing approach.

Scalability and availability

Since data access patterns of individual users are independent of one another, we expect most components in the system are horizontally scalable.

For better availability, data is replicated across multiple data centers. Users communicate with a mail server that is physically closer to them in the network topology. During a network partition, users can access messages from other data centers (Figure 8.12).

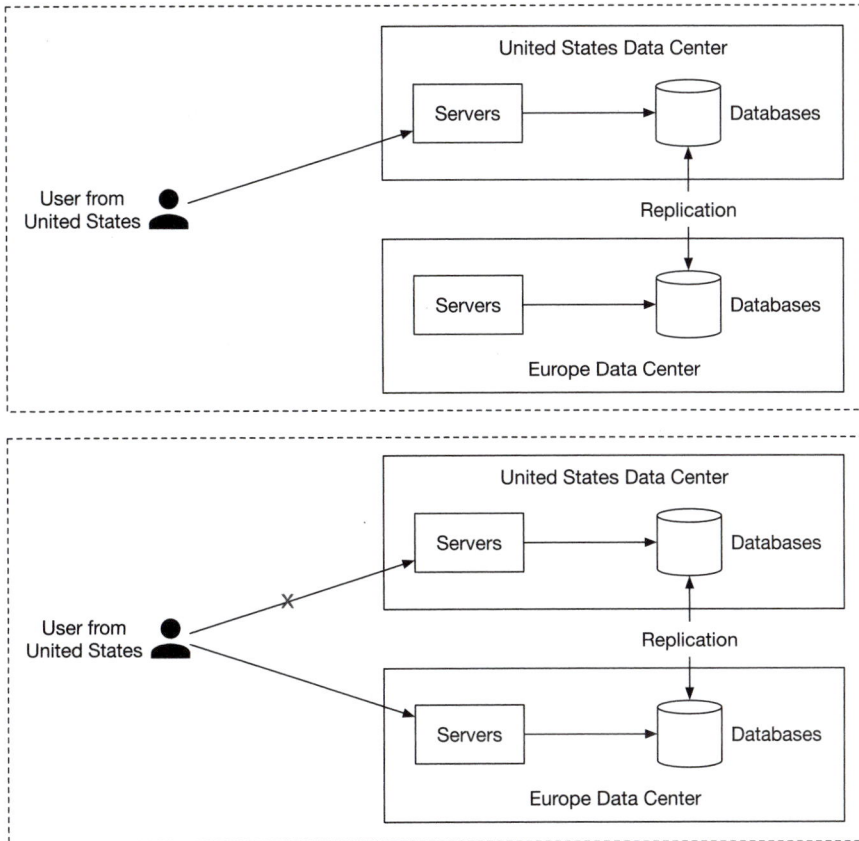

Figure 8.12: Multi-data center setup

Step 4 - Wrap Up

In this chapter, we have presented a design for building large-scale email servers. We started by gathering requirements and doing some back-of-the-envelope calculations to get a good idea of the scale. In the high-level design, we discussed how traditional email servers were designed and why they cannot satisfy modern use cases. We also discussed email APIs and high-level designs for sending and receiving flows. Finally, we dived deep into metadata database design, email deliverability, search, and scalability.

If there is extra time at the end of the interview, here are a few additional talking points:

- Fault tolerance. Many parts of the system can fail, and you can talk about how to handle node failures, network issues, event delays, etc.
- Compliance. Email service works all around the world and there are legal regulations to comply with. For instance, we need to handle and store personally identifiable information (PII) from Europe in a way that complies with General Data Protection Regulation (GDPR) [28]. Legal intercept is another typical feature in this area [29].
- Security. Email security is important because emails contain sensitive information.

Gmail provides safety features such as phishing protections, safe browsing, proactive alerts, account safety, confidential mode, and email encryption [30].

- Optimizations. Sometimes, the same email is sent to multiple recipients, and the same email attachment is stored several times in the object store (S3) in the group emails. One optimization we could do is to check the existence of the attachment in storage, before performing the expensive save operation.

Congratulations on getting this far! Now give yourself a pat on the back. Good job!

Chapter summary

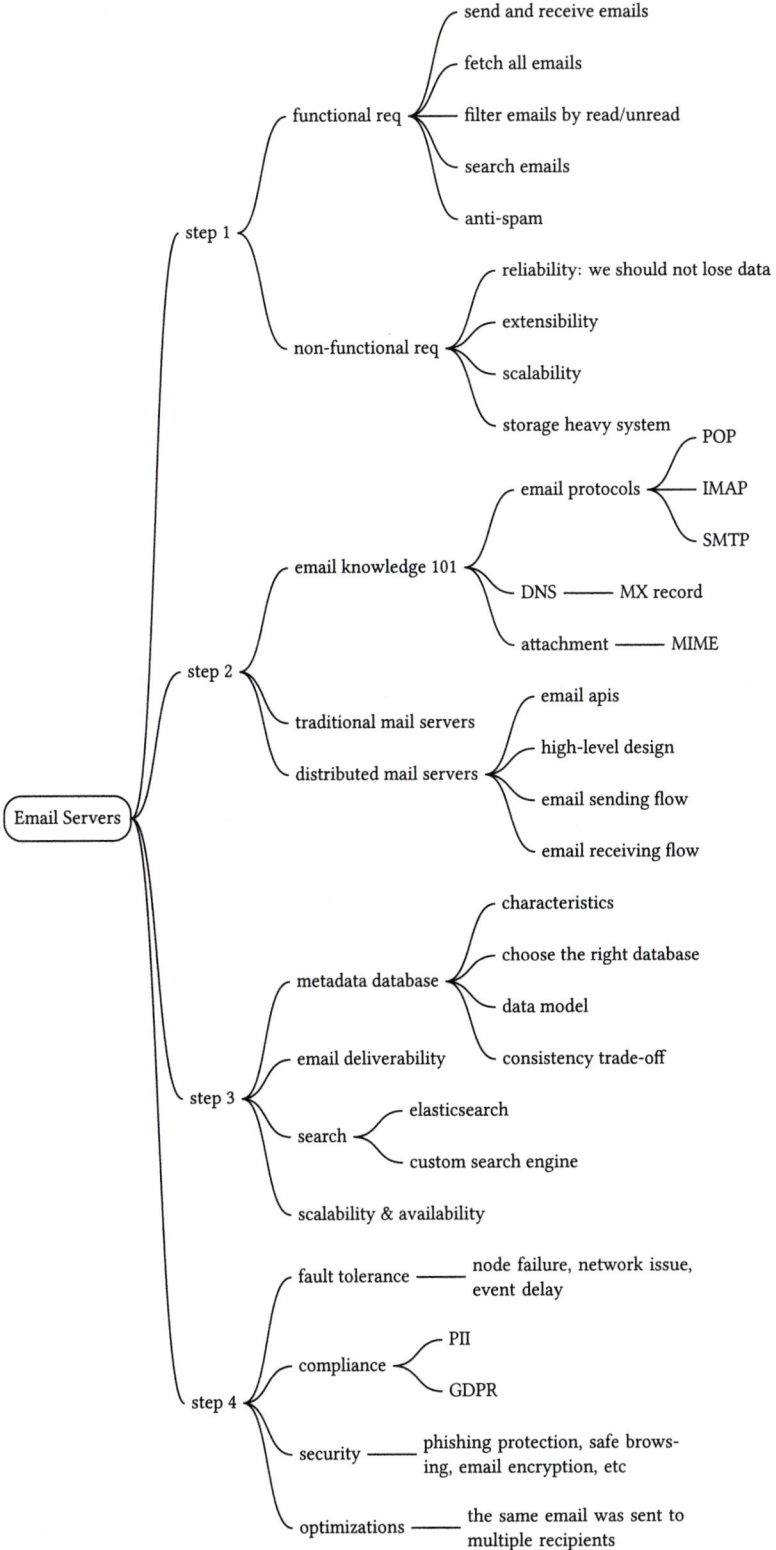

Email Servers

- step 1
  - functional req
    - send and receive emails
    - fetch all emails
    - filter emails by read/unread
    - search emails
    - anti-spam
  - non-functional req
    - reliability: we should not lose data
    - extensibility
    - scalability
    - storage heavy system

- step 2
  - email knowledge 101
    - email protocols
      - POP
      - IMAP
      - SMTP
    - DNS —— MX record
    - attachment —— MIME
  - traditional mail servers
  - distributed mail servers
    - email apis
    - high-level design
    - email sending flow
    - email receiving flow

- step 3
  - metadata database
    - characteristics
    - choose the right database
    - data model
    - consistency trade-off
  - email deliverability
  - search
    - elasticsearch
    - custom search engine
  - scalability & availability

- step 4
  - fault tolerance —— node failure, network issue, event delay
  - compliance
    - PII
    - GDPR
  - security —— phishing protection, safe browsing, email encryption, etc
  - optimizations —— the same email was sent to multiple recipients

Reference Material

[1] Number of Active Gmail Users. https://financesonline.com/number-of-active-gmail-users/.

[2] Outlook. https://en.wikipedia.org/wiki/Outlook.com.

[3] How Many Emails Are Sent Per Day in 2021? https://review42.com/resources/how-many-emails-are-sent-per-day/.

[4] RFC 1939 - Post Office Protocol - Version 3. http://www.faqs.org/rfcs/rfc1939.html.

[5] ActiveSync. https://en.wikipedia.org/wiki/ActiveSync.

[6] Email attachment. https://en.wikipedia.org/wiki/Email_attachment.

[7] MIME. https://en.wikipedia.org/wiki/MIME.

[8] Threading. https://en.wikipedia.org/wiki/Conversation_threading.

[9] IMAP LIST Extension for Special-Use Mailboxes. https://datatracker.ietf.org/doc/html/rfc6154.

[10] Apache James. https://james.apache.org/.

[11] A JSON Meta Application Protocol (JMAP) Subprotocol for WebSocket. https://tools.ietf.org/id/draft-ietf-jmap-websocket-07.html#RFC7692.

[12] Cassandra Limitations. https://cwiki.apache.org/confluence/display/CASSANDRA2/CassandraLimitations.

[13] Inverted index. https://en.wikipedia.org/wiki/Inverted_index.

[14] Exponential backoff. https://en.wikipedia.org/wiki/Exponential_backoff.

[15] QQ Email System Optimization (in Chinese). https://www.slideshare.net/areyouok/06-qq-5431919.

[16] IOPS. https://en.wikipedia.org/wiki/IOPS.

[17] UUID and timeuuid types. https://docs.datastax.com/en/cql-oss/3.3/cql/cql_reference/uuid_type_r.html.

[18] Message threading. https://www.jwz.org/doc/threading.html.

[19] Global spam volume. https://www.statista.com/statistics/420391/spam-email-traffic-share/.

[20] Warming up dedicated IP addresses. https://docs.aws.amazon.com/ses/latest/dg/dedicated-ip-warming.html.

[21] 2018 Data Breach Investigations Report. https://enterprise.verizon.com/resources/reports/DBIR_2018_Report.pdf.

[22] Sender Policy Framework. https://en.wikipedia.org/wiki/Sender_Policy_Framew ork.

[23] DomainKeys Identified Mail. https://en.wikipedia.org/wiki/DomainKeys_Identifie d_Mail.

[24] Domain-based Message Authentication, Reporting & Conformance. https://dmarc. org/.

[25] DB-Engines Ranking of Search Engines. https://db-engines.com/en/ranking/sear ch+engine.

[26] Log-structured merge-tree. https://en.wikipedia.org/wiki/Log-structured_merge-t ree.

[27] Microsoft Exchange Conference 2014 Search in Exchange. https://www.youtube.co m/watch?v=5EXGCSzzQak&t=2173s.

[28] General Data Protection Regulation. https://en.wikipedia.org/wiki/General_Data _Protection_Regulation.

[29] Lawful interception. https://en.wikipedia.org/wiki/Lawful_interception.

[30] Email safety. https://safety.google/intl/en_us/gmail/.

9   S3-like Object Storage

In this chapter, we design an object storage service similar to Amazon Simple Storage Service (S3). S3 is a service offered by Amazon Web Services (AWS) that provides object storage through a RESTful API-based interface. Here are some facts about AWS S3:

- Launched in June 2006.
- S3 added versioning, bucket policy, and multipart upload support in 2010.
- S3 added server-side encryption, multi-object delete, and object expiration in 2011.
- Amazon reported 2 trillion objects stored in S3 by 2013.
- Life cycle policy, event notification, and cross-region replication support were introduced in 2014 and 2015.
- Amazon reported over 100 trillion objects stored in S3 by 2021.

Before we dig into object storage, let's first review storage systems in general and define some terminologies.

Storage System 101

At a high-level, storage systems fall into three broad categories:

- Block storage
- File storage
- Object storage

Block storage

Block storage came first, in the 1960s. Common storage devices like hard disk drives (HDD) and solid-state drives (SSD) that are physically attached to servers are all considered as block storage.

Block storage presents the raw blocks to the server as a volume. This is the most flexible and versatile form of storage. The server can format the raw blocks and use them as a file system, or it can hand control of those blocks to an application. Some applications like a database or a virtual machine engine manage these blocks directly in order to squeeze every drop of performance out of them.

Block storage is not limited to physically attached storage. Block storage could be connected to a server over a high-speed network or over industry-standard connectivity protocols like Fibre Channel (FC) [1] and iSCSI [2]. Conceptually, the network-attached block storage still presents raw blocks. To the servers, it works the same as physically attached block storage.

File storage

File storage is built on top of block storage. It provides a higher-level abstraction to make it easier to handle files and directories. Data is stored as files under a hierarchical directory structure. File storage is the most common general-purpose storage solution. File storage could be made accessible by a large number of servers using common file-level network protocols like SMB/CIFS [3] and NFS [4]. The servers accessing file storage do not need to deal with the complexity of managing the blocks, formatting volume, etc. The simplicity of file storage makes it a great solution for sharing a large number of files and folders within an organization.

Object storage

Object storage is new. It makes a very deliberate tradeoff to sacrifice performance for high durability, vast scale, and low cost. It targets relatively "cold" data and is mainly used for archival and backup. Object storage stores all data as objects in a flat structure. There is no hierarchical directory structure. Data access is normally provided via a RESTful API. It is relatively slow compared to other storage types. Most public cloud service providers have an object storage offering, such as AWS S3, Google object storage, and Azure blob storage.

Comparison

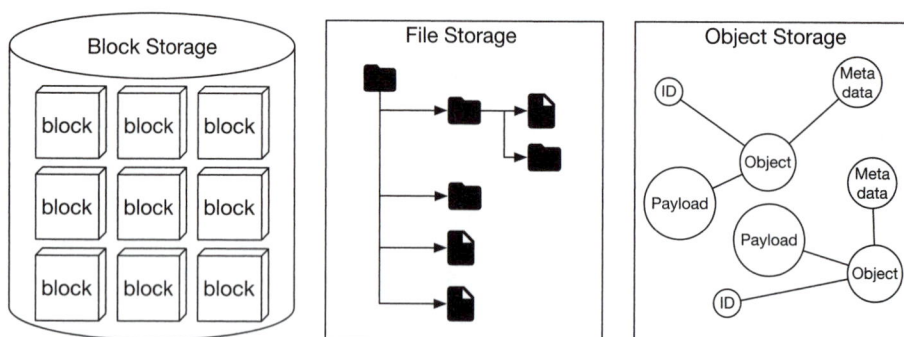

Figure 9.1: Three different storage options

Table 9.1 compares block storage, file storage, and object storage.

	Block storage	**File storage**	**Object storage**
Mutable Content	Y	Y	N (object versioning is supported, in-place update is not)
Cost	High	Medium to high	Low
Performance	Medium to high, very high	Medium to high	Low to medium
Consistency	Strong consistency	Strong consistency	Strong consistency [5]
Data access	SAS [6]/iSCSI/FC	Standard file access, CIFS/SMB, and NFS	RESTful API
Scalability	Medium scalability	High scalability	Vast scalability
Good for	Virtual machines (VM), high-performance applications like database	General-purpose file system access	Binary data, unstructured data

Table 9.1: Storage options

Terminology

To design S3-like object storage, we need to understand some core object storage concepts first. This section provides an overview of the terms that apply to object storage.

Bucket. A logical container for objects. The bucket name is globally unique. To upload data to S3, we must first create a bucket.

Object. An object is an individual piece of data we store in a bucket. It contains object data (also called payload) and metadata. Object data can be any sequence of bytes we want to store. The metadata is a set of name-value pairs that describe the object.

Versioning. A feature that keeps multiple variants of an object in the same bucket. It is enabled at bucket-level. This feature enables users to recover objects that are deleted or overwritten by accident.

Uniform Resource Identifier (URI). The object storage provides RESTful APIs to access its resources, namely, buckets and objects. Each resource is uniquely identified by its URI.

Service-level agreement (SLA). A service-level agreement is a contract between a service provider and a client. For example, the Amazon S3 Standard-Infrequent Access storage class provides the following SLA [7]:

- Designed for durability of 99.999999999% of objects across multiple Availability Zones.
- Data is resilient in the event of one entire Availability Zone destruction.

- Designed for 99.9% availability.

Step 1 - Understand the Problem and Establish Design Scope

The following questions help to clarify the requirements and narrow down the scope.

Candidate: Which features should be included in the design?
Interviewer: We would like you to design an S3-like object storage system with the following functionalities:

- Bucket creation.
- Object uploading and downloading.
- Object versioning.
- Listing objects in a bucket. It's similar to the aws S3 ls command [8].

Candidate: What is the typical data size?
Interviewer: We need to store both massive objects (a few GBs or more) and a large number of small objects (tens of KBs,) efficiently.

Candidate: How much data do we need to store in one year?
Interviewer: 100 petabytes (PB).

Candidate: Can we assume data durability is 6 nines (99.9999%) and service availability is 4 nines (99.99%)?
Interviewer: Yes, that sounds reasonable.

Non-functional requirements

- 100PB of data
- Data durability is 6 nines
- Service availability is 4 nines
- Storage efficiency. Reduce storage costs while maintaining a high degree of reliability and performance.

Back-of-the-envelope estimation

Object storage is likely to have bottlenecks in either disk capacity or disk IO per second (IOPS). Let's take a look.

- Disk capacity. Let's assume objects follow the distribution listed below:
  - 20% of all objects are small objects (less than 1MB).
  - 60% of objects are medium-sized objects (1 MB ~ 64MB).

- 20% are large objects (larger than 64MB).

- IOPS. Let's assume one hard disk (SATA interface, 7200 rpm) is capable of doing $100 \sim 150$ random seeks per second ($100 \sim 150$ IOPS).

With those assumptions, we can estimate the total number of objects the system can persist. To simplify the calculation, let's use the median size for each object type (0.5MB for small objects, 32MB for medium objects, and 200MB for large objects). A 40% storage usage ratio gives us:

- $100\,\mathrm{PB} = 100 \times 1000 \times 1000 \times 1000\,\mathrm{MB} = 10^{11}\,\mathrm{MB}$
- $\dfrac{10^{11} \times 0.4}{(0.2 \times 0.5\,\mathrm{MB} + 0.6 \times 32\,\mathrm{MB} + 0.2 \times 200\,\mathrm{MB})} = 0.68$ billion objects.
- If we assume the metadata of an object is about 1KB in size, we need 0.68TB space to store all metadata information.

Even though we may not use those numbers, it's good to have a general idea about the scale and constraint of the system.

Step 2 - Propose High-level Design and Get Buy-in

Before diving into the design, let's explore a few interesting properties of object storage, as they may influence it.

Object immutability. One of the main differences between object storage and the other two types of storage systems is that the objects stored inside of object storage are immutable. We may delete them or replace them entirely with a new version, but we cannot make incremental changes.

Key-value store. We could use object URI to retrieve object data (Listing 9.1). The object URI is the key and object data is the value.

```
Request:
GET /bucket1/object1.txt HTTP/1.1

Response:
HTTP/1.1 200 OK
Content-Length: 4567

[4567 bytes of object data]
```

Listing 9.1: Use object URI to retrieve object data

Write once, read many times. The data access pattern for object data is written once and read many times. According to the research done by LinkedIn, 95% of requests are read operations [9].

Support both small and large objects. Object size may vary and we need to support both.

The design philosophy of object storage is very similar to that of the UNIX file system. In UNIX, when we save a file in the local file system, it does not save the filename and file data together. Instead, the filename is stored in a data structure called "inode" [10], and the file data is stored in different disk locations. The inode contains a list of file block pointers that point to the disk locations of the file data. When we access a local file, we first fetch the metadata in the inode. We then read the file data by following the file block pointers to the actual disk locations.

The object storage works similarly. The inode becomes the metadata store that stores all the object metadata. The hard disk becomes the data store that stores the object data. In the UNIX file system, the inode uses the file block pointer to record the location of data on the hard disk. In object storage, the metadata store uses the ID of the object to find the corresponding object data in the data store, via a network request. Figure 9.2 shows the UNIX file system and the object storage.

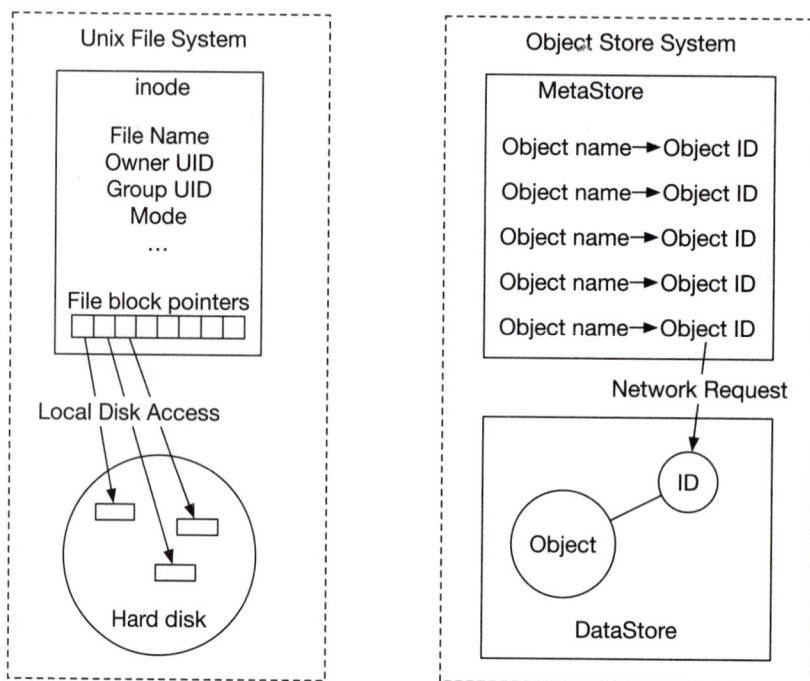

Figure 9.2: UNIX file system and object store

Separating metadata and object data simplifies the design. The data store contains immutable data while the metadata store contains mutable data. This separation enables us to implement and optimize these two components independently. Figure 9.3 shows what the bucket and object look like.

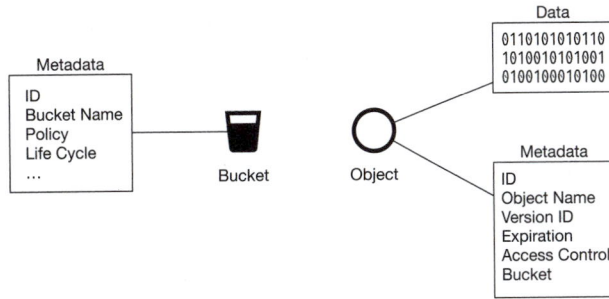

Figure 9.3: Bucket & object

High-level design

Figure 9.4 shows the high-level design.

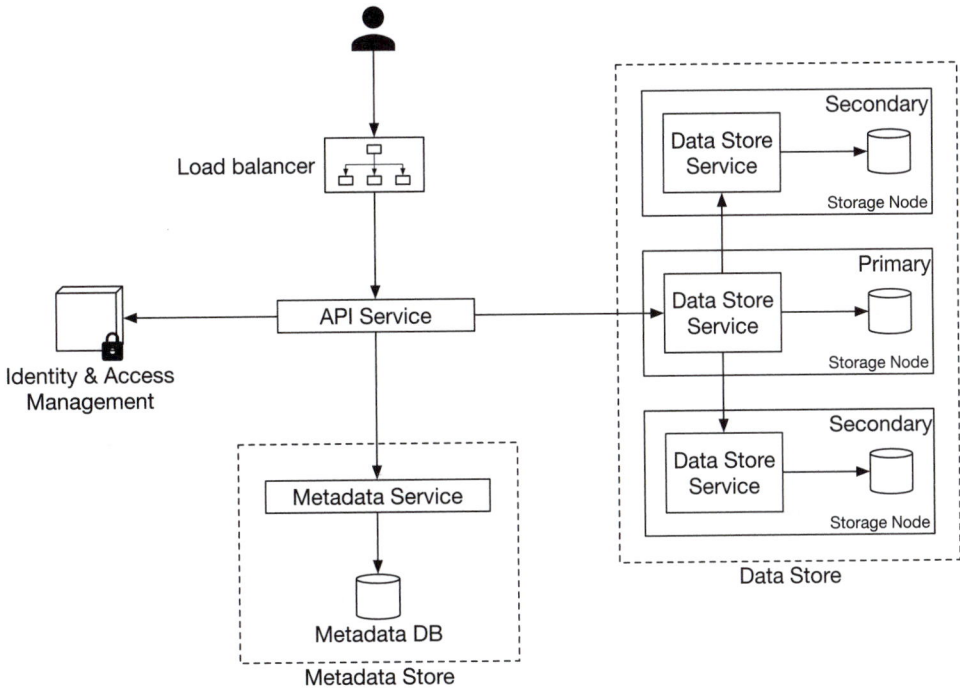

Figure 9.4: High-level design

Let's go over the components one by one.

Load balancer. Distributes RESTful API requests across a number of API servers.

API service. Orchestrates remote procedure calls to the identity and access management service, metadata service, and storage stores. This service is stateless so it can be horizontally scaled.

Identity and access management (IAM). The central place to handle authentication, authorization, and access control. Authentication verifies who you are, and authorization validates what operations you could perform based on who you are.

Data store. Stores and retrieves the actual data. All data-related operations are based on object ID (UUID).

Metadata store. Stores the metadata of the objects.

Note that the metadata and data stores are just logical components, and there are different ways to implement them. For example, in Ceph's Rados Gateway [11], there is no stand-alone metadata store. Everything, including the object bucket, is persisted as one or multiple Rados objects.

Now we have a basic understanding of the high-level design, let's explore some of the most important workflows in object storage.

- Uploading an object.
- Downloading an object.
- Object versioning and listing objects in a bucket. They will be explained in the "design deep dive" section on page 261.

Uploading an object

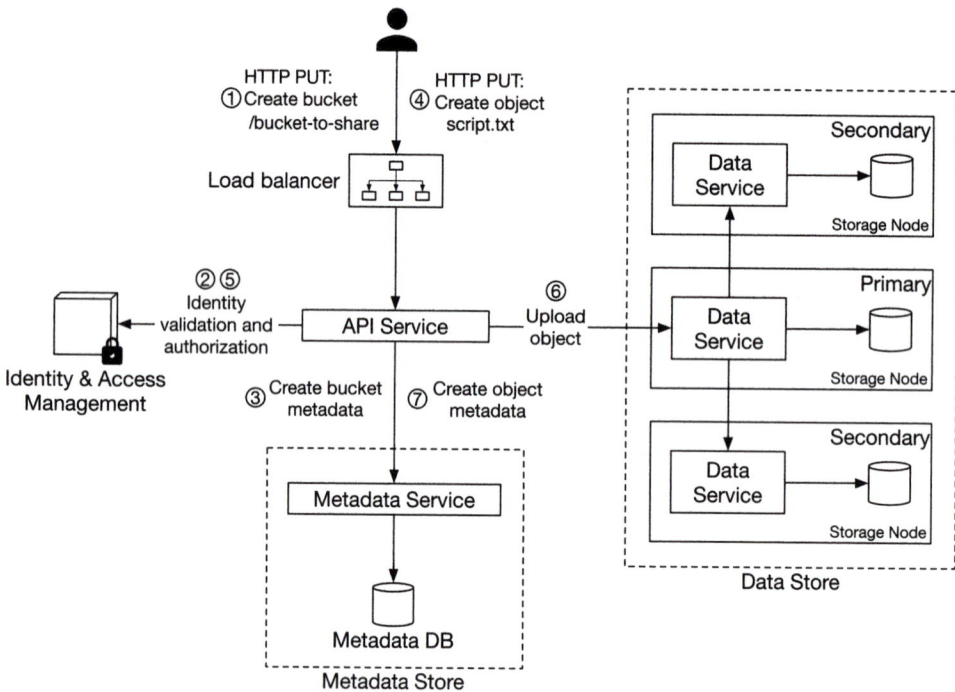

Figure 9.5: Uploading an object

An object has to reside in a bucket. In this example, we first create a bucket named bucket-to-share and then upload a file named script.txt to the bucket. Figure 9.5 explains how this flow works in 7 steps.

1. The client sends an HTTP PUT request to create a bucket named bucket-to-share. The

request is forwarded to the API service.

2. The API service calls the IAM to ensure the user is authorized and has WRITE permission.

3. The API service calls the metadata store to create an entry with the bucket info in the metadata database. Once the entry is created, a success message is returned to the client.

4. After the bucket is created, the client sends an HTTP PUT request to create an object named script.txt.

5. The API service verifies the user's identity and ensures the user has WRITE permission on the bucket.

6. Once validation succeeds, the API service sends the object data in the HTTP PUT payload to the data store. The data store persists the payload as an object and returns the UUID of the object.

7. The API service calls the metadata store to create a new entry in the metadata database. It contains important metadata such as the object_id (UUID), bucket_id (which bucket the object belongs to), object_name, etc. A sample entry is shown in Table 9.2.

object_name	object_id	bucket_id
script.txt	239D5866-0052-00F6-014E-C914E61ED42B	82AA1B2E-F599-4590-B5E4-1F51AAE5F7E4

Table 9.2: Sample entry

The API to upload an object could look like this:

```
PUT /bucket-to-share/script.txt HTTP/1.1
Host: foo.s3example.org
Date: Sun, 12 Sept 2021 17:51:00 GMT
Authorization: authorization string
Content-Type: text/plain
Content-Length: 4567
x-amz-meta-author: Alex

[4567 bytes of object data]
```

Listing 9.2: Uploading an object

Downloading an object

A bucket has no directory hierarchy. However, we can create a logical hierarchy by concatenating the bucket name and the object name to simulate a folder structure. For example, we name the object bucket-to-share/script.txt instead of script.txt. To get an object, we specify the object name in the GET request. The API to download an object looks like this:

```
GET /bucket-to-share/script.txt HTTP/1.1
Host: foo.s3example.org
Date: Sun, 12 Sept 2021 18:30:01 GMT
Authorization: authorization string
```

Listing 9.3: Downloading an object

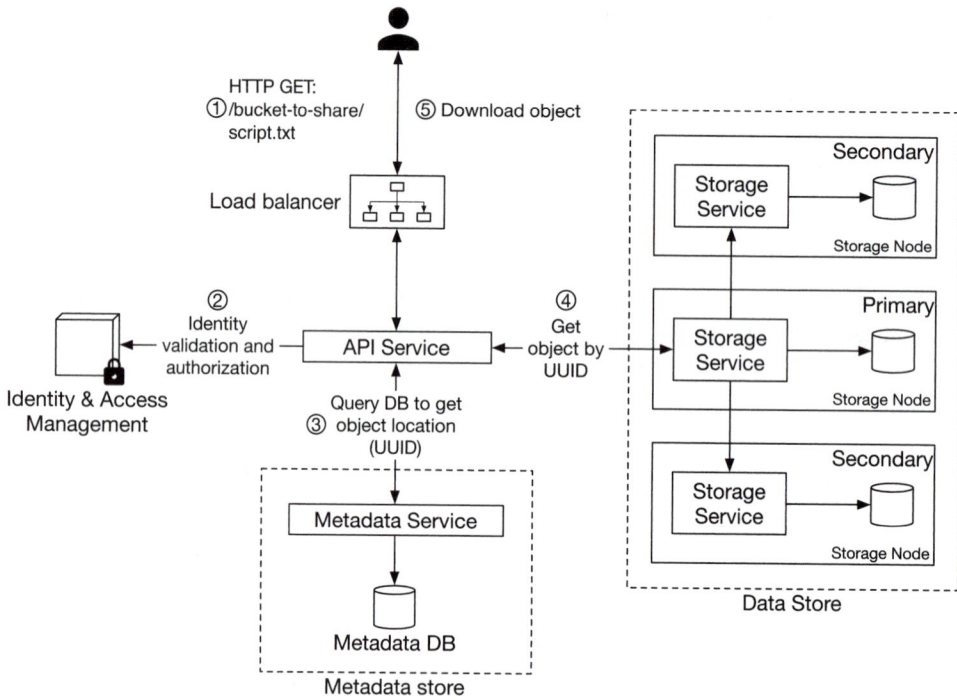

Figure 9.6: Downloading an object

As mentioned earlier, the data store does not store the name of the object and it only supports object operations via object_id (UUID). In order to download the object, we first map the object name to the UUID. The workflow of downloading an object is shown below:

1. The client sends an HTTP GET request to the load balancer: GET /bucket-to-share/sc ript.txt

2. The API service queries the IAM to verify that the user has READ access to the bucket.

3. Once validated, the API service fetches the corresponding object's UUID from the metadata store.

4. Next, the API service fetches the object data from the data store by its UUID.

5. The API service returns the object data to the client in HTTP GET response.

Step 3 - Design Deep Dive

In this section, we dive deep into a few areas:

- Data store
- Metadata data model
- Listing objects in a bucket
- Object versioning
- Optimizing uploads of large files
- Garbage collection

Data store

Let's take a closer look at the design of the data store. As discussed previously, the API service handles external requests from users and calls different internal services to fulfill those requests. To persist or retrieve an object, the API service calls the data store. Figure 9.7 shows the interactions between the API service and the data store for uploading and downloading an object.

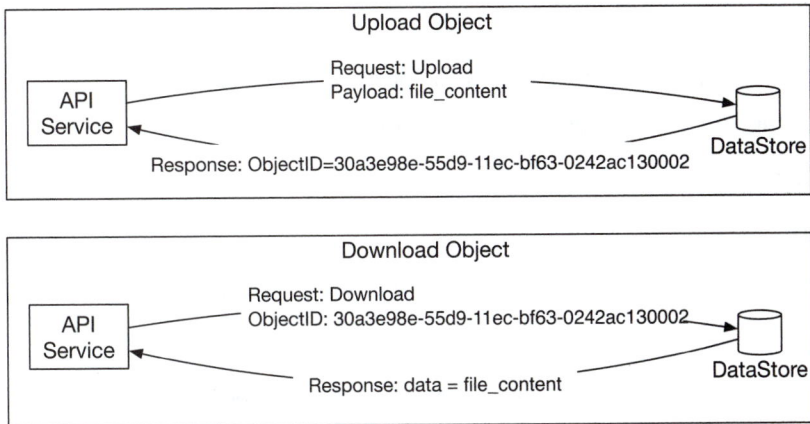

Figure 9.7: Upload and download an object

High-level design for the data store

The data store has three main components as shown in Figure 9.8.

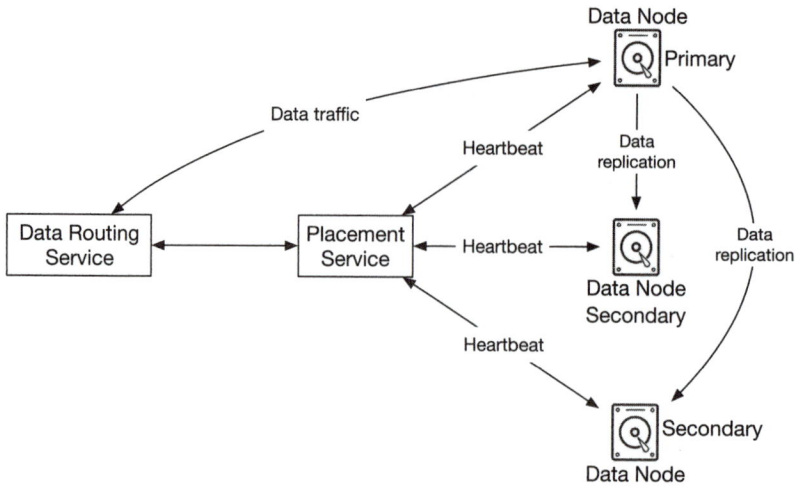

Figure 9.8: Data store components

Data routing service

The data routing service provides RESTful or gRPC [12] APIs to access the data node cluster. It is a stateless service that can scale by adding more servers. This service has the following responsibilities:

- Query the placement service to get the best data node to store data.
- Read data from data nodes and return it to the API service.
- Write data to data nodes.

Placement service

The placement service determines which data nodes (primary and replicas) should be chosen to store an object. It maintains a virtual cluster map, which provides the physical topology of the cluster. The virtual cluster map contains location information for each data node which the placement service uses to make sure the replicas are physically separated. This separation is key to high durability. See the "Durability" section on page 268 for details. An example of the virtual cluster map is shown in Figure 9.9.

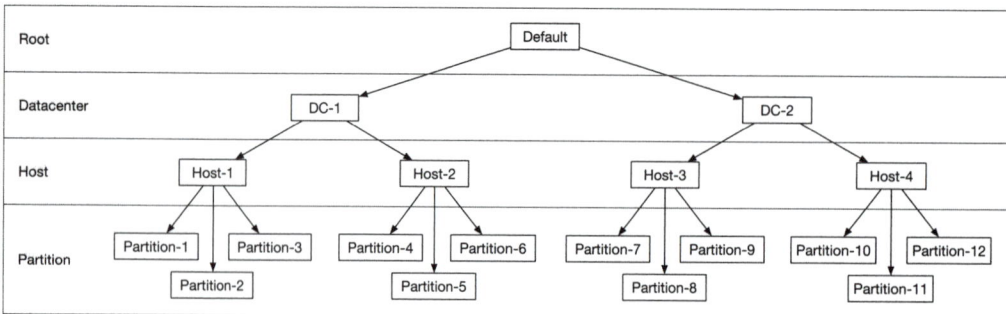

Figure 9.9: Virtual cluster map

The placement service continuously monitors all data nodes through heartbeats. If a data node doesn't send a heartbeat within a configurable 15-second grace period, the placement service marks the node as "down" in the virtual cluster map.

This is a critical service, so we suggest building a cluster of 5 or 7 placement service nodes with Paxos [13] or Raft [14] consensus protocol. The consensus protocol ensures that as long as more than half of the nodes are healthy, the service as a whole continues to work. For example, if the placement service cluster has 7 nodes, it can tolerate a 3 node failure. To learn more about consensus protocols, refer to the reference materials [13] [14].

Data node

The data node stores the actual object data. It ensures reliability and durability by replicating data to multiple data nodes, also called a replication group.

Each data node has a data service daemon running on it. The data service daemon continuously sends heartbeats to the placement service. The heartbeat message includes the following essential information:

- How many disk drives (HDD or SSD) does the data node manage?
- How much data is stored on each drive?

When the placement service receives the heartbeat for the first time, it assigns an ID for this data node, adds it to the virtual cluster map, and returns the following information:

- a unique ID of the data node
- the virtual cluster map
- where to replicate data

Data persistence flow

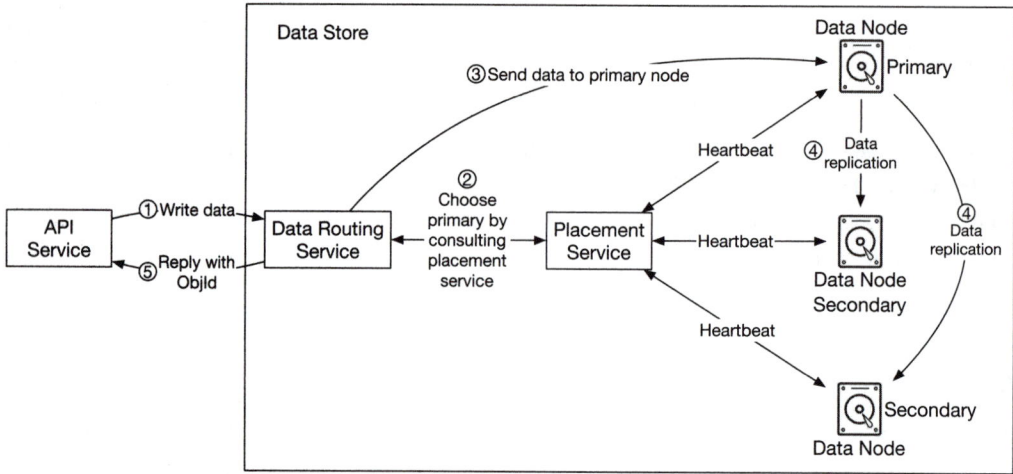

Figure 9.10: Data persistence flow

Now let's take a look at how data is persisted in the data node.

1. The API service forwards the object data to the data store.

2. The data routing service generates a UUID for this object and queries the placement service for the data node to store this object. The placement service checks the virtual cluster map and returns the primary data node.

3. The data routing service sends data directly to the primary data node, together with its UUID.

4. The primary data node saves the data locally and replicates it to two secondary data nodes. The primary node responds to the data routing service when data is successfully replicated to all secondary nodes.

5. The UUID of the object (ObjId) is returned to the API service.

In step 2, given a UUID for the object as an input, the placement service returns the replication group for the object. How does the placement service do this? Keep in mind that this lookup needs to be deterministic, and it must survive the addition or removal of replication groups. Consistent hashing is a common implementation of such a lookup function. Refer to [15] for more information.

In step 4, the primary data node replicates data to all secondary nodes before it returns a response. This makes data strongly consistent among all data nodes. This consistency comes with latency costs because we have to wait until the slowest replica finishes. Figure 9.11 shows the trade-offs between consistency and latency.

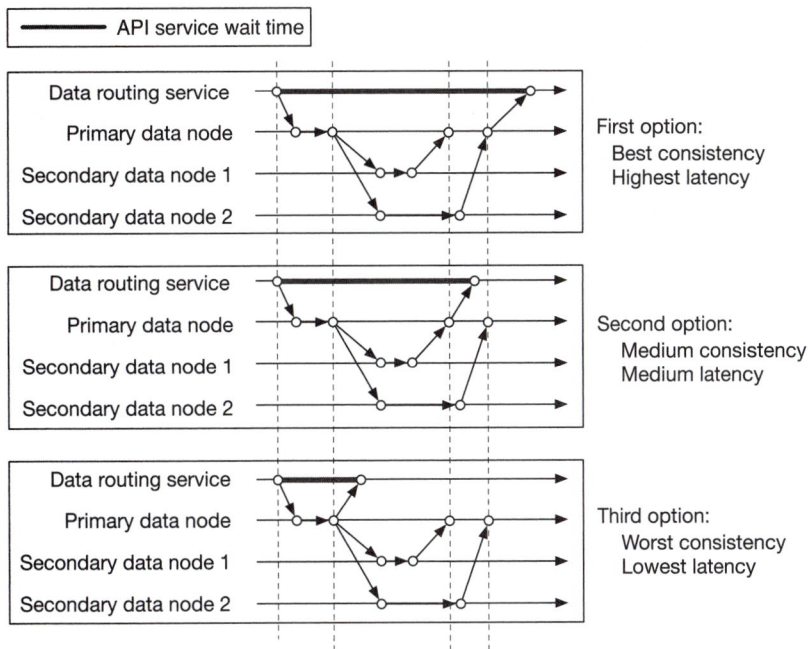

Figure 9.11: Trade-off between consistency and latency

1. Data is considered as successfully saved after all three nodes store the data. This approach has the best consistency but the highest latency.

2. Data is considered as successfully saved after the primary and one of the secondaries store the data. This approach has a medium consistency and medium latency.

3. Data is considered as successfully saved after the primary persists the data. This approach has the worst consistency but the lowest latency.

Both 2 and 3 are forms of eventual consistency.

How data is organized

Now let's take a look at how each data node manages the data. A simple solution is to store each object in a stand-alone file. This works, but the performance suffers when there are many small files. Two issues arise when having too many small files on a file system. First, it wastes many data blocks. A file system stores files in discrete disk blocks. Disk blocks have the same size, and the size is fixed when the volume is initialized. The typical block size is around 4KB. For a file smaller than 4KB, it would still consume the entire disk block. If the file system holds a lot of small files, it wastes a lot of disk blocks, with each one only lightly filled with a small file.

Second, it could exceed the system's inode capacity. The file system stores the location and other information about a file in a special type of block called inode. For most file systems, the number of inodes is fixed when the disk is initialized. With millions of small files, it runs the risk of consuming all inodes. Also, the operating system does not handle a large number of inodes very well, even with aggressive caching of file system metadata. For these reasons, storing small objects as individual files does not work well in practice.

To address these issues, we can merge many small objects into a larger file. It works conceptually like a write-ahead log (WAL). When we save an object, it is appended to an existing read-write file. When the read-write file reaches its capacity threshold (usually set to a few GBs), the read-write file is marked as read-only and a new read-write file is created to receive new objects. Once a file is marked as read-only, it can only serve read requests. Figure 9.12 explains how this process works.

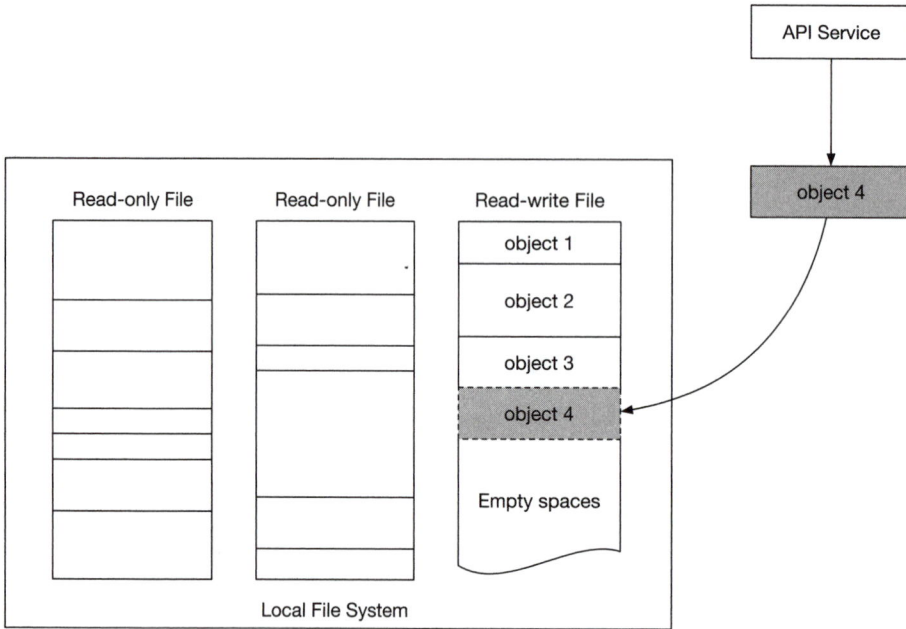

Figure 9.12: Store multiple small objects in one big file

Note that write access to the read-write file must be serialized. As shown in Figure 9.12, objects are stored in order, one after the other, in the read-write file. To maintain this on-disk layout, multiple cores processing incoming write requests in parallel must take their turns to write to the read-write file. For a modern server with a large number of cores processing many incoming requests in parallel, this seriously restricts write throughput. To fix this, we could provide dedicated read-write files, one for each core processing incoming requests.

Object lookup

With each data file holding many small objects, how does the data node locate an object by UUID? The data node needs the following information:

- The data file that contains the object
- The starting offset of the object in the data file
- The size of the object

The database schema to support this lookup is shown in Table 9.3.

object_mapping
object_id
file_name
start_offset
object_size

Table 9.3: Object_mapping table

Field	Description
object_id	UUID of the object
file_name	The name of the file that contains the object
start_offset	Beginning address of the object in the file
object_size	The number of bytes in the object

Table 9.4: Object_mapping fields

We considered two options for storing this mapping: a file-based key-value store such as RocksDB [16] or a relational database. RocksDB is based on SSTable [17], and it is fast for writes but slower for reads. A relational database usually uses a B+ tree [18] based storage engine, and it is fast for reads but slower for writes. As mentioned earlier, the data access pattern is write once and read multiple times. Since a relational database provides better read performance, it is a better choice than RocksDB.

How should we deploy this relational database? At our scale, the data volume for the mapping table is massive. Deploying a single large cluster to support all data nodes could work, but is difficult to manage. Note that this mapping data is isolated within each data node. There is no need to share this across data nodes. To take advantage of this property, we could simply deploy a simple relational database on each data node. SQLite [19] is a good choice here. It is a file-based relational database with a solid reputation.

Updated data persistence flow

Since we have made quite a few changes to the data node, let's revisit how to save a new object in the data node (Figure 9.13).

1. The API service sends a request to save a new object named object 4.

2. The data node service appends the object named object 4 at the end of the read-write file named /data/c.

3. A new record of object 4 is inserted into the object_mapping table.

4. The data node service returns the UUID to the API service.

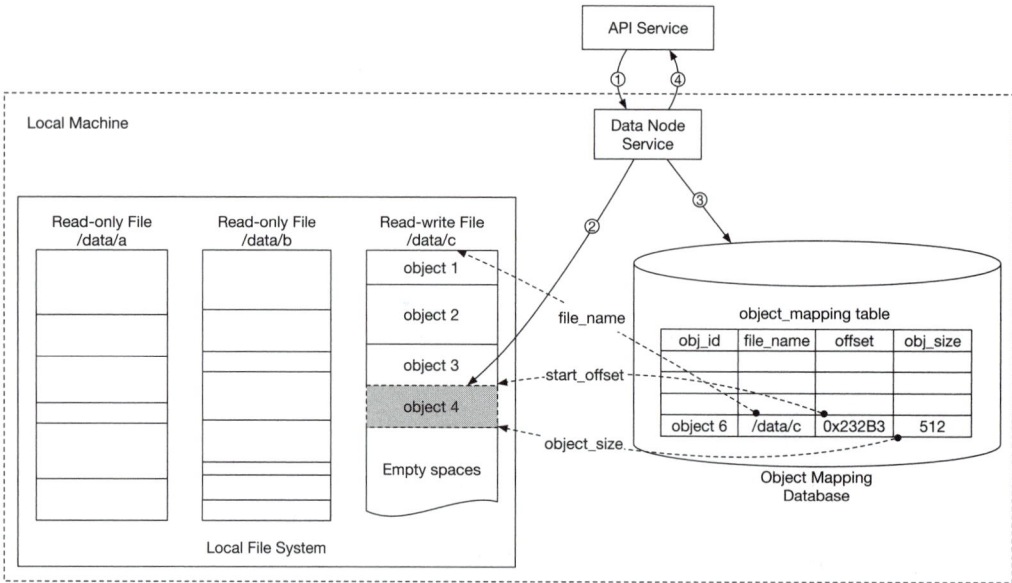

Figure 9.13: Updated data persistence flow

Durability

Data reliability is extremely important for data storage systems. How can we create a storage system that offers six nines of durability? Each failure case has to be carefully considered and data needs to be properly replicated.

Hardware failure and failure domain

Hard drive failures are inevitable no matter which media we use. Some storage media may have better durability than others, but we cannot rely on a single hard drive to achieve our durability objective. A proven way to increase durability is to replicate data to multiple hard drives, so a single disk failure does not impact the data availability, as a whole. In our design, we replicate data three times.

Let's assume the spinning hard drive has an annual failure rate of 0.81% [20]. This number highly depends on the model and make. Making 3 copies of data gives us $1 - 0.0081^3 =\sim 0.999999$ reliability. This is a very rough estimate. For more sophisticated calculations, please read [20].

For a complete durability evaluation, we also need to consider the impacts of different failure domains. A failure domain is a physical or logical section of the environment that is negatively affected when a critical service experiences problems. In a modern data center, a server is usually put into a rack [21], and the racks are grouped into rows/floors/-rooms. Since each rack shares network switches and power, all the servers in a rack are in a rack-level failure domain. A modern server shares components like the motherboard, processors, power supply, HDD drives, etc. The components in a server are in a node-level failure domain.

Here is a good example of a large-scale failure domain isolation. Typically, data centers divide infrastructure that shares nothing into different Availability Zones (AZs). We replicate our data to different AZs to minimize the failure impact (Figure 9.14). Note that the choice of failure domain level doesn't directly increase the durability of data, but it will result in better reliability in extreme cases, such as large-scale power outages, cooling system failures, natural disasters, etc.

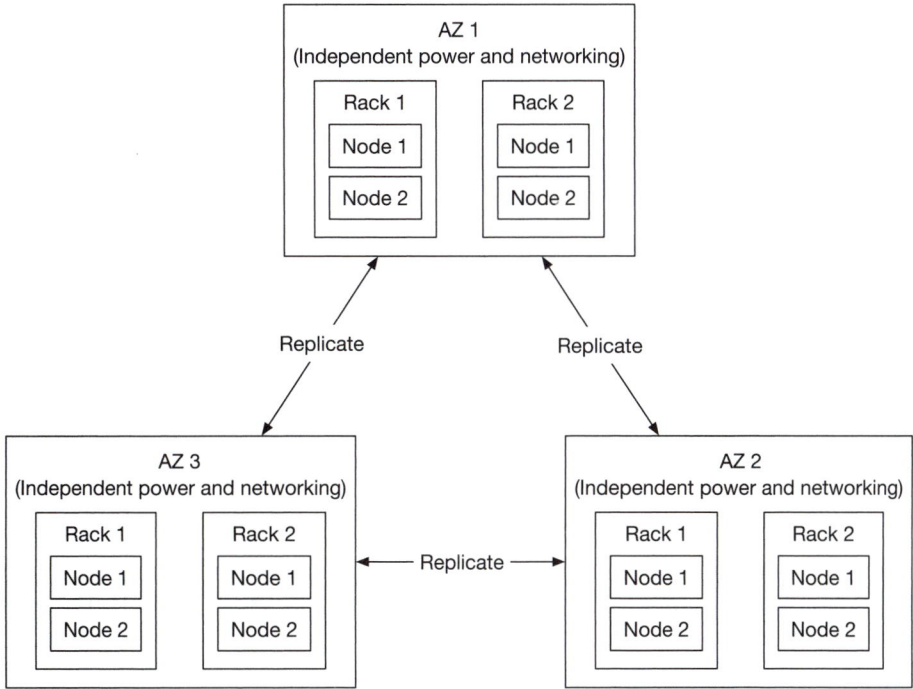

Figure 9.14: Multi-Datacenter replication

Erasure coding

Making three full copies of data gives us roughly 6 nines of data durability. Are there other options to further increase durability? Yes, erasure coding is one option. Erasure coding [22] deals with data durability differently. It chunks data into smaller pieces (placed on different servers) and creates parities for redundancy. In the event of failures, we can use chunk data and parities to reconstruct the data. Let's take a look at a concrete example (4 + 2 erasure coding) as shown in Figure 9.15.

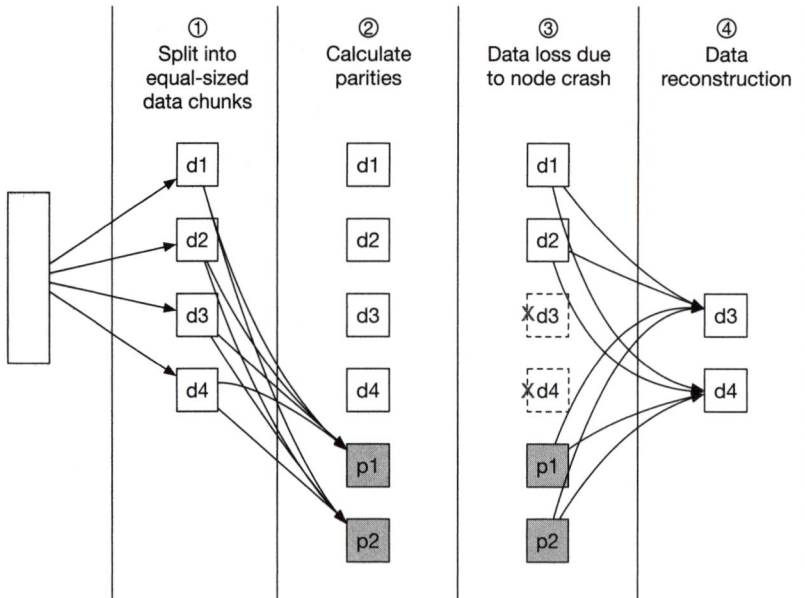

Figure 9.15: Erasure coding

1. Data is broken up into four even-sized data chunks d1, d2, d3, and d4.

2. The mathematical formula [23] is used to calculate the parities p1 and p2. To give a much simplified example, $p1 = d1 + 2 \times d2 - d3 + 4 \times d4$ and $p2 = -d1 + 5 \times d2 + d3 - 3 \times d4$ [24].

3. Data d3 and d4 are lost due to node crashes.

4. The mathematical formula is used to reconstruct lost data d3 and d4, using the known values of d1, d2, p1, and p2.

Let's take a look at another example as shown in Figure 9.16 to better understand how erasure coding works with failure domains. An $(8+4)$ erasure coding setup breaks up the original data evenly into 8 chunks and calculates 4 parities. All 12 pieces of data have the same size. All 12 chunks of data are distributed across 12 different failure domains. The mathematics behind erasure coding ensures that the original data can be reconstructed when at most 4 nodes are down.

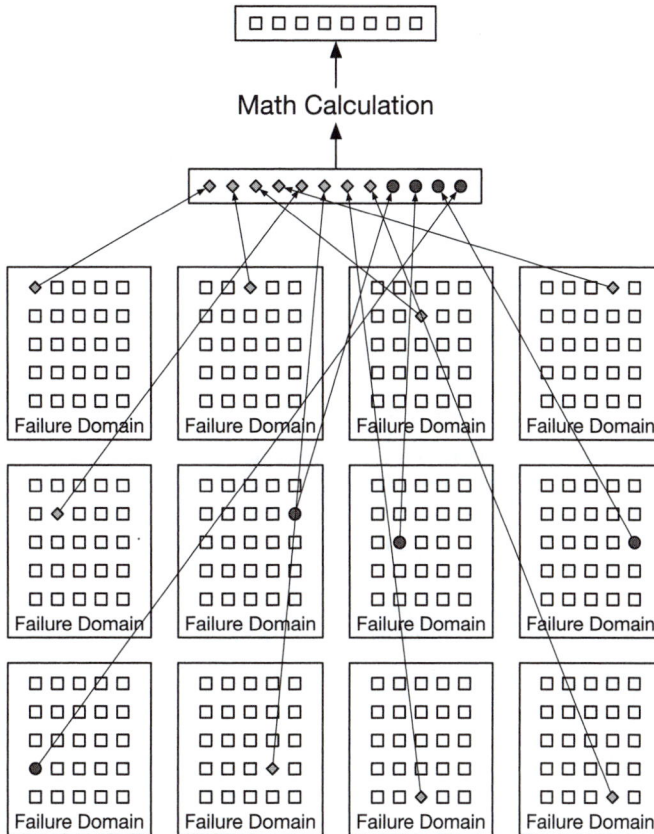

Figure 9.16: $(8 + 4)$ erasure coding

Compared to replication where the data router only needs to read data for an object from one healthy node, in erasure coding the data router has to read data from at least 8 healthy nodes. This is an architectural design tradeoff. We use a more complex solution with a slower access speed, in exchange for higher durability and lower storage cost. For object storage where the main cost is storage, this tradeoff might be worth it.

How much extra space does erasure coding need? For every two chunks of data, we need one parity block, so the storage overhead is 50% (Figure 9.17). While in 3-copy replication, the storage overhead is 200% (Figure 9.17).

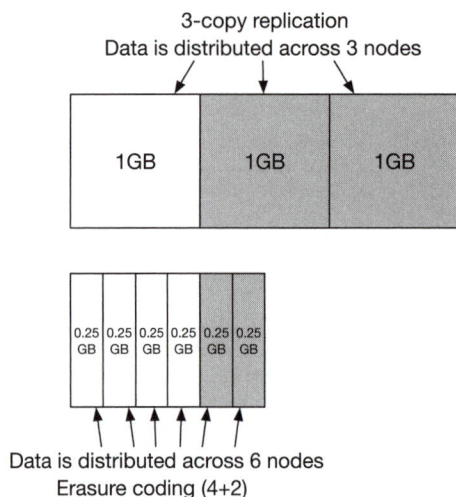

Figure 9.17: Extra space for replication and erasure coding

Does erasure coding increase data durability? Let's assume a node has a 0.81% annual failure rate. According to the calculation done by Backblaze [20], erasure coding can achieve 11 nines durability. The calculation requires complicated math. If you're interested, refer to [20] for details.

Table 9.5 compares the pros and cons of replication and erasure coding.

	Replication	**Erasure coding**
Durability	6 nines of durability (data copied 3 times)	11 nines of durability (8 + 4 erasure coding). **Erasure coding wins.**
Storage efficiency	200% storage overhead.	50% storage overhead. **Erasure coding wins.**
Compute resource	No computation. **Replication wins.**	Higher usage of computation resources to calculate parities.
Write performance	Replicating data to multiple nodes. No calculation is needed. **Replication wins.**	Increased write latency because we need to calculate parities before data is written to disk.
Read performance	In normal operation, reads are served from the same replica. Reads under a failure mode are not impacted because reads can be served from a non-fault replica. **Replication wins.**	In normal operation, every read has to come from multiple nodes in the cluster. Reads under a failure mode are slower because the missing data must be reconstructed first.

Table 9.5: Replication vs erasure coding

In summary, replication is widely adopted in latency-sensitive applications while erasure coding is often used to minimize storage cost. Erasure coding is attractive for its cost efficiency and durability, but it greatly complicates the data node design. Therefore, for this design, we mainly focus on replication.

Correctness verification

Erasure coding increases data durability at comparable storage costs. Now we can move on to solve another hard challenge: data corruption.

If a disk fails completely and the failure can be detected, it can be treated as a data node failure. In this case, we can reconstruct data using erasure coding. However, in-memory data corruption is a regular occurrence in large-scale systems.

This problem can be addressed by verifying checksums [25] between process boundaries. A checksum is a small-sized block of data that is used to detect data errors. Figure 9.18 illustrates how the checksum is generated.

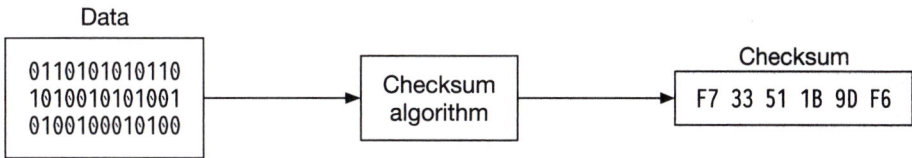

Figure 9.18: Generate checksum

If we know the checksum of the original data, we can compute the checksum of the data after transmission:

- If they are different, data is corrupted.
- If they are the same, there is a very high probability the data is not corrupted. The probability is not 100%, but in practice, we could assume they are the same.

Figure 9.19: Compare checksums

There are many checksum algorithms, such as MD5 [26], SHA1 [27], HMAC [28], etc. A good checksum algorithm usually outputs a significantly different value even for a small change made to the input. For this chapter, we choose a simple checksum algorithm such as MD5.

In our design, we append the checksum at the end of each object. Before a file is marked as read-only, we add a checksum of the entire file at the end. Figure 9.20 shows the layout.

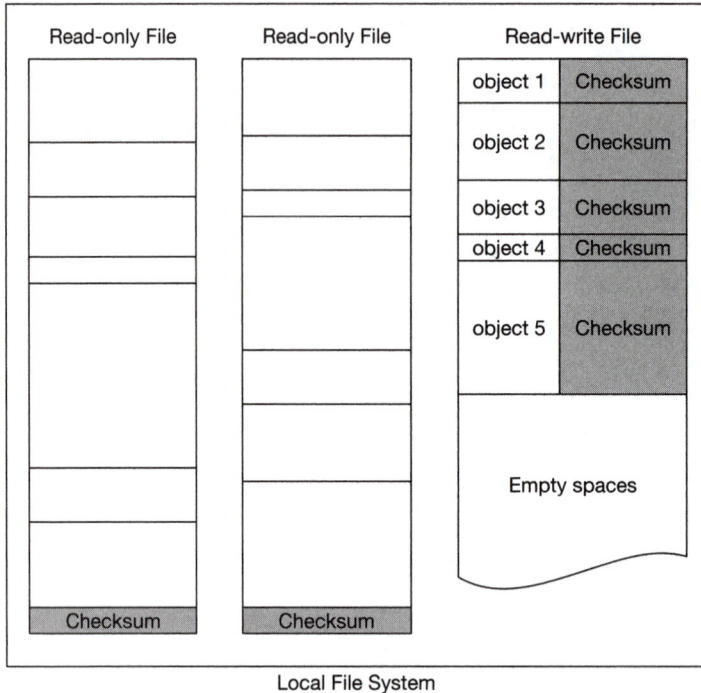

Figure 9.20: Add checksum to data node

With $(8 + 4)$ erasure coding and checksum verification, this is what happens when we read data:

1. Fetch the object data and the checksum.
2. Compute the checksum against the data received.
   (a) If the two checksums match, the data is error-free.
   (b) If the checksums are different, the data is corrupted. We will try to recover by reading the data from other failure domains.
3. Repeat steps 1 and 2 until all 8 pieces of data are returned. We then reconstruct the data and send it back to the client.

Metadata data model

In this section, we first discuss the database schema and then dive into scaling the database.

Schema

The database schema needs to support the following 3 queries:

Query 1: Find the object ID by object name.

Query 2: Insert and delete an object based on the object name.

Query 3: List objects in a bucket sharing the same prefix.

Figure 9.21 shows the schema design. We need two database tables: bucket and object.

bucket
bucket_name
bucket_id
owner_id
enable_versioning

object
bucket_name
object_name
object_version
object_id

Figure 9.21: Database tables

Scale the bucket table

Since there is usually a limit on the number of buckets a user can create, the size of the bucket table is small. Let's assume we have 1 million customers, each customer owns 10 buckets and each record takes 1KB. That means we need 10GB (1 million $\times 10 \times$ 1KB) of storage space. The whole table can easily fit in a modern database server. However, a single database server might not have enough CPU or network bandwidth to handle all read requests. If so, we can spread the read load among multiple database replicas.

Scale the object table

The object table holds the object metadata. The dataset at our design scale will likely not fit in a single database instance. We can scale the object table by sharding.

One option is to shard by the bucket_id so all the objects under the same bucket are stored in one shard. This doesn't work because it causes hotspot shards as a bucket might contain billions of objects.

Another option is to shard by object_id. The benefit of this sharding scheme is that it evenly distributes the load. But we will not be able to execute query 1 and query 2 efficiently because those two queries are based on the URI.

We choose to shard by a combination of bucket_name and object_name. This is because most of the metadata operations are based on the object URI, for example, finding the object ID by URI or uploading an object via URI. To evenly distribute the data, we can use the hash of the <bucket_name, object_name> as the sharding key.

With this sharding scheme, it is straightforward to support the first two queries, but the last query is less obvious. Let's take a look.

Listing objects in a bucket

The object store arranges files in a flat structure instead of a hierarchy, like in a file system. An object can be accessed using a path in this format, s3://bucket-name/object-name. For example, s3://mybucket/abc/d/e/f/file.txt contains:

- Bucket name: mybucket
- Object name: abc/d/e/f/file.txt

To help users organize their objects in a bucket, S3 introduces a concept called 'prefixes'. A prefix is a string at the beginning of the object name. S3 uses prefixes to organize the data in a way similar to directories. However, prefixes are not directories. Listing a bucket by prefix limits the results to only those object names that begin with the prefix.

In the example above with the path s3://mybucket/abc/d/e/f/file.txt, the prefix is abc/d/e/f/.

The AWS S3 listing command has 3 typical uses:

1. List all buckets owned by a user. The command looks like this:

   ```
   aws s3 list-buckets
   ```

2. List all objects in a bucket that are at the same level as the specified prefix. The command looks like this:

   ```
   aws s3 ls s3://mybucket/abc/
   ```

   In this mode, objects with more slashes in the name after the prefix are rolled up into a common prefix. For example, with these objects in the bucket:

   ```
   CA/cities/losangeles.txt
   CA/cities/sanfranciso.txt
   NY/cities/ny.txt
   federal.txt
   ```

   Listing the bucket with the "/" prefix would return these results, with everything under CA/ and NY/ rolled up into them:

   ```
   CA/
   NY/
   federal.txt
   ```

3. Recursively list all objects in a bucket that shares the same prefix. The command looks like this:

   ```
   aws s3 ls s3://mybucket/abc/ --recursive
   ```

   Using the same example as above, listing the bucket with the CA/ prefix would return these results:

   ```
   CA/cities/losangeles.txt
   CA/cities/sanfranciso.txt
   ```

Single database

Let's first explore how we would support the listing command with a single database. To list all buckets owned by a user, we run the following query:

```
SELECT * FROM bucket WHERE owner_id={id}
```

To list all objects in a bucket that share the same prefix, we run a query like this.

```
SELECT * FROM object
WHERE bucket_id = "123" AND object_name LIKE `abc/%`
```

In this example, we find all objects with bucket_id equals to 123 that share the prefix abc/. Any objects with more slashes in their names after the specified prefix are rolled up in the application code as stated earlier in use case 2.

The same query would support the recursive listing mode, as stated in use case 3 previously. The application code would list every object sharing the same prefix, without performing any rollups.

Distributed databases

When the metadata table is sharded, it's difficult to implement the listing function because we don't know which shards contain the data. The most obvious solution is to run a search query on all shards and then aggregate the results. To achieve this, we can do the following:

1. The metadata service queries every shard by running the following query:

```
SELECT * FROM object
WHERE bucket_id = "123" AND object_name LIKE `a/b/%`
```

2. The metadata service aggregates all objects returned from each shard and returns the result to the caller.

This solution works, but implementing pagination for this is a bit complicated. Before we explain why, let's review how pagination works for a simple case with a single database. To return pages of listing with 10 objects for each page, the SELECT query would start with this:

```
SELECT * FROM object
WHERE bucket_id = "123" AND object_name LIKE `a/b/%`
ORDER BY object_name OFFSET 0 LIMIT 10
```

The OFFSET and LIMIT would restrict the results to the first 10 objects. In the next call, the user sends the request with a hint to the server, so it knows to construct the query for the second page with an OFFSET of 10. This hint is usually done with a cursor that the server returns with each page to the client. The offset information is encoded in the cursor. The client would include the cursor in the request for the next page. The server decodes the cursor and uses the offset information embedded in it to construct the query for the next page. To continue with the example above, the query for the second page looks like this:

```
SELECT * FROM metadata
WHERE bucket_id = "123" AND object_name LIKE `a/b/%`
ORDER BY object_name OFFSET 10 LIMIT 10
```

This client-server request loop continues until the server returns a special cursor that marks the end of the entire listing.

Now, let's explore why it's complicated to support pagination for sharded databases. Since the objects are distributed across shards, the shards would likely return a varying number of results. Some shards would contain a full page of 10 objects, while others would be partial or empty. The application code would receive results from every shard, aggregate and sort them, and return only a page of 10 in our example. The objects that don't get included in the current round must be considered again for the next round. This means that each shard would likely have a different offset. The server must track the offsets for all the shards and associate those offsets with the cursor. If there are hundreds of shards, there will be hundreds of offsets to track.

We have a solution that can solve the problem, but there are some tradeoffs. Since object storage is tuned for vast scale and high durability, object listing performance is rarely a priority. In fact, all commercial object storage supports object listing with sub-optimal performance. To take advantage of this, we could denormalize the listing data into a separate table sharded by bucket ID. This table is only used for listing objects. With this setup, even buckets with billions of objects would offer acceptable performance. This isolates the listing query to a single database which greatly simplifies the implementation.

Object versioning

Versioning is a feature that keeps multiple versions of an object in a bucket. With versioning, we can restore objects that are accidentally deleted or overwritten. For example, we may modify a document and save it under the same name, inside the same bucket. Without versioning, the old version of the document metadata is replaced by the new version in the metadata store. The old version of the document is marked as deleted, so its storage space will be reclaimed by the garbage collector. With versioning, the object storage keeps all previous versions of the document in the metadata store, and the old versions of the document are never marked as deleted in the object store.

Figure 9.22 explains how to upload a versioned object. For this to work, we first need to enable versioning on the bucket.

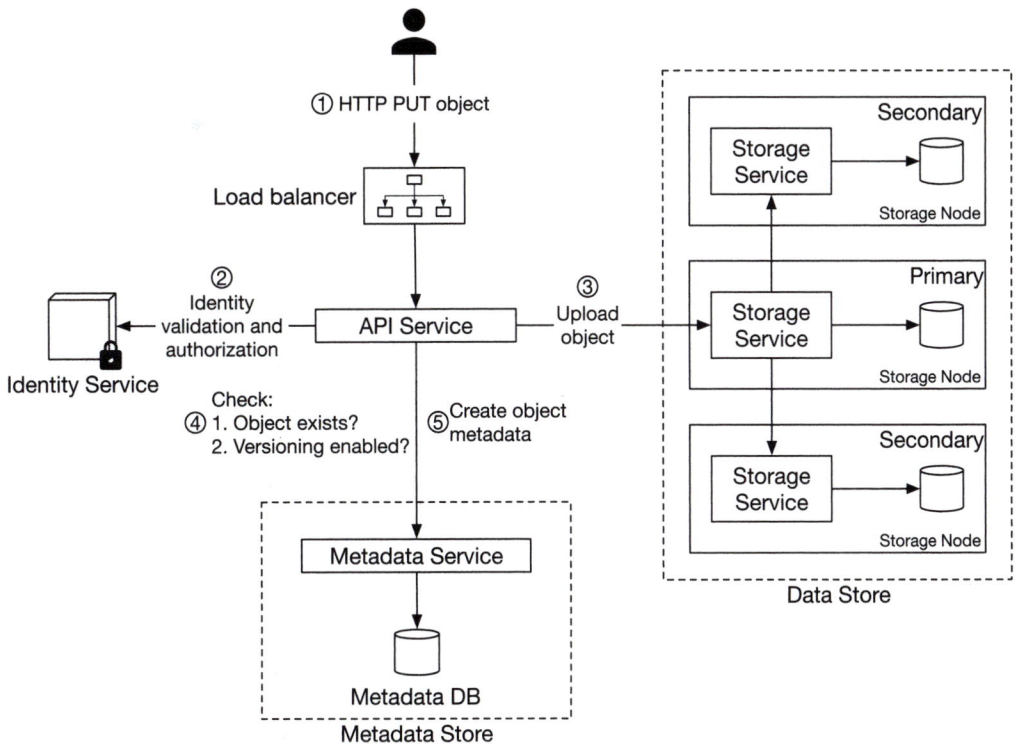

Figure 9.22: Object versioning

1. The client sends an HTTP PUT request to upload an object named script.txt.

2. The API service verifies the user's identity and ensures that the user has WRITE permission on the bucket.

3. Once verified, the API service uploads the data to the data store. The data store persists the data as a new object and returns a new UUID to the API service.

4. The API service calls the metadata store to store the metadata information of this object.

5. To support versioning, the object table for the metadata store has a column called object_version that is only used if versioning is enabled. Instead of overwriting the existing record, a new record is inserted with the same bucket_id and object_name as the old record, but with a new object_id and object_version. The object_id is the UUID for the new object returned in step 3. The object_version is a TIMEUUID [29] generated when the new row is inserted. No matter which database we choose for the metadata store, it should be efficient to look up the current version of an object. The current version has the largest TIMEUUID of all the entries with the same object_name. See Figure 9.23 for an illustration of how we store versioned metadata.

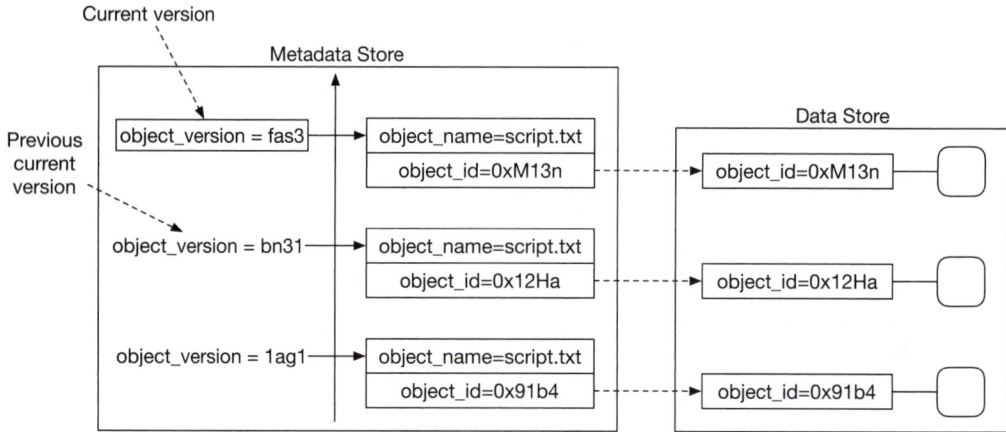

Figure 9.23: Versioned metadata

In addition to uploading a versioned object, it can also be deleted. Let's take a look.

When we delete an object, all versions remain in the bucket and we insert a delete marker, as shown in Figure 9.24.

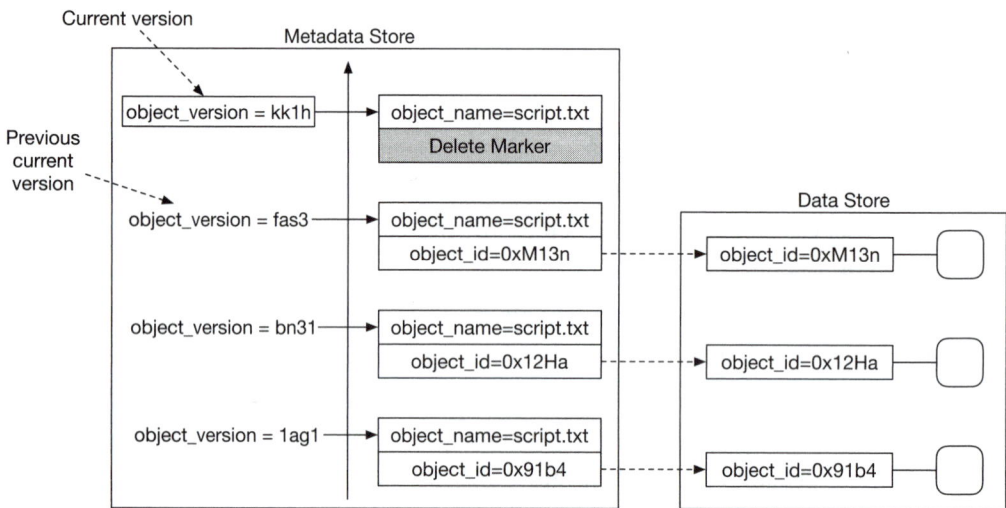

Figure 9.24: Delete object by inserting a delete marker

A delete marker is a new version of the object, and it becomes the current version of the object once inserted. Performing a GET request when the current version of the object is a delete marker returns a 404 Object Not Found error.

Optimizing uploads of large files

In the back-of-the-envelope estimation, we estimated that 20% of the objects are large. Some might be larger than a few GBs. It is possible to upload such a large object file directly, but it could take a long time. If the network connection fails in the middle of the upload, we have to start over. A better solution is to slice a large object into smaller parts and upload them independently. After all the parts are uploaded, the object store re-assembles the object from the parts. This process is called multipart upload.

Figure 9.25 illustrates how multipart upload works:

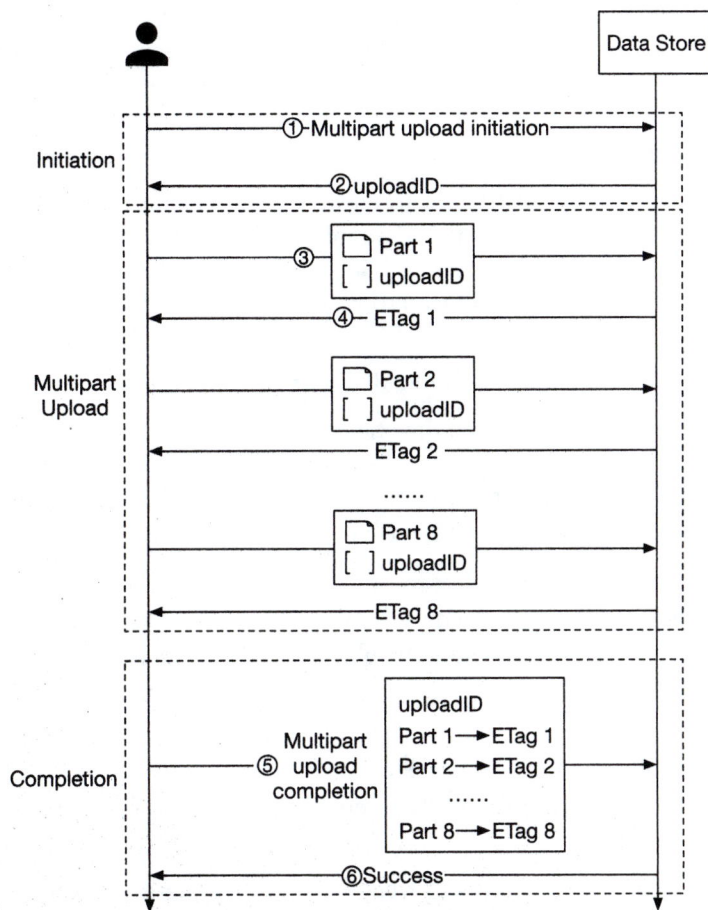

Figure 9.25: Multipart upload

1. The client calls the object storage to initiate a multipart upload.

2. The data store returns an uploadID, which uniquely identifies the upload.

3. The client splits the large file into small objects and starts uploading. Let's assume the size of the file is 1.6GB and the client splits it into 8 parts, so each part is 200MB in size. The client uploads the first part to the data store together with the uploadID it received in step 2.

4. When a part is uploaded, the data store returns an ETag, which is essentially the md5 checksum of that part. It is used to verify multipart uploads.

5. After all parts are uploaded, the client sends a complete multipart upload request, which includes the uploadID, part numbers, and ETags.

6. The data store reassembles the object from its parts based on the part number. Since the object is really large, this process may take a few minutes. After reassembly is

complete, it returns a success message to the client.

One potential problem with this approach is that old parts are no longer useful after the object has been reassembled from them. To solve this problem, we can introduce a garbage collection service responsible for freeing up space from parts that are no longer needed.

Garbage collection

Garbage collection is the process of automatically reclaiming storage space that is no longer used. There are a few ways that data might become garbage:

- Lazy object deletion. An object is marked as deleted at delete time without actually being deleted.
- Orphan data. For example, half uploaded data or abandoned multipart uploads.
- Corrupted data. Data that failed the checksum verification.

The garbage collector does not remove objects from the data store, right away. Deleted objects will be periodically cleaned up with a compaction mechanism.

The garbage collector is also responsible for reclaiming unused space in replicas. For replication, we delete the object from both primary and backup nodes. For erasure coding, if we use $(8 + 4)$ setup, we delete the object from all 12 nodes.

Figure 9.26 shows an example of how compaction works.

1. The garbage collector copies objects from /data/b to a new file named /data/d. Note the garbage collector skips "Object 2" and "Object 5" because the delete flag is set to true for both of them.

2. After all objects are copied, the garbage collector updates the object_mapping table. For example, the obj_id and object_size fields of "Object 3" remain the same, but file_name and start_offset are updated to reflect its new location. To ensure data consistency, it's a good idea to wrap the update operations to file_name and start_offset in a database transaction.

object_mapping table

obj_id	file_name	offset	obj_size
object 3	/data/b	0x232B3	

object_mapping table

obj_id	file_name	offset	obj_size
object 3	/data/d	0x10013	

/data/b

X Object 2
Object 3

X Object 5

Read-only File

Before Compaction

/data/d

Object 3

Read-only File

After Compaction

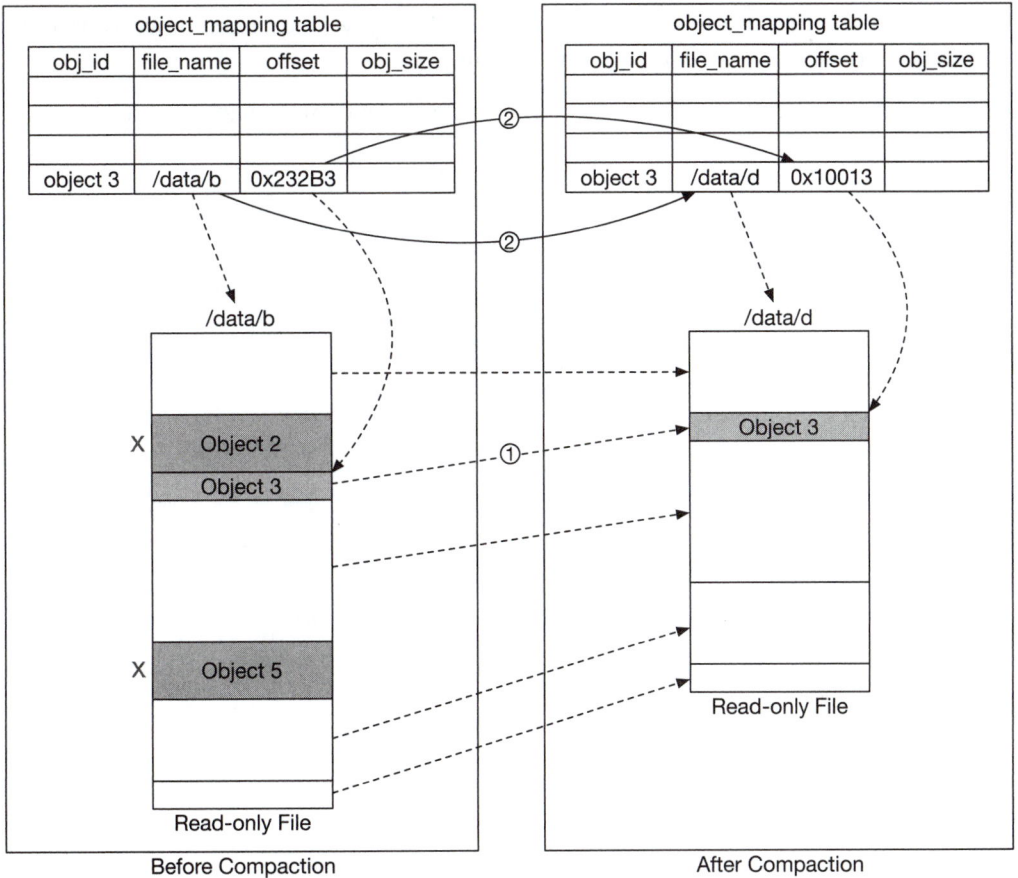

Figure 9.26: Compaction

As we can see from Figure 9.26, the size of the new file after compaction is smaller than the old file. To avoid creating a lot of small files, the garbage collector usually waits until there are a large number of read-only files to compact, and the compaction process appends objects from many read-only files into a few large new files.

Step 4 - Wrap Up

In this chapter, we described the high-level design for S3-like object storage. We compared the differences between block storage, file storage, and object storage.

The focus of this interview is on the design of object storage, so we listed how the uploading, downloading, listing objects in a bucket, and versioning of objects are typically done in object storage.

Then we dived deeper into the design. Object storage is composed of a data store and a metadata store. We explained how the data is persisted into the data store and discussed two methods for increasing reliability and durability: replication and erasure coding. For the metadata store, we explained how the multipart upload is executed and how to design the database schema to support typical use cases. Lastly, we explained how to shard the metadata store to support even larger data volume.

Congratulations on getting this far! Now give yourself a pat on the back. Good job!

Chapter Summary

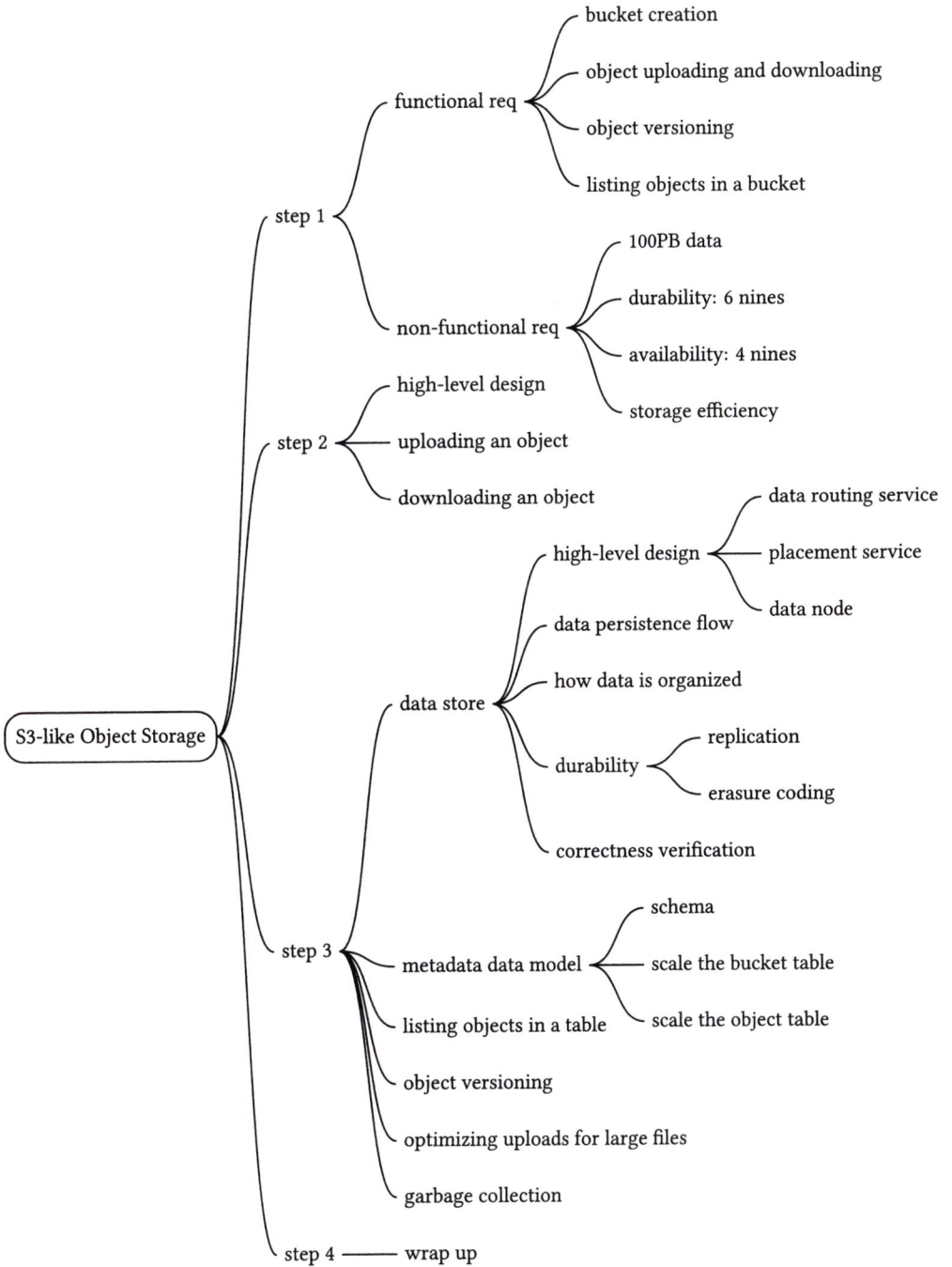

S3-like Object Storage

- step 1
  - functional req
    - bucket creation
    - object uploading and downloading
    - object versioning
    - listing objects in a bucket
  - non-functional req
    - 100PB data
    - durability: 6 nines
    - availability: 4 nines
    - storage efficiency
- step 2
  - high-level design
  - uploading an object
  - downloading an object
- step 3
  - data store
    - high-level design
      - data routing service
      - placement service
      - data node
    - data persistence flow
    - how data is organized
    - durability
      - replication
      - erasure coding
    - correctness verification
  - metadata data model
    - schema
    - scale the bucket table
    - scale the object table
  - listing objects in a table
  - object versioning
  - optimizing uploads for large files
  - garbage collection
- step 4 — wrap up

Reference Material

[1] Fibre channel. https://en.wikipedia.org/wiki/Fibre_Channel.

[2] iSCSI. https://en.wikipedia.org/wiki/ISCSI.

[3] Server Message Block. https://en.wikipedia.org/wiki/Server_Message_Block.

[4] Network File System. https://en.wikipedia.org/wiki/Network_File_System.

[5] Amazon S3 Strong Consistency. https://aws.amazon.com/s3/consistency/.

[6] Serial Attached SCSI. https://en.wikipedia.org/wiki/Serial_Attached_SCSI.

[7] AWS CLI ls command. https://docs.aws.amazon.com/cli/latest/reference/s3/ls.html.

[8] Amazon S3 Service Level Agreement. https://aws.amazon.com/s3/sla/.

[9] Ambry. LinkedIn'sScalableGeo-DistributedObjectStore:https://assured-cloud-com puting.illinois.edu/files/2014/03/Ambry-LinkedIns-Scalable-GeoDistributed-Objec t-Store.pdf.

[10] inode. https://en.wikipedia.org/wiki/Inode.

[11] Ceph's Rados Gateway. https://docs.ceph.com/en/pacific/radosgw/index.html.

[12] grpc. https://grpc.io/.

[13] Paxos. https://en.wikipedia.org/wiki/Paxos_(computer_science).

[14] Raft. https://raft.github.io/.

[15] Consistent hashing. https://www.toptal.com/big-data/consistent-hashing.

[16] RocksDB. https://github.com/facebook/rocksdb.

[17] SSTable. https://www.igvita.com/2012/02/06/sstable-and-log-structured-storage-l eveldb/.

[18] B+ tree. https://en.wikipedia.org/wiki/B%2B_tree.

[19] SQLite. https://www.sqlite.org/index.html.

[20] Data Durability Calculation. https://www.backblaze.com/blog/cloud-storage-dur ability/.

[21] Rack. https://en.wikipedia.org/wiki/19-inch_rack.

[22] Erasure Coding. https://en.wikipedia.org/wiki/Erasure_code.

[23] Reed–Solomon error correction. https://en.wikipedia.org/wiki/Reed%E2%80%93Sol omon_error_correction.

[24] Erasure Coding Demystified. https://www.youtube.com/watch?v=Q5kVuM7zEUI.

[25] Checksum. https://en.wikipedia.org/wiki/Checksum.

[26] Md5. https://en.wikipedia.org/wiki/MD5.

[27] Sha1. https://en.wikipedia.org/wiki/SHA-1.

[28] Hmac. https://en.wikipedia.org/wiki/HMAC.

[29] TIMEUUID. https://docs.datastax.com/en/cql-oss/3.3/cql/cql_reference/timeuuid_functions_r.html.

10 Real-time Gaming Leaderboard

In this chapter, we are going to walk through the challenge of designing a leaderboard for an online mobile game.

What is a leaderboard? Leaderboards are common in gaming and elsewhere to show who is leading a particular tournament or competition. Users are assigned points for completing tasks or challenges, and whoever has the most points is at the top of the leaderboard. Figure 10.1 shows an example of a mobile game leaderboard. The leaderboard shows the ranking of the leading competitors and also displays the position of the user on it.

Rank	Player	Points
⭐ 1	Aquaboys	976
⭐ 2	B team	956
⭐ 3	Berlin's Angels	890
☆ 4	GrendelTeam	878

Figure 10.1: Leaderboard

Step 1 - Understand the Problem and Establish Design Scope

Leaderboards can be pretty straightforward, but there are a number of different matters that can add complexity. We should clarify the requirements.

Candidate: How is the score calculated for the leaderboard?

Interviewer: The user gets a point when they win a match. We can go with a simple point system in which each user has a score associated with them. Each time the user wins a match, we should add a point to their total score.

Candidate: Are all players included in the leaderboard?
Interviewer: Yes.

Candidate: Is there a time segment associated with the leaderboard?
Interviewer: Each month, a new tournament kicks off which starts a new leaderboard.

Candidate: Can we assume we only care about the top 10 users?
Interviewer: We want to display the top 10 users as well as the position of a specific user on the leaderboard. If time allows, let's also discuss how to return users who are four places above and below a specific user.

Candidate: How many users are in a tournament?
Interviewer: Average of 5 million daily active users (DAU) and 25 million monthly active users (MAU).

Candidate: How many matches are played on average during a tournament?
Interviewer: Each player plays 10 matches per day on average.

Candidate: How do we determine the rank if two players have the same score?
Interviewer: In this case, their ranks are the same. If time allows, we can talk about ways to break ties.

Candidate: Does the leaderboard need to be real-time?
Interviewer: Yes, we want to present real-time results, or as close as possible. It is not okay to present a batched history of results.

Now that we've gathered all the requirements, let's list the functional requirements.

- Display top 10 players on the leaderboard.
- Show a user's specific rank.
- Display players who are four places above and below the desired user (bonus).

Other than clarifying functional requirements, it's important to understand non-functional requirements.

Non-functional requirements

- Real-time update on scores.
- Score update is reflected on the leaderboard in real-time.
- General scalability, availability, and reliability requirements.

Back-of-the-envelope estimation

Let's take a look at some back-of-the-envelope calculations to determine the potential scale and challenges our solution will need to address.

With 5 million DAU, if the game had an even distribution of players during a 24-hour period, we would have an average of 50 users per second $\left(\frac{5,000,000 \text{ DAU}}{10^5 \text{ seconds}} =\sim 50 \right)$. However, we know that usages most likely aren't evenly distributed, and potentially there are peaks during evenings when many people across different time zones have time to play. To account for this, we could assume that peak load would be 5 times the average. Therefore we'd want to allow for a peak load of 250 users per second.

QPS for users scoring a point: if a user plays 10 games per day on average, the QPS for users scoring a point is: $50 \times 10 =\sim 500$. Peak QPS is 5x of the average: $500 \times 5 = 2,500$.

QPS for fetching the top 10 leaderboard: assume a user opens the game once a day and the top 10 leaderboard is loaded only when a user first opens the game. The QPS for this is around 50.

Step 2 - Propose High-level Design and Get Buy-in

In this section, we will discuss API design, high-level architecture, and data models.

API design

At a high level, we need the following three APIs:

POST /v1/scores

Update a user's position on the leaderboard when a user wins a game. The request parameters are listed below. This should be an internal API that can only be called by the game servers. The client should not be able to update the leaderboard score directly.

Field	Description
user_id	The user who wins a game.
points	The number of points a user gained by winning a game.

Table 10.1: Request parameters

Response:

Name	Description
200 OK	Successfully updated a user's score.
400 Bad Request	Failed to update a user's score.

Table 10.2: Response

GET /v1/scores

Fetch the top 10 players from the leaderboard.

Sample response:

```
{
  "data": [
    {
      "user_id": "user_id1",
      "user_name": "alice",
      "rank": 1,
      "score": 976
    },
    {
      "user_id": "user_id2",
      "user_name": "bob",
      "rank": 2,
      "score": 965
    }
  ],
  ...
  "total": 10
}
```

GET /v1/scores/{:user_id}

Fetch the rank of a specific user.

Field	Description
user_id	The ID of the user whose rank we would like to fetch.

Table 10.3: Request parameters

Sample response:

```
{
  "user_info": {
    "user_id": "user5",
    "score": 940,
    "rank": 6,
  }
}
```

High-level architecture

The high-level design diagram is shown in Figure 10.2. There are two services in this design. The game service allows users to play the game and the leaderboard service creates and displays a leaderboard.

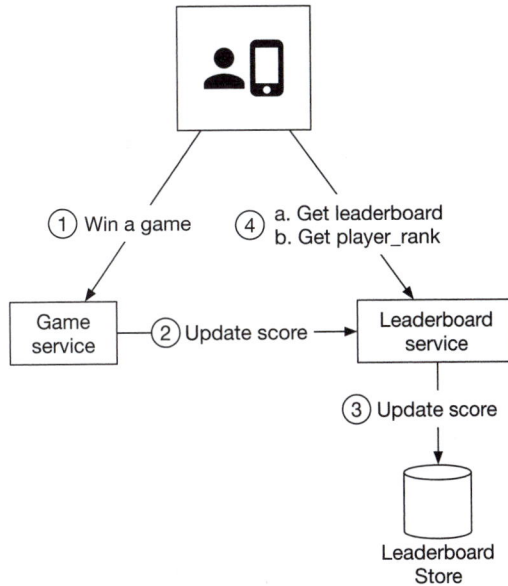

Figure 10.2: High-level design

1. When a player wins a game, the client sends a request to the game service.

2. The game service ensures the win is valid and calls the leaderboard service to update the score.

3. The leaderboard service updates the user's score in the leaderboard store.

4. A player makes a call to the leaderboard service directly to fetch leaderboard data, including:

   (a) top 10 leaderboard.

   (b) the rank of the player on the leaderboard.

Before settling on this design, we considered a few alternatives and decided against them. It might be helpful to go through the thought process of this and to compare different options.

Should the client talk to the leaderboard service directly?

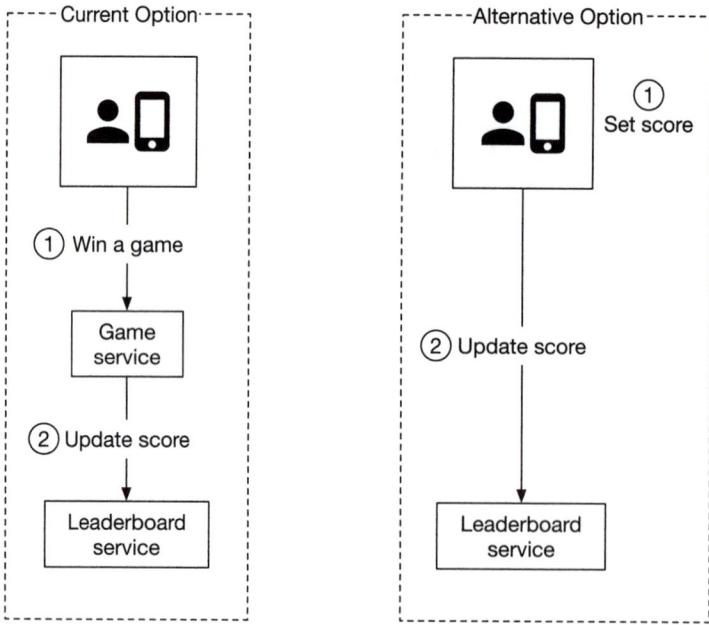

Figure 10.3: Who sets the leaderboard score

In the alternative design, the score is set by the client. This option is not secure because it is subject to man-in-the-middle attack [1], where players can put in a proxy and change scores at will. Therefore, we need the score to be set on the server-side.

Note that for server authoritative games such as online poker, the client may not need to call the game server explicitly to set scores. The game server handles all game logic, and it knows when the game finishes and could set the score without any client intervention.

Do we need a message queue between the game service and the leaderboard service?

The answer to this question highly depends on how the game scores are used. If the data is used in other places or supports multiple functionalities, then it might make sense to put data in Kafka as shown in Figure 10.4. This way, the same data can be consumed by multiple consumers, such as leaderboard service, analytics service, push notification service, etc. This is especially true when the game is a turn-based or multi-player game in which we need to notify other players about the score update. As this is not an explicit requirement based on the conversation with the interviewer, we do not use a message queue in our design.

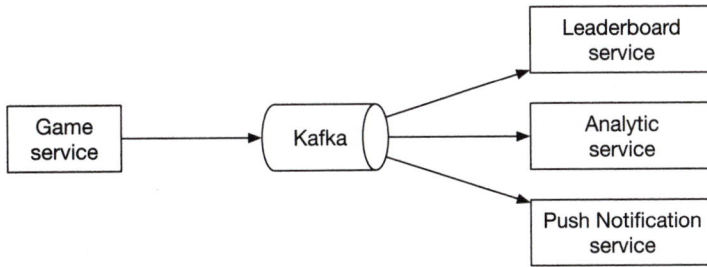

Figure 10.4: Game scores are used by multiple services

Data models

One of the key components in the system is the leaderboard store. We will discuss three potential solutions: relational database, Redis, and NoSQL (NoSQL solution is explained in deep dive section on page 308).

Relational database solution

First, let's take a step back and start with the simplest solution. What if the scale doesn't matter and we have only a few users?

We would most likely opt to have a simple leaderboard solution using a relational database system (RDS). Each monthly leaderboard could be represented as a database table containing user id and score columns. When the user wins a match, either award the user 1 point if they are new, or increase their existing score by 1 point. To determine a user's ranking on the leaderboard, we would sort the table by the score in descending order. The details are explained below.

Leaderboard DB table:

Figure 10.5: Leaderboard table

In reality, the leaderboard table has additional information, such as a game_id, a timestamp, etc. However, the underlying logic of how to query and update the leaderboard remains the same. For simplicity, we assume only the current month's leaderboard data is stored in the leaderboard table.

A user wins a point:

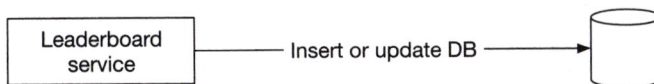

Figure 10.6: A user wins a point

Assume every score update would be an increment of 1. If a user doesn't yet have an entry in the leaderboard for the month, the first insert would be:

```
INSERT INTO leaderboard (user_id, score) VALUES ('mary1934', 1)
;
```

An update to the user's score would be:

```
UPDATE leaderboard set score=score + 1 where user_id='mary1934';
```

Find a user's leaderboard position:

Figure 10.7: Find a user's leaderboard position

To fetch the user rank, we would sort the leaderboard table and rank by the score:

```
SELECT (@rownum := @rownum + 1) AS rank, user_id, score
FROM leaderboard
ORDER BY score DESC;
```

The result of the SQL query looks like this:

rank	user_id	score
1	happy_tomato	987
2	mallow	902
3	smith	870
4	mary1934	850

Table 10.4: Result sorted by score

This solution works when the data set is small, but the query becomes very slow when there are millions of rows. Let's take a look at why.

To figure out the rank of a user, we need to sort every single player into their correct spot on the leaderboard so we can determine exactly what the correct rank is. Remember that there can be duplicate scores as well, so the rank isn't just the position of the user in the list.

SQL databases are not performant when we have to process large amounts of continuously changing information. Attempting to do a rank operation over millions of rows is going to take 10s of seconds, which is not acceptable for the desired real-time approach. Since the data is constantly changing, it is also not feasible to consider a cache.

A relational database is not designed to handle the high load of read queries this implementation would require. An RDS could be used successfully if done as a batch operation, but that would not align with the requirement to return a real-time position for the user on the leaderboard.

One optimization we can do is to add an index and limit the number of pages to scan with the LIMIT clause. The query looks like this:

```
SELECT (@rownum := @rownum + 1) AS rank, user_id, score
FROM leaderboard
ORDER BY score DESC
LIMIT 10
```

However, this approach doesn't scale well. First, finding a user's rank is not performant because it essentially requires a table scan to determine the rank. Second, this approach doesn't provide a straightforward solution for determining the rank of a user who is not at the top of the leaderboard.

Redis solution

We want to find a solution that gives us predictable performance even for millions of users and allows us to have easy access to common leaderboard operations, without needing to fall back on complex DB queries.

Redis provides a potential solution to our problem. Redis is an in-memory data store supporting key-value pairs. Since it works in memory, it allows for fast reads and writes. Redis has a specific data type called **sorted sets** that are ideal for solving leaderboard system design problems.

What are sorted sets?

A sorted set is a data type similar to a set. Each member of a sorted set is associated with a score. The members of a set must be unique, but scores may repeat. The score is used to rank the sorted set in ascending order.

Our leaderboard use case maps perfectly to sorted sets. Internally, a sorted set is implemented by two data structures: a hash table and a skip list [2]. The hash table maps users to scores and the skip list maps scores to users. In sorted sets, users are sorted by scores. A good way to understand a sorted set is to picture it as a table with score and member columns as shown in Figure 10.8. The table is sorted by score in descending order.

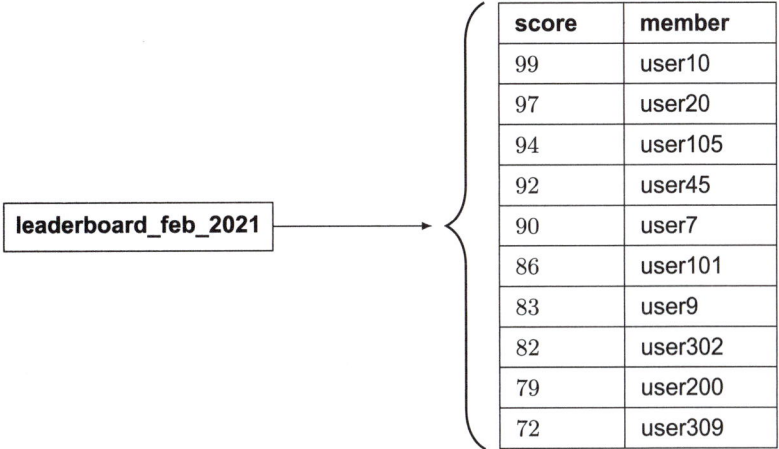

score	member
99	user10
97	user20
94	user105
92	user45
90	user7
86	user101
83	user9
82	user302
79	user200
72	user309

leaderboard_feb_2021 ⟶

Figure 10.8: February leaderboard is represented by the sorted set

In this chapter, we don't go into the full detail of the sorted set implementation, but we do go over the high-level ideas.

A skip list is a list structure that allows for fast search. It consists of a base sorted linked list and multi-level indexes. Let's take a look at an example. In Figure 10.9, the base list is a sorted singly-linked list. The time complexity of insertion, removal, and search operations is $O(n)$.

How can we make those operations faster? One idea is to get to the middle quickly, as the binary search algorithm does. To achieve that, we add a level 1 index that skips every other node, and then a level 2 index that skips every other node of the level 1 indexes. We keep introducing additional levels, with each new level skipping every other nodes of the previous level. We stop this addition when the distance between nodes is $\frac{n}{2} - 1$, where n is the total number of nodes. As shown in Figure 10.9, searching for number 45 is a lot faster when we have multi-level indexes.

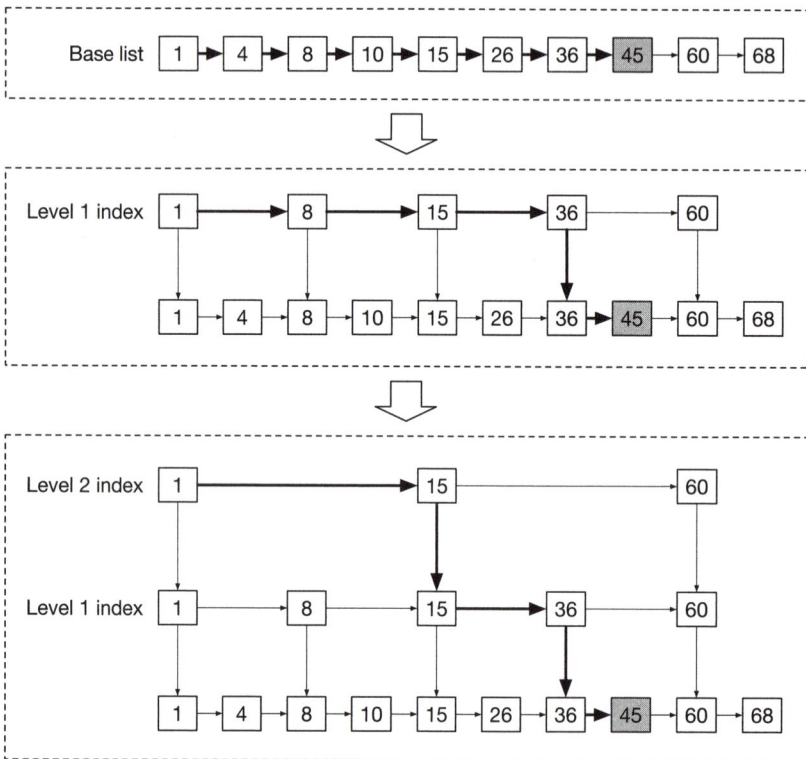

Figure 10.9: Skip list

When the data set is small, the speed improvement using the skip list isn't obvious. Figure 10.10 shows an example of a skip list with 5 levels of indexes. In the base linked list, it needs to travel 62 nodes to reach the correct node. In the skip list, it only needs to traverse 11 nodes [3].

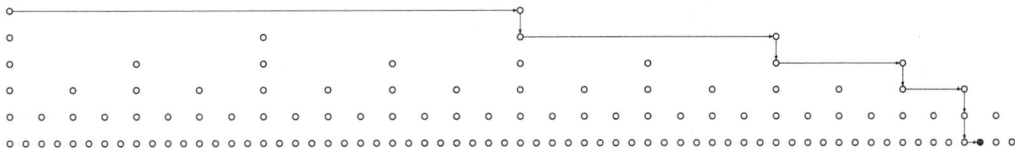

Figure 10.10: Skip list with 5 levels of indexes

Sorted sets are more performant than a relational database because each element is automatically positioned in the right order during insert or update, as well as the fact that the complexity of an add or find operation in a sorted set is logarithmic: $O(\log(n))$.

In contrast, to calculate the rank of a specific user in a relational database, we need to run nested queries:

```
SELECT *,(SELECT COUNT(*) FROM leaderboard lb2
WHERE lb2.score >= lb1.score) RANK
FROM leaderboard lb1
WHERE lb1.user_id = {:user_id};
```

Implementation using Redis sorted sets

Now that we know sorted sets are fast, let's take a look at the Redis operations we will use to build our leaderboard [4] [5] [6] [7]:

- ZADD: insert the user into the set if they don't yet exist. Otherwise, update the score for the user. It takes $O(\log(n))$ to execute.

- ZINCRBY: increment the score of the user by the specified increment. If the user doesn't exist in the set, then it assumes the score starts at 0. It takes $O(\log(n))$ to execute.

- ZRANGE/ZREVRANGE: fetch a range of users sorted by the score. We can specify the order (range vs. revrange), the number of entries, and the position to start from. This takes $O(\log(n)+m)$ to execute, where m is the number of entries to fetch (which is usually small in our case), and n is the number of entries in the sorted set.

- ZRANK/ZREVRANK: fetch the position of any user sorting in ascending/descending order in logarithmic time.

Workflow with sorted sets

1. A user scores a point

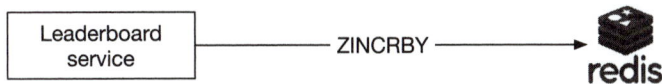

Figure 10.11: A user scores a point

Every month we create a new leaderboard sorted set and the previous ones are moved to historical data storage. When a user wins a match, they score 1 point; so we call ZINCRBY to increment the user's score by 1 in that month's leaderboard, or add the user to the leaderboard set if they weren't already there. The syntax for ZINCRBY is:

```
ZINCRBY <key> <increment> <user>
```

The following command adds a point to user mary1934 after they win a match.

```
ZINCRBY leaderboard_feb_2021 1 'mary1934'
```

2. A user fetches the top 10 global leaderboard

Figure 10.12: Fetch top 10 global leaderboard

We will call ZREVRANGE to obtain the members in descending order because we want the highest scores, and pass the WITHSCORES attribute to ensure that it also returns the total score for each user, as well as the set of users with the highest scores. The following command fetches the top 10 players on the Feb-2021 leaderboard.

```
ZREVRANGE leaderboard_feb_2021 0 9 WITHSCORES
```

This returns a list like this:

```
[(user2,score2),(user1,score1),(user5,score5)...]
```

3. A user wants to fetch their leaderboard position

Figure 10.13: Fetch a user's leaderboard position

To fetch the position of a user in the leaderboard, we will call ZREVRANK to retrieve their rank on the leaderboard. Again, we call the rev version of the command because we want to rank scores from high to low.

```
ZREVRANK leaderboard_feb_2021 'mary1934'
```

4. Fetch the relative position in the leaderboard for a user. An example is shown in Figure 10.14.

Rank	Player	Points
267	Aquaboys	876
258	B team	845
259	Berlin's Angels	832
360	GrendelTeam	799
361	Mallow007	785
362	Woo78	743
363	milan~114	732
364	G3^^^^2	726
365	Mailso_91_	712

Figure 10.14: Fetch 4 players above and below

While not an explicit requirement, we can easily fetch the relative position for a user by leveraging ZREVRANGE with the number of results above and below the desired player. For example, if user Mallow007's rank is 361 and we want to fetch 4 players above and below them, we would run the following command.

```
ZREVRANGE leaderboard_feb_2021 357 365
```

Storage requirement

At a minimum, we need to store the user id and score. The worst-case scenario is that all 25 million monthly active users have won at least one game, and they all have entries in the leaderboard for the month. Assuming the id is a 24-character string and the score is a 16-bit integer (or 2 bytes), we need 26 bytes of storage per leaderboard entry. Given the worst-case scenario of one leaderboard entry per MAU, we would need 26 bytes $\times 25$ million $= 650$ million bytes or ~ 650MB for leaderboard storage in the Redis cache. Even if we double the memory usage to account for the overhead of the skip list and the hash for the sorted set, one modern Redis server is more than enough to hold the data.

Another related factor to consider is CPU and I/O usage. Our peak QPS from the back-of-the-envelope estimation is 2500 updates/sec. This is well within the performance envelope of a single Redis server.

One concern about the Redis cache is persistence, as a Redis node might fail. Luckily, Redis does support persistence, but restarting a large Redis instance from disk is slow. Usually, Redis is configured with a read replica, and when the main instance fails, the read replica is promoted, and a new read replica is attached.

Besides, we need to have 2 supporting tables (user and point) in a relational database like

MySQL. The user table would store the user ID and user's display name (in a real-world application, this would contain a lot more data). The point table would contain the user id, score, and timestamp when they won a game. This can be leveraged for other game functions such as play history, and can also be used to recreate the Redis leaderboard in the event of an infrastructure failure.

As a small performance optimization, it may make sense to create an additional cache of the user details, potentially for the top 10 players since they are retrieved most frequently. However, this doesn't amount to a large amount of data.

Step 3 - Design Deep Dive

Now that we've discussed the high-level design, let's dive into the following:

- Whether or not to use a cloud provider
    - Manage our own services
    - Leverage cloud service providers like Amazon Web Services (AWS)
- Scaling Redis
- Alternative solution: NoSQL
- Other considerations

To use a cloud provider or not

Depending on the existing infrastructure, we generally have two options for deploying our solution. Let's take a look at each of them.

Manage our own services

In this approach, we will create a leaderboard sorted set each month to store the leaderboard data for that period. The sorted set stores member and score information. The rest of the details about the user, such as their name and profile image, are stored in MySQL databases. When fetching the leaderboard, besides the leaderboard data, API servers also query the database to fetch corresponding users' names and profile images to display on the leaderboard. If this becomes too inefficient in the long term, we can leverage a user profile cache to store users' details for the top 10 players. The design is shown in Figure 10.15.

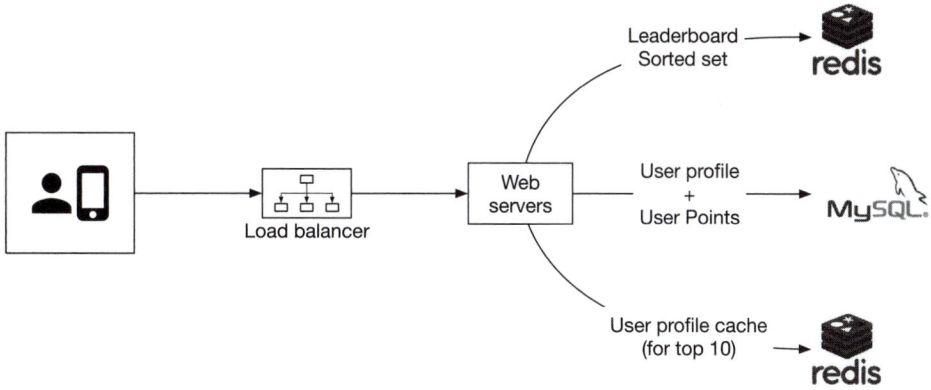

Figure 10.15: Manage our own services

Build on the cloud

The second approach is to leverage cloud infrastructures. In this section, we assume our existing infrastructure is built on AWS and that it's a natural fit to build the leaderboard on the cloud. We will use two major AWS technologies in this design: Amazon API Gateway and AWS Lambda function [8]. The Amazon API gateway provides a way to define the HTTP endpoints of a RESTful API and connect it to any backend services. We use it to connect to our AWS lambda functions. The mapping between Restful APIs and Lambda functions is shown in Table 10.5.

APIs	Lambda function
`GET /v1/scores`	`LeaderboardFetchTop10`
`GET /v1/scores/{:user_id}`	`LeaderboardFetchPlayerRank`
`POST /v1/scores`	`LeaderboardUpdateScore`

Table 10.5: Lambda functions

AWS Lambda is one of the most popular serverless computing platforms. It allows us to run code without having to provision or manage the servers ourselves. It runs only when needed and will scale automatically based on traffic. Serverless is one of the hottest topics in cloud services and is supported by all major cloud service providers. For example, Google Cloud has Google Cloud Functions [9] and Microsoft has named its offering Microsoft Azure Functions [10].

At a high level, our game calls the Amazon API Gateway, which in turn invokes the appropriate lambda functions. We will use AWS Lambda functions to invoke the appropriate commands on the storage layer (both Redis and MySQL), return the results back to the API Gateway, and then to the application.

We can leverage Lambda functions to perform the queries we need without having to spin up a server instance. AWS provides support for Redis clients that can be called from the Lambda functions. This also allows for auto-scaling as needed with DAU growth. Design diagrams for a user scoring a point and retrieving the leaderboard are shown below:

Use case 1: scoring a point

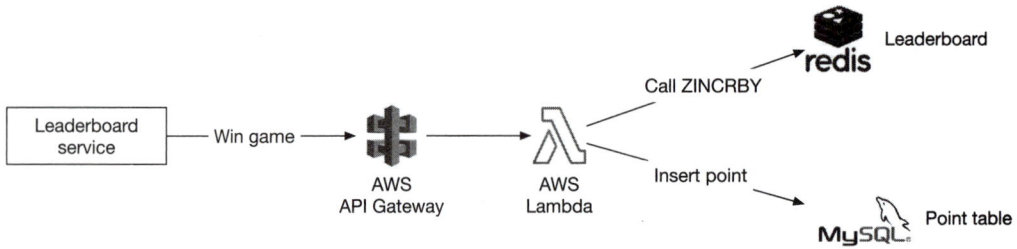

Figure 10.16: Score a point

Use case 2: retrieving leaderboard

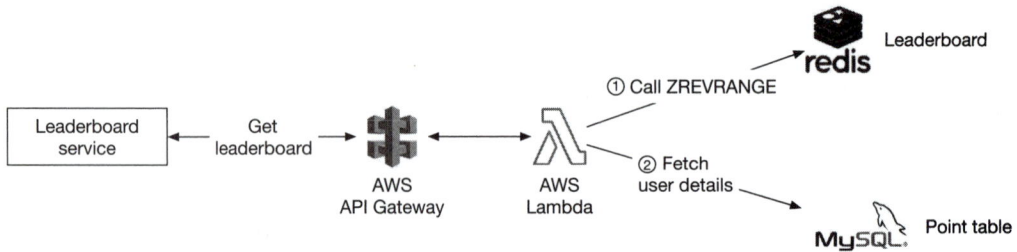

Figure 10.17: Retrieve leaderboard

Lambdas are great because they are a serverless approach, and the infrastructure will take care of auto-scaling the function as needed. This means we don't need to manage the scaling and environment setup and maintenance. Given this, we recommend going with a serverless approach if we build the game from the ground up.

Scaling Redis

With 5 million DAU, we can get away with one Redis cache from both a storage and QPS perspective. However, let's imagine we have 500 million DAU, which is 100 times our original scale. Now our worst-case scenario for the size of the leaderboard goes up to 65GB (650MB $\times$ 100), and our QPS goes up to 250,000 (2,500 $\times$ 100) queries per second. This calls for a sharding solution.

Data sharding

We consider sharding in one of the following two ways: fixed or hash partitions.

Fixed partition

One way to understand fixed partitions is to look at the overall range of points on the leaderboard. Let's say that the number of points won in one month ranges from 1 to 1000, and we break up the data by range. For example, we could have 10 shards and each shard would have a range of 100 scores (For example, $1 \sim 100, 101 \sim 200, 201 \sim 300, ...$) as shown in Figure 10.18.

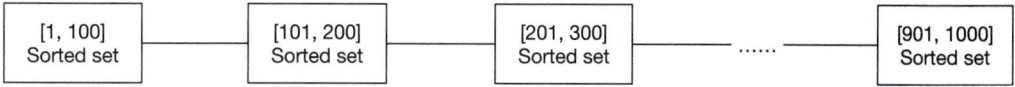

Figure 10.18: Fixed partition

For this to work, we want to ensure there is an even distribution of scores across the leaderboard. Otherwise, we need to adjust the score range in each shard to make sure of a relatively even distribution. In this approach, we shard the data ourselves in the application code.

When we are inserting or updating the score for a user, we need to know which shard they are in. We could do this by calculating the user's current score from the MySQL database. This can work, but a more performant option is to create a secondary cache to store the mapping from user ID to score. We need to be careful when a user increases their score and moves between shards. In this case, we need to remove the user from their current shard and move them to the new shard.

To fetch the top 10 players in the leaderboard, we would fetch the top 10 players from the shard (sorted set) with the highest scores. In Figure 10.18, the last shard with scores $[901, 1000]$ contains the top 10 players.

To fetch the rank of a user, we would need to calculate the rank within their current shard (local rank), as well as the total number of players with higher scores in all of the shards. Note that the total number of players in a shard can be retrieved by running the info keyspace command in $O(1)$ [11].

Hash partition

A second approach is to use the Redis cluster, which is desirable if the scores are very clustered or clumped. Redis cluster provides a way to shard data automatically across multiple Redis nodes. It doesn't use consistent hashing but a different form of sharding, where every key is part of a **hash slot**. There are 16384 hash slots [12] and we can compute the hash slot of a given key by doing CRC16(key) %16384 [13]. This allows us to add and remove nodes in the cluster easily without redistributing all the keys. In Figure 10.19, we have 3 nodes, where:

- The first node contains hash slots $[0, 5500]$.
- The second node contains hash slots $[5501, 11000]$.
- The third node contains hash slots $[11001, 16383]$.

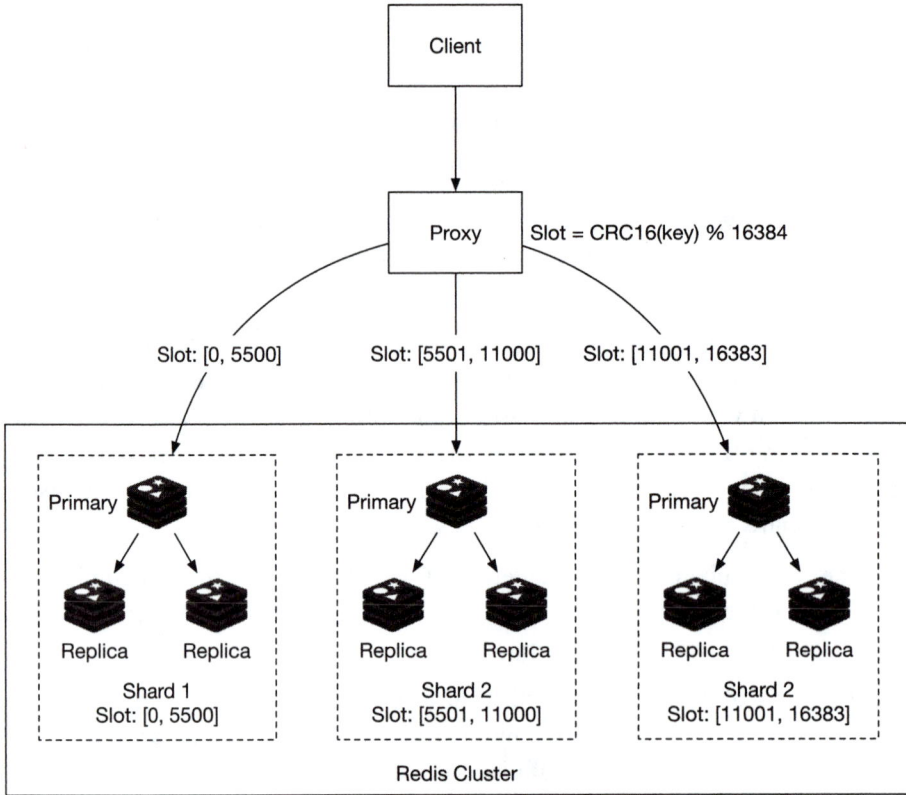

Figure 10.19: Hash partition

An update would simply change the score of the user in the corresponding shard (determined by CRC16(key) %16384). Retrieving the top 10 players on the leaderboard is more complicated. We need to gather the top 10 players from each shard and have the application sort the data. A concrete example is shown in Figure 10.20. Those queries can be parallelized to reduce latency.

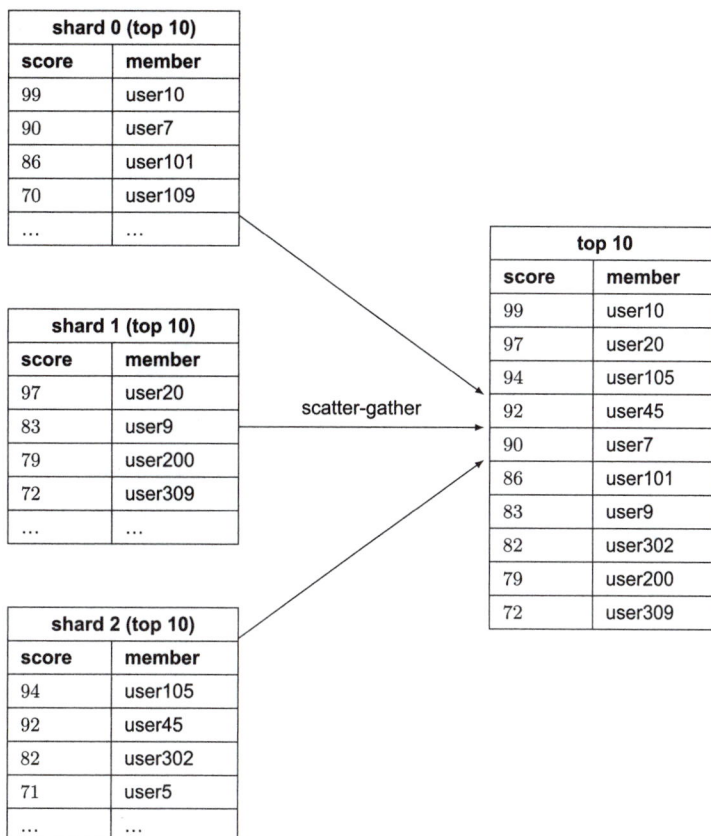

Figure 10.20: Scatter-gather

This approach has a few limitations:

- When we need to return top k results (where k is a very large number) on the leaderboard, the latency is high because a lot of entries are returned from each shard and need to be sorted.

- Latency is high if we have lots of partitions because the query has to wait for the slowest partition.

- Another issue with this approach is that it doesn't provide a straightforward solution for determining the rank of a specific user.

Therefore, we lean towards the first proposal: fixed partition.

Sizing a Redis node

There are multiple things to consider when sizing the Redis nodes [14]. Write-heavy applications require much more available memory, since we need to be able to accommodate all of the writes to create the snapshot in case of a failure. To be safe, allocate twice the amount of memory for write-heavy applications.

Redis provides a tool called Redis-benchmark that allows us to benchmark the performance of the Redis setup, by simulating multiple clients executing multiple queries and returning the number of requests per second for the given hardware. To learn more about Redis-benchmark, see [15].

Alternative solution: NoSQL

An alternative solution to consider is NoSQL databases. What kind of NoSQL should we use? Ideally, we want to choose a NoSQL that has the following properties:

- Optimized for writes.
- Efficiently sort items within the same partition by score.

NoSQL databases such as Amazon's DynamoDB [16], Cassandra, or MongoDB can be a good fit. In this chapter, we use DynamoDB as an example. DynamoDB is a fully managed NoSQL database that offers reliable performance and great scalability. To allow efficient access to data with attributes other than the primary key, we can leverage global secondary indexes [17] in DynamoDB. A global secondary index contains a selection of attributes from the parent table, but they are organized using a different primary key. Let's take a look at an example.

The updated system diagram is shown in Figure 10.21. Redis and MySQL are replaced with DynamoDB.

Figure 10.21: DynamoDB solution

Assume we design the leaderboard for a chess game and our initial table is shown in Figure 10.22. It is a denormalized view of the leaderboard and user tables and contains everything needed to render a leaderboard.

Primary key	Attributes			
user_id	score	email	profile_pic	leaderboard_name
lovelove	309	love@test.com	https://cdn.example/3.png	chess#2020-02
i_love_tofu	209	test@test.com	https://cdn.example/p.png	chess#2020-02
golden_gate	103	gold@test.com	https://cdn.example/2.png	chess#2020-03
pizza_or_bread	203	piz@test.com	https://cdn.example/31.png	chess#2021-05
ocean	10	oce@test.com	https://cdn.example/32.png	chess#2020-02
...	...	...	...	...

Figure 10.22: Denormalized view of the leaderboard and user tables

This table scheme works, but it doesn't scale well. As more rows are added, we have to scan the entire table to find the top scores.

To avoid a linear scan, we need to add indexes. Our first attempt is to use game_name#{year-month} as the partition key and the score as the sort key, as shown in Figure 10.23.

Global Secondary Index		Attributes		
Partition key (PK)	Sort key (score)	user_id	email	profile_pic
chess#2020-02	309	lovelove	love@test.com	https://cdn.example/3.png
chess#2020-02	209	i_love_tofu	test@test.com	https://cdn.example/p.png
chess#2020-03	103	golden_gate	gold@test.com	https://cdn.example/2.png
chess#2020-02	203	pizza_or_bread	piz@test.com	https://cdn.example/31.png
chess#2020-02	10	ocean	oce@test.com	https://cdn.example/32.png
...	...	...	...	...

Figure 10.23: Partition key and sort key

This works, but it runs into issues at a high load. DynamoDB splits data across multiple nodes using consistent hashing. Each item lives in a corresponding node based on its partition key. We want to structure the data so that data is evenly distributed across partitions. In our table design (Figure 10.23), all the data for the most recent month would be stored in one partition and that partition becomes a hot partition. How can we solve this problem?

We can split data into n partitions and append a partition number (user_id % number_of_partitions) to the partition key. This pattern is called write sharding. Write sharding adds complexity for both read and write operations, so we should consider the trade-offs carefully.

The second question we need to answer is, how many partitions should we have? It can be based on write volume or DAU. The important thing to remember is that there is a trade-off between load on partitions and read complexity. Because data for the same month is spread evenly across multiple partitions, the load for a single partition is much lighter. However, to read items for a given month, we have to query all the partitions and merge the results, which adds read complexity.

The partition key looks something like this: game_name#{year-month}#p{partition_number}. Figure 10.24 shows the updated schema table.

Global Secondary Index		Attributes		
Partition key (PK)	Sort key (score)	user_id	email	profile_pic
chess#2020-02#p0	309	lovelove	love@test.com	https://cdn.example/3.png
chess#2020-02#p1	209	i_love_tofu	test@test.com	https://cdn.example/p.png
chess#2020-03#p2	103	golden_gate	gold@test.com	https://cdn.example/2.png
chess#2020-02#p1	203	pizza_or_bread	piz@test.com	https://cdn.example/31.png
chess#2020-02#p2	10	ocean	oce@test.com	https://cdn.example/32.png
…	…	…	…	…

Figure 10.24: Updated partition key

The global secondary index uses `game_name#{year-month}#p{partition_number}` as the partition key and the score as the sort key. What we end up with are n partitions that are all sorted within their own partition (locally sorted). If we assume we had 3 partitions, then in order to fetch the top 10 leaderboard, we would use the approach called "scatter-gather" mentioned earlier. We would fetch the top 10 results in each of the partitions (this is the "scatter" portion), and then we would allow the application to sort the results among all the partitions (this is the "gather" portion). An example is shown in Figure 10.25.

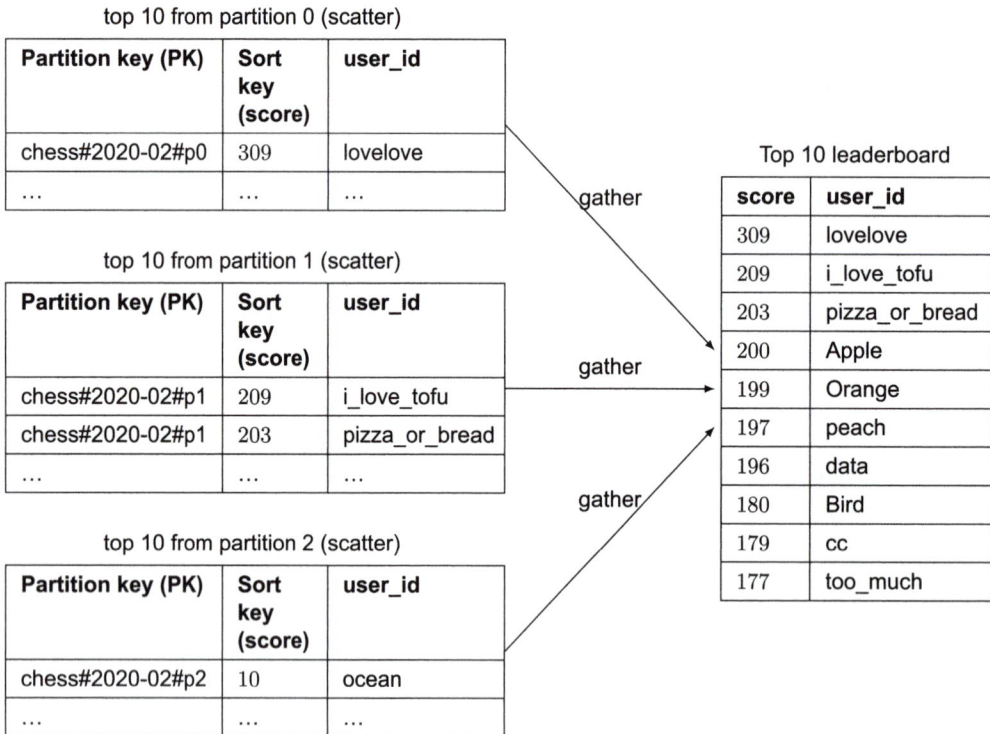

top 10 from partition 0 (scatter)

Partition key (PK)	Sort key (score)	user_id
chess#2020-02#p0	309	lovelove
…	…	…

top 10 from partition 1 (scatter)

Partition key (PK)	Sort key (score)	user_id
chess#2020-02#p1	209	i_love_tofu
chess#2020-02#p1	203	pizza_or_bread
…	…	…

top 10 from partition 2 (scatter)

Partition key (PK)	Sort key (score)	user_id
chess#2020-02#p2	10	ocean
…	…	…

Top 10 leaderboard

score	user_id
309	lovelove
209	i_love_tofu
203	pizza_or_bread
200	Apple
199	Orange
197	peach
196	data
180	Bird
179	cc
177	too_much

gather
gather
gather

Figure 10.25: Scatter-gather

How do we decide on the number of partitions? This might require some careful benchmarking. More partitions decrease the load on each partition but add complexity, as we need to scatter across more partitions to build the final leaderboard. By employing benchmarking, we can see the trade-off more clearly.

However, similar to the Redis partition solution mentioned earlier, this approach doesn't provide a straightforward solution for determining the relative rank of a user. But it is possible to get the percentile of a user's position, which could be good enough. In real life, telling a player that they are in the top $10 \sim 20\%$ might be better than showing the exact rank at eg. 1,200,001. Therefore, if the scale is large enough that we needed to shard, we could assume that the score distributions are roughly the same across all shards. If this assumption is true, we could have a cron job that analyzes the distribution of the score for each shard, and caches that result.

The result would look something like this:

10th percentile = score < 100
20th percentile = score < 500

$\vdots$ $\qquad\qquad\quad$ $\vdots$

90th percentile = score < 6500

Then we could quickly return a user's relative ranking (say 90th percentile).

Step 4 - Wrap Up

In this chapter, we have created a solution for building a real-time game leaderboard with the scale of millions of DAU. We explored the straightforward solution of using a MySQL database and rejected that approach because it does not scale to millions of users. We then designed the leaderboard using Redis sorted sets. We also looked into scaling the solution to 500 million DAU, by leveraging sharding across different Redis caches. We also proposed an alternative NoSQL solution.

In the event you have some extra time at the end of the interview, you can cover a few more topics:

Faster retrieval and breaking tie

A Redis Hash provides a map between string fields and values. We could leverage a hash for 2 use cases:

1. To store a map of the user id to the user object that we can display on the leaderboard. This allows for faster retrieval than having to go to the database to fetch the user object.

2. In the case of two players having the same scores, we could rank the users based on who received that score first. When we increment the score of the user, we can also store a map of the user id to the timestamp of the most recently won game. In the case of a tie, the user with the older timestamp ranks higher.

System failure recovery

The Redis cluster can potentially experience a large-scale failure. Given the design above, we could create a script that leverages the fact that the MySQL database records an entry with a timestamp each time a user won a game. We could iterate through all of the entries for each user, and call ZINCRBY once per entry, per user. This would allow us to recreate the leaderboard offline if necessary, in case of a large-scale outage.

Congratulations on getting this far! Now give yourself a pat on the back. Good job!

Chapter Summary

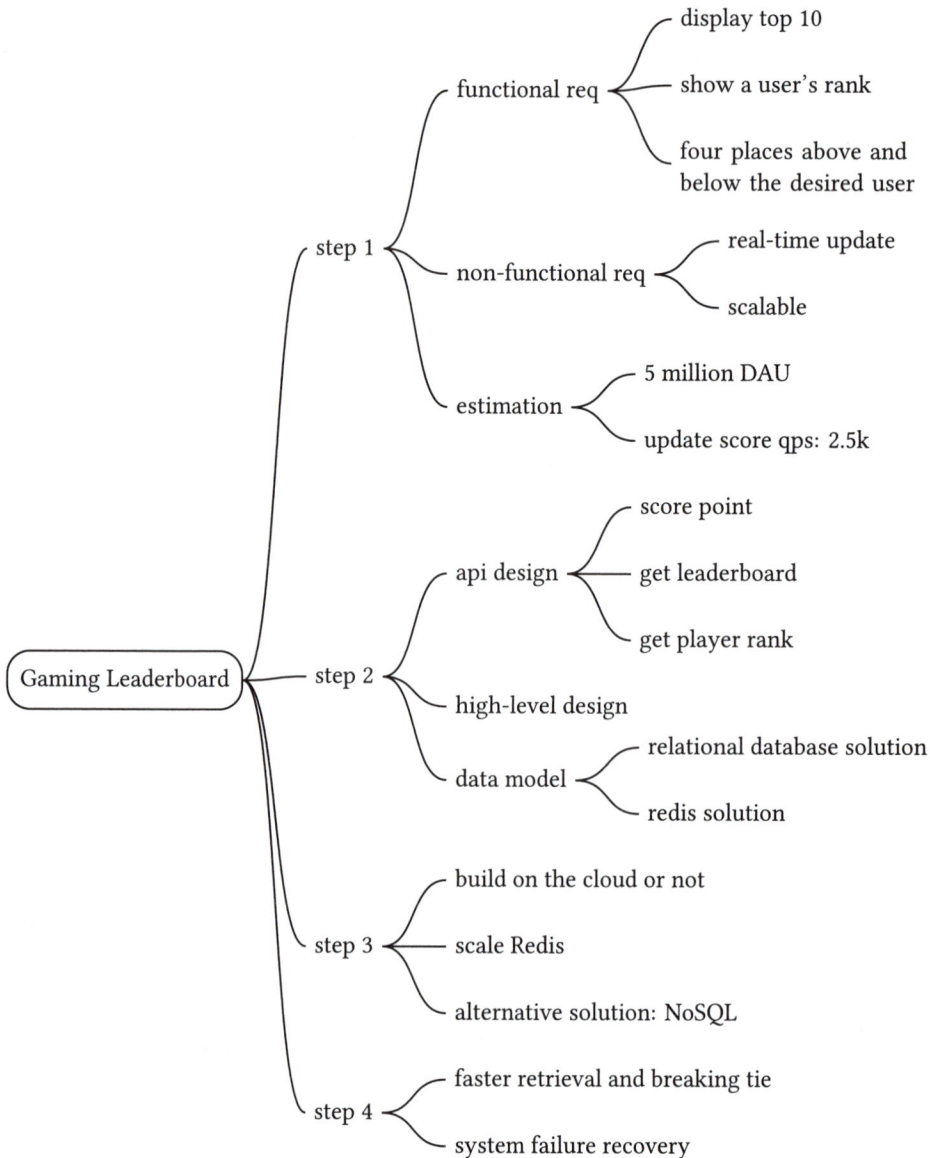

A mind map titled "Gaming Leaderboard" with the following branches:

- **step 1**
  - functional req
    - display top 10
    - show a user's rank
    - four places above and below the desired user
  - non-functional req
    - real-time update
    - scalable
  - estimation
    - 5 million DAU
    - update score qps: 2.5k
- **step 2**
  - api design
    - score point
    - get leaderboard
    - get player rank
  - high-level design
  - data model
    - relational database solution
    - redis solution
- **step 3**
  - build on the cloud or not
  - scale Redis
  - alternative solution: NoSQL
- **step 4**
  - faster retrieval and breaking tie
  - system failure recovery

Reference Material

[1] Man-in-the-middle attack. https://en.wikipedia.org/wiki/Man-in-the-middle_atta ck.

[2] Redis Sorted Set source code. https://github.com/redis/redis/blob/unstable/src/t_z set.c.

[3] Geekbang. https://static001.geekbang.org/resource/image/46/a9/46d283cd82c987 153b3fe0c76dfba8a9.jpg.

[4] Building real-time Leaderboard with Redis. https://medium.com/@sandeep4.ver ma/building-real-time-leaderboard-with-redis-82c98aa47b9f.

[5] Build a real-time gaming leaderboard with Amazon ElastiCache for Redis. https: //aws.amazon.com/blogs/database/building-a-real-time-gaming-leaderboard-wit h-amazon-elasticache-for-redis.

[6] How we created a real-time Leaderboard for a million Users. https://levelup.gitcon nected.com/how-we-created-a-real-time-leaderboard-for-a-million-users-555aa a3ccf7b.

[7] Leaderboards. https://redislabs.com/solutions/use-cases/leaderboards/.

[8] Lambda. https://aws.amazon.com/lambda/.

[9] Google Cloud Functions. https://cloud.google.com/functions.

[10] Azure Functions. https://azure.microsoft.com/en-us/services/functions/.

[11] Info command. https://redis.io/commands/INFO.

[12] Why redis cluster only have 16384 slots. https://stackoverflow.com/questions/3620 3532/why-redis-cluster-only-have-16384-slots.

[13] Cyclic redundancy check. https://en.wikipedia.org/wiki/Cyclic_redundancy_chec k.

[14] Choosing your node size. https://docs.aws.amazon.com/AmazonElastiCache/latest /red-ug/nodes-select-size.html.

[15] How fast is Redis? https://redis.io/topics/benchmarks.

[16] Using Global Secondary Indexes in DynamoDB. https://docs.aws.amazon.com/am azondynamodb/latest/developerguide/GSI.html.

[17] Leaderboard & Write Sharding. https://www.dynamodbguide.com/leaderboard-w rite-sharding/.

11   Payment System

In this chapter, we design a payment system. E-commerce has exploded in popularity across the world in recent years. What makes every transaction possible is a payment system running behind the scenes. A reliable, scalable, and flexible payment system is essential.

What is a payment system? According to Wikipedia, "a payment system is any system used to settle financial transactions through the transfer of monetary value. This includes the institutions, instruments, people, rules, procedures, standards, and technologies that make its exchange possible" [1].

A payment system is easy to understand on the surface but is also intimidating for many developers to work on. A small slip could potentially cause significant revenue loss and destroy credibility among users. But fear not! In this chapter, we demystify payment systems.

Step 1 - Understand the Problem and Establish Design Scope

A payment system can mean very different things to different people. Some may think it's a digital wallet like Apple Pay or Google Pay. Others may think it's a backend system that handles payments such as PayPal or Stripe. It is very important to determine the exact requirements at the beginning of the interview. These are some questions you can ask the interviewer:

Candidate: What kind of payment system are we building?
Interviewer: Assume you are building a payment backend for an e-commerce application like Amazon.com. When a customer places an order on Amazon.com, the payment system handles everything related to money movement.

Candidate: What payment options are supported? Credit cards, PayPal, bank cards, etc?

Interviewer: The payment system should support all of these options in real life. However, in this interview, we can use credit card payment as an example.

Candidate: Do we handle credit card payment processing ourselves?
Interviewer: No, we use third-party payment processors, such as Stripe, Braintree, Square, etc.

Candidate: Do we store credit card data in our system?
Interviewer: Due to extremely high security and compliance requirements, we do not store card numbers directly in our system. We rely on third-party payment processors to handle sensitive credit card data.

Candidate: Is the application global? Do we need to support different currencies and international payments?
Interviewer: Great question. Yes, the application would be global but we assume only one currency is used in this interview.

Candidate: How many payment transactions per day?
Interviewer: 1 million transactions per day.

Candidate: Do we need to support the pay-out flow, which an e-commerce site like Amazon uses to pay sellers every month?
Interviewer: Yes, we need to support that.

Candidate: I think I have gathered all the requirements. Is there anything else I should pay attention to?
Interviewer: Yes. A payment system interacts with a lot of internal services (accounting, analytics, etc.) and external services (payment service providers). When a service fails, we may see inconsistent states among services. Therefore, we need to perform reconciliation and fix any inconsistencies. This is also a requirement.

With these questions, we get a clear picture of both the functional and non-functional requirements. In this interview, we focus on designing a payment system that supports the following.

Functional requirements
- Pay-in flow: payment system receives money from customers on behalf of sellers.
- Pay-out flow: payment system sends money to sellers around the world.

Non-functional requirements
- Reliability and fault tolerance. Failed payments need to be carefully handled.
- A reconciliation process between internal services (payment systems, accounting systems) and external services (payment service providers) is required. The process asynchronously verifies that the payment information across these systems is consistent.

Back-of-the-envelope estimation

The system needs to process 1 million transactions per day, which is 1,000,000 transactions $/10^5$ seconds $= 10$ transactions per second (TPS). 10 TPS is not a big number for a typical database, which means the focus of this system design interview is on how to correctly handle payment transactions, rather than aiming for high throughput.

Step 2 - Propose High-level Design and Get Buy-in

At a high level, the payment flow is broken down into two steps to reflect how money flows:

- Pay-in flow
- Pay-out flow

Take the e-commerce site, Amazon, as an example. After a buyer places an order, the money flows into Amazon's bank account, which is the pay-in flow. Although the money is in Amazon's bank account, Amazon does not own all of the money. The seller owns a substantial part of it and Amazon only works as the money custodian for a fee. Later, when the products are delivered and money is released, the balance after fees then flows from Amazon's bank account to the seller's bank account. This is the pay-out flow. The simplified pay-in and pay-out flows are shown in Figure 11.1.

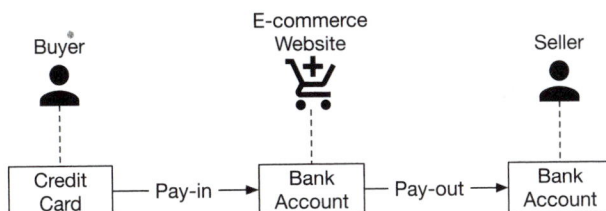

Figure 11.1: Simplified pay-in and pay-out flow

Pay-in flow

The high-level design diagram for the pay-in flow is shown in Figure 11.2. Let's take a look at each component of the system.

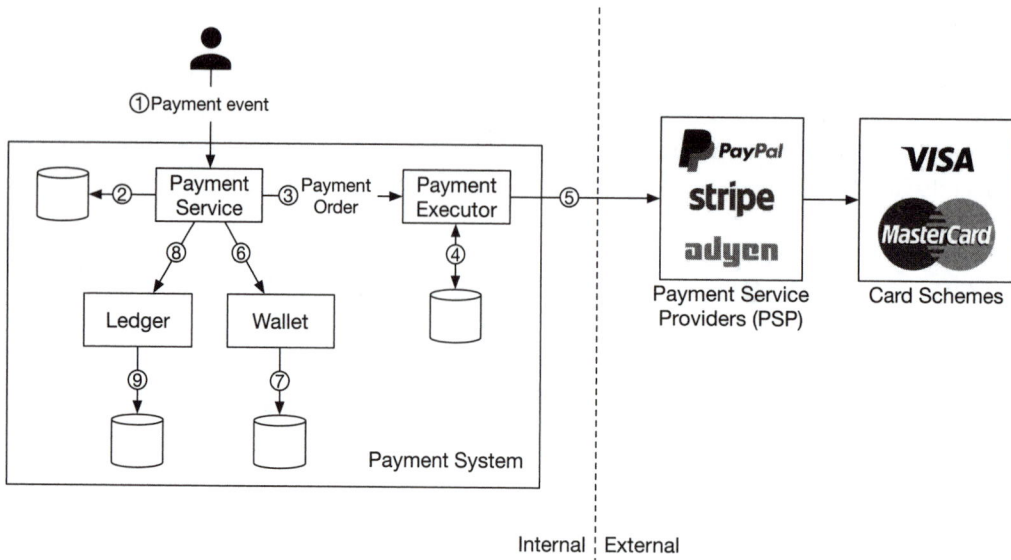

Figure 11.2: Pay-in flow

Payment service

The payment service accepts payment events from users and coordinates the payment process. The first thing it usually does is a risk check, assessing for compliance with regulations such as AML/CFT [2], and for evidence of criminal activity such as money laundering or financing of terrorism. The payment service only processes payments that pass this risk check. Usually, the risk check service uses a third-party provider because it is very complicated and highly specialized.

Payment executor

The payment executor executes a single payment order via a Payment Service Provider (PSP). A payment event may contain several payment orders.

Payment Service Provider (PSP)

A PSP moves money from account A to account B. In this simplified example, the PSP moves the money out of the buyer's credit card account.

Card schemes

Card schemes are the organizations that process credit card operations. Well known card schemes are Visa, MasterCard, Discovery, etc. The card scheme ecosystem is very complex [3].

Ledger

The ledger keeps a financial record of the payment transaction. For example, when a user pays the seller $1, we record it as debit $1 from the user and credit $1 to the seller. The ledger system is very important in post-payment analysis, such as calculating the total revenue of the e-commerce website or forecasting future revenue.

Wallet

The wallet keeps the account balance of the merchant. It may also record how much a given user has paid in total.

As shown in Figure 11.2, a typical pay-in flow works like this:

1. When a user clicks the "place order" button, a payment event is generated and sent to the payment service.
2. The payment service stores the payment event in the database.
3. Sometimes, a single payment event may contain several payment orders. For example, you may select products from multiple sellers in a single checkout process. If the e-commerce website splits the checkout into multiple payment orders, the payment service calls the payment executor for each payment order.
4. The payment executor stores the payment order in the database.
5. The payment executor calls an external PSP to process the credit card payment.
6. After the payment executor has successfully processed the payment, the payment service updates the wallet to record how much money a given seller has.
7. The wallet server stores the updated balance information in the database.
8. After the wallet service has successfully updated the seller's balance information, the payment service calls the ledger to update it.
9. The ledger service appends the new ledger information to the database.

APIs for payment service

We use the RESTful API design convention for the payment service.

POST /v1/payments

This endpoint executes a payment event. As mentioned above, a single payment event may contain multiple payment orders. The request parameters are listed below:

Field	Description	Type
buyer_info	The information of the buyer	json
checkout_id	A globally unique ID for this checkout	string
credit_card_info	This could be encrypted credit card information or a payment token. The value is PSP-specific.	json
payment_orders	A list of the payment orders	list

Table 11.1: API request parameters (execute a payment event)

The payment_orders look like this:

Field	Description	Type
`seller_account`	Which seller will receive the money	string
`amount`	The transaction amount for the order	string
`currency`	The currency for the order	string (ISO 4217 [4])
`payment_order_id`	A globally unique ID for this payment	string

Table 11.2: payment_orders

Note that the `payment_order_id` is globally unique. When the payment executor sends a payment request to a third-party PSP, the `payment_order_id` is used by the PSP as the deduplication ID, also called the idempotency key.

You may have noticed that the data type of the "amount" field is "string," rather than "double". Double is not a good choice because:

1. Different protocols, software, and hardware may support different numeric precisions in serialization and deserialization. This difference might cause unintended rounding errors.

2. The number could be extremely big (for example, Japan's GDP is around 5×10^{14} yen for the calendar year 2020), or extremely small (for example, a satoshi of Bitcoin is 10^{-8}).

It is recommended to keep numbers in string format during transmission and storage. They are only parsed to numbers when used for display or calculation.

`GET /v1/payments/{:id}`

This endpoint returns the execution status of a single payment order based on `payment_order_id`.

The payment API mentioned above is similar to the API of some well-known PSPs. If you are interested in a more comprehensive view of payment APIs, check out Stripe's API documentation [5].

The data model for payment service

We need two tables for the payment service: payment event and payment order. When we select a storage solution for a payment system, performance is usually not the most important factor. Instead, we focus on the following:

1. Proven stability. Whether the storage system has been used by other big financial firms for many years (for example more than 5 years) with positive feedback.

2. The richness of supporting tools, such as monitoring and investigation tools.

3. Maturity of the database administrator (DBA) job market. Whether we can recruit experienced DBAs is a very important factor to consider.

Usually, we prefer a traditional relational database with ACID transaction support over NoSQL/NewSQL.

The payment event table contains detailed payment event information. This is what it looks like:

Name	Type
checkout_id	string **PK**
buyer_info	string
seller_info	string
credit_card_info	depends on the card provider
is_payment_done	boolean

Table 11.3: Payment event

The payment order table stores the execution status of each payment order. This is what it looks like:

Name	Type
payment_order_id	String **PK**
buyer_account	string
amount	string
currency	string
checkout_id	string **FK**
payment_order_status	string
ledger_updated	boolean
wallet_updated	boolean

Table 11.4: Payment order

Before we dive into the tables, let's take a look at some background information.

- The checkout_id is the foreign key. A single checkout creates a payment event that may contain several payment orders.
- When we call a third-party PSP to deduct money from the buyer's credit card, the money is not directly transferred to the seller. Instead, the money is transferred to the e-commerce website's bank account. This process is called pay-in. When the pay-out condition is satisfied, such as when the products are delivered, the seller initiates a pay-out. Only then is the money transferred from the e-commerce website's bank account to the seller's bank account. Therefore, during the pay-in flow, we only need the buyer's card information, not the seller's bank account information.

In the payment order table (Table 11.4), payment_order_status is an enumerated type (enum) that keeps the execution status of the payment order. Execution status includes NOT_STARTED, EXECUTING, SUCCESS, FAILED. The update logic is:

1. The initial status of payment_order_status is NOT_STARTED.

2. When the payment service sends the payment order to the payment executor, the `payment_order_status` is `EXECUTING`.

3. The payment service updates the `payment_order_status` to `SUCCESS` or `FAILED` depending on the response of the payment executor.

Once the `payment_order_status` is `SUCCESS`, the payment service calls the wallet service to update the seller balance and update the `wallet_updated` field to `TRUE`. Here we simplify the design by assuming wallet updates always succeed.

Once it is done, the next step for the payment service is to call the ledger service to update the ledger database by updating the `ledger_updated` field to `TRUE`.

When all payment orders under the same `checkout_id` are processed successfully, the payment service updates the `is_payment_done` to `TRUE` in the payment event table. A scheduled job usually runs at a fixed interval to monitor the status of the in-flight payment orders. It sends an alert when a payment order does not finish within a threshold so that engineers can investigate it.

Double-entry ledger system

There is a very important design principle in the ledger system: the double-entry principle (also called double-entry accounting/bookkeeping [6]). Double-entry system is fundamental to any payment system and is key to accurate bookkeeping. It records every payment transaction into two separate ledger accounts with the same amount. One account is debited and the other is credited with the same amount (Table 11.5).

Account	Debit	Credit
buyer	$1	
seller		$1

Table 11.5: Double-entry system

The double-entry system states that the sum of all the transaction entries must be 0. One cent lost means someone else gains a cent. It provides end-to-end traceability and ensures consistency throughout the payment cycle. To find out more about implementing the double-entry system, see Square's engineering blog about immutable double-entry accounting database service [7].

Hosted payment page

Most companies prefer not to store credit card information internally because if they do, they have to deal with complex regulations such as Payment Card Industry Data Security Standard (PCI DSS) [8] in the United States. To avoid handling credit card information, companies use hosted credit card pages provided by PSPs. For websites, it is a widget or an iframe, while for mobile applications, it may be a pre-built page from the payment SDK. Figure 11.3 illustrates an example of the checkout experience with PayPal integration. The key point here is that the PSP provides a hosted payment page that captures the customer card information directly, rather than relying on our payment service.

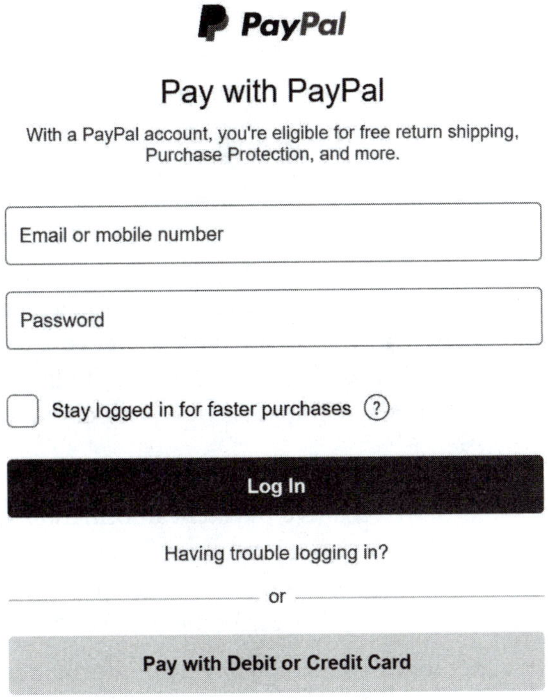

P *PayPal*

Pay with PayPal

With a PayPal account, you're eligible for free return shipping,
Purchase Protection, and more.

Email or mobile number

Password

☐ Stay logged in for faster purchases (?)

Log In

Having trouble logging in?

—————————————— or ——————————————

Pay with Debit or Credit Card

Figure 11.3: Hosted pay with PayPal page

Pay-out flow

The components of the pay-out flow are very similar to the pay-in flow. One difference is that instead of using PSP to move money from the buyer's credit card to the e-commerce website's bank account, the pay-out flow uses a third-party pay-out provider to move money from the e-commerce website's bank account to the seller's bank account.

Usually, the payment system uses third-party account payable providers like Tipalti [9] to handle pay-outs. There are a lot of bookkeeping and regulatory requirements with pay-outs as well.

Step 3 - Design Deep Dive

In this section, we focus on making the system faster, more robust, and secure. In a distributed system, errors and failures are not only inevitable but common. For example, what happens if a customer pressed the "pay" button multiple times? Will they be charged multiple times? How do we handle payment failures caused by poor network connections? In this section, we dive deep into several key topics.

- PSP integration
- Reconciliation
- Handling payment processing delays

- Communication among internal services
- Handling failed payments
- Exact-once delivery
- Consistency
- Security

PSP integration

If the payment system can directly connect to banks or card schemes such as Visa or MasterCard, payment can be made without a PSP. These direct connections are uncommon and highly specialized. They are usually reserved for really large companies that can justify such an investment. For most companies, the payment system integrates with a PSP instead, in one of two ways:

1. If a company can safely store sensitive payment information and chooses to do so, PSP can be integrated using API. The company is responsible for developing the payment web pages, collecting and storing sensitive payment information. PSP is responsible for connecting to banks or card schemes.

2. If a company chooses not to store sensitive payment information due to complex regulations and security concerns, PSP provides a hosted payment page to collect card payment details and securely store them in PSP. This is the approach most companies take.

We use Figure 11.4 to explain how the hosted payment page works in detail.

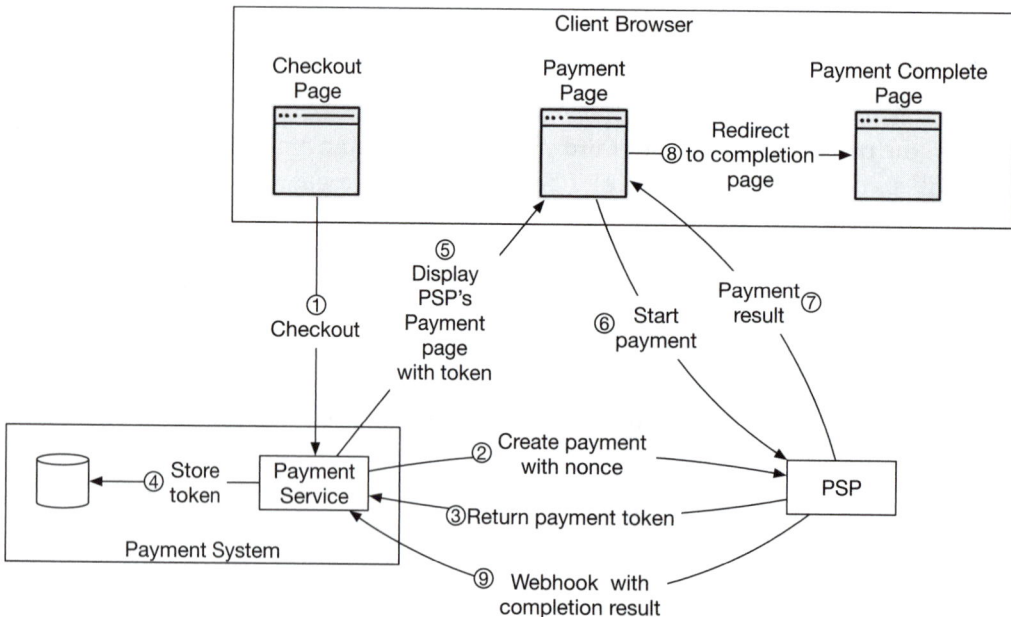

Figure 11.4: Hosted payment flow

We omitted the payment executor, ledger, and wallet in Figure 11.4 for simplicity. The payment service orchestrates the whole payment process.

1. The user clicks the "checkout" button in the client browser. The client calls the payment service with the payment order information.

2. After receiving the payment order information, the payment service sends a payment registration request to the PSP. This registration request contains payment information, such as the amount, currency, expiration date of the payment request, and the redirect URL. Because a payment order should be registered only once, there is a UUID field to ensure the exactly-once registration. This UUID is also called nonce [10]. Usually, this UUID is the ID of the payment order.

3. The PSP returns a token back to the payment service. A token is a UUID on the PSP side that uniquely identifies the payment registration. We can examine the payment registration and the payment execution status later using this token.

4. The payment service stores the token in the database before calling the PSP-hosted payment page.

5. Once the token is persisted, the client displays a PSP-hosted payment page. Mobile applications usually use the PSP's SDK integration for this functionality. Here we use Stripe's web integration as an example (Figure 11.5). Stripe provides a JavaScript library that displays the payment UI, collects sensitive payment information, and calls the PSP directly to complete the payment. Sensitive payment information is collected by Stripe. It never reaches our payment system. The hosted payment page usually needs two pieces of information:

   (a) The token we received in step 4. The PSP's javascript code uses the token to retrieve detailed information about the payment request from the PSP's backend. One important piece of information is how much money to collect.

   (b) Another important piece of information is the redirect URL. This is the web page URL that is called when the payment is complete. When the PSP's JavaScript finishes the payment, it redirects the browser to the redirect URL. Usually, the redirect URL is an e-commerce web page that shows the status of the checkout. Note that the redirect URL is different from the webhook [11] URL in step 9.

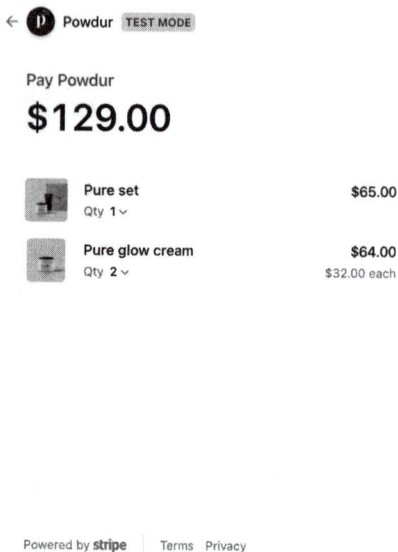

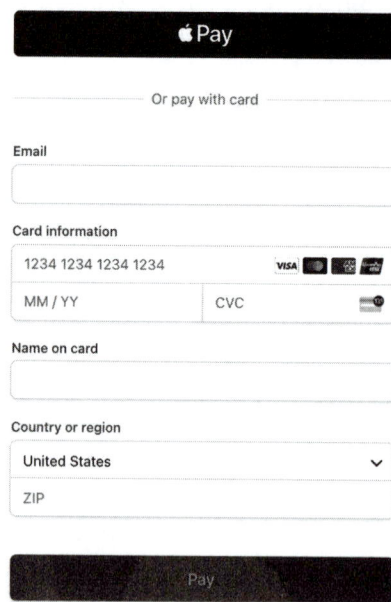

Figure 11.5: Hosted payment page by Stripe

6. The user fills in the payment details on the PSP's web page, such as the credit card number, holder's name, expiration date, etc, then clicks the pay button. The PSP starts the payment processing.

7. The PSP returns the payment status.

8. The web page is now redirected to the redirect URL. The payment status that is received in step 7 is typically appended to the URL. For example, the full redirect URL could be [12]: `https://your-company.com/?tokenID=JIOUIQ123NSF&payResult=X32 4FSa`

9. Asynchronously, the PSP calls the payment service with the payment status via a webhook. The webhook is an URL on the payment system side that was registered with the PSP during the initial setup with the PSP. When the payment system receives payment events through the webhook, it extracts the payment status and updates the `payment_order_status` field in the Payment Order database table.

So far, we explained the happy path of the hosted payment page. In reality, the network connection could be unreliable and all 9 steps above could fail. Is there any systematic way to handle failure cases? The answer is reconciliation.

Reconciliation

When system components communicate asynchronously, there is no guarantee that a message will be delivered, or a response will be returned. This is very common in the payment business, which often uses asynchronous communication to increase system performance. External systems, such as PSPs or banks, prefer asynchronous communication as well. So how can we ensure correctness in this case?

The answer is reconciliation. This is a practice that periodically compares the states among related services in order to verify that they are in agreement. It is usually the last line of defense in the payment system.

Every night the PSP or banks send a settlement file to their clients. The settlement file contains the balance of the bank account, together with all the transactions that took place on this bank account during the day. The reconciliation system parses the settlement file and compares the details with the ledger system. Figure 11.6 below shows where the reconciliation process fits in the system.

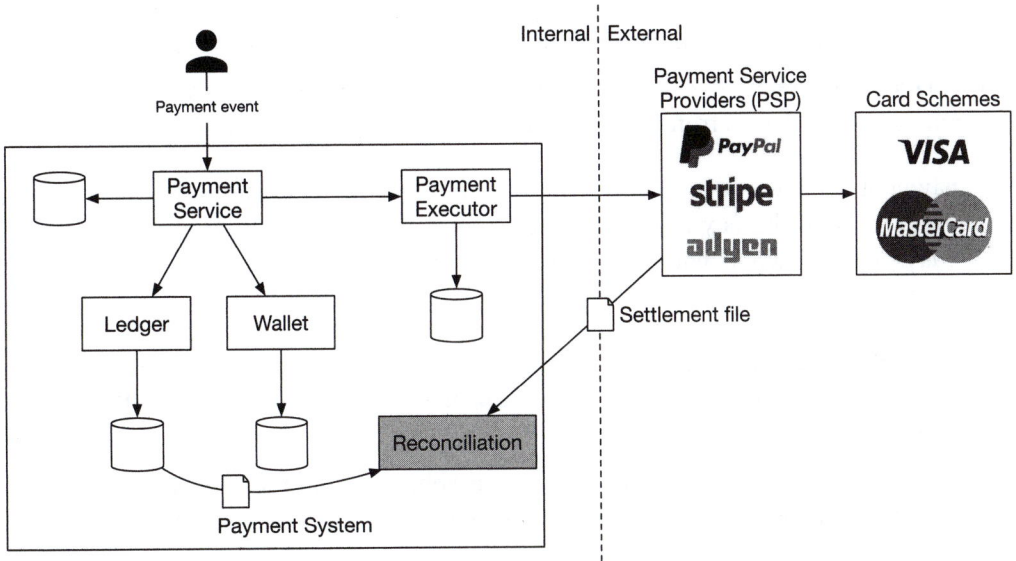

Figure 11.6: Reconciliation

Reconciliation is also used to verify that the payment system is internally consistent. For example, the states in the ledger and wallet might diverge and we could use the reconciliation system to detect any discrepancy.

To fix mismatches found during reconciliation, we usually rely on the finance team to perform manual adjustments. The mismatches and adjustments are usually classified into three categories:

1. The mismatch is classifiable and the adjustment can be automated. In this case, we know the cause of the mismatch, how to fix it, and it is cost-effective to write a program to automate the adjustment. Engineers can automate both the mismatch classification and adjustment.

2. The mismatch is classifiable, but we are unable to automate the adjustment. In this case, we know the cause of the mismatch and how to fix it, but the cost of writing an auto adjustment program is too high. The mismatch is put into a job queue and the finance team fixes the mismatch manually.

3. The mismatch is unclassifiable. In this case, we do not know how the mismatch happens. The mismatch is put into a special job queue. The finance team investigates it manually.

Handling payment processing delays

As discussed previously, an end-to-end payment request flows through many components and involves both internal and external parties. While in most cases a payment request would complete in seconds, there are situations where a payment request would stall and sometimes take hours or days before it is completed or rejected. Here are some examples where a payment request could take longer than usual:

- The PSP deems a payment request high risk and requires a human to review it.
- A credit card requires extra protection like 3D Secure Authentication [13] which requires extra details from a card holder to verify a purchase.

The payment service must be able to handle these payment requests that take a long time to process. If the buy page is hosted by an external PSP, which is quite common these days, the PSP would handle these long-running payment requests in the following ways:

- The PSP would return a pending status to our client. Our client would display that to the user. Our client would also provide a page for the customer to check the current payment status.
- The PSP tracks the pending payment on our behalf, and notifies the payment service of any status update via the webhook the payment service registered with the PSP.

When the payment request is finally completed, the PSP calls the registered webhook mentioned above. The payment service updates its internal system and completes the shipment to the customer.

Alternatively, instead of updating the payment service via a webhook, some PSP would put the burden on the payment service to poll the PSP for status updates on any pending payment requests.

Communication among internal services

There are two types of communication patterns that internal services use to communicate: synchronous vs asynchronous. Both are explained below.

Synchronous communication

Synchronous communication like HTTP works well for small-scale systems, but its shortcomings become obvious as the scale increases. It creates a long request and response cycle that depends on many services. The drawbacks of this approach are:

- Low performance. If any one of the services in the chain doesn't perform well, the whole system is impacted.

- Poor failure isolation. If PSPs or any other services fail, the client will no longer receive a response.

- Tight coupling. The request sender needs to know the recipient.

- Hard to scale. Without using a queue to act as a buffer, it's not easy to scale the system to support a sudden increase in traffic.

Asynchronous communication

Asynchronous communication can be divided into two categories:

- Single receiver: each request (message) is processed by one receiver or service. It's usually implemented via a shared message queue. The message queue can have multiple subscribers, but once a message is processed, it gets removed from the queue. Let's take a look at a concrete example. In Figure 11.7, service A and service B both subscribe to a shared message queue. When m1 and m2 are consumed by service A and service B respectively, both messages are removed from the queue as shown in Figure 11.8.

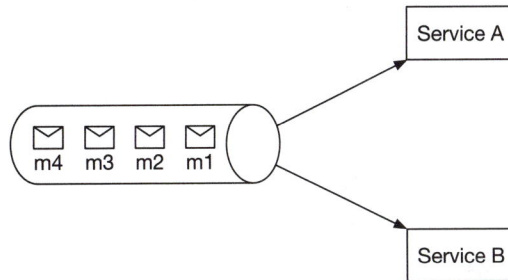

Figure 11.7: Message queue

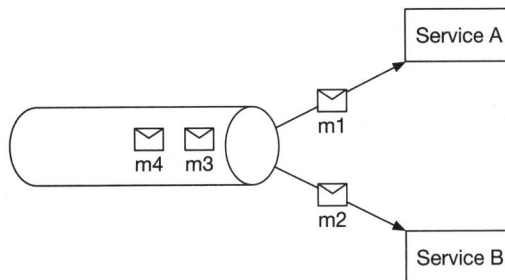

Figure 11.8: Single receiver for each message

- Multiple receivers: each request (message) is processed by multiple receivers or services. Kafka works well here. When consumers receive messages, they are not removed from Kafka. The same message can be processed by different services. This model maps well to the payment system, as the same request might trigger multiple side effects such as sending push notifications, updating financial reporting, analytics, etc. An example is illustrated in Figure 11.9. Payment events are published to Kafka and consumed by different services such as the payment system, analytics service, and billing service.

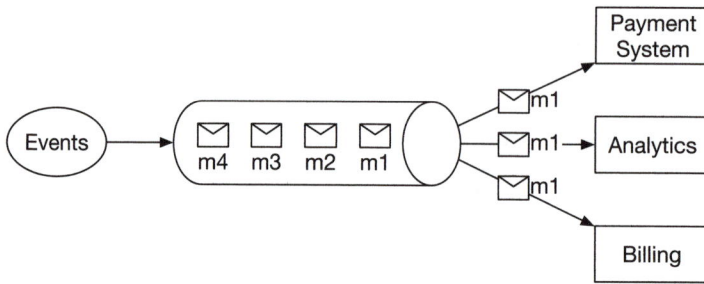

Figure 11.9: Multiple receivers for the same message

Generally speaking, synchronous communication is simpler in design, but it doesn't allow services to be autonomous. As the dependency graph grows, the overall performance suffers. Asynchronous communication trades design simplicity and consistency for scalability and failure resilience. For a large-scale payment system with complex business logic and a large number of third-party dependencies, asynchronous communication is a better choice.

Handling failed payments

Every payment system has to handle failed transactions. Reliability and fault tolerance are key requirements. We review some of the techniques for tackling those challenges.

Tracking payment state

Having a definitive payment state at any stage of the payment cycle is crucial. Whenever a failure happens, we can determine the current state of a payment transaction and decide whether a retry or refund is needed. The payment state can be persisted in an append-only database table.

Retry queue and dead letter queue

To gracefully handle failures, we utilize the retry queue and dead letter queue, as shown in Figure 11.10.

- Retry queue: retryable errors such as transient errors are routed to a retry queue.

- Dead letter queue [14]: if a message fails repeatedly, it eventually lands in the dead letter queue. A dead letter queue is useful for debugging and isolating problematic messages for inspection to determine why they were not processed successfully.

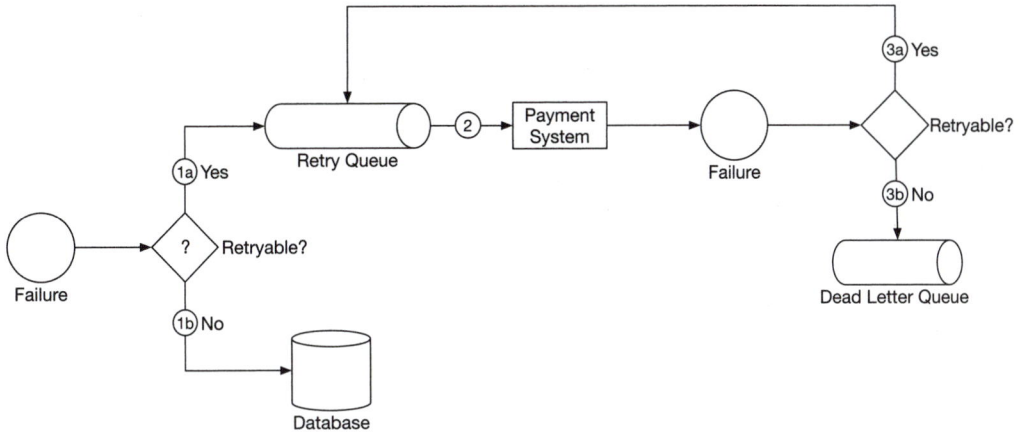

Figure 11.10: Handle failed payments

1. Check whether the failure is retryable.

   (a) Retryable failures are routed to a retry queue.

   (b) For non-retryable failures such as invalid input, errors are stored in a database.

2. The payment system consumes events from the retry queue and retries failed payment transactions.

3. If the payment transaction fails again:

   (a) If the retry count doesn't exceed the threshold, the event is routed to the retry queue.

   (b) If the retry count exceeds the threshold, the event is put in the dead letter queue. Those failed events might need to be investigated.

If you are interested in a real-world example of using those queues, take a look at Uber's payment system that utilizes Kafka to meet the reliability and fault-tolerance requirements [15].

Exactly-once delivery

One of the most serious problems a payment system can have is to double charge a customer. It is important to guarantee in our design that the payment system executes a payment order exactly-once [16].

At first glance, exactly-once delivery seems very hard to tackle, but if we divide the problem into two parts, it is much easier to solve. Mathematically, an operation is executed exactly-once if:

1. It is executed at-least-once.

2. At the same time, it is executed at-most-once.

We will explain how to implement at-least-once using retry, and at-most-once using idempotency check.

Retry

Occasionally, we need to retry a payment transaction due to network errors or timeout. Retry provides the at-least-once guarantee. For example, as shown in Figure 11.11, where the client tries to make a $10 payment, but the payment request keeps failing due to a poor network connection. In this example, the network eventually recovered and the request succeeded at the fourth attempt.

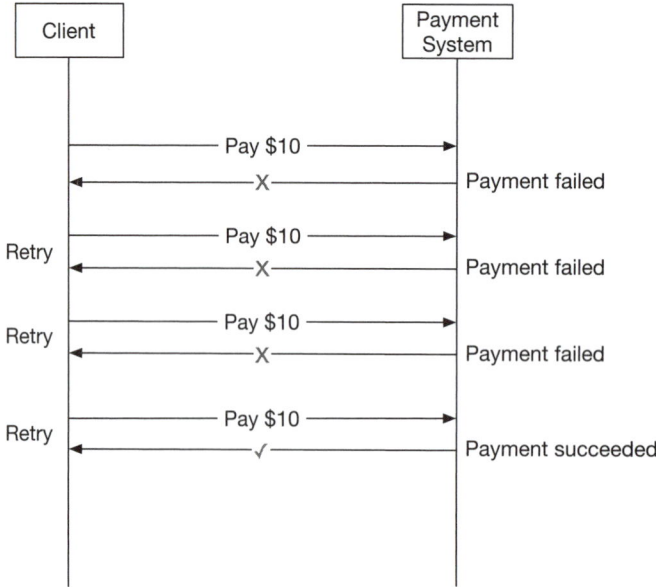

Figure 11.11: Retry

Deciding the appropriate time intervals between retries is important. Here are a few common retry strategies.

- Immediate retry: client immediately resends a request.
- Fixed intervals: wait a fixed amount of time between the time of the failed payment and a new retry attempt.
- Incremental intervals: client waits for a short time for the first retry, and then incrementally increases the time for subsequent retries.
- Exponential backoff [17]: double the waiting time between retries after each failed retry. For example, when a request fails for the first time, we retry after 1 second; if it fails a second time, we wait 2 seconds before the next retry; if it fails a third time, we wait 4 seconds before another retry.
- Cancel: the client can cancel the request. This is a common practice when the failure is permanent or repeated requests are unlikely to be successful.

Determining the appropriate retry strategy is difficult. There is no "one size fits all" solution. As a general guideline, use exponential backoff if the network issue is unlikely to be resolved in a short amount of time. Overly aggressive retry strategies waste computing resources and can cause service overload. A good practice is to provide an error code with a `Retry-After` header.

A potential problem of retrying is double payments. Let us take a look at two scenarios.

Scenario 1: The payment system integrates with PSP using a hosted payment page, and the client clicks the pay button twice.

Scenario 2: The payment is successfully processed by the PSP, but the response fails to reach our payment system due to network errors. The user clicks the "pay" button again or the client retries the payment.

In order to avoid double payment, the payment has to be executed at-most-once. This at-most-once guarantee is also called idempotency.

Idempotency

Idempotency is key to ensuring the at-most-once guarantee. According to Wikipedia, "idempotence is the property of certain operations in mathematics and computer science whereby they can be applied multiple times without changing the result beyond the initial application" [18]. From an API standpoint, idempotency means clients can make the same call repeatedly and produce the same result.

For communication between clients (web and mobile applications) and servers, an idempotency key is usually a unique value that is generated by the client and expires after a certain period of time. A UUID is commonly used as an idempotency key and it is recommended by many tech companies such as Stripe [19] and PayPal [20]. To perform an idempotent payment request, an idempotency key is added to the HTTP header: `<idempotency-key: key_value>`.

Now that we understand the basics of idempotency, let's take a look at how it helps to solve the double payment issues mentioned above.

Scenario 1: what if a customer clicks the "pay" button quickly twice?

In Figure 11.12, when a user clicks "pay," an idempotency key is sent to the payment system as part of the HTTP request. In an e-commerce website, the idempotency key is usually the ID of the shopping cart right before the checkout.

For the second request, it's treated as a retry because the payment system has already seen the idempotency key. When we include a previously specified idempotency key in the request header, the payment system returns the latest status of the previous request.

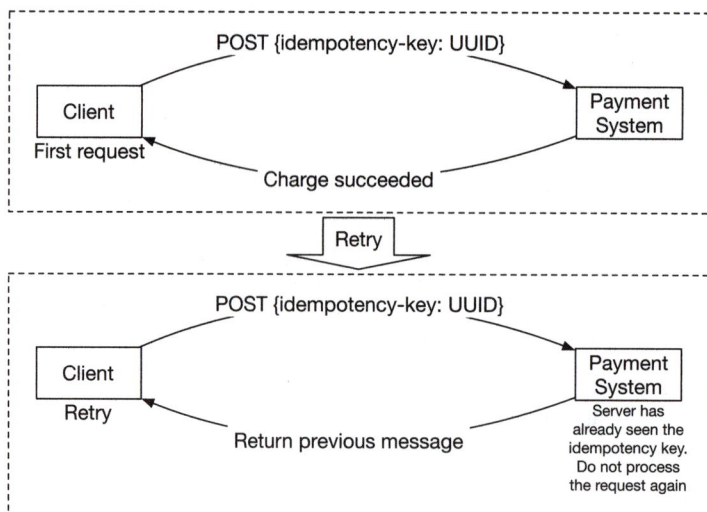

Figure 11.12: Idempotency

If multiple concurrent requests are detected with the same idempotency key, only one request is processed and the others receive the 429 Too Many Requests status code.

To support idempotency, we can use the database's unique key constraint. For example, the primary key of the database table is served as the idempotency key. Here is how it works:

1. When the payment system receives a payment, it tries to insert a row into the database table.

2. A successful insertion means we have not seen this payment request before.

3. If the insertion fails because the same primary key already exists, it means we have seen this payment request before. The second request will not be processed.

Scenario 2: The payment is successfully processed by the PSP, but the response fails to reach our payment system due to network errors. Then the user clicks the "pay" button again.

As shown in Figure 11.4 (step 2 and step 3), the payment service sends the PSP a nonce and the PSP returns a corresponding token. The nonce uniquely represents the payment order, and the token uniquely maps to the nonce. Therefore, the token uniquely maps to the payment order.

When the user clicks the "pay" button again, the payment order is the same, so the token sent to the PSP is the same. Because the token is used as the idempotency key on the PSP side, it is able to identify the double payment and return the status of the previous execution.

Consistency

Several stateful services are called in a payment execution:

1. The payment service keeps payment-related data such as nonce, token, payment order, execution status, etc.

2. The ledger keeps all accounting data.

3. The wallet keeps the account balance of the merchant.

4. The PSP keeps the payment execution status.

5. Data might be replicated among different database replicas to increase reliability.

In a distributed environment, the communication between any two services can fail, causing data inconsistency. Let's take a look at some techniques to resolve data inconsistency in a payment system.

To maintain data consistency between internal services, ensuring exactly-once processing is very important.

To maintain data consistency between the internal service and external service (PSP), we usually rely on idempotency and reconciliation. If the external service supports idempotency, we should use the same idempotency key for payment retry operations. Even if an external service supports idempotent APIs, reconciliation is still needed because we shouldn't assume the external system is always right.

If data is replicated, replication lag could cause inconsistent data between the primary database and the replicas. There are generally two options to solve this:

1. Serve both reads and writes from the primary database only. This approach is easy to set up, but the obvious drawback is scalability. Replicas are used to ensure data reliability, but they don't serve any traffic, which wastes resources.

2. Ensure all replicas are always in-sync. We could use consensus algorithms such as Paxos [21] and Raft [22], or use consensus-based distributed databases such as YugabyteDB [23] or CockroachDB [24].

Payment security

Payment security is very important. In the final part of this system design, we briefly cover a few techniques for combating cyberattacks and card thefts.

Problem	Solution
Request/response eavesdropping	Use HTTPS
Data tampering	Enforce encryption and integrity monitoring
Man-in-the-middle attack	Use SSL with certificate pinning
Data loss	Database replication across multiple regions and take snapshots of data
Distributed denial-of-service attack (DDoS)	Rate limiting and firewall [25]
Card theft	Tokenization. Instead of using real card numbers, tokens are stored and used for payment
PCI compliance	PCI DSS is an information security standard for organizations that handle branded credit cards
Fraud	Address verification, card verification value (CVV), user behavior analysis, etc. [26] [27]

Table 11.6: Payment security

Step 4 - Wrap Up

In this chapter, we investigated the pay-in flow and pay-out flow. We went into great depth about retry, idempotency, and consistency. Payment error handling and security are also covered at the end of the chapter.

A payment system is extremely complex. Even though we have covered many topics, there are still more worth mentioning. The following is a representative but not an exhaustive list of relevant topics.

- Monitoring. Monitoring key metrics is a critical part of any modern application. With extensive monitoring, we can answer questions like "What is the average acceptance rate for a specific payment method?", "What is the CPU usage of our servers?", etc. We can create and display those metrics on a dashboard.

- Alerting. When something abnormal occurs, it is important to alert on-call developers so they respond promptly.

- Debugging tools. "Why does a payment fail?" is a common question. To make debugging easier for engineers and customer support, it is important to develop tools that allow staff to review the transaction status, processing server history, PSP records, etc. of a payment transaction.

- Currency exchange. Currency exchange is an important consideration when designing a payment system for an international user base.

- Geography. Different regions might have completely different sets of payment methods.

- Cash payment. Cash payment is very common in India, Brazil, and some other countries. Uber [28] and Airbnb [29] wrote detailed engineering blogs about how they handled cash-based payment.

- Google/Apple pay integration. Please read [30] if interested.

Congratulations on getting this far! Now give yourself a pat on the back. Good job!

Chapter Summary

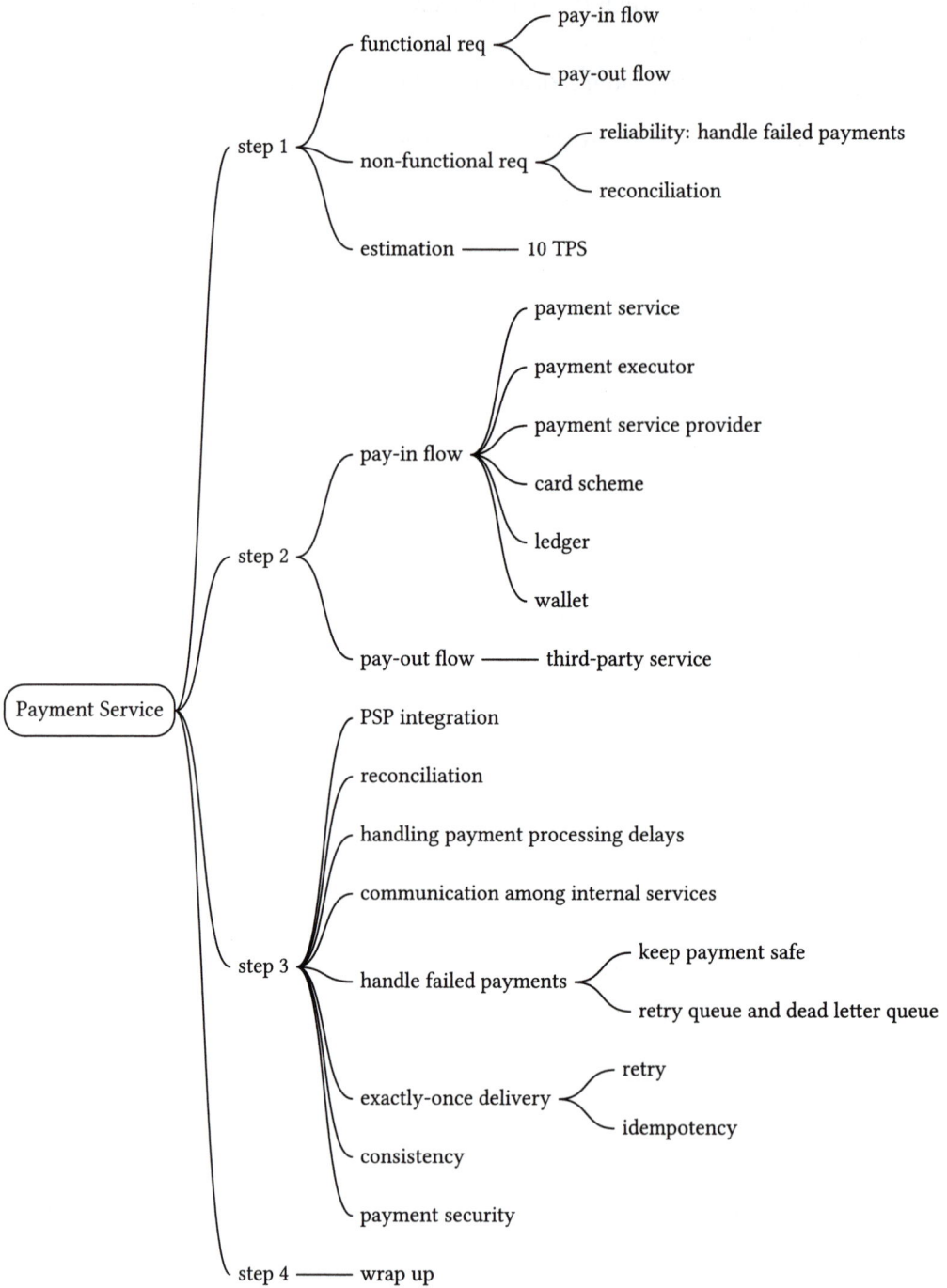

- **Payment Service**
  - **step 1**
    - functional req
      - pay-in flow
      - pay-out flow
    - non-functional req
      - reliability: handle failed payments
      - reconciliation
    - estimation —— 10 TPS
  - **step 2**
    - pay-in flow
      - payment service
      - payment executor
      - payment service provider
      - card scheme
      - ledger
      - wallet
    - pay-out flow —— third-party service
  - **step 3**
    - PSP integration
    - reconciliation
    - handling payment processing delays
    - communication among internal services
    - handle failed payments
      - keep payment safe
      - retry queue and dead letter queue
    - exactly-once delivery
      - retry
      - idempotency
    - consistency
    - payment security
  - **step 4** —— wrap up

Reference Material

[1] Payment system. https://en.wikipedia.org/wiki/Payment_system.

[2] AML/CFT. https://en.wikipedia.org/wiki/Money_laundering.

[3] Card scheme. https://en.wikipedia.org/wiki/Card_scheme.

[4] ISO 4217. https://en.wikipedia.org/wiki/ISO_4217.

[5] Stripe API Reference. https://stripe.com/docs/api.

[6] Double-entry bookkeeping. https://en.wikipedia.org/wiki/Double-entry_bookkeeping.

[7] Books, an immutable double-entry accounting database service. https://developer.squareup.com/blog/books-an-immutable-double-entry-accounting-database-service/.

[8] Payment Card Industry Data Security Standard. https://en.wikipedia.org/wiki/Payment_Card_Industry_Data_Security_Standard.

[9] Tipalti. https://tipalti.com/.

[10] Nonce. https://en.wikipedia.org/wiki/Cryptographic_nonce.

[11] Webhooks. https://stripe.com/docs/webhooks.

[12] Customize your success page. https://stripe.com/docs/payments/checkout/custom-success-page.

[13] 3D Secure. https://en.wikipedia.org/wiki/3-D_Secure.

[14] Kafka Connect Deep Dive – Error Handling and Dead Letter Queues. https://www.confluent.io/blog/kafka-connect-deep-dive-error-handling-dead-letter-queues/.

[15] Reliable Processing in a Streaming Payment System. https://www.youtube.com/watch?v=5TD8m7w1xE0&list=PLLEUtp5eGr7Dz3fWGUpiSiG3d_WgJe-KJ.

[16] Chain Services with Exactly-Once Guarantees. https://www.confluent.io/blog/chain-services-exactly-guarantees/.

[17] Exponential backoff. https://en.wikipedia.org/wiki/Exponential_backoff.

[18] Idempotence. https://en.wikipedia.org/wiki/Idempotence.

[19] Stripe idempotent requests. https://stripe.com/docs/api/idempotent_requests.

[20] Idempotency. https://developer.paypal.com/docs/platforms/develop/idempotency/.

[21] Paxos. https://en.wikipedia.org/wiki/Paxos_(computer_science).

[22] Raft. https://raft.github.io/.

[23] YogabyteDB. https://www.yugabyte.com/.

[24] Cockroachdb. https://www.cockroachlabs.com/.

[25] What is DDoS attack. https://www.cloudflare.com/learning/ddos/what-is-a-ddos-attack/.

[26] How Payment Gateways Can Detect and Prevent Online Fraud. https://www.chargebee.com/blog/optimize-online-billing-stop-online-fraud/.

[27] Advanced Technologies for Detecting and Preventing Fraud at Uber. https://eng.uber.com/advanced-technologies-detecting-preventing-fraud-uber/.

[28] Re-Architecting Cash and Digital Wallet Payments for India with Uber Engineering. https://eng.uber.com/india-payments/.

[29] Scaling Airbnb's Payment Platform. https://medium.com/airbnb-engineering/scaling-airbnbs-payment-platform-43ebfc99b324.

[30] Payments Integration at Uber: A Case Study – Gergely Orosz. https://www.youtube.com/watch?v=yooCE5B0SRA.

12   Digital Wallet

Payment platforms usually provide a digital wallet service to clients, so they can store money in the wallet and spend it later. For example, you can add money to your digital wallet from your bank card and when you buy products online, you are given the option to pay using the money in your wallet. Figure 12.1 shows this process.

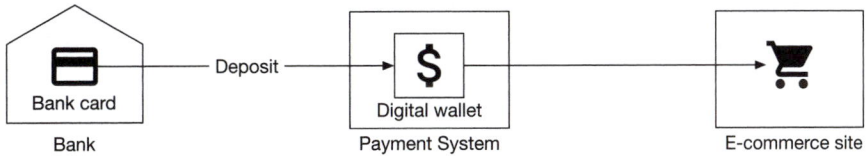

Figure 12.1: Digital wallet

Spending money is not the only feature that the digital wallet provides. For a payment platform like PayPal, we can directly transfer money to somebody else's wallet on the same payment platform. Compared with the bank-to-bank transfer, direct transfer between digital wallets is faster, and most importantly, it usually does not charge an extra fee. Figure 12.2 shows a cross-wallet balance transfer operation.

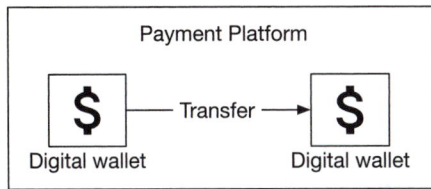

Figure 12.2: Cross-wallet balance transfer

Suppose we are asked to design the backend of a digital wallet application that supports the cross-wallet balance transfer operation. At the beginning of the interview, we will ask clarification questions to nail down the requirements.

Step 1 - Understand the Problem and Establish Design Scope

Candidate: Should we only focus on balance transfer operations between two digital wallets? Do we need to worry about other features?
Interviewer: Let's focus on balance transfer operations only.

Candidate: How many transactions per second (TPS) does the system need to support?
Interviewer: Let's assume 1,000,000 TPS.

Candidate: A digital wallet has strict requirements for correctness. Can we assume transactional guarantees [1] are sufficient?
Interviewer: That sounds good.

Candidate: Do we need to prove correctness?
Interviewer: This is a good question. Correctness is usually only verifiable after a transaction is complete. One way to verify is to compare our internal records with statements from banks. The limitation of reconciliation is that it only shows discrepancies and cannot tell how a difference was generated. Therefore, we would like to design a system with reproducibility, meaning we could always reconstruct historical balance by replaying the data from the very beginning.

Candidate: Can we assume the availability requirement is 99.99%
Interviewer: Sounds good.

Candidate: Do we need to take foreign exchange into consideration?
Interviewer: No, it's out of scope.

In summary, our digital wallet needs to support the following:

- Support balance transfer operation between two digital wallets.
- Support 1,000,000 TPS.
- Reliability is at least 99.99%.
- Support transactions.
- Support reproducibility.

Back-of-the-envelope estimation

When we talk about TPS, we imply a transactional database will be used. Today, a relational database running on a typical data center node can support a few thousand transactions per second. For example, reference [2] contains the performance benchmark of some of the popular transactional database servers. Let's assume a database node can support 1,000 TPS. In order to reach 1 million TPS, we need 1,000 database nodes.

However, this calculation is slightly inaccurate. Each transfer command requires two operations: deducting money from one account and depositing money to the other account. To support 1 million transfers per second, the system actually needs to handle up to 2 million TPS, which means we need 2,000 nodes.

Table 12.1 shows the total number of nodes required when the "per-node TPS" (the TPS a single node can handle) changes. Assuming hardware remains the same, the more transactions a single node can handle per second, the lower the total number of nodes required, indicating lower hardware cost. So one of our design goals is to increase the number of transactions a single node can handle.

Per-node TPS	Node Number
100	20,000
1,000	2,000
10,000	200

Table 12.1: Mapping between pre-node TPS and node number

Step 2 - Propose High-level Design and Get Buy-in

In this section, we will discuss the following:

- API design
- Three high-level designs
    1. Simple in-memory solution
    2. Database-based distributed transaction solution
    3. Event sourcing solution with reproducibility

API design

We will use the RESTful API convention. For this interview, we only need to support one API:

API	Detail
POST /v1/wallet/balance_transfer	Transfer balance from one wallet to another

Request parameters are:

Field	Description	Type
from_account	The debit account	string
to_account	The credit account	string
amount	The amount of money	string
currency	The currency type	string (ISO 4217 [3])
transaction_id	ID used for deduplication	uuid

Sample response body:

```
{
  "Status": "success"
  "Transaction_id": "01589980-2664-11ec-9621-0242ac130002"
}
```

One thing worth mentioning is that the data type of the "amount" field is "string," rather than "double". We explained the reasoning in Chapter 11 Payment System on page 320.

In practice, many people still choose float or double representation of numbers because it is supported by almost every programming language and database. It is a proper choice as long as we understand the potential risk of losing precision.

In-memory sharding solution

The wallet application maintains an account balance for every user account. A good data structure to represent this <user,balance> relationship is a map, which is also called a hash table (map) or key-value store.

For in-memory stores, one popular choice is Redis. One Redis node is not enough to handle 1 million TPS. We need to set up a cluster of Redis nodes and evenly distribute user accounts among them. This process is called partitioning or sharding.

To distribute the key-value data among n partitions, we could calculate the hash value of the key and divide it by n. The remainder is the destination of the partition. The pseudocode below shows the sharding process:

```
String accountID = "A";
Int partitionNumber = 7;
Int myPartition = accountID.hashCode() % partitionNumber;
```

The number of partitions and addresses of all Redis nodes can be stored in a centralized place. We could use ZooKeeper [4] as a highly-available configuration storage solution.

The final component of this solution is a service that handles the transfer commands. We call it the wallet service and it has several key responsibilities.

1. Receives the transfer command
2. Validates the transfer command
3. If the command is valid, it updates the account balances for the two users involved in the transfer. In a cluster, the account balances are likely to be in different Redis nodes

The wallet service is stateless. It is easy to scale horizontally. Figure 12.3 shows the in-memory solution.

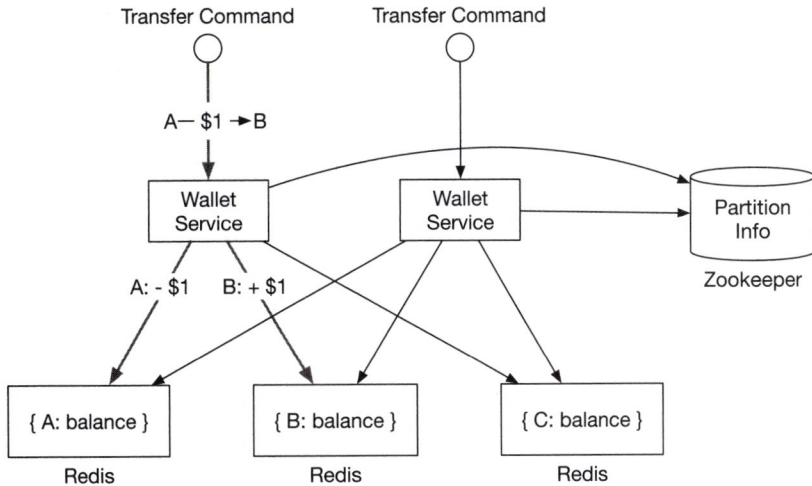

Figure 12.3: In-memory solution

In this example, we have 3 Redis nodes. There are three clients, A, B, and C. Their account balances are evenly spread across these three Redis nodes. There are two wallet service nodes in this example that handle the balance transfer requests. When one of the wallet service nodes receives the transfer command which is to move $1 from client A to client B, it issues two commands to two Redis nodes. For the Redis node that contains client A's account, the wallet service deducts $1 from the account. For client B, the wallet service adds $1 to the account.

Candidate: In this design, account balances are spread across multiple Redis nodes. ZooKeeper is used to maintain the sharding information. The stateless wallet service uses the sharding information to locate the Redis nodes for the clients and updates the account balances accordingly.

Interviewer: This design works, but it does not meet our correctness requirement. The wallet service updates two Redis nodes for each transfer. There is no guarantee that both updates would succeed. If, for example, the wallet service node crashes after the first update has gone through but before the second update is done, it would result in an incomplete transfer. The two updates need to be in a single atomic transaction.

Distributed transactions

Database sharding

How do we make the updates to two different storage nodes atomic? The first step is to replace each Redis node with a transactional relational database node. Figure 12.4 shows the architecture. This time, clients A, B, and C are partitioned into 3 relational databases, rather than in 3 Redis nodes.

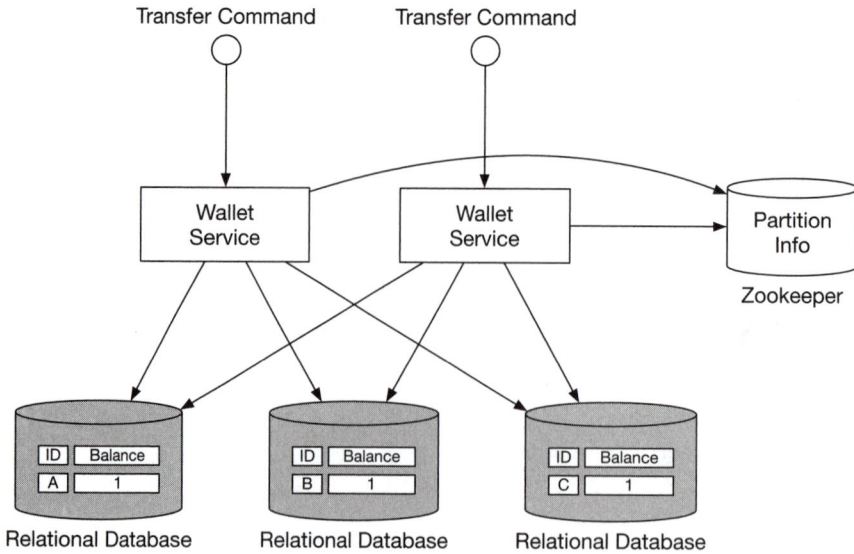

Figure 12.4: Relational database

Using transactional databases only solves part of the problem. As mentioned in the last section, it is very likely that one transfer command will need to update two accounts in two different databases. There is no guarantee that two update operations will be handled at exactly the same time. If the wallet service restarted right after it updated the first account balance, how can we make sure the second account will be updated as well?

Distributed transaction: Two-phase commit

In a distributed system, a transaction may involve multiple processes on multiple nodes. To make a transaction atomic, the distributed transaction might be the answer. There are two ways to implement a distributed transaction: a low-level solution and a high-level solution. We will examine each of them.

The low-level solution relies on the database itself. The most commonly used algorithm is called two-phase commit (2PC). As the name implies, it has two phases, as in Figure 12.5.

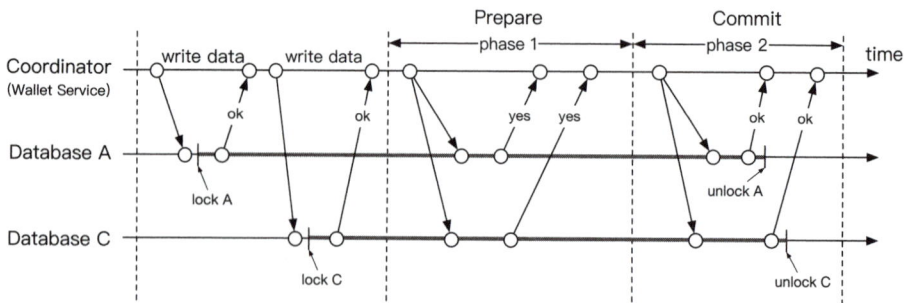

Figure 12.5: Two-phase commit (source [5])

1. The coordinator, which in our case is the wallet service, performs read and write operations on multiple databases as normal. As shown in Figure 12.5, both databases A and C are locked.

2. When the application is about to commit the transaction, the coordinator asks all databases to prepare the transaction.

3. In the second phase, the coordinator collects replies from all databases and performs the following:

   (a) If all databases reply with a yes, the coordinator asks all databases to commit the transaction they have received.

   (b) If any database replies with a no, the coordinator asks all databases to abort the transaction.

It is a low-level solution because the prepare step requires a special modification to the database transaction. For example, there is an X/Open XA [6] standard that coordinates heterogeneous databases to achieve 2PC. The biggest problem with 2PC is that it's not performant, as locks can be held for a very long time while waiting for a message from the other nodes. Another issue with 2PC is that the coordinator can be a single point of failure, as shown in Figure 12.6.

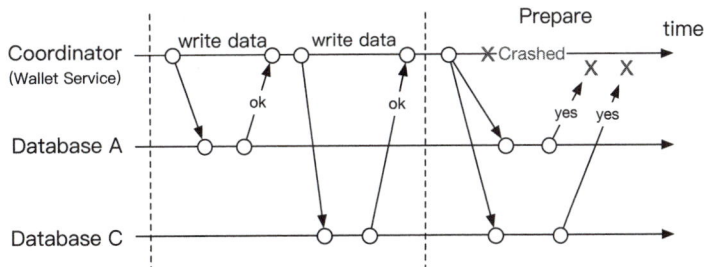

Figure 12.6: Coordinator crashes

Distributed transaction: Try-Confirm/Cancel (TC/C)

TC/C is a type of compensating transaction [7] that has two steps:

1. In the first phase, the coordinator asks all databases to reserve resources for the transaction.

2. In the second phase, the coordinator collects replies from all databases:
   (a) If all databases reply with yes, the coordinator asks all databases to confirm the operation, which is the Try-Confirm process.

   (b) If any database replies with no, the coordinator asks all databases to cancel the operation, which is the Try-Cancel process.

It's important to note that the two phases in 2PC are wrapped in the same transaction, but in TC/C each phase is a separate transaction.

TC/C example

It would be much easier to explain how TC/C works with a real-world example. Suppose we want to transfer $1 from account A to account C. Table 12.2 gives a summary of how TC/C is executed in each phase.

Phase	Operation	A	C
1	Try	Balance change: −$1	Do nothing
2	Confirm	Do nothing	Balance change: +$1
	Cancel	Balance change: +$1	Do Nothing

Table 12.2: TC/C example

Let's assume the wallet service is the coordinator of the TC/C. At the beginning of the distributed transaction, account A has $1 in its balance, and account C has $0.

First phase: Try In the Try phase, the wallet service, which acts as the coordinator, sends two transaction commands to two databases:

1. For the database that contains account A, the coordinator starts a local transaction that reduces the balance of A by $1.

2. For the database that contains account C, the coordinator gives it a NOP (no operation). To make the example adaptable for other scenarios, let's assume the coordinator sends to this database a NOP command. The database does nothing for NOP commands and always replies to the coordinator with a success message.

The Try phase is shown in Figure 12.7. The thick line indicates that a lock is held by the transaction.

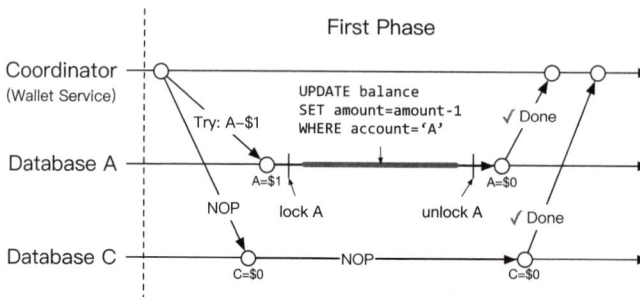

Figure 12.7: Try phase

Second phase: Confirm If both databases reply yes, the wallet service starts the next Confirm phase.

Account A's balance has already been updated in the first phase. The wallet service does not need to change its balance here. However, account C has not yet received its $1 from account A in the first phase. In the Confirm phase, the wallet service has to add $1 to account C's balance.

The Confirm process is shown in Figure 12.8.

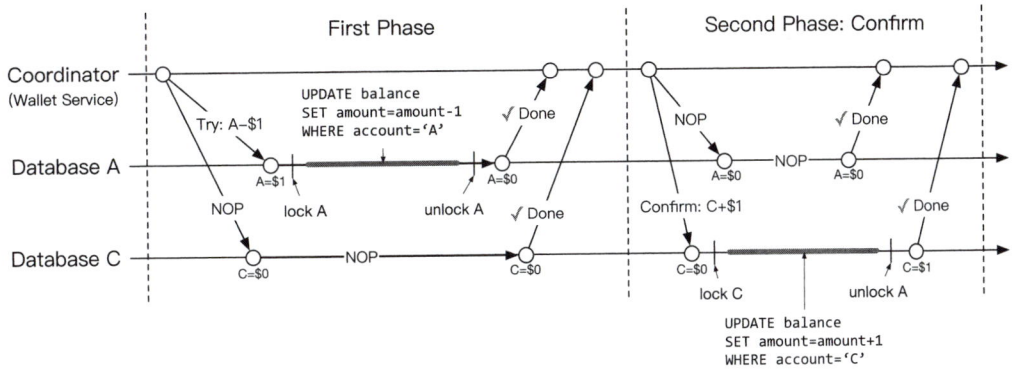

Figure 12.8: Confirm phase

Second phase: Cancel What if the first Try phase fails? In the example above we have assumed the NOP operation on account C always succeeds, although in practice it may fail. For example, account C might be an illegal account, and the regulator has mandated that no money can flow into or out of this account. In this case, the distributed transaction must be canceled and we have to clean up.

Because the balance of account A has already been updated in the transaction in the Try phase, it is impossible for the wallet service to cancel a completed transaction. What it can do is to start another transaction that reverts the effect of the transaction in the Try phase, which is to add $1 back to account A.

Because account C was not updated in the Try phase, the wallet service just needs to send a NOP operation to account C's database.

The Cancel process is shown in Figure 12.9.

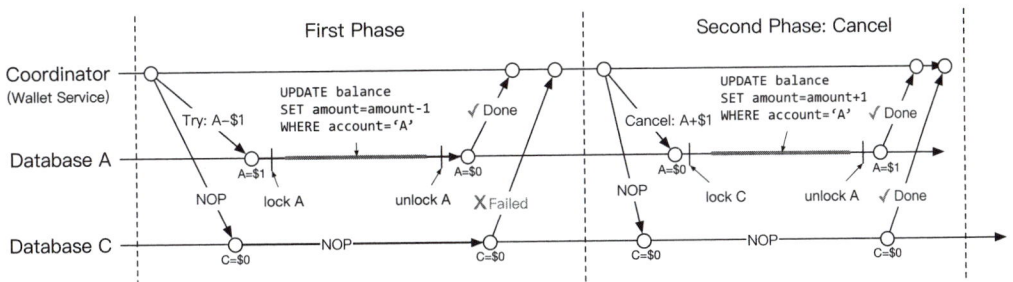

Figure 12.9: Cancel phase

Comparison between 2PC and TC/C

Table 12.3 shows that there are many similarities between 2PC and TC/C, but there are also differences. In 2PC, all local transactions are not done (still locked) when the second phase starts, while in TC/C, all local transactions are done (unlocked) when the second phase starts. In other words, the second phase of 2PC is about completing an unfinished transaction, such as an abort or commit, while in TC/C, the second phase is about using a reverse operation to offset the previous transaction result when an error occurs. The following table summarizes their differences.

	First Phase	Second Phase: success	Second Phase: fail
2PC	Local transactions are not done yet	Commit all local transactions	Cancel all local transactions
TC/C	All local transactions are completed, either committed or canceled	Execute new local transactions if needed	Reverse the side effect of the already committed transaction, or called "undo"

Table 12.3: 2PC v.s. TC/C

TC/C is also called a distributed transaction by compensation. It is a high-level solution because the compensation, also called the "undo," is implemented in the business logic. The advantage of this approach is that it is database-agnostic. As long as a database supports transactions, TC/C will work. The disadvantage is that we have to manage the details and handle the complexity of the distributed transactions in the business logic at the application layer.

Phase status table

We still have not yet answered the question asked earlier; what if the wallet service restarts in the middle of TC/C? When it restarts, all previous operation history might be lost, and the system may not know how to recover.

The solution is simple. We can store the progress of a TC/C as phase status in a transactional database. The phase status includes at least the following information.

- The ID and content of a distributed transaction.
- The status of the Try phase for each database. The status could be not sent yet, has been sent, and response received.
- The name of the second phase. It could be Confirm or Cancel. It could be calculated using the result of the Try phase.
- The status of the second phase.
- An out-of-order flag (explained soon in the section "out-of-order Execution").

Where should we put the phase status tables? Usually, we store the phase status in the database that contains the wallet account from which money is deducted. The updated architecture diagram is shown in Figure 12.10.

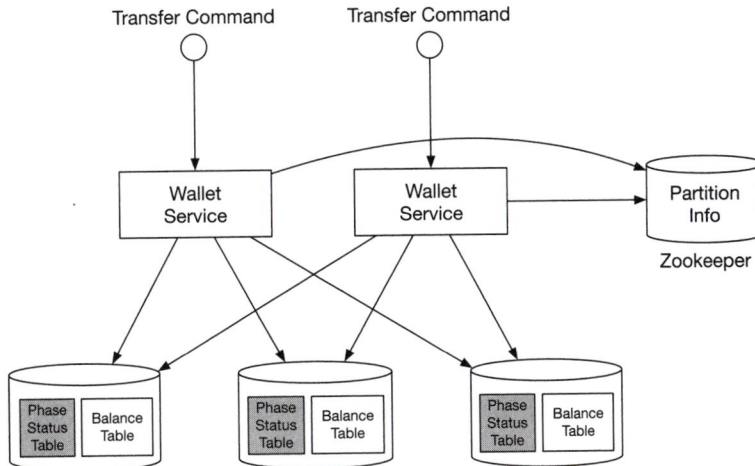

Figure 12.10: Phase status table

Unbalanced state

Have you noticed that by the end of the Try phase, $1 is missing (Figure 12.11)?

Assuming everything goes well, by the end of the Try phase, $1 is deducted from account A and account C remains unchanged. The sum of account balances in A and C will be $0, which is less than at the beginning of the TC/C. It violates a fundamental rule of accounting that the sum should remain the same after a transaction.

The good news is that the transactional guarantee is still maintained by TC/C. TC/C comprises several independent local transactions. Because TC/C is driven by application, the application itself is able to see the intermediate result between these local transactions. On the other hand, the database transaction or 2PC version of the distributed transaction was maintained by databases that are invisible to high-level applications.

There are always data discrepancies during the execution of distributed transactions. The discrepancies might be transparent to us because lower-level systems such as databases already fixed the discrepancies. If not, we have to handle it ourselves (for example, TC/C).

The unbalanced state is shown in Figure 12.11.

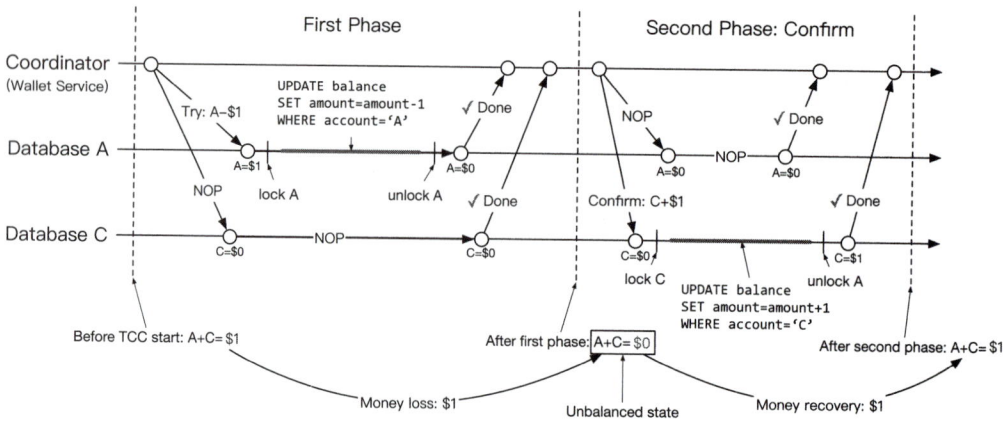

Figure 12.11: Unbalanced state

Valid operation orders

There are three choices for the Try phase:

Try phase choices	Account A	Account C
Choice 1	−$1	NOP
Choice 2	NOP	+$1
Choice 3	−$1	+$1

Table 12.4: Try phase choices

All three choices look plausible, but some are not valid.

For choice 2, if the Try phase on account C is successful, but has failed on account A (NOP), the wallet service needs to enter the Cancel phase. There is a chance that somebody else may jump in and move the $1 away from account C. Later when the wallet service tries to deduct $1 from account C, it finds nothing is left, which violates the transactional guarantee of a distributed transaction.

For choice 3, if $1 is deducted from account A and added to account C concurrently, it introduces lots of complications. For example, $1 is added to account C, but it fails to deduct the money from account A. What should we do in this case?

Therefore, choice 2 and choice 3 are flawed choices and only choice 1 is valid.

Out-of-order execution

One side effect of TC/C is the out-of-order execution. It will be much easier to explain using an example.

We reuse the above example which transfers $1 from account A to account C. As Figure 12.12 shows, in the Try phase, the operation against account A fails and it returns a failure to the wallet service, which then enters the Cancel phase and sends the cancel operation to both account A and account C.

Let's assume that the database that handles account C has some network issues and it receives the Cancel instruction before the Try instruction. In this case, there is nothing to cancel.

The out-of-order execution is shown in Figure 12.12.

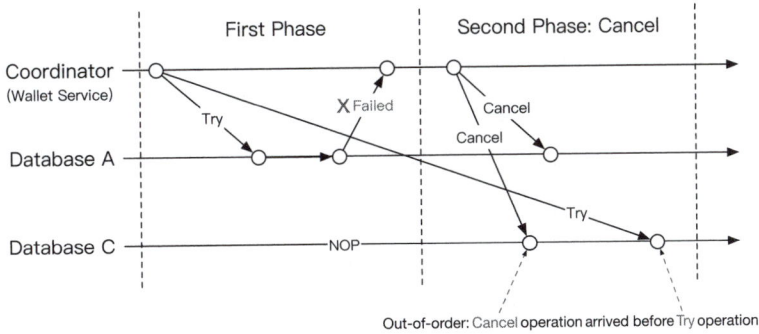

Figure 12.12: Out-of-order execution

To handle out-of-order operations, each node is allowed to Cancel a TC/C without receiving a Try instruction, by enhancing the existing logic with the following updates:

- The out-of-order Cancel operation leaves a flag in the database indicating that it has seen a Cancel operation, but it has not seen a Try operation yet.
- The Try operation is enhanced so it always checks whether there is an out-of-order flag, and it returns a failure if there is.

This is why we added an out-of-order flag to the phase status table in the "Phase Status Table" section.

Distributed transaction: Saga

Linear order execution

There is another popular distributed transaction solution called Saga [8]. Saga is the de-facto standard in a microservice architecture. The idea of Saga is simple:

1. All operations are ordered in a sequence. Each operation is an independent transaction on its own database.

2. Operations are executed from the first to the last. When one operation has finished, the next operation is triggered.

3. When an operation has failed, the entire process starts to roll back from the current operation to the first operation in reverse order, using compensating transactions. So if a distributed transaction has n operations, we need to prepare $2n$ operations: n operations for the normal case and another n for the compensating transaction during rollback.

It is easier to understand this by using an example. Figure 12.13 shows the Saga workflow to transfer $1 from account A to account C. The top horizontal line shows the normal order of execution. The two vertical lines show what the system should do when there is an error. When it encounters an error, the transfer operations are rolled back and the client receives an error message. As we mentioned in the "Valid operation orders" section on page 352, we have to put the deduction operation before the addition operation.

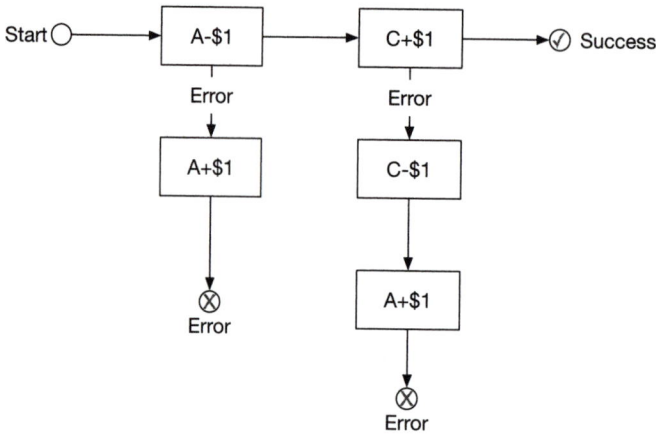

Figure 12.13: Saga workflow

How do we coordinate the operations? There are two ways to do it:

1. Choreography. In a microservice architecture, all the services involved in the Saga distributed transaction do their jobs by subscribing to other services' events. So it is fully decentralized coordination.

2. Orchestration. A single coordinator instructs all services to do their jobs in the correct order.

The choice of which coordination model to use is determined by the business needs and goals. The challenge of the choreography solution is that services communicate in a fully asynchronous way, so each service has to maintain an internal state machine in order to understand what to do when other services emit an event. It can become hard to manage when there are many services. The orchestration solution handles complexity well, so it is usually the preferred solution in a digital wallet system.

Comparison between TC/C and Saga

TC/C and Saga are both application-level distributed transactions. Table 12.5 summarizes their similarities and differences.

	TC/C	Saga
Compensating action	In Cancel phase	In rollback phase
Central coordination	Yes	Yes (orchestration mode)
Operation execution order	any	linear
Parallel execution possibility	Yes	No (linear execution)
Could see the partial inconsistent status	Yes	Yes
Application or database logic	Application	Application

Table 12.5: TC/C vs Saga

Which one should we use in practice? The answer depends on the latency requirement. As Table 12.5 shows, operations in Saga have to be executed in linear order, but it is possible to execute them in parallel in TC/C. So the decision depends on a few factors:

1. If there is no latency requirement, or there are very few services, such as our money transfer example, we can choose either of them. If we want to go with the trend in microservice architecture, choose Saga.

2. If the system is latency-sensitive and contains many services/operations, TC/C might be a better option.

Candidate: To make the balance transfer transactional, we replace Redis with a relational database, and use TC/C or Saga to implement distributed transactions.

Interviewer: Great work! The distributed transaction solution works, but there might be cases where it doesn't work well. For example, users might enter the wrong operations at the application level. In this case, the money we specified might be incorrect. We need a way to trace back the root cause of the issue and audit all account operations. How can we do this?

Event sourcing

Background

In real life, a digital wallet provider may be audited. These external auditors might ask some challenging questions, for example:

1. Do we know the account balance at any given time?

2. How do we know the historical and current account balances are correct?

3. How do we prove that the system logic is correct after a code change?

One design philosophy that systematically answers those questions is event sourcing, which is a technique developed in Domain-Driven Design (DDD) [9].

Definition

There are four important terms in event sourcing.

1. Command
2. Event
3. State
4. State machine

Command

A command is the intended action from the outside world. For example, if we want to transfer $1 from client A to client C, this money transfer request is a command.

In event sourcing, it is very important that everything has an order. So commands are usually put into a FIFO (first in, first out) queue.

Event

Command is an intention and not a fact because some commands may be invalid and cannot be fulfilled. For example, the transfer operation will fail if the account balance becomes negative after the transfer.

A command must be validated before we do anything about it. Once the command passes the validation, it is valid and must be fulfilled. The result of the fulfillment is called an event.

There are two major differences between command and event.

1. Events must be executed because they represent a validated fact. In practice, we usually use the past tense for an event. If the command is "transfer $1 from A to C", the corresponding event would be "transfer**red** $1 from A to C".
2. Commands may contain randomness or I/O, but events must be deterministic. Events represent historical facts.

There are two important properties of the event generation process.

1. One command may generate any number of events. It could generate zero or more events.
2. Event generation may contain randomness, meaning it is not guaranteed that a command always generates the same event(s). The event generation may contain external I/O or random numbers. We will revisit this property in more detail near the end of the chapter.

The order of events must follow the order of commands. So events are stored in a FIFO queue, as well.

State

State is what will be changed when an event is applied. In the wallet system, state is the balances of all client accounts, which can be represented with a map data structure. The key is the account name or ID, and the value is the account balance. Key-value stores are usually used to store the map data structure. The relational database can also be viewed as a key-value store, where keys are primary keys and values are table rows.

State machine

A state machine drives the event sourcing process. It has two major functions.

1. Validate commands and generate events.
2. Apply event to update state.

Event sourcing requires the behavior of the state machine to be deterministic. Therefore, the state machine itself should never contain any randomness. For example, it should never read anything random from the outside using I/O, or use any random numbers. When it applies an event to a state, it should always generate the same result.

Figure 12.14 shows the static view of event sourcing architecture. The state machine is responsible for converting the command to an event and for applying the event. Because state machine has two primary functions, we usually draw two state machines, one for validating commands and the other for applying events.

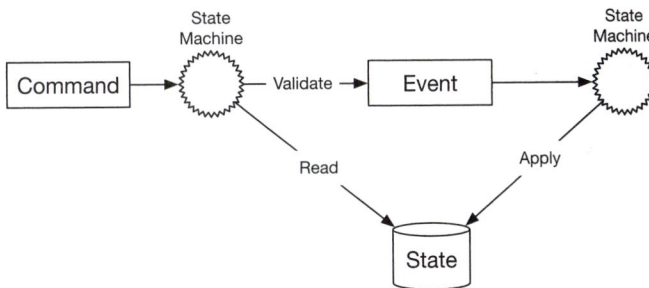

Figure 12.14: Static view of event sourcing

If we add the time dimension, Figure 12.15 shows the dynamic view of event sourcing. The system keeps receiving commands and processing them, one by one.

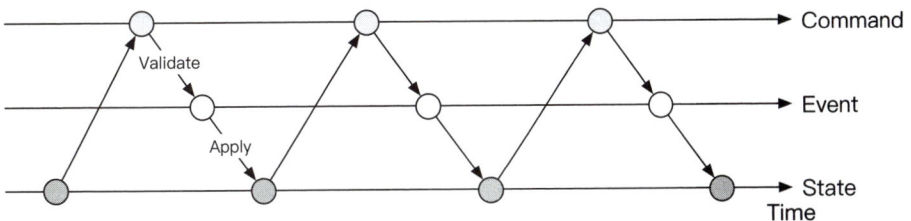

Figure 12.15: Dynamic view of event sourcing

Wallet service example

For the wallet service, the commands are balance transfer requests. These commands are put into a FIFO queue. One popular choice for the command queue is Kafka [10]. The command queue is shown in Figure 12.16.

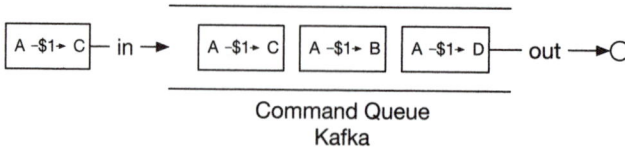

Figure 12.16: Command queue

Let us assume the state (the account balance) is stored in a relational database. The state machine examines each command one by one in FIFO order. For each command, it checks whether the account has a sufficient balance. If yes, the state machine generates an event for each account. For example, if the command is "A → $1 → C", the state machine generates two events: "A:−$1" and "C:+$1".

Figure 12.17 shows how the state machine works in 5 steps.

1. Read commands from the command queue.
2. Read balance state from the database.
3. Validate the command. If it is valid, generate two events for each of the accounts.
4. Read the next event.
5. Apply the event by updating the balance in the database.

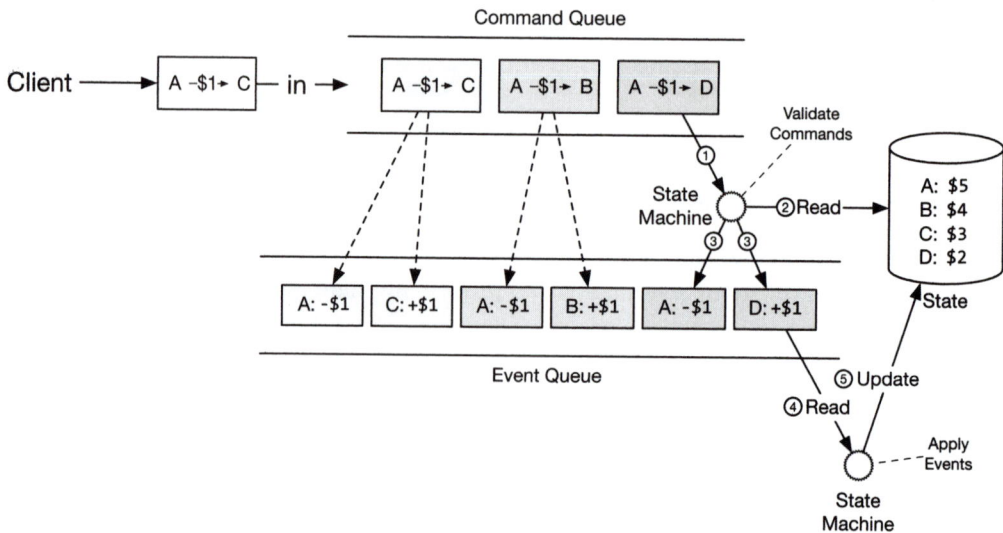

Figure 12.17: How state machine works

Reproducibility

The most important advantage that event sourcing has over other architectures is reproducibility.

In the distributed transaction solutions mentioned earlier, a wallet service saves the updated account balance (the state) into the database. It is difficult to know why the account balance was changed. Meanwhile, historical balance information is lost during the update operation. In the event sourcing design, all changes are saved first as immutable history. The database is only used as an updated view of what balance looks like at any given point in time.

We could always reconstruct historical balance states by replaying the events from the very beginning. Because the event list is immutable and the state machine logic is deterministic, it is guaranteed that the historical states generated from each replay are the same.

Figure 12.18 shows how to reproduce the states of the wallet service by replaying the events.

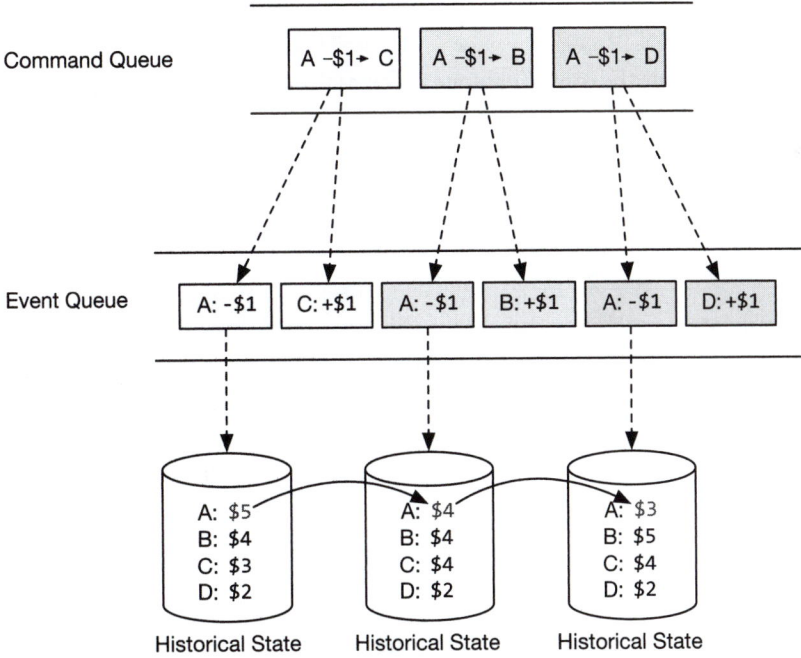

Figure 12.18: Reproduce states

Reproducibility helps us answer the difficult questions that the auditors ask at the beginning of the section. We repeat the questions here.

1. Do we know the account balance at any given time?

2. How do we know the historical and current account balances are correct?

3. How do we prove the system logic is correct after a code change?

For the first question, we could answer it by replaying events from the start, up to the point in time where we would like to know the account balance.

For the second question, we could verify the correctness of the account balance by recalculating it from the event list.

For the third question, we can run different versions of the code against the events and verify that their results are identical.

Because of the audit capability, event sourcing is often chosen as the de facto solution for the wallet service.

Command-query responsibility segregation (CQRS)

So far, we have designed the wallet service to move money from one account to another efficiently. However, the client still does not know what the account balance is. There needs to be a way to publish state (balance information) so the client, which is outside of the event sourcing framework, can know what the state is.

Intuitively, we can create a read-only copy of the database (historical state) and share it with the outside world. Event sourcing answers this question in a slightly different way.

Rather than publishing the state (balance information), event sourcing publishes all the events. The external world could rebuild any customized state itself. This design philosophy is called CQRS [11].

In CQRS, there is one state machine responsible for the write part of the state, but there can be many read-only state machines, which are responsible for building views of the states. Those views could be used for queries.

These read-only state machines can derive different state representations from the event queue. For example, clients may want to know their balances and a read-only state machine could save state in a database to serve the balance query. Another state machine could build state for a specific time period to help investigate issues like possible double charges. The state information is an audit trail that could help to reconcile the financial records.

The read-only state machines lag behind to some extent, but will always catch up. The architecture design is eventually consistent.

Figure 12.19 shows a classic CQRS architecture.

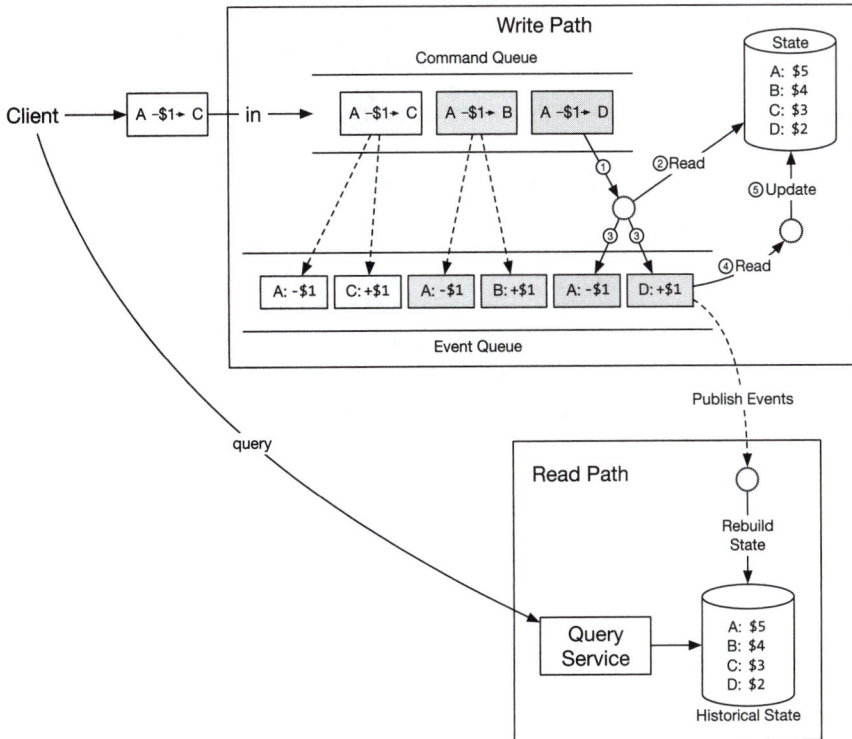

Figure 12.19: CQRS architecture

Candidate: In this design, we use event sourcing architecture to make the whole system reproducible. All valid business records are saved in an immutable event queue which could be used for correctness verification.

Interviewer: That's great. But the event sourcing architecture you proposed only handles one event at a time and it needs to communicate with several external systems. Can we make it faster?

Step 3 - Design Deep Dive

In this section, we dive deep into techniques for achieving high performance, reliability, and scalability.

High-performance event sourcing

In the earlier example, we used Kafka as the command and event store, and the database as a state store. Let's explore some optimizations.

File-based command and event list

The first optimization is to save commands and events to a local disk, rather than to a remote store like Kafka. This avoids transit time across the network. The event list uses an append-only data structure. Appending is a sequential write operation, which is generally very fast. It works well even for magnetic hard drives because the operating system is heavily optimized for sequential reads and writes. According to this article [12], sequential disk access can be faster than random memory access in some cases.

The second optimization is to cache recent commands and events in memory. As we explained before, we process commands and events right after they are persisted. We may cache them in memory to save the time of loading them back from the local disk.

We are going to explore some implementation details. A technique called mmap [13] is great for implementing the optimizations mentioned previously. Mmap can write to a local disk and cache recent content in memory at the same time. It maps a disk file to memory as an array. The operating system caches certain sections of the file in memory to accelerate the read and write operations. For append-only file operations, it is almost guaranteed that all data are saved in memory, which is very fast.

Figure 12.20 shows the file-based command and event storage.

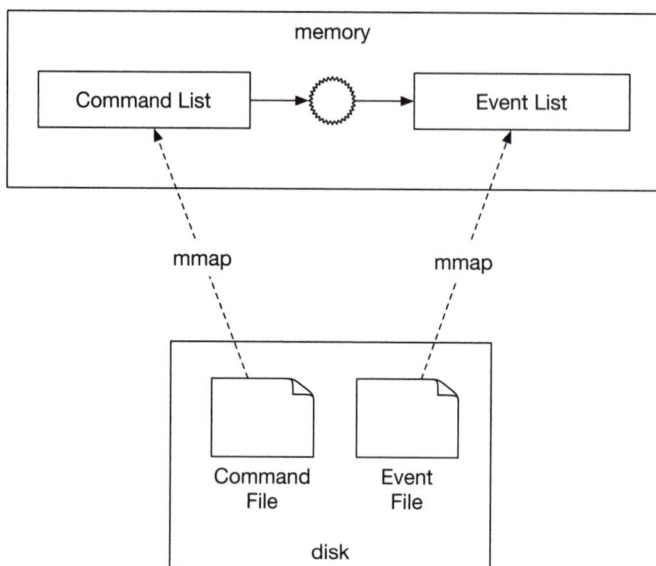

Figure 12.20: File-based command and event storage

File-based state

In the previous design, state (balance information) is stored in a relational database. In a production environment, a database usually runs in a stand-alone server that can only be accessed through networks. Similar to the optimizations we did for command and event, state information can be saved to the local disk, as well.

More specifically, we can use SQLite [14], which is a file-based local relational database or use RocksDB [15], which is a local file-based key-value store.

RocksDB is chosen because it uses a log-structured merge-tree (LSM), which is optimized for write operations. To improve read performance, the most recent data is cached.

Figure 12.21 shows the file-based solution for command, event, and state.

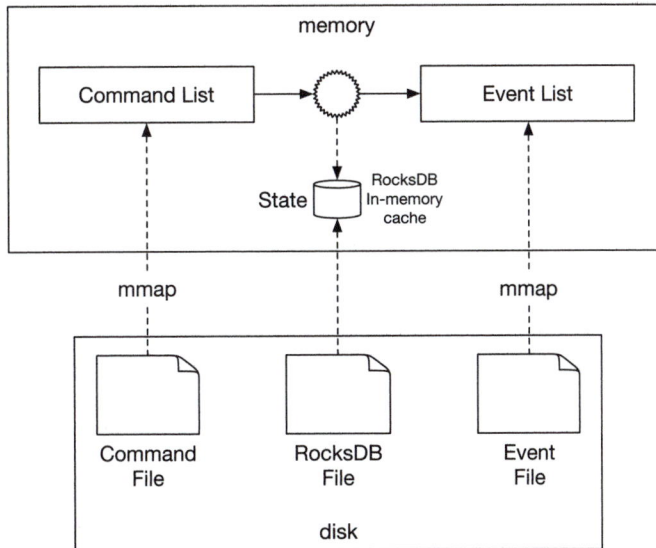

Figure 12.21: File-based solution for command, event, and state

Snapshot

Once everything is file-based, let us consider how to accelerate the reproducibility process. When we first introduced reproducibility, the state machine had to process events from the very beginning, every time. What we could optimize is to periodically stop the state machine and save the current state into a file. This is called a snapshot.

A snapshot is an immutable view of a historical state. Once a snapshot is saved, the state machine does not have to restart from the very beginning anymore. It can read data from a snapshot, verify where it left off, and resume processing from there.

For financial applications such as wallet service, the finance team often requires a snapshot to be taken at 00:00 so they can verify all transactions that happened during that day. When we first introduced CQRS of event sourcing, the solution was to set up a read-only state machine that reads from the beginning until the specified time is met. With snapshots, a read-only state machine only needs to load one snapshot that contains the data.

A snapshot is a giant binary file and a common solution is to save it in an object storage solution, such as HDFS [16].

Figure 12.22 shows the file-based event sourcing architecture. When everything is file-based, the system can fully utilize the maximum I/O throughput of the computer hardware.

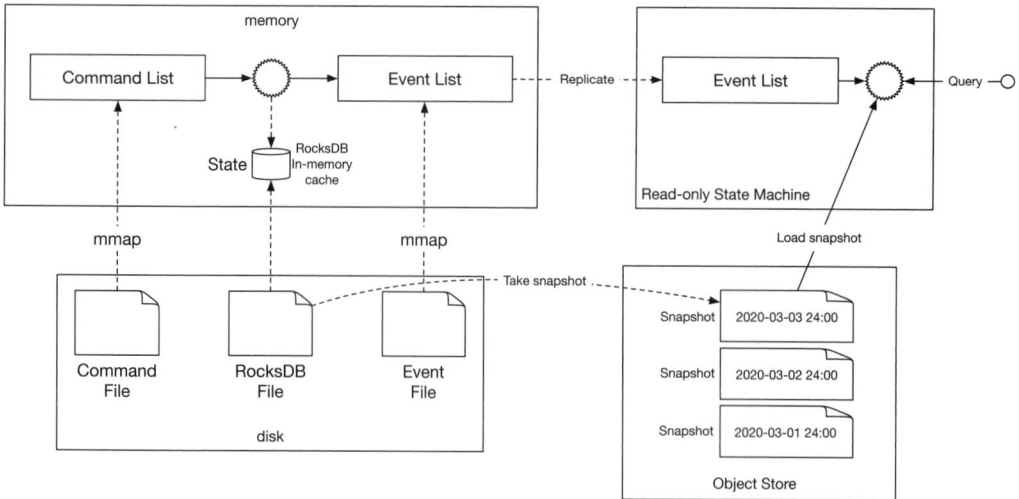

Figure 12.22: Snapshot

Candidate: We could refactor the design of event sourcing so the command list, event list, state, and snapshot are all saved in files. Event sourcing architecture processes the event list in a linear manner, which fits well into the design of hard disks and operating system cache.

Interviewer: The performance of the local file-based solution is better than the system that requires accessing data from remote Kafka and databases. However, there is another problem: because data is saved on a local disk, a server is now stateful and becomes a single point of failure. How do we improve the reliability of the system?

Reliable high-performance event sourcing

Before we explain the solution, let's examine the parts of the system that need the reliability guarantee.

Reliability analysis

Conceptually, everything a node does is around two concepts; data and computation. As long as data is durable, it's easy to recover the computational result by running the same code on another node. This means we only need to worry about the reliability of data because if data is lost, it is lost forever. The reliability of the system is mostly about the reliability of the data.

There are four types of data in our system.

1. File-based command
2. File-based event
3. File-based state
4. State snapshot

Let us take a close look at how to ensure the reliability of each type of data.

State and snapshot can always be regenerated by replaying the event list. To improve the reliability of state and snapshot, we just need to ensure the event list has strong reliability.

Now let us examine command. On the face of it, event is generated from command. We might think providing a strong reliability guarantee for command should be sufficient. This seems to be correct at first glance, but it misses something important. Event generation is not guaranteed to be deterministic, and also it may contain random factors such as random numbers, external I/O, etc. So command cannot guarantee reproducibility of events.

Now it's time to take a close look at event. Event represents historical facts that introduce changes to the state (account balance). Event is immutable and can be used to rebuild the state.

From this analysis, we conclude that event data is the only one that requires a high-reliability guarantee. We will explain how to achieve this in the next section.

Consensus

To provide high reliability, we need to replicate the event list across multiple nodes. During the replication process, we have to guarantee the following properties.

1. No data loss.
2. The relative order of data within a log file remains the same across nodes.

To achieve those guarantees, consensus-based replication is a good fit. The consensus algorithm makes sure that multiple nodes reach a consensus on what the event list is. Let's use the Raft [17] consensus algorithm as an example.

The Raft algorithm guarantees that as long as more than half of the nodes are online, the append-only lists on them have the same data. For example, if we have 5 nodes and use the Raft algorithm to synchronize their data, as long as at least 3 (more than $\frac{1}{2}$) of the nodes are up as Figure 12.23 shows, the system can still work properly as a whole:

Figure 12.23: Raft

A node can have three different roles in the Raft algorithm.

1. Leader
2. Candidate
3. Follower

We can find the implementation of the Raft algorithm in the Raft paper. We will only cover the high level concepts here and not go into detail. In Raft, at most one node is the leader of the cluster and the remaining nodes are followers. The leader is responsible for receiving external commands and replicating data reliably across nodes in the cluster.

With the Raft algorithm, the system is reliable as long as the majority of the nodes are operational. For example, if there are 3 nodes in the cluster, it could tolerate the failure of 1 node, and if there are 5 nodes, it can tolerate the failure of 2 nodes.

Reliable solution

With replication, there won't be a single point of failure in our file-based event sourcing architecture. Let's take a look at the implementation details. Figure 12.24 shows the event sourcing architecture with the reliability guarantee.

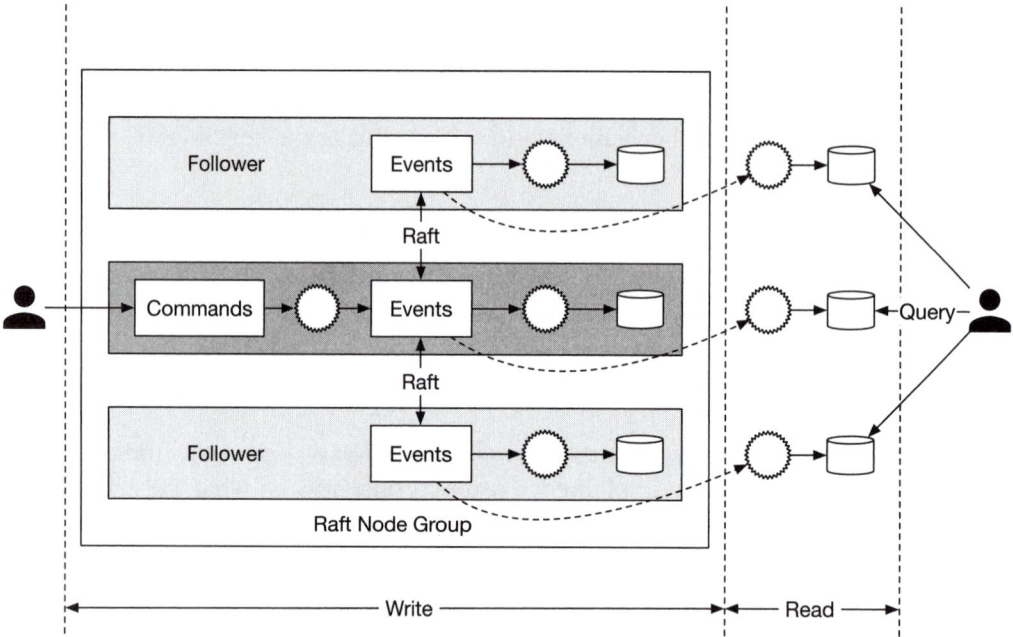

Figure 12.24: Raft node group

In Figure 12.24, we set up 3 event sourcing nodes. These nodes use the Raft algorithm to synchronize the event list reliably.

The leader takes incoming command requests from external users, converts them into events, and appends events into the local event list. The Raft algorithm replicates newly added events to the followers.

All nodes, including the followers, process the event list and update the state. The Raft algorithm ensures the leader and followers have the same event lists, while event sourcing guarantees all states are the same, as long as the event lists are the same.

A reliable system needs to handle failures gracefully, so let's explore how node crashes are handled.

If the leader crashes, the Raft algorithm automatically selects a new leader from the remaining healthy nodes. This newly elected leader takes responsibility for accepting commands from external users. It is guaranteed that the cluster as a whole can provide continued service when a node goes down.

When the leader crashes, it is possible that the crash happens before the command list is converted to events. In this case, the client would notice the issue either by a timeout or by receiving an error response. The client needs to resend the same command to the newly elected leader.

In contrast, follower crashes are much easier to handle. If a follower crashes, requests sent to it will fail. Raft handles failures by retrying indefinitely until the crashed node is restarted or a new one replaces it.

Candidate: In this design, we use the Raft consensus algorithm to replicate the event list across multiple nodes. The leader receives commands and replicates events to other nodes.

Interviewer: Yes, the system is more reliable and fault-tolerant. However, in order to handle 1 million TPS, one server is not enough. How can we make the system more scalable?

Distributed event sourcing

In the previous section, we explained how to implement a reliable high-performance event sourcing architecture. It solves the reliability issue, but it has two limitations.

1. When a digital wallet is updated, we want to receive the updated result immediately. But in the CQRS design, the request/response flow can be slow. This is because a client doesn't know exactly when a digital wallet is updated and the client may need to rely on periodic polling.
2. The capacity of a single Raft group is limited. At a certain scale, we need to shard the data and implement distributed transactions.

Let's take a look at how those two problems are solved.

Pull vs push

In the pull model, an external user periodically polls execution status from the read-only state machine. This model is not real-time and may overload the wallet service if the polling frequency is set too high. Figure 12.25 shows the pulling model.

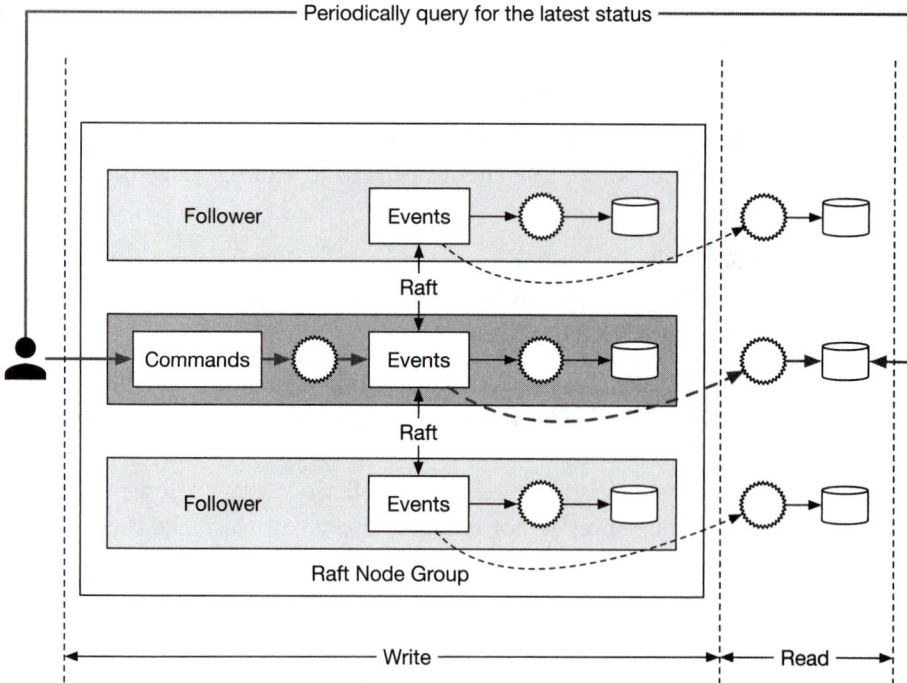

Figure 12.25: Periodical pulling

The naive pull model can be improved by adding a reverse proxy [18] between the external user and the event sourcing node. In this design, the external user sends a command to the reverse proxy, which forwards the command to event sourcing nodes and periodically polls the execution status. This design simplifies the client logic, but the communication is still not real-time.

Figure 12.26 shows the pull model with a reverse proxy added.

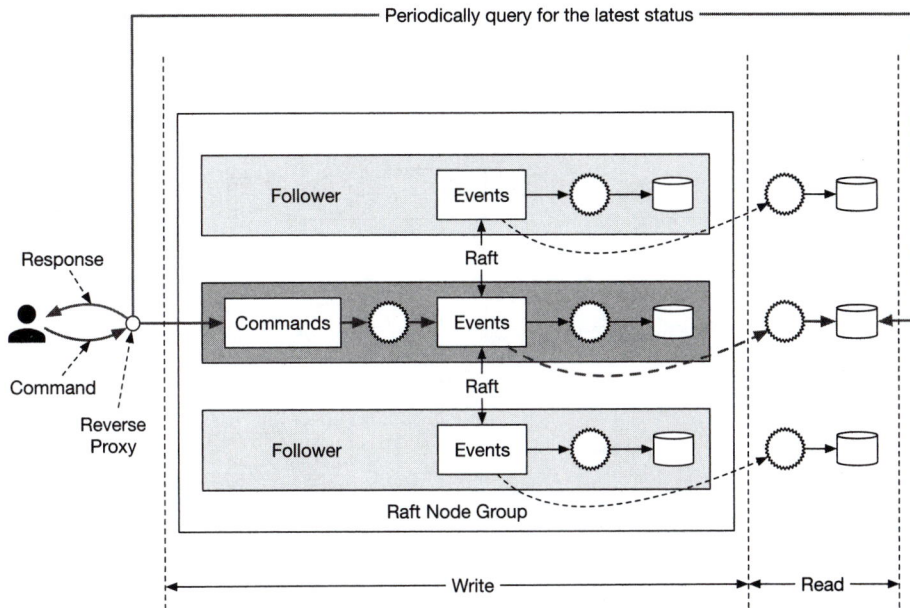

Figure 12.26: Pull model with reverse proxy

Once we have the reverse proxy, we could make the response faster by modifying the read-only state machine. As we mentioned earlier, the read-only state machine could have its own behavior. For example, one behavior could be that the read-only state machine pushes execution status back to the reverse proxy, as soon as it receives the event. This will give the user a feeling of real-time response.

Figure 12.27 shows the push-based model.

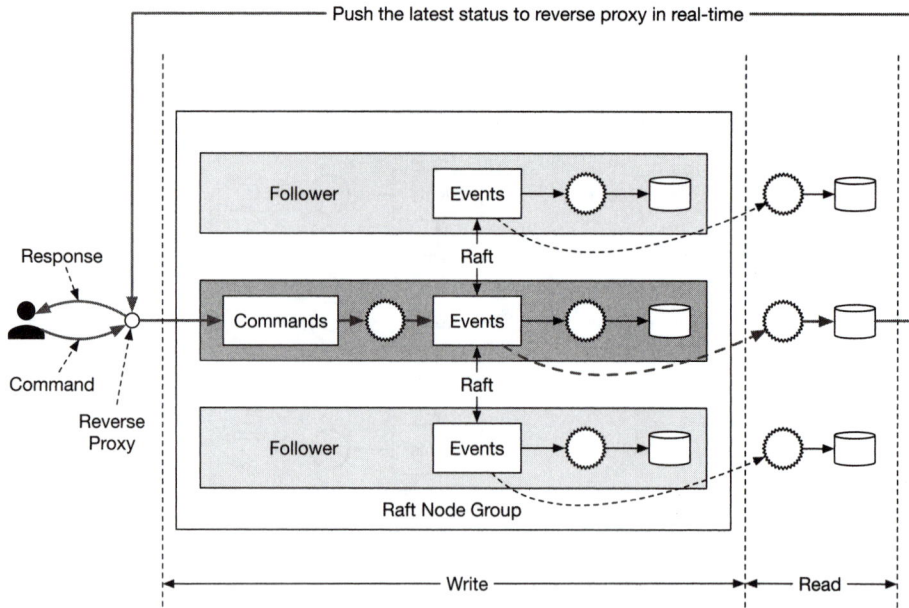

Figure 12.27: Push model

Distributed transaction

Once synchronous execution is adopted for every event sourcing node group, we can reuse the distributed transaction solution, TC/C or Saga. Assume we partition the data by dividing the hash value of keys by 2.

Figure 12.28 shows the updated design.

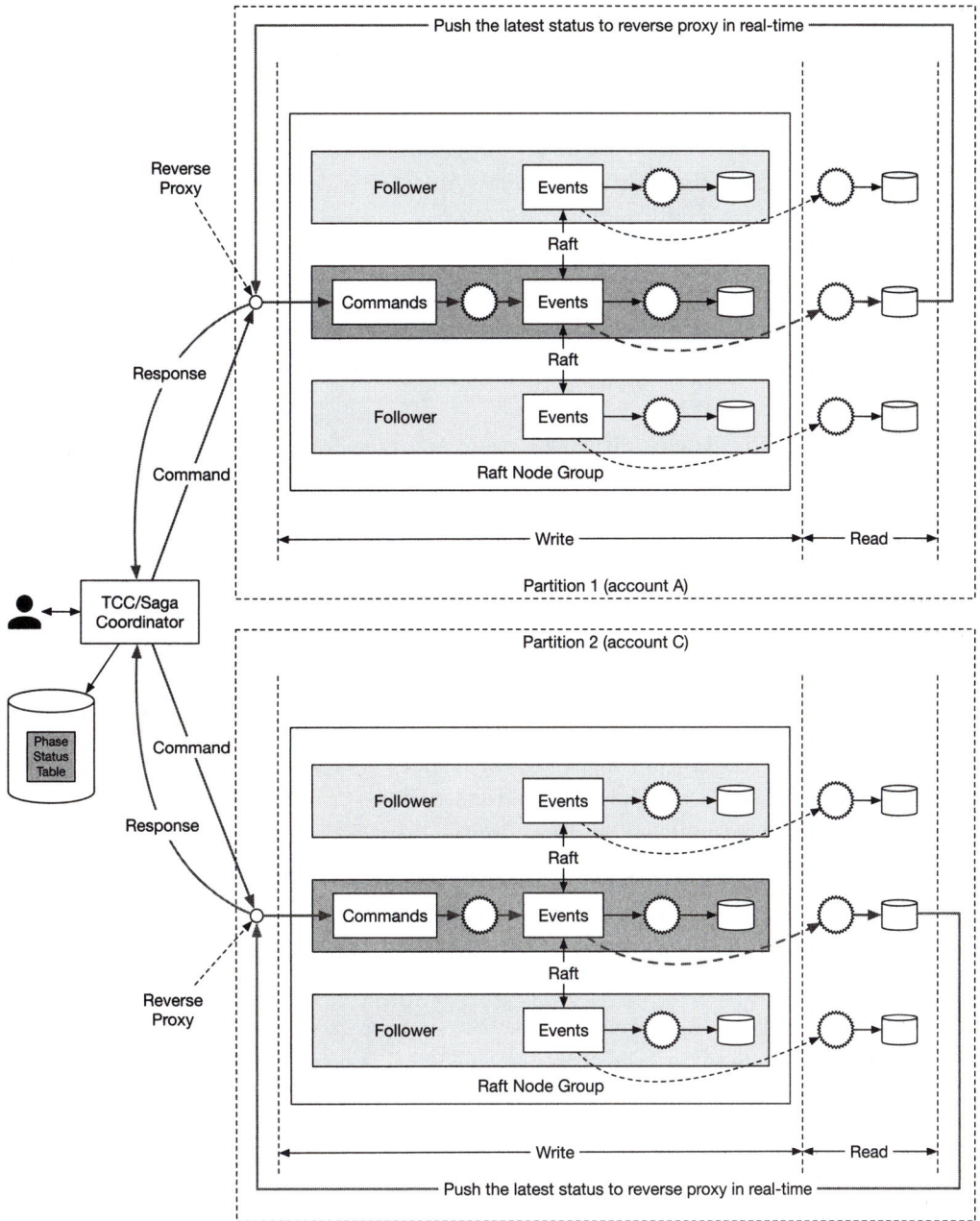

Figure 12.28: Final design

Let's take a look at how the money transfer works in the final distributed event sourcing architecture. To make it easier to understand, we use the Saga distributed transaction model and only explain the happy path without any rollback.

The money transfer operation contains 2 distributed operations: A:−$1 and C:+$1. The Saga coordinator coordinates the execution as shown in Figure 12.29:

1. User A sends a distributed transaction to the Saga coordinator. It contains two op-

erations: A:−$1 and C:+$1.

2. Saga coordinator creates a record in the phase status table to trace the status of a transaction.

3. Saga coordinator examines the order of operations and determines that it needs to handle A:−$1 first. The coordinator sends A:−$1 as a command to Partition 1, which contains account A's information.

4. Partition 1's Raft leader receives the A−$1 command and stores it in the command list. It then validates the command. If it is valid, it is converted into an event. The Raft consensus algorithm is used to synchronize data across different nodes. The event (deducting $1 from A's account balance) is executed after synchronization is complete.

5. After the event is synchronized, the event sourcing framework of Partition 1 synchronizes the data to the read path using CQRS. The read path reconstructs the state and the status of execution.

6. The read path of Partition 1 pushes the status back to the caller of the event sourcing framework, which is the Saga coordinator.

7. Saga coordinator receives the success status from Partition 1.

8. The Saga coordinator creates a record, indicating the operation in Partition 1 is successful, in the phase status table.

9. Because the first operation succeeds, the Saga coordinator executes the second operation, which is C:+$1. The coordinator sends C:+$1 as a command to Partition 2 which contains account C's information.

10. Partition 2's Raft leader receives the C:+$1 command and saves it to the command list. If it is valid, it is converted into an event. The Raft consensus algorithm is used to synchronize data across different nodes. The event (add $1 to C's account) is executed after synchronization is complete.

11. After the event is synchronized, the event sourcing framework of Partition 2 synchronizes the data to the read path using CQRS. The read path reconstructs the state and the status of execution.

12. The read path of Partition 2 pushes the status back to the caller of the event sourcing framework, which is the Saga coordinator.

13. The Saga coordinator receives the success status from Partition 2.

14. The Saga coordinator creates a record, indicating the operation in Partition 2 is successful in the phase status table.

15. At this time, all operations succeed and the distributed transaction is completed. The Saga coordinator responds to its caller with the result.

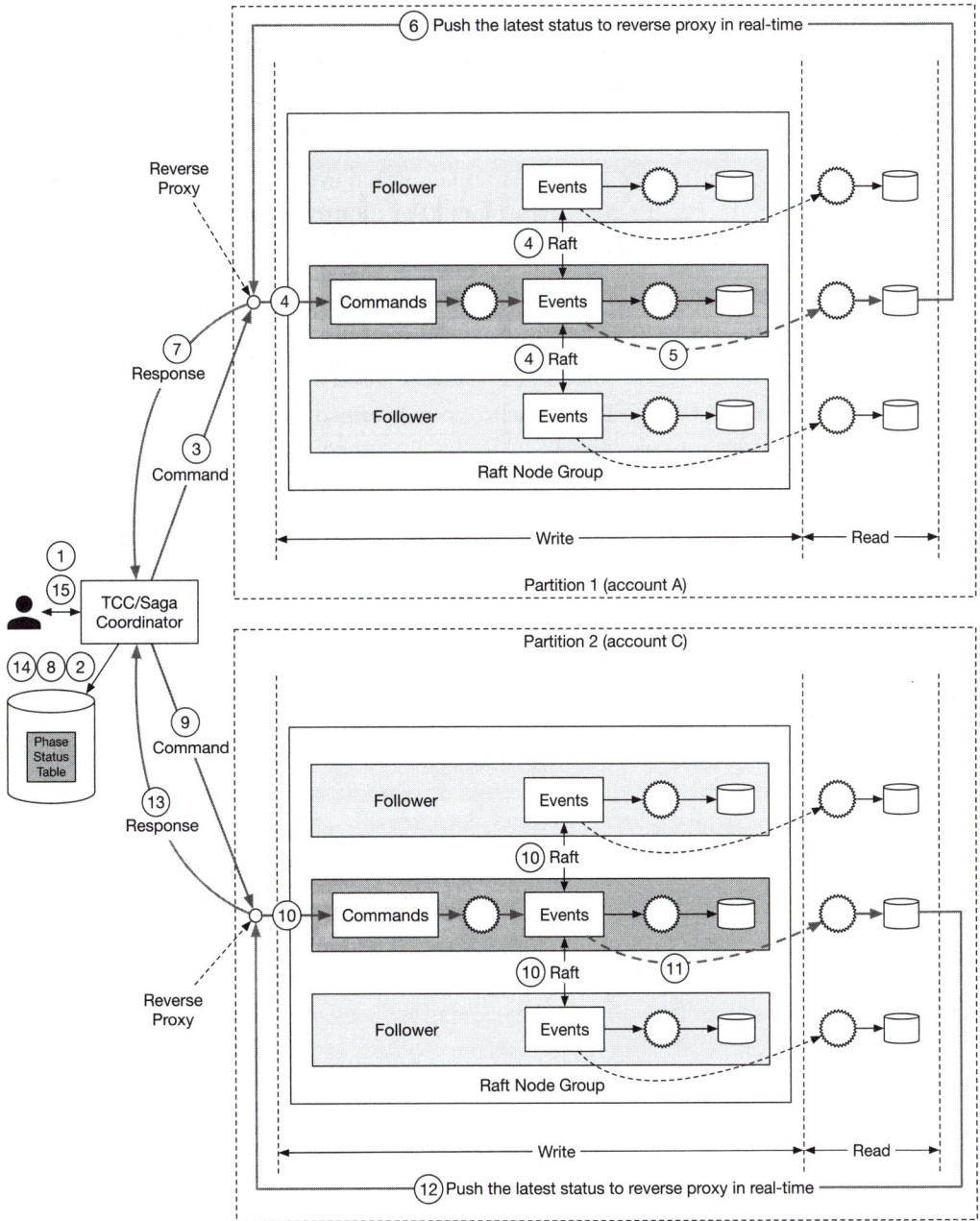

Figure 12.29: Final design in a numbered sequence

Step 4 - Wrap Up

In this chapter, we designed a wallet service that is capable of processing over 1 million payment commands per second. After a back-of-the-envelope estimation, we concluded that a few thousand nodes are required to support such a load.

In the first design, a solution using in-memory key-value stores like Redis is proposed. The problem with this design is that data isn't durable.

In the second design, the in-memory cache is replaced by transactional databases. To support multiple nodes, different transactional protocols such as 2PC, TC/C, and Saga are proposed. The main issue with transaction-based solutions is that we cannot conduct a data audit easily.

Next, event sourcing is introduced. We first implemented event sourcing using an external database and queue, but it's not performant. We improved performance by storing command, event, and state in a local node.

A single node means a single point of failure. To increase the system reliability, we use the Raft consensus algorithm to replicate the event list onto multiple nodes.

The last enhancement we made was to adopt the CQRS feature of event sourcing. We added a reverse proxy to change the asynchronous event sourcing framework to a synchronous one for external users. The TC/C or Saga protocol is used to coordinate Command executions across multiple node groups.

Congratulations on getting this far! Now give yourself a pat on the back. Good job!

Chapter Summary

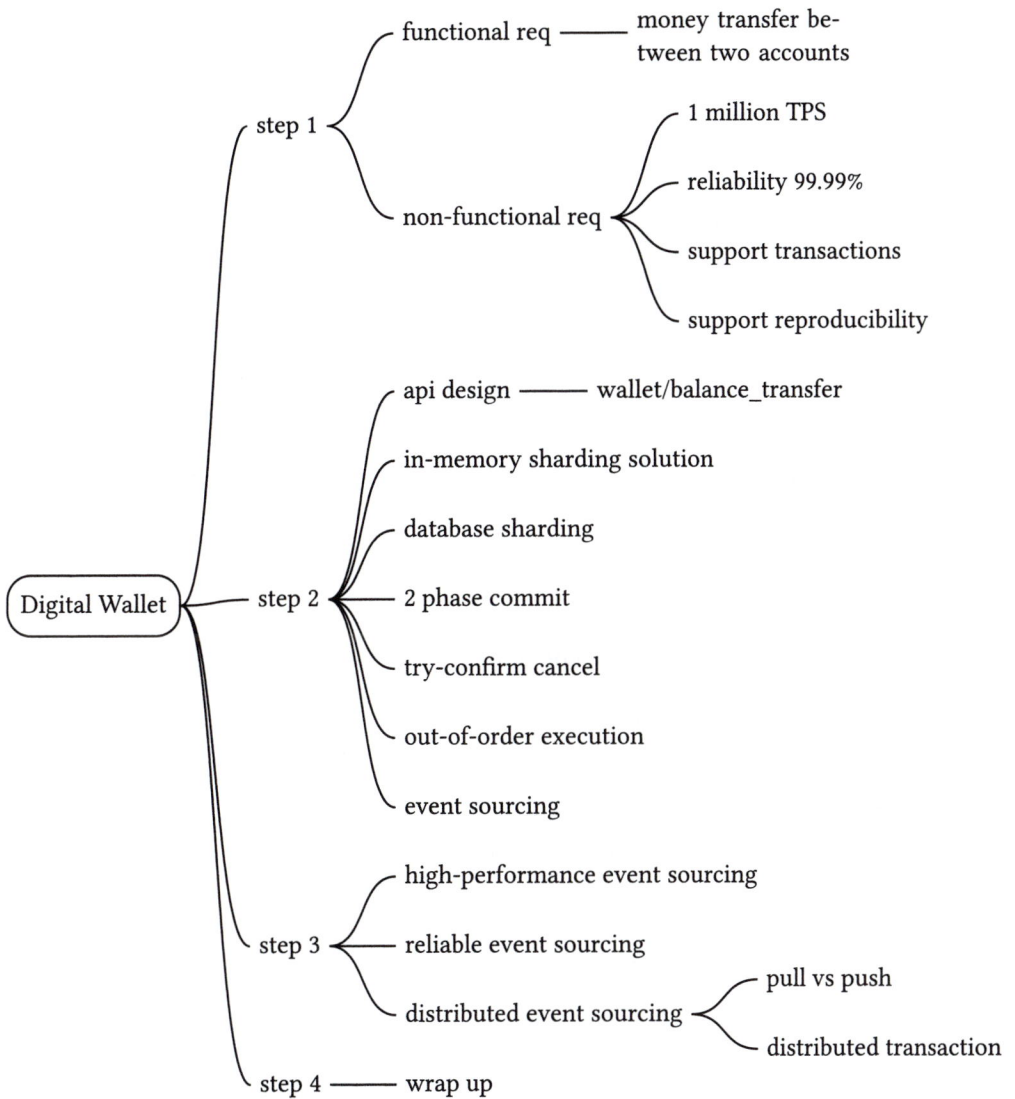

```
Digital Wallet
│
├── step 1
│     ├── functional req ────── money transfer be-
│     │                          tween two accounts
│     └── non-functional req
│           ├── 1 million TPS
│           ├── reliability 99.99%
│           ├── support transactions
│           └── support reproducibility
│
├── step 2
│     ├── api design ────── wallet/balance_transfer
│     ├── in-memory sharding solution
│     ├── database sharding
│     ├── 2 phase commit
│     ├── try-confirm cancel
│     ├── out-of-order execution
│     └── event sourcing
│
├── step 3
│     ├── high-performance event sourcing
│     ├── reliable event sourcing
│     └── distributed event sourcing
│           ├── pull vs push
│           └── distributed transaction
│
└── step 4 ────── wrap up
```

Reference Material

[1] Transactional guarantees. https://docs.oracle.com/cd/E17275_01/html/programm er_reference/rep_trans.html.

[2] TPC-E Top Price/Performance Results. http://tpc.org/tpce/results/tpce_price_perf _results5.asp?resulttype=all.

[3] ISO 4217 CURRENCY CODES. https://en.wikipedia.org/wiki/ISO_4217.

[4] Apache ZooKeeper. https://zookeeper.apache.org/.

[5] Martin Kleppmann. *Designing Data-Intensive Applications*. O'Reilly Media, 2017.

[6] X/Open XA. https://en.wikipedia.org/wiki/X/Open_XA.

[7] Compensating transaction. https://en.wikipedia.org/wiki/Compensating_transacti on.

[8] SAGAS, HectorGarcia-Molina. https://www.cs.cornell.edu/andru/cs711/2002fa/re ading/sagas.pdf.

[9] Eric Evans. *Domain-Driven Design: Tackling Complexity in the Heart of Software*. Addison-Wesley Professional, 2003.

[10] Apache Kafka. https://kafka.apache.org/.

[11] CQRS. https://martinfowler.com/bliki/CQRS.html.

[12] Comparing Random and Sequential Access in Disk and Memory. https://delivery images.acm.org/10.1145/1570000/1563874/jacobs3.jpg.

[13] mmap. https://man7.org/linux/man-pages/man2/mmap.2.html.

[14] SQLite. https://www.sqlite.org/index.html.

[15] RocksDB. https://rocksdb.org/.

[16] Apache Hadoop. https://hadoop.apache.org/.

[17] Raft. https://raft.github.io/.

[18] Reverse proxy. https://en.wikipedia.org/wiki/Reverse_proxy.

13   Stock Exchange

In this chapter, we design an electronic stock exchange system.

The basic function of an exchange is to facilitate the matching of buyers and sellers efficiently. This fundamental function has not changed over time. Before the rise of computing, people exchanged tangible goods by bartering and shouting at each other to get matched. Today, orders are processed silently by supercomputers, and people trade not only for the exchange of products, but also for speculation and arbitrage. Technology has greatly changed the landscape of trading and exponentially boosted electronic market trading volume.

When it comes to stock exchanges, most people think about major market players like The New York Stock exchange (NYSE) or Nasdaq, which have existed for over fifty years. In fact, there are many other types of exchange. Some focus on vertical segmentation of the financial industry and place special focus on technology [1], while others have an emphasis on fairness [2]. Before diving into the design, it is important to check with the interviewer about the scale and the important characteristics of the exchange in question.

Just to get a taste of the kind of problem we are dealing with; NYSE is trading billions of matches per day [3], and HKEX about 200 billion shares per day [4]. Figure 13.1 shows the big exchanges in the "trillion-dollar club" by market capitalization.

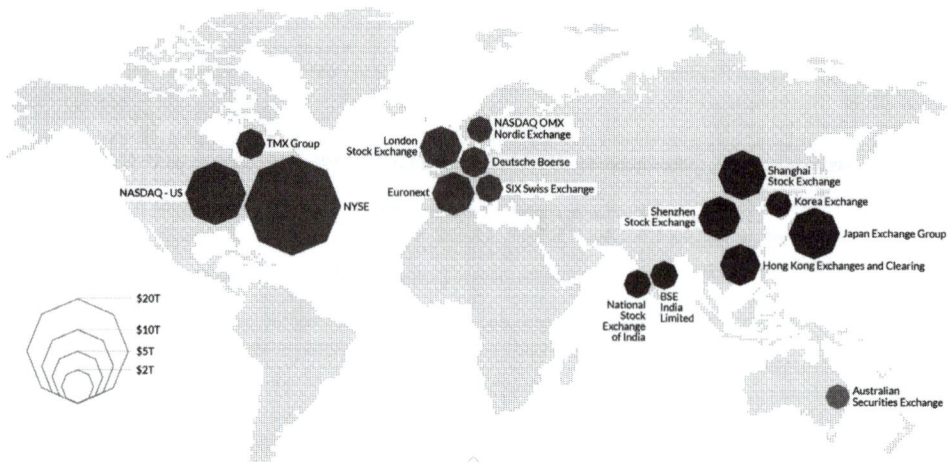

Figure 13.1: Largest stock exchanges (Source: [5])

Step 1 - Understand the Problem and Establish Design Scope

A modern exchange is a complicated system with stringent requirements on latency, throughput, and robustness. Before we start, let's ask the interviewer a few questions to clarify the requirements.

Candidate: Which securities are we going to trade? Stocks, options, or futures?
Interviewer: For simplicity, only stocks.

Candidate: Which types of order operations are supported: placing a new order, canceling an order, or replacing an order? Do we need to support limit order, market order, or conditional order?
Interviewer: We need to support the following: placing a new order and canceling an order. For the order type, we only need to consider the limit order.

Candidate: Does the system need to support after-hours trading?
Interviewer: No, we just need to support the normal trading hours.

Candidate: Could you describe the basic functions of the exchange? And the scale of the exchange, such as how many users, how many symbols, and how many orders?
Interviewer: A client can place new limit orders or cancel them, and receive matched trades in real-time. A client can view the real-time order book (the list of buy and sell orders). The exchange needs to support at least tens of thousands of users trading at the same time, and it needs to support at least 100 symbols. For the trading volume, we should support billions of orders per day. Also, the exchange is a regulated facility, so we need to make sure it runs risk checks.

Candidate: Could you please elaborate on risk checks?
Interviewer: Let's just do simple risk checks. For example, a user can only trade a maximum of 1 million shares of Apple stock in one day.

Candidate: I noticed you didn't mention user wallet management. Is it something we also need to consider?

Interviewer: Good catch! We need to make sure users have sufficient funds when they place orders. If an order is waiting in the order book to be filled, the funds required for the order need to be withheld to prevent overspending.

Non-functional requirements

After checking with the interviewer for the functional requirements, we should determine the non-functional requirements. In fact, requirements like "at least 100 symbols" and "tens of thousands of users" tell us that the interviewer wants us to design a small-to-medium scale exchange. On top of this, we should make sure the design can be extended to support more symbols and users. Many interviewers focus on extensibility as an area for follow-up questions.

Here is a list of non-functional requirements:

- **Availability.** At least 99.99%. Availability is crucial for exchanges. Downtime, even seconds, can harm reputation.

- **Fault tolerance.** Fault tolerance and a fast recovery mechanism are needed to limit the impact of a production incident.

- **Latency.** The round-trip latency should be at the millisecond level, with a particular focus on the 99th percentile latency. The round trip latency is measured from the moment a market order enters the exchange to the point where the market order returns as a filled execution. A persistently high 99th percentile latency causes a terrible user experience for a small number of users.

- **Security.** The exchange should have an account management system. For legal and compliance, the exchange performs a KYC (Know Your Client) check to verify a user's identity before a new account is opened. For public resources, such as web pages containing market data, we should prevent distributed denial-of-service (DDoS) [6] attacks.

Back-of-the-envelope estimation

Let's do some simple back-of-the-envelope calculations to understand the scale of the system:

- 100 symbols

- 1 billion orders per day

- NYSE Stock exchange is open Monday through Friday from 9:30 am to 4:00 pm Eastern Time. That's 6.5 hours in total.

- QPS: $\dfrac{1 \text{ billion}}{6.5 \times 3{,}600} = \sim 43{,}000$

- Peak QPS: $5 \times$ QPS $= 215{,}000$. The trading volume is significantly higher when the market first opens in the morning and before it closes in the afternoon.

Step 2 - Propose High-Level Design and Get Buy-In

Before we dive into the high-level design, let's briefly discuss some basic concepts and terminology that are helpful for designing an exchange.

Business Knowledge 101

Broker

Most retail clients trade with an exchange via a broker. Some brokers whom you might be familiar with include Charles Schwab, Robinhood, E*Trade, Fidelity, etc. These brokers provide a friendly user interface for retail users to place trades and view market data.

Institutional client

Institutional clients trade in large volumes using specialized trading software. Different institutional clients operate with different requirements. For example, pension funds aim for a stable income. They trade infrequently, but when they do trade, the volume is large. They need features like order splitting to minimize the market impact [7] of their sizable orders. Some hedge funds specialize in market making and earn income via commission rebates. They need low latency trading abilities, so obviously they cannot simply view market data on a web page or a mobile app, as retail clients do.

Limit order

A limit order is a buy or sell order with a fixed price. It might not find a match immediately, or it might just be partially matched.

Market order

A market order doesn't specify a price. It is executed at the prevailing market price immediately. A market order sacrifices cost in order to guarantee execution. It is useful in certain fast-moving market conditions.

Market data levels

The US stock market has three tiers of price quotes: L1 (level 1), L2, and L3. L1 market data contains the best bid price, ask price, and quantities (Figure 13.2). Bid price refers to the highest price a buyer is willing to pay for a stock. Ask price refers to the lowest price a seller is willing to sell the stock.

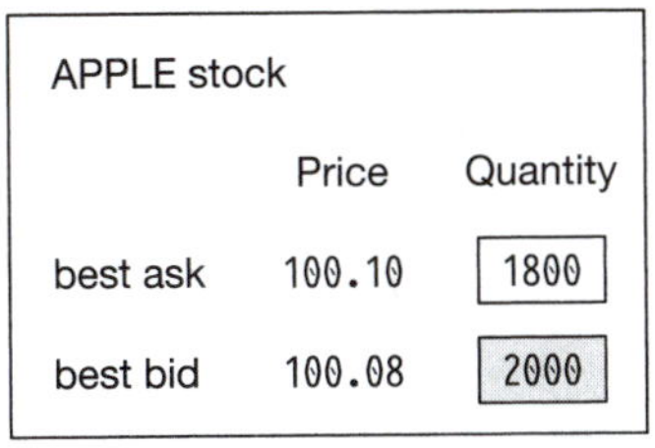

Figure 13.2: Level 1 data

L2 includes more price levels than L1 (Figure 13.3).

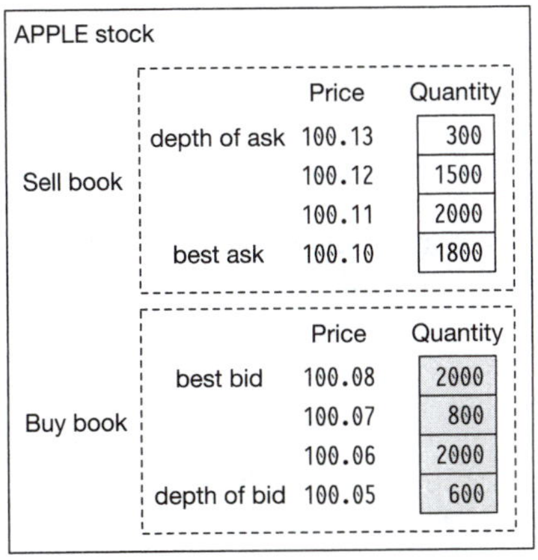

Figure 13.3: Level 2 data

L3 shows price levels and the queued quantity at each price level (Figure 13.4).

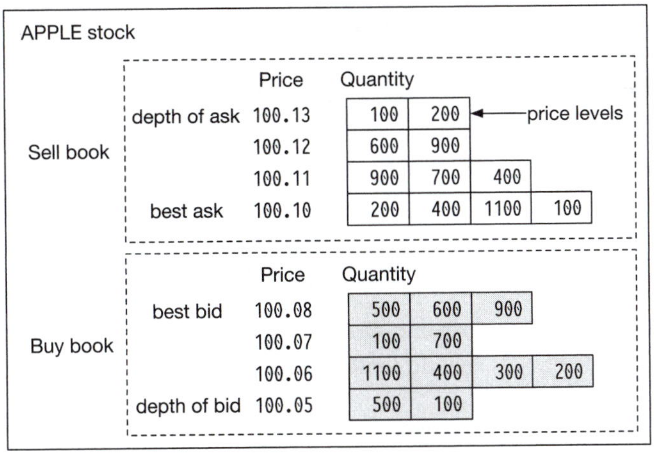

Figure 13.4: Level 3 data

Candlestick chart

A candlestick chart represents the stock price for a certain period of time. A typical candlestick looks like this (Figure 13.5). A candlestick shows the market's open, close, high, and low price for a time interval. The common time intervals are one-minute, five-minute, one-hour, one-day, one-week, and one-month.

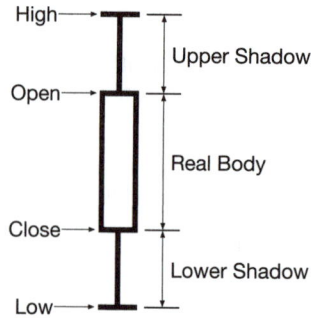

Figure 13.5: A single candlestick chart

FIX

FIX protocol [8], which stands for Financial Information exchange protocol, was created in 1991. It is a vendor-neutral communications protocol for exchanging securities transaction information. See below for an example of a securities transaction encoded in FIX [8].

```
8=FIX.4.2 | 9=176 | 35=8 | 49=PHLX | 56=PERS |
52=20071123-05:30:00.000 | 11=ATOMNOCCC9990900 | 20=3 | 150=E | 39=E
| 55=MSFT | 167=CS | 54=1 | 38=15 | 40=2 | 44=15 | 58=PHLX EQUITY
TESTING | 59=0 | 47=C | 32=0 | 31=0 | 151=15 | 14=0 | 6=0 | 10=128 |
```

High-level design

Now that we have some basic understanding of the key concepts, let's take a look at the high-level design, as shown in Figure 13.6.

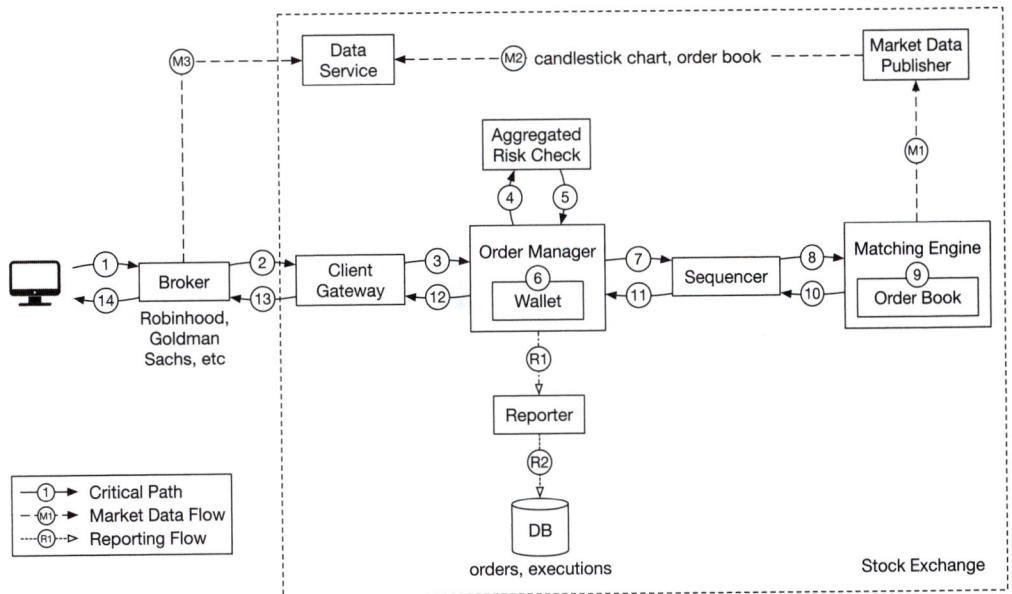

Figure 13.6: High-level design

Let's trace the life of an order through various components in the diagram to see how the pieces fit together.

First, we follow the order through the **trading flow**. This is the critical path with strict latency requirements. Everything has to happen fast in the flow:

Step 1: A client places an order via the broker's web or mobile app.

Step 2: The broker sends the order to the exchange.

Step 3: The order enters the exchange through the client gateway. The client gateway performs basic gatekeeping functions such as input validation, rate limiting, authentication, normalization, etc. The client gateway then forwards the order to the order manager.

Step 4 ∼ 5: The order manager performs risk checks based on rules set by the risk manager.

Step 6: After passing risk checks, the order manager verifies there are sufficient funds in the wallet for the order.

Step 7 ∼ 9: The order is sent to the matching engine. When a match is found, the matching engine emits two executions (also called fills), with one each for the buy and sell sides. To guarantee that matching results are deterministic when replayed, both orders and executions are sequenced in the sequencer (more on the sequencer later).

Step 10 ∼ 14: The executions are returned to the client.

Next, we follow the **market data flow** and trace the order executions from the matching engine to the broker via the data service.

Step M1: The matching engine generates a stream of executions (fills) as matches are made. The stream is sent to the market data publisher.

Step M2: The market data publisher constructs the candlestick charts and the order books as market data from the stream of executions and orders. It then sends market data to the data service.

Step M3: The market data is saved to specialized storage for real-time analytics. Brokers connect to the data service to obtain timely market data. Brokers relay market data to their clients.

Lastly, we examine the **reporting flow**.

Step R1~R2 (reporting flow): The reporter collects all the necessary reporting fields (e.g. `client_id`, `price`, `quantity`, `order_type`, `filled_quantity`, `remaining_quantity`) from orders and executions, and writes the consolidated records to the database.

Note that the trading flow (steps 1 to 14) is on the critical path, while the market data flow and reporting flow are not. They have different latency requirements.

Now let's examine each of the three flows in more detail.

Trading flow

The trading flow is on the critical path of the exchange. Everything must happen fast. The heart of the trading flow is the matching engine. Let's go over that first.

Matching engine

The matching engine is also called the cross engine. Here are the primary responsibilities of the matching engine:

1. Maintain the order book for each symbol. An order book is a list of buy and sell orders for a symbol. We explain the construction of an order book in the Data models section later.

2. Match buy and sell orders. A match results in two executions (one from the buy side and the other from the sell side). The matching function must be fast and accurate.

3. Distribute the execution stream as market data.

A highly available matching engine implementation must be able to produce matches in a deterministic order. That is, given a known sequence of orders as an input, the matching engine must produce the same sequence of executions (fills) as an output when the sequence is replayed. This determinism is a foundation of high availability which we will discuss at length in the deep dive section.

Sequencer

The sequencer is the key component that makes the matching engine deterministic. It stamps every incoming order with a sequence ID before it is processed by the matching engine. It also stamps every pair of executions (fills) completed by the matching engine with sequence IDs. In other words, the sequencer has an inbound and an outbound instance, with each maintaining its own sequences. The sequence generated by each sequencer must be sequential numbers, so that any missing numbers can be easily detected. See Figure 13.7 for details.

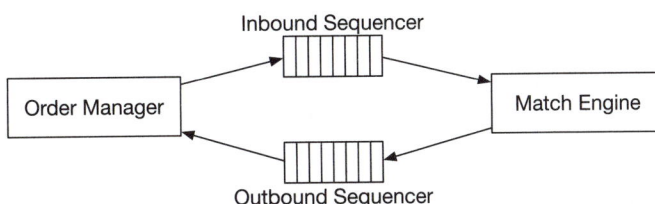

Figure 13.7: Inbound and outbound sequencers

The incoming orders and outgoing executions are stamped with sequence IDs for these reasons:

1. Timeliness and fairness
2. Fast recovery / replay
3. Exactly-once guarantee

The sequencer does not only generate sequence IDs. It also functions as a message queue. There is one to send messages (incoming orders) to the matching engine, and another one to send messages (executions) back to the order manager. It is also an event store for the orders and executions. It is similar to having two Kafka event streams connected to the matching engine, one for incoming orders and the other for outgoing executions. In fact, we could have used Kafka if its latency was lower and more predictable. We discuss how the sequencer is implemented in a low-latency exchange environment in the deep dive section.

Order manager

The order manager receives orders on one end and receives executions on the other. It manages the orders' states. Let's look at it closely.

The order manager receives inbound orders from the client gateway and performs the following:

- It sends the order for risk checks. Our requirements for risk checking are simple. For example, we verify that a user's trade volume is below $1M a day.

- It checks the order against the user's wallet and verifies that there are sufficient funds to cover the trade. The wallet was discussed at length in the "Digital Wallet" chapter on page 341. Refer to that chapter for an implementation that would work in the exchange.

- It sends the order to the sequencer where the order is stamped with a sequence ID. The sequenced order is then processed by the matching engine. There are many attributes in a new order, but there is no need to send all the attributes to the matching engine. To reduce the size of the message in data transmission, the order manager only sends the necessary attributes.

On the other end, the order manager receives executions from the matching engine via the sequencer. The order manager returns the executions for the filled orders to the brokers via the client gateway.

The order manager should be fast, efficient, and accurate. It maintains the current states for the orders. In fact, the challenge of managing the various state transitions is the major source of complexity for the order manager. There can be tens of thousands of cases involved in a real exchange system. Event sourcing [9] is perfect for the design of an order manager. We discuss an event sourcing design in the deep dive section.

Client gateway

The client gateway is the gatekeeper for the exchange. It receives orders placed by clients and routes them to the order manager. The gateway provides the following functions as shown in Figure 13.8.

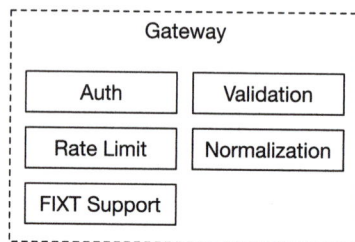

Figure 13.8: Client gateway components

The client gateway is on the critical path and is latency-sensitive. It should stay lightweight. It passes orders to the correct destinations as quickly as possible. The functions above, while critical, must be completed as quickly as possible. It is a design trade-off to decide what functionality to put in the client gateway, and what to leave out. As a general guideline, we should leave complicated functions to the matching engine and risk check.

There are different types of client gateways for retail and institutional clients. The main considerations are latency, transaction volume, and security requirements. For instance, institutions like the market makers provide a large portion of liquidity for the exchange. They require very low latency. Figure 13.9 shows different client gateway connections to an exchange. An extreme example is the colocation (colo) engine. It is the trading engine software running on some servers rented by the broker in the exchange's data center. The latency is literally the time it takes for light to travel from the colocated server to the exchange server [10].

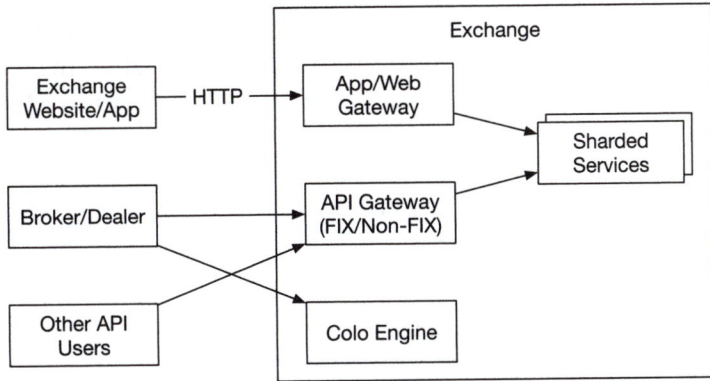

Figure 13.9: Client gateway

Market data flow

The market data publisher (MDP) receives executions from the matching engine and builds the order books and candlestick charts from the stream of executions. The order books and candlestick charts, which we discuss in the Data Models section later, are collectively called market data. The market data is sent to the data service where they are made available to subscribers. Figure 13.10 shows an implementation of MDP and how it fits with the other components in the market data flow.

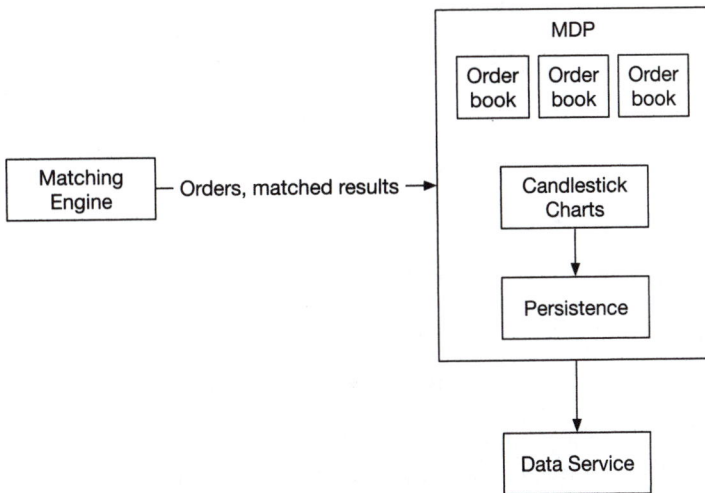

Figure 13.10: Market Data Publisher

Reporting flow

One essential part of the exchange is reporting. The reporter is not on the trading critical path, but it is a critical part of the system. It provides trading history, tax reporting, compliance reporting, settlements, etc. Efficiency and latency are critical for the trading flow, but the reporter is less sensitive to latency. Accuracy and compliance are key factors for the reporter.

It is common practice to piece attributes together from both incoming orders and outgoing executions. An incoming new order contains order details, and outgoing execution usually only contains order ID, price, quantity, and execution status. The reporter merges the attributes from both sources for the reports. Figure 13.11 shows how the components in the reporting flow fit together.

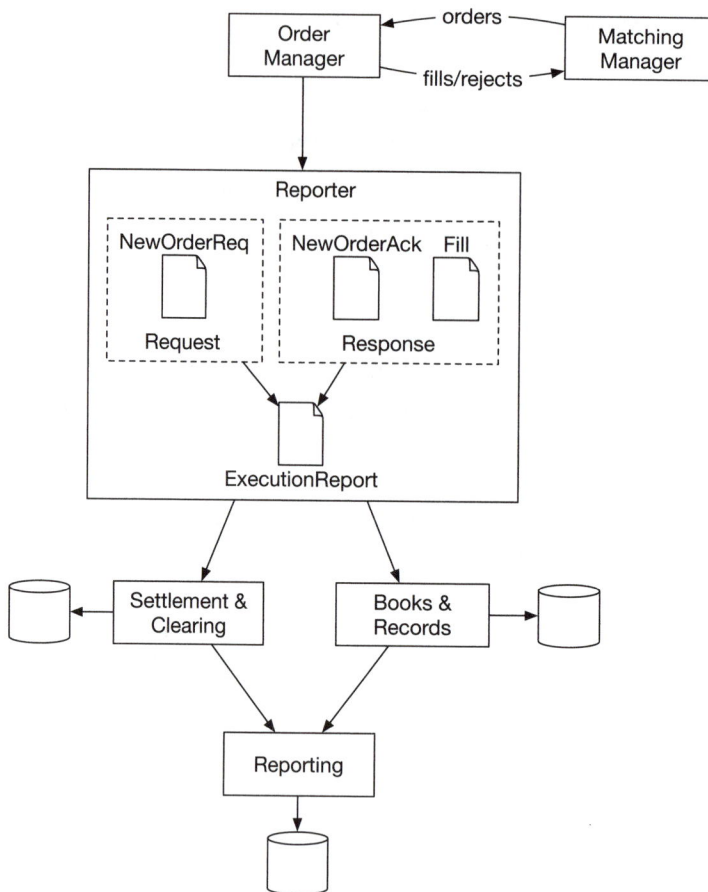

Figure 13.11: Reporter

A sharp reader might notice that the section order of "Step 2 - Propose High-Level Design and Get Buy-In" looks a little different than other chapters. In this chapter, the API design and data models sections come after the high-level design. The sections are arranged this way because these other sections require some concepts that were introduced in the high-level design.

API Design

Now that we understand the high-level design, let's take a look at the API design.

Clients interact with the stock exchange via the brokers to place orders, view executions, view market data, download historical data for analysis, etc. We use the RESTful conventions for the API below to specify the interface between the brokers and the client gateway. Refer to the "Data models" section on page 391 for the resources mentioned below.

Note that the RESTful API might not satisfy the latency requirements of institutional clients like hedge funds. The specialized software built for these institutions likely uses a different protocol, but no matter what it is, the basic functionality mentioned below needs to be supported.

Order

`POST /v1/order`

This endpoint places an order. It requires authentication.

Parameters

  `symbol`: the stock symbol. String
  `side`: buy or sell. String
  `price`: the price of the limit order. Long
  `orderType`: limit or market (note we only support limit orders in our design). String
  `quantity`: the quantity of the order. Long

Response

Body:

    `id`: the ID of the order. Long
    `creationTime`: the system creation time of the order. Long
    `filledQuantity`: the quantity that has been successfully executed. Long
    `remainingQuantity`: the quantity still to be executed. Long
    `status`: new/canceled/filled. String
    rest of the attributes are the same as the input parameters

Code:

    200: successful
    40x: parameter error/access denied/unauthorized
    500: server error

Execution

`GET /v1/execution?symbol={:symbol}&orderId={:orderId}&startTime={:startTime}&endTime={:endTime}`

This endpoint queries execution info. It requires authentication.

Parameters

  `symbol`: the stock symbol. String
  `orderId`: the ID of the order. Optional. String
  `startTime`: query start time in epoch [11]. Long
  `endTime`: query end time in epoch. Long

Response

Body:

executions: array with each execution in scope (see attributes below). Array

  id: the ID of the execution. Long

  orderId: the ID of the order. Long

  symbol: the stock symbol. String

  side: buy or sell. String

  price: the price of the execution. Long

  orderType: limit or market. String

  quantity: the filled quantity. Long

Code:

  200: successful

  40x: parameter error/not found/access denied/unauthorized

  500: server error

Order book

GET /v1/marketdata/orderBook/L2?symbol={:symbol}&depth={:depth}

This endpoint queries L2 order book information for a symbol with designated depth.

Parameters

  symbol: the stock symbol. String

  depth: order book depth per side. Int

  startTime: query start time in epoch. Long

  endTime: query end time in epoch. Long

Response

Body:

  bids: array with price and size. Array

  asks: array with price and size.Array

Code:

  200: successful

  40x: parameter error/not found/access denied/unauthorized

  500: server error

Historical prices (candlestick charts)

GET /v1/marketdata/candles?symbol={:symbol}&resolution={:resolution}&startTime
{:startTime}&endTime={:endTime}

This endpoint queries candlestick chart data (see candlestick chart in data models section) for a symbol given a time range and resolution.

Parameters

symbol: the stock symbol. String
resolution: window length of the candlestick chart in seconds. Long
startTime: start time of the window in epoch. Long
endTime: end time of the window in epoch. Long

Response

Body:

candles: array with each candlestick data (attributes listed below). Array
open: open price of each candlestick. Double
close: close price of each candlestick. Double
high: high price of each candlestick. Double
low: low price of each candlestick. Double

Code:

200: successful
40x: parameter error/not found/access denied/unauthorized
500: server error

Data models

There are three main types of data in the stock exchange. Let's explore them one by one.

- Product, order, and execution
- Order book
- Candlestick chart

Product, order, execution

A product describes the attributes of a traded symbol, like product type, trading symbol, UI display symbol, settlement currency, lot size, tick size, etc. This data doesn't change frequently. It is primarily used for UI display. The data can be stored in any database and is highly cacheable.

An order represents the inbound instruction for a buy or sell order. An execution represents the outbound matched result. An execution is also called a fill. Not every order has an execution. The output of the matching engine contains two executions, representing the buy and sell sides of a matched order.

See Figure 13.12 for the logical model diagram that shows the relationships between the three entities. Note it is not a database schema.

Order

+ orderID: UUID
+ productID: int
+ price: long
+ quantity: long
+ side: Side
+ orderStatus: OrderStatus
+ orderType: OrderType
+ timeInForce: TimeInForce
+ symbol: long
+ userID: long
+ clientOrderID: string
+ broker: string
+ accountID: long
+ entryTime: long
+ transactionTime: long

Execution

+ execID: UUID
+ orderID: UUID
+ price: long
+ quantity: long
+ side: Side
+ orderStatus: OrderStatus
+ orderType: OrderType
+ symbol: long
+ userID: long
+ feeCurrency: Currency
+ feeRate: long
+ feeAmount: long
+ accountID: long
+ execStatus: ExecStatus
+ transactionTime: long

1 → 0..n

Product

+ productID: int
+ symbol: type
+ lotSize: int
+ tickSize: decimal
+ quoteCurrency: Currency
+ settleCurrency: Currency
+ description: string
+ field: type

1 → 1

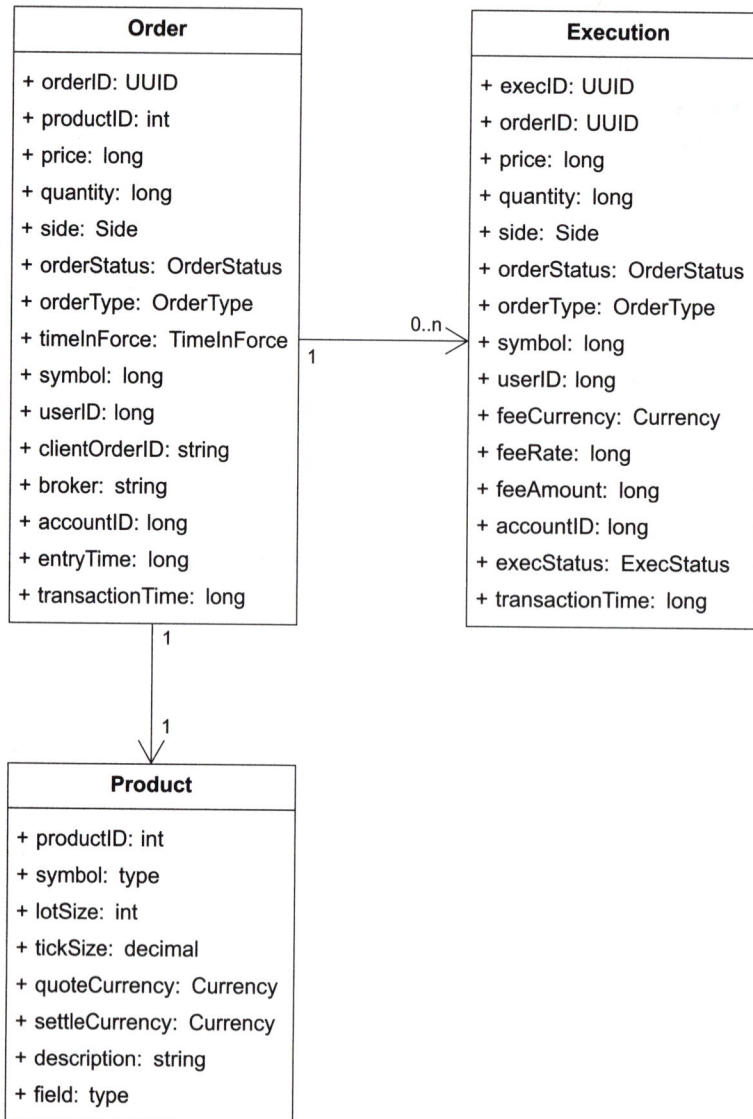

Figure 13.12: Product, order, execution

Orders and executions are the most important data in the exchange. We encounter them in all three flows mentioned in the high-level design, in slightly different forms.

- In the critical trading path, orders and executions are not stored in a database. To achieve high performance, this path executes trades in memory and leverages hard disk or shared memory to persist and share orders and executions. Specifically, orders and executions are stored in the sequencer for fast recovery, and data is archived after the market closes. We discuss an efficient implementation of the sequencer in the deep dive section.

- The reporter writes orders and executions to the database for reporting use cases like reconciliation and tax reporting.

- Executions are forwarded to the market data processor to reconstruct the order book and candlestick chart data. We discuss these data types next.

Order book

An order book is a list of buy and sell orders for a specific security or financial instrument, organized by price level [12] [13]. It is a key data structure in the matching engine for fast order matching. An efficient data structure for an order book must satisfy these requirements:

- Constant lookup time. Operation includes: getting volume at a price level or between price levels.

- Fast add/cancel/execute operations, preferably $O(1)$ time complexity. Operations include: placing a new order, canceling an order, and matching an order.

- Fast update. Operation: replacing an order.

- Query best bid/ask.

- Iterate through price levels.

Let's walk through an example order execution against an order book, as illustrated in Figure 13.13.

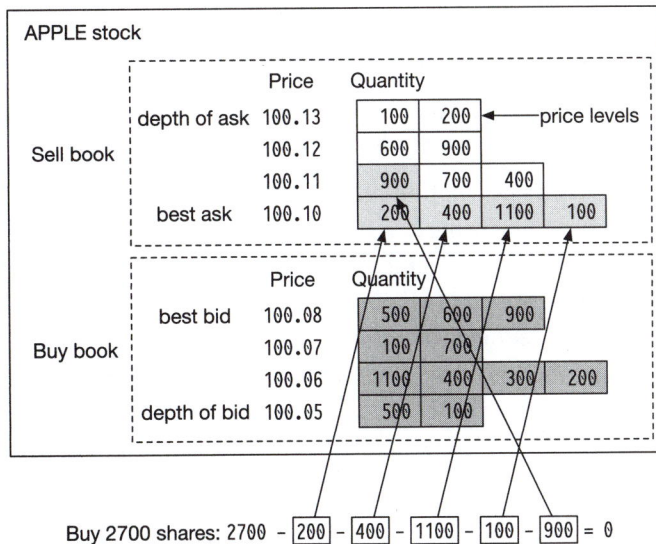

Buy 2700 shares: 2700 – 200 – 400 – 1100 – 100 – 900 = 0

Figure 13.13: Limit order book illustrated

In the example above, there is a large market buy order for 2,700 shares of Apple. The buy order matches all the sell orders in the best ask queue and the first sell order in the 100.11 price queue. After fulfilling this large order, the bid/ask spread widens, and the price increases by one level (best ask is 100.11 now).

The following code snippet shows an implementation of the order book.

```
class PriceLevel{
  private Price limitPrice;
  private long totalVolume;
  private List<Order> orders;
}
class Book<Side> {
  private Side side;
  private Map<Price, PriceLevel> limitMap;
}
class OrderBook {
  private Book<Buy> buyBook;
  private Book<Sell> sellBook;
  private PriceLevel bestBid;
  private PriceLevel bestOffer;
  private Map<OrderID, Order> orderMap;
}
```

Does the code meet all the design requirements stated above? For example, when adding/canceling a limit order, is the time complexity $O(1)$? The answer is no since we are using a plain list here (private List<Order> orders). To have a more efficient order book, change the data structure of "orders" to a doubly-linked list so that the deletion type of operation (cancel and match) is also $O(1)$. Let's review how we achieve $O(1)$ time complexity for these operations:

1. Placing a new order means adding a new Order to the tail of the PriceLevel. This is $O(1)$ time complexity for a doubly-linked list.

2. Matching an order means deleting an Order from the head of the PriceLevel. This is $O(1)$ time complexity for a doubly-linked list.

3. Canceling an order means deleting an Order from the OrderBook. We leverage the helper data structure Map<OrderID, Order> orderMap in the OrderBook to find the Order to cancel in $O(1)$ time. Once the order is found, if the "orders" list was a singly-linked list, the code would have to traverse the entire list to locate the previous pointer in order to delete the order. That would have taken $O(n)$ time. Since the list is now doubly-linked, the order itself has a pointer to the previous order, which allows the code to delete the order without traversing the entire order list.

Figure 13.14 explains how these three operations work.

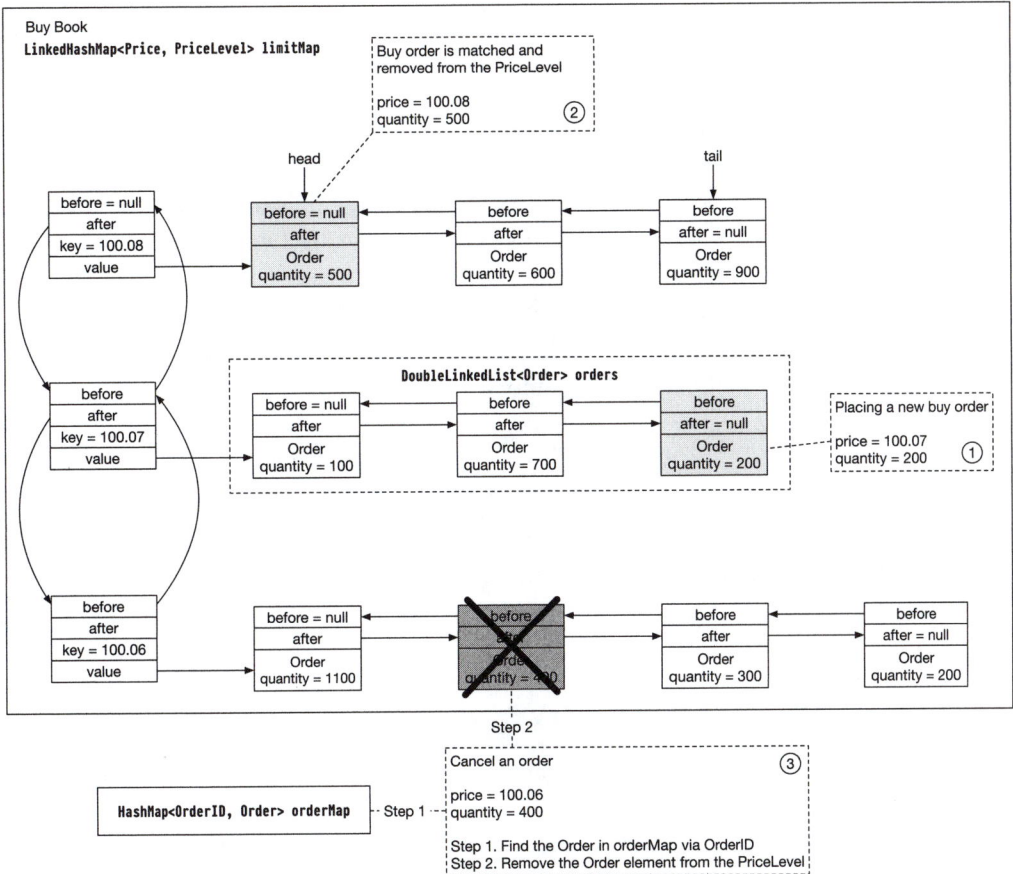

Buy Book
`LinkedHashMap<Price, PriceLevel> limitMap`

Buy order is matched and removed from the PriceLevel
price = 100.08
quantity = 500 ②

Placing a new buy order
price = 100.07
quantity = 200 ①

Cancel an order ③
price = 100.06
quantity = 400
Step 1. Find the Order in orderMap via OrderID
Step 2. Remove the Order element from the PriceLevel

`HashMap<OrderID, Order> orderMap` — Step 1

Figure 13.14: Place, match, and cancel an order in $O(1)$

See the reference material for more details [14].

It is worth noting that the order book data structure is also heavily used in the market data processor to reconstruct the L1, L2, and L3 data from the streams of executions generated by the matching engine.

Candlestick chart

Candlestick chart is another key data structure (alongside order book) in the market data processor to produce market data.

We model this with a `Candlestick` class and a `CandlestickChart` class. When the interval for the candlestick has elapsed, a new `Candlestick` class is instantiated for the next interval and added to the linked list in the `CandleStickChart` instance.

```
class Candlestick {
    private long openPrice;
    private long closePrice;
    private long highPrice;
    private long lowPrice;
    private long volume;
    private long timestamp;
```

```
    private int interval;
  }
  class CandlestickChart {
    private LinkedList<Candlestick> sticks;
  }
```

Tracking price history in candlestick charts for many symbols at many time intervals consumes a lot of memory. How can we optimize it? Here are two ways:

1. Use pre-allocated ring buffers to hold sticks to reduce the number of new object allocations.

2. Limit the number of sticks in the memory and persist the rest to disk.

We will examine the optimizations in the "Market data publisher" section in deep dive on page 407.

The market data is usually persisted in an in-memory columnar database (for example, KDB [15]) for real-time analytics. After the market is closed, data is persisted in a historical database.

Step 3 - Design Deep Dive

Now that we understand how an exchange works at a high level, let's investigate how a modern exchange has evolved to become what it is today. What does a modern exchange look like? The answer might surprise a lot of readers. Some large exchanges run almost everything on a single gigantic server. While it might sound extreme, we can learn many good lessons from it.

Let's dive in.

Performance

As discussed in the non-functional requirements, latency is very important for an exchange. Not only does the average latency need to be low, but the overall latency must also be stable. A good measure for the level of stability is the 99th percentile latency.

Latency can be broken down into its components as shown in the formula below:

$$\text{Latency} = \sum \text{executionTimeAlongCriticalPath}$$

There are two ways to reduce latency:

1. Decrease the number of tasks on the critical path.

2. Shorten the time spent on each task:

   a. By reducing or eliminating network and disk usage

   b. By reducing execution time for each task

Let's review the first point. As shown in the high-level design, the critical trading path includes the following:

gateway → order manager → sequencer → matching engine

The critical path only contains the necessary components, even logging is removed from the critical path to achieve low latency.

Now let's look at the second point. In the high-level design, the components on the critical path run on individual servers connected over the network. The round trip network latency is about 500 microseconds. When there are multiple components all communicating over the network on the critical path, the total network latency adds up to single-digit milliseconds. In addition, the sequencer is an event store that persists events to disk. Even assuming an efficient design that leverages the performance advantage of sequential writes, the latency of disk access still measures in tens of milliseconds. To learn more about network and disk access latency, see "Latency Numbers Every Programmer Should Know" [16].

Accounting for both network and disk access latency, the total end-to-end latency adds up to tens of milliseconds. While this number was respectable in the early days of the exchange, it is no longer sufficient as exchanges compete for ultra-low latency.

To stay ahead of the competition, exchanges over time evolve their design to reduce the end-to-end latency on the critical path to tens of microseconds, primarily by exploring options to reduce or eliminate network and disk access latency. A time-tested design eliminates the network hops by putting everything on the same server. When all components are on the same server, they can communicate via mmap [17] as an event store (more on this later).

Figure 13.15 shows a low-latency design with all the components on a single server:

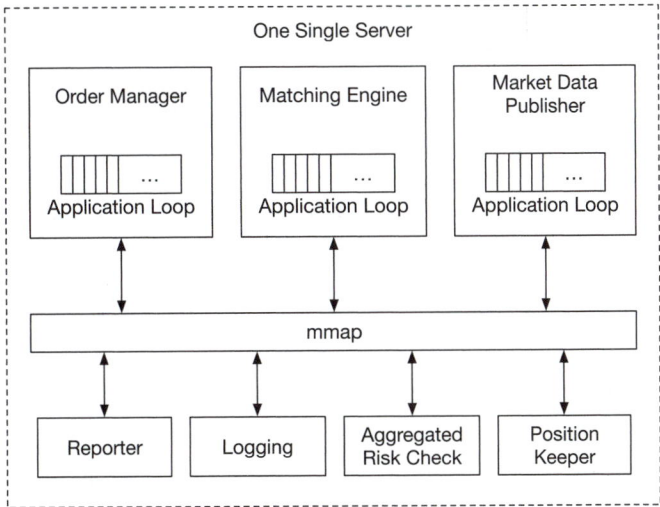

Figure 13.15: A low latency single server exchange design

There are a few interesting design decisions that are worth a closer look at.

Let's first focus on the application loops in the diagram above. An application loop is an interesting concept. It keeps polling for tasks to execute in a while loop and is the primary task execution mechanism. To meet the strict latency budget, only the most mission-critical tasks should be processed by the application loop. Its goal is to reduce the execution time for each component and to guarantee a highly predictable execution time (i.e., a low 99th percentile latency). Each box in the diagram represents a component. A component is a process on the server. To maximize CPU efficiency, each application loop (think of it as the main processing loop) is single-threaded, and the thread is pinned to a fixed CPU core. Using the order manager as an example, it looks like the following diagram (Figure 13.16).

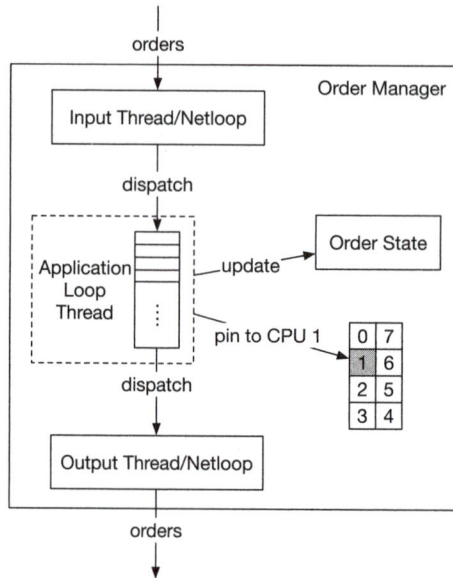

Figure 13.16: Application loop thread in Order Manager

In this diagram, the application loop for the order manager is pinned to CPU 1. The benefits of pinning the application loop to the CPU are substantial:

1. No context switch [18]. CPU 1 is fully allocated to the order manager's application loop.
2. No locks and therefore no lock contention, since there is only one thread that updates states.

Both of these contribute to a low 99th percentile latency.

The tradeoff of CPU pinning is that it makes coding more complicated. Engineers need to carefully analyze the time each task takes to keep it from occupying the application loop thread for too long, as it can potentially block subsequent tasks.

Next, let's focus our attention on the long rectangle labeled "mmap" at the center of

Figure 13.15. "mmap" refers to a POSIX-compliant UNIX system call named mmap(2) that maps a file into the memory of a process.

mmap(2) provides a mechanism for high-performance sharing of memory between processes. The performance advantage is compounded when the backing file is in /dev/shm. /dev/shm is a memory-backed file system. When mmap(2) is done over a file in /dev/shm, the access to the shared memory does not result in any disk access at all.

Modern exchanges take advantage of this to eliminate as much disk access from the critical path as possible. mmap(2) is used in the server to implement a message bus over which the components on the critical path communicate. The communication pathway has no network or disk access, and sending a message on this mmap message bus takes sub-microsecond. By leveraging mmap to build an event store, coupled with the event sourcing design paradigm which we will discuss next, modern exchanges can build low-latency microservices inside a server.

Event sourcing

We discussed event sourcing in the "Digital Wallet" chapter on page 341. Please refer to that chapter for an in-depth review of event sourcing.

The concept of event sourcing is not hard to understand. In a traditional application, states are persisted in a database. When something goes wrong, it is hard to trace the source of the issue. The database only keeps the current states, and there are no records of the events that have led to the current states.

In event sourcing, instead of storing the current states, it keeps an immutable log of all state-changing events. These events are the golden source of truth. See Figure 13.17 for a comparison.

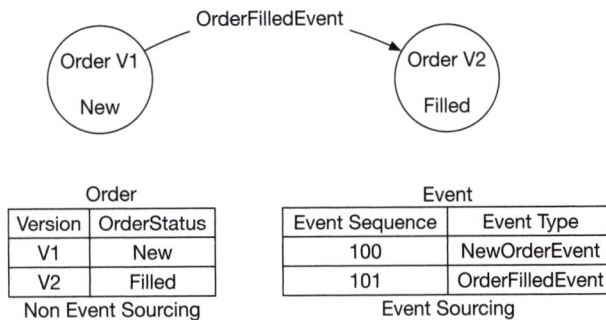

Order

Version	OrderStatus
V1	New
V2	Filled

Non Event Sourcing

Event

Event Sequence	Event Type
100	NewOrderEvent
101	OrderFilledEvent

Event Sourcing

Figure 13.17: Non-event sourcing vs event sourcing

On the left is a classic database schema. It keeps track of the order status for an order, but it does not contain any information about how an order arrives at the current state. On the right is the event sourcing counterpart. It tracks all the events that change the order states, and it can recover order states by replaying all the events in sequence.

Figure 13.18 shows an event sourcing design using the mmap event store as a message bus. This looks very much like the Pub-Sub model in Kafka. In fact, if there is no strict latency requirement, Kafka could be used.

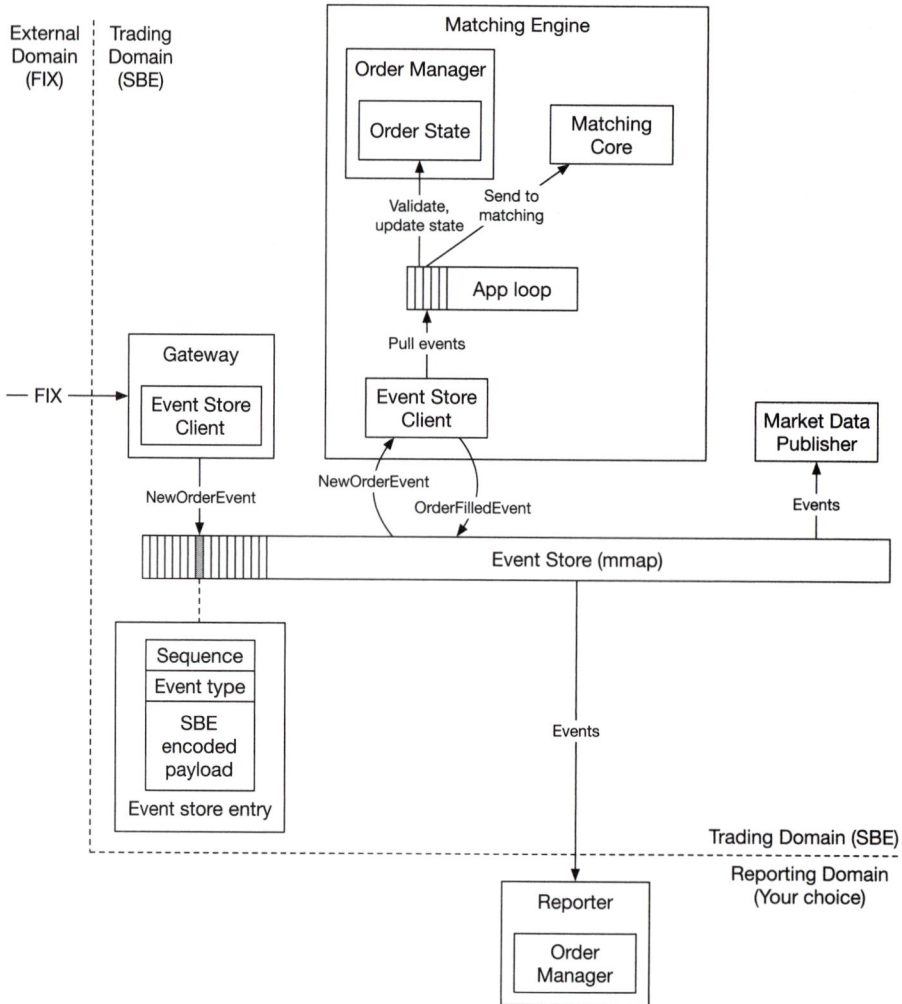

Figure 13.18: An event sourcing design

In the diagram, the external domain communicates with the trading domain using FIX
that we introduced in the Business Knowledge 101 section on page 380.

- The gateway transforms FIX to "FIX over Simple Binary Encoding" (SBE) for fast
  and compact encoding and sends each order as a NewOrderEvent via the Event Store
  Client in a pre-defined format (see event store entry in the diagram).

- The order manager (embedded in the matching engine) receives the NewOrderEvent
  from the event store, validates it, and adds it to its internal order states. The order is
  then sent to the matching core.

- If the order gets matched, an OrderFilledEvent is generated and sent to the event
  store.

- Other components such as the market data processor and the reporter subscribe to the event store and process those events accordingly.

This design follows the high-level design closely, but there are some adjustments to make it work more efficiently in the event sourcing paradigm.

The first difference is the order manager. The order manager becomes a reusable library that is embedded in different components. It makes sense for this design because the states of the orders are important for multiple components. Having a centralized order manager for other components to update or query the order states would hurt latency, especially if those components are not on the critical trading path, as is the case for the reporter in the diagram. Although each component maintains the order states by itself, with event sourcing the states are guaranteed to be identical and replayable.

Another key difference is that the sequencer is nowhere to be seen. What happened to it?

With the event sourcing design, we have one single event store for all messages. Note that the event store entry contains a sequence field. This field is injected by the sequencer.

There is only one sequencer for each event store. It is a bad practice to have multiple sequencers, as they will fight for the right to write to the event store. In a busy system like an exchange, a lot of time would be wasted on lock contention. Therefore, the sequencer is a single writer which sequences the events before sending them to the event store. Unlike the sequencer in the high-level design which also functions as a message store, the sequencer here only does one simple thing and is super fast. Figure 13.19 shows a design for the sequencer in a memory-map (mmap) environment.

The sequencer pulls events from the ring buffer that is local to each component. For each event, it stamps a sequence ID on the event and sends it to the event store. We can have backup sequencers for high availability in case the primary sequencer goes down.

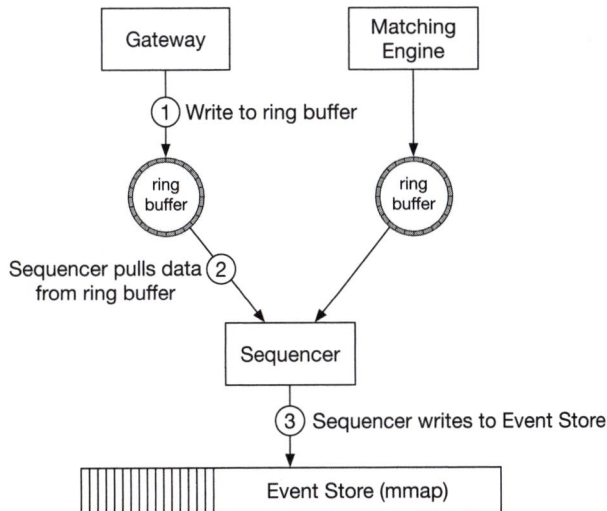

Figure 13.19: Sample design of Sequencer

High availability

For high availability, our design aims for 4 nines (99.99%). This means the exchange can only have 8.64 seconds of downtime per day. It requires almost immediate recovery if a service goes down.

To achieve high availability, consider the following:

- First, identify single-point-of-failures in the exchange architecture. For example, the failure of the matching engine could be a disaster for the exchange. Therefore, we set up redundant instances alongside the primary instance.

- Second, detection of failure and the decision to failover to the backup instance should be fast.

For stateless services such as the client gateway, they could easily be horizontally scaled by adding more servers. For stateful components, such as the order manager and matching engine, we need to be able to copy state data across replicas.

Figure 13.20 shows an example of how to copy data. The hot matching engine works as the primary instance, and the warm engine receives and processes the exact same events but does not send any event out onto the event store. When the primary goes down, the warm instance can immediately take over as the primary and send out events. When the warm secondary instance goes down, upon restart, it can always recover all the states from the event store. Event sourcing is a great fit for the exchange architecture. The inherent determinism makes state recovery easy and accurate.

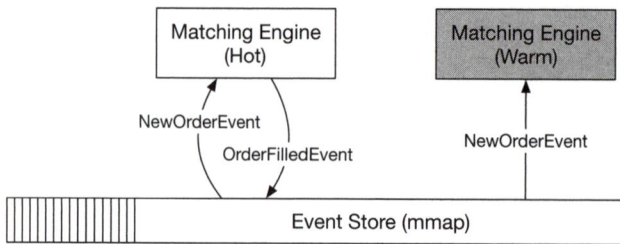

Figure 13.20: Hot-warm matching engine

We need to design a mechanism to detect potential problems in the primary. Besides normal monitoring of hardware and processes, we can also send heartbeats from the matching engine. If a heartbeat is not received in time, the matching engine might be experiencing problems.

The problem with this hot-warm design is that it only works within the boundary of a single server. To achieve high availability, we have to extend this concept across multiple machines or even across data centers. In this setting, an entire server is either hot or warm, and the entire event store is replicated from the hot server to all warm replicas. Replicating the entire event store across machines takes time. We could use reliable UDP [19] to efficiently broadcast the event messages to all warm servers. Refer to the design of Aeron [20] for an example.

In the next section, we discuss an improvement to the hot-warm design to achieve high availability.

Fault tolerance

The hot-warm design above is relatively simple. It works reasonably well, but what happens if the warm instances go down as well? This is a low probability but catastrophic event, so we should prepare for it.

This is a problem large tech companies face. They tackle it by replicating core data to data centers in multiple cities. It mitigates the risk of a natural disaster such as an earthquake or a large-scale power outage. To make the system fault-tolerant, we have to answer many questions:

1. If the primary instance goes down, how and when do we decide to failover to the backup instance?
2. How do we choose the leader among backup instances?
3. What is the recovery time needed (RTO - Recovery Time Objective)?
4. What functionalities need to be recovered (RPO - Recovery Point Objective)? Can our system operate under degraded conditions?

Let's answer these questions one by one.

First, we have to understand what "down" really means. This is not as straightforward as it seems. Consider these situations.

1. The system might send out false alarms, which cause unnecessary failovers.
2. Bugs in the code might cause the primary instance to go down. The same bug could bring down the backup instance after the failover. When all backup instances are knocked out by the bug, the system is no longer available.

These are tough problems to solve. Here are some suggestions. When we first release a new system, we might need to perform failovers manually. Only when we gather enough signals and operational experience and gain more confidence in the system do we automate the failure detection process. Chaos engineering [21] is a good practice to surface edge cases and gain operational experience faster.

Once the decision to failover is correctly made, how do we decide which server takes over? Fortunately, this is a well-understood problem. There are many battle-tested leader-election algorithms. We use Raft [22] as an example.

Figure 13.21 shows a Raft cluster with 5 servers with their own event stores. The current leader sends data to all the other instances (followers). The minimum number of votes required to perform an operation in Raft is $\frac{n}{2} + 1$, where n is the number of members in the cluster. In this example, the minimum is $\frac{5}{2} + 1 = 3$.

The following diagram (Figure 13.21) shows the followers receiving new events from the leader over RPC. The events are saved to the follower's own mmap event store.

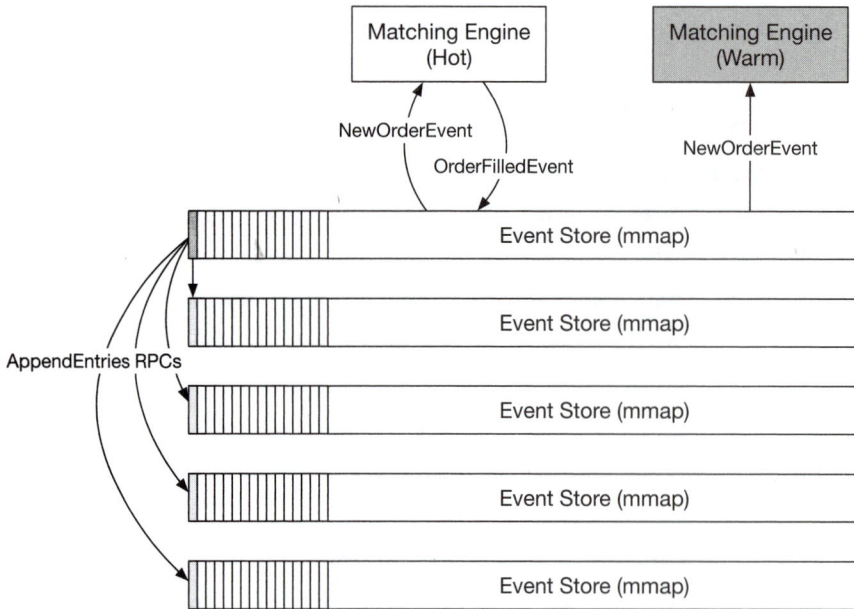

Figure 13.21: Event replication in Raft cluster

Let's briefly examine the leader election process. The leader sends heartbeat messages (AppendEnties with no content as shown in Figure 13.21) to its followers. If a follower has not received heartbeat messages for a period of time, it triggers an election timeout that initiates a new election. The first follower that reaches election timeout becomes a candidate, and it asks the rest of the followers to vote (RequestVote). If the first follower receives a majority of votes, it becomes the new leader. If the first follower has a lower term value than the new node, it cannot be the leader. If multiple followers become candidates at the same time, it is called a "split vote". In this case, the election times out, and a new election is initiated. See Figure 13.22 for the explanation of "term". Time is divided into arbitrary intervals in Raft to represent normal operation and election.

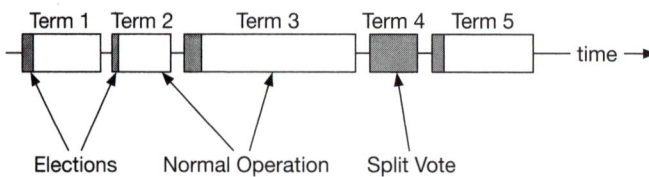

Figure 13.22: Raft terms (Source: [23])

Next, let's take a look at recovery time. Recovery Time Objective (RTO) refers to the amount of time an application can be down without causing significant damage to the business. For a stock exchange, we need to achieve a second-level RTO, which definitely requires automatic failover of services. To do this, we categorize services based on priority and define a degradation strategy to maintain a minimum service level.

Finally, we need to figure out the tolerance for data loss. Recovery Point Objective (RPO) refers to the amount of data that can be lost before significant harm is done to the business, i.e. the loss tolerance. In practice, this means backing up data frequently. For a stock exchange, data loss is not acceptable, so RPO is near zero. With Raft, we have many copies of the data. it guarantees that state consensus is achieved among cluster nodes. If the current leader crashes, the new leader should be able to function immediately.

Matching algorithms

Let's take a slight detour and dive into the matching algorithms. The pseudo-code below explains how matching works at a high level.

```
Context handleOrder(OrderBook orderBook, OrderEvent orderEvent) {
    if (orderEvent.getSequenceId() != nextSequence) {
        return Error(OUT_OF_ORDER, nextSequence);
    }

    if (!validateOrder(symbol, price, quantity)) {
        return ERROR(INVALID_ORDER, orderEvent);
    }

    Order order = createOrderFromEvent(orderEvent);
    switch (msgType):
        case NEW:
            return handleNew(orderBook, order);
        case CANCEL:
            return handleCancel(orderBook, order);
        default:
            return ERROR(INVALID_MSG_TYPE, msgType);

}

Context handleNew(OrderBook orderBook, Order order) {
    if (BUY.equals(order.side)) {
        return match(orderBook.sellBook, order);
    } else {
        return match(orderBook.buyBook, order);
    }
}

Context handleCancel(OrderBook orderBook, Order order) {
    if (!orderBook.orderMap.contains(order.orderId)) {
        return ERROR(CANNOT_CANCEL_ALREADY_MATCHED, order);
    }
    removeOrder(order);
    setOrderStatus(order, CANCELED);
    return SUCCESS(CANCEL_SUCCESS, order);
}

Context match(OrderBook book, Order order) {
    Quantity leavesQuantity = order.quantity - order.matchedQuantity;
    Iterator<Order> limitIter = book.limitMap.get(order.price).orders;
    while (limitIter.hasNext() && leavesQuantity > 0) {
        Quantity matched = min(limitIter.next.quantity, order.quantity);
        order.matchedQuantity += matched;
        leavesQuantity = order.quantity - order.matchedQuantity;
```

```
        remove(limitIter.next);
        generateMatchedFill();
    }
    return SUCCESS(MATCH_SUCCESS, order);
}
```

The pseudocode uses the FIFO (First In First Out) matching algorithm. The order that comes in first at a certain price level gets matched first, and the last one gets matched last.

There are many matching algorithms. These algorithms are commonly used in futures trading. For example, a FIFO with LMM (Lead Market Maker) algorithm allocates a certain quantity to the LMM based on a predefined ratio ahead of the FIFO queue, which the LMM firm negotiates with the exchange for the privilege. See more matching algorithms on the CME website [24]. The matching algorithms are used in many other scenarios. A typical one is a dark pool [25].

Determinism

There is both functional determinism and latency determinism. We have covered functional determinism in previous sections. The design choices we make, such as sequencer and event sourcing, guarantee that if the events are replayed in the same order, the results will be the same.

With functional determinism, the actual time when the event happens does not matter most of the time. What matters is the order of the events. In Figure 13.23, event timestamps from discrete uneven dots in the time dimension are converted to continuous dots, and the time spent on replay/recovery can be greatly reduced.

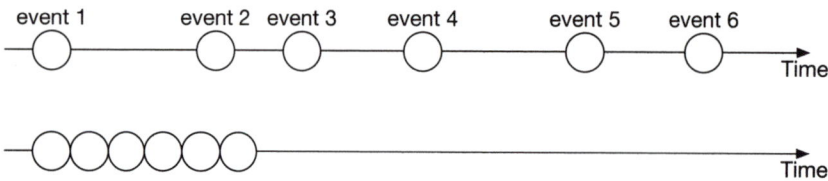

Figure 13.23: Time in event sourcing

Latency determinism means having almost the same latency through the system for each trade. This is key to the business. There is a mathematical way to measure this: the 99th percentile latency, or even more strictly, the 99.99th percentile latency. We can leverage HdrHistogram [26] to calculate latency. If the 99th percentile latency is low, the exchange offers stable performance across almost all the trades.

It is important to investigate large latency fluctuations. For example, in Java, safe points are often the cause. The HotSpot JVM [27] Stop-the-World garbage collection is a well-known example.

This concludes our deep dive on the critical trading path. In the remainder of this chapter, we take a closer look at some of the more interesting aspects of other parts of the exchange.

Market data publisher optimizations

As we can see from the matching algorithm, the L3 order book data gives us a better view of the market. We can get free one-day candlestick data from Google Finance, but it is expensive to get the more detailed L2/L3 order book data. Many hedge funds record the data themselves via the exchange real-time API to build their own candlestick charts and other charts for technical analysis.

The market data publisher (MDP) receives matched results from the matching engine and rebuilds the order book and candlestick charts based on that. It then publishes the data to the subscribers.

The order book rebuild is similar to the pseudocode mentioned in the matching algorithms section above. MDP is a service with many levels. For example, a retail client can only view 5 levels of L2 data by default and needs to pay extra to get 10 levels. MDP's memory cannot expand forever, so we need to have an upper limit on the candlesticks. Refer to the data models section for a review of the candlestick charts. The design of the MDP is in Figure 13.24.

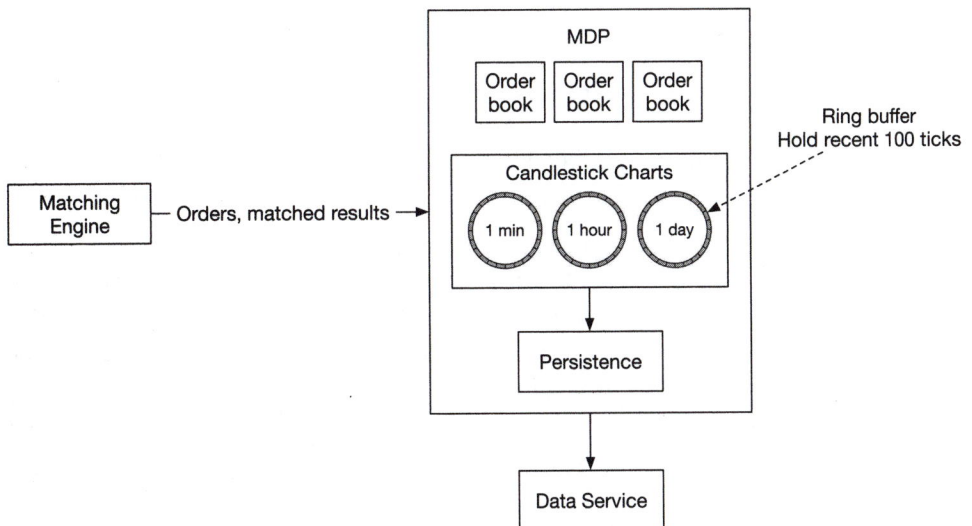

Figure 13.24: Market Data Publisher

This design utilizes ring buffers. A ring buffer, also called a circular buffer, is a fixed-size queue with the head connected to the tail. A producer continuously produces data and one or more consumers pull data off it. The space in a ring buffer is pre-allocated. There is no object creation or deallocation necessary. The data structure is also lock-free. There are other techniques to make the data structure even more efficient. For example, padding ensures that the ring buffer's sequence number is never in a cache line with anything else. Refer to [28] for more detail.

Distribution fairness of market data

In stock trading, having lower latency than others is like having an oracle that can see the future. For a regulated exchange, it is important to guarantee that all the receivers of market data get that data at the same time. Why is this important? For example, the MDP holds a list of data subscribers, and the order of the subscribers is decided by the order in which they connect to the publisher, with the first one always receiving data first. Guess what happens, then? Smart clients will fight to be the first on the list when the market opens.

There are some ways to mitigate this. Multicast using reliable UDP is a good solution to broadcast updates to many participants at once. The MDP could also assign a random order when the subscriber connects to it. We look at multicast in more detail.

Multicast

Data can be transported over the internet by three different types of protocols. Let's take a quick look.

1. Unicast: from one source to one destination.
2. Broadcast: from one source to an entire subnetwork.
3. Multicast: from one source to a set of hosts that can be on different subnetworks.

Multicast is a commonly-used protocol in exchange design. By configuring several receivers in the same multicast group, they will in theory receive data at the same time. However, UDP is an unreliable protocol and the datagram might not reach all the receivers. There are solutions to handle retransmission [29].

Colocation

While we are on the subject of fairness, it is a fact that a lot of exchanges offer colocation services, which put hedge funds or brokers' servers in the same data center as the exchange. The latency in placing an order to the matching engine is essentially proportional to the length of the cable. Colocation does not break the notion of fairness. It can be considered as a paid-for VIP service.

Network security

An exchange usually provides some public interfaces and a DDoS attack is a real challenge. Here are a few techniques to combat DDoS:

1. Isolate public services and data from private services, so DDoS attacks don't impact the most important clients. In case the same data is served, we can have multiple read-only copies to isolate problems.
2. Use a caching layer to store data that is infrequently updated. With good caching, most queries won't hit databases.
3. Harden URLs against DDoS attacks. For example, with an URL like `https://my.website.com/data?from=123&to=456`, an attacker can easily generate many different requests by changing the query string. Instead, URLs like this work better: `https://my.website.com/data/recent`. It can also be cached at the CDN layer.
4. An effective safelist/blocklist mechanism is needed. Many network gateway prod-

ucts provide this type of functionality.

5. Rate limiting is frequently used to defend against DDoS attacks.

Step 4 - Wrap Up

After reading this chapter, you may come to the conclusion that an ideal deployment model for a big exchange is to put everything on a single gigantic server or even one single process. Indeed, this is exactly how some exchanges are designed!

With the recent development of the cryptocurrency industry, many crypto exchanges use cloud infrastructure to deploy their services [30]. Some decentralized finance projects are based on the notion of AMM (Automatic Market Making) and don't even need an order book.

The convenience provided by the cloud ecosystem changes some of the designs and lowers the threshold for entering the industry. This will surely inject innovative energy into the financial world.

Congratulations on getting this far! Now give yourself a pat on the back. Good job!

Chapter Summary

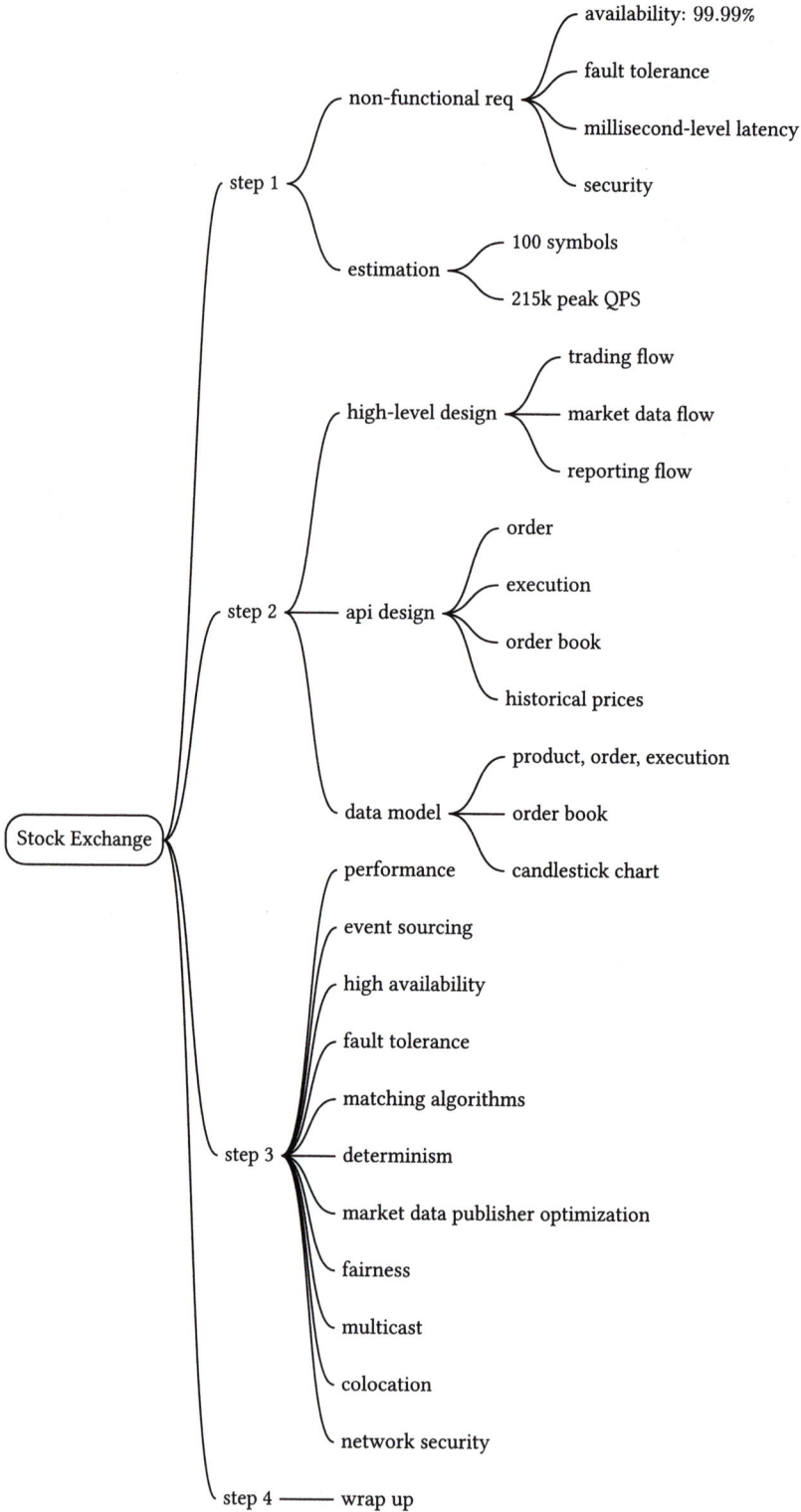

Stock Exchange
- step 1
  - non-functional req
    - availability: 99.99%
    - fault tolerance
    - millisecond-level latency
    - security
  - estimation
    - 100 symbols
    - 215k peak QPS
- step 2
  - high-level design
    - trading flow
    - market data flow
    - reporting flow
  - api design
    - order
    - execution
    - order book
    - historical prices
  - data model
    - product, order, execution
    - order book
    - candlestick chart
- step 3
  - performance
  - event sourcing
  - high availability
  - fault tolerance
  - matching algorithms
  - determinism
  - market data publisher optimization
  - fairness
  - multicast
  - colocation
  - network security
- step 4 — wrap up

Reference Material

[1] LMAX exchange was famous for its open-source Disruptor. https://www.lmax.com/exchange.

[2] IEX attracts investors by "playing fair", also is the "Flash Boys Exchange". https://en.wikipedia.org/wiki/IEX.

[3] NYSE matched volume. https://www.nyse.com/markets/us-equity-volumes.

[4] HKEX daily trading volume. https://www.hkex.com.hk/Market-Data/Statistics/Consolidated-Reports/Securities-Statistics-Archive/Trading_Value_Volume_And_Number_Of_Deals?sc_lang=en#select1=0.

[5] All of the World's Stock Exchanges by Size. http://money.visualcapitalist.com/all-of-the-worlds-stock-exchanges-by-size/.

[6] Denial of service attack. https://en.wikipedia.org/wiki/Denial-of-service_attack.

[7] Market impact. https://en.wikipedia.org/wiki/Market_impact.

[8] Fix trading. https://www.fixtrading.org/.

[9] Event Sourcing. https://martinfowler.com/eaaDev/EventSourcing.html.

[10] CME Co-Location and Data Center Services. https://www.cmegroup.com/trading/colocation/co-location-services.html.

[11] Epoch. https://www.epoch101.com/.

[12] Order book. https://www.investopedia.com/terms/o/order-book.asp.

[13] Order book. https://en.wikipedia.org/wiki/Order_book.

[14] How to Build a Fast Limit Order Book. https://bit.ly/3ngMtEO.

[15] Developing with kdb+ and the q language. https://code.kx.com/q/.

[16] Latency Numbers Every Programmer Should Know. https://gist.github.com/jboner/2841832.

[17] mmap. https://en.wikipedia.org/wiki/Memory_map.

[18] Context switch. https://bit.ly/3pva7A6.

[19] Reliable User Datagram Protocol. https://en.wikipedia.org/wiki/Reliable_User_Datagram_Protocol.

[20] Aeron. https://github.com/real-logic/aeron/wiki/Design-Overview.

[21] Chaos engineering. https://en.wikipedia.org/wiki/Chaos_engineering.

[22] Raft. https://raft.github.io/.

[23] Designing for Understandability: the Raft Consensus Algorithm. https://raft.githu b.io/slides/uiuc2016.pdf.

[24] Supported Matching Algorithms. https://bit.ly/3aYoCEo.

[25] Dark pool. https://www.investopedia.com/terms/d/dark-pool.asp.

[26] HdrHistogram: A High Dynamic Range Histogram. http://hdrhistogram.org/.

[27] HotSpot (virtual machine). https://en.wikipedia.org/wiki/HotSpot_(virtual_mach ine).

[28] Cache line padding. https://bit.ly/3lZTFWz.

[29] NACK-Oriented Reliable Multicast. https://en.wikipedia.org/wiki/NACK-Oriente d_Reliable_Multicast.

[30] AWS Coinbase Case Study. https://aws.amazon.com/solutions/case-studies/coinb ase/.

Afterword

Congratulations! You have completed this interview guide. You have accumulated skills and knowledge with which to design complex systems. Not everyone has the discipline to do what you have done, to learn what you have learned. Take a moment to pat yourself on the back. Your hard work will pay off.

Landing your dream job is a long journey and requires lots of time and effort. Practice makes perfect. Best of luck!

Thank you for buying and reading this book. Without readers like you, our work would not exist. We hope you have enjoyed the book!

If you have comments or questions about this book, feel free to send us an email at hi@bytebytego.com. If you notice any errors, please let us know so we can make corrections for the next edition. Thank you!

Join the community

We created a members-only Discord group. It is designed for community discussions on the following topics:

- System design fundamentals.
- Showcasing design diagrams and getting feedback.
- Finding mock interview buddies.
- General chat with community members.

Come join us and introduce yourself to the community, today! Use the link below or scan the QR code.

http://bit.ly/systemdiscord

Index

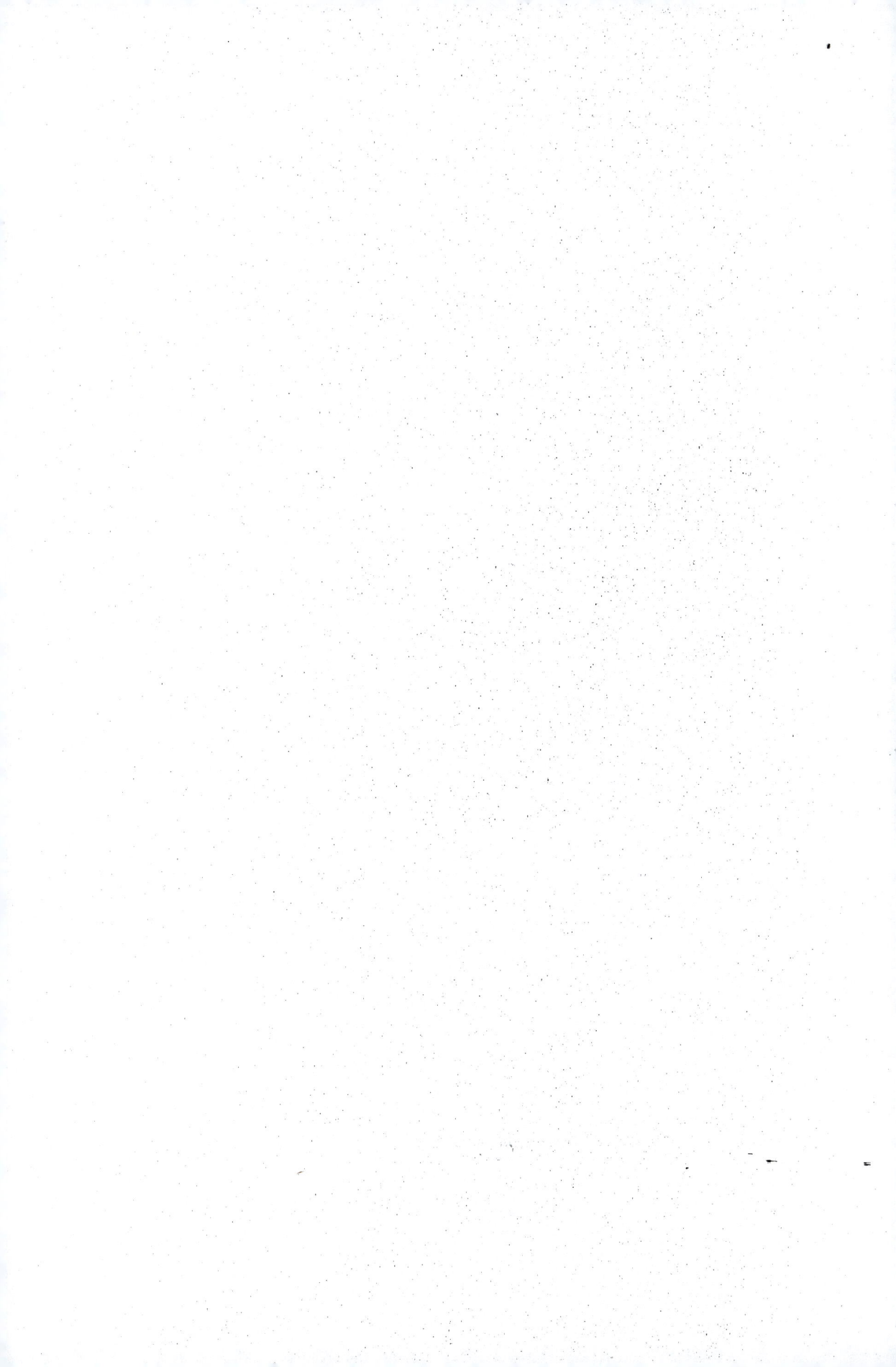